INTERNATIONAL LABOUR AND THE
ORIGINS OF THE COLD WAR

INTERNATIONAL LABOUR AND THE ORIGINS OF THE COLD WAR

DENIS MACSHANE

CLARENDON PRESS · OXFORD
1992

Oxford University Press, Walton Street, Oxford OX2 6DP
Oxford New York Toronto
Delhi Bombay Calcutta Madras Karachi
Petaling Jaya Singapore Hong Kong Tokyo
Nairobi Dar es Salaam Cape Town
Melbourne Auckland
and associated companies in
Berlin Ibadan

Oxford is a trade mark of Oxford University Press

Published in the United States
by Oxford University Press, New York

British Library Cataloguing in Publication Data
Data available

Library of Congress Cataloging-in-Publication Data
MacShane, Denis.
International labour and the origins of the Cold War/Denis MacShane.
p. cm.
Includes bibliographical references (p.   ) and index.
1. Trade-unions and foreign policy—History.   2. Cold War.
I. Title.
HD6490.F58M38   1992   322'.2—dc20   91–33653
ISBN 0–19–827366–5

Typeset by Pentacor PLC, High Wycombe, Bucks
Printed and bound in
Great Britain by Bookcraft (Bath) Ltd
Midsomer Norton, Avon

Preface

THIS book could not have been written without the help of several trade-unions which let me have access to their private archives. I should like to thank the officers and staff of the International Metalworkers' Federation in Geneva; the Amalgamated Engineering Union, the International Transport Workers' Federation, the Iron and Steel Trades Confederation, and the Trades Union Congress in London; the International Association of Machinists in Washington DC, the United Automobile Workers' Union of America in Detroit, and the United Steelworkers of America in Pittsburgh; and IG Metall in Frankfurt for access to their archives. Librarians at Nuffield College, Oxford, the Walter Reuther Memorial Library at Wayne State University, Detroit, the Catholic University, Washington DC, and the Geneva University Library have been most helpful. I am grateful to Noreen Branson for permission to quote from her forthcoming book on the British Communist Party in the 1940s. I have translated from French or German various archival or secondary source citations. Translations into English in union documents have been left as they originally appeared.

I am grateful to the following participants in events described in this book for talking to me about their involvement and impressions of the period: Alfred Dannenberg, Eddie Frow, Herman Rebhan, Victor Reuther, and I. F. Stone. I have profited from discussions on the themes discussed in the study with Gary Busch, Nelson Lichtenstein, and Peter Weiler. Mark Cousins, Geoffrey Hamilton, and Ben Pimlott have been a source of calm advice and encouragement. Collin Gonze, Piers Gray, John Lloyd, Colin MacCabe, Daniel Pham Minh Duong, Don Stillman, Werner Thönnessen, and Anne Trebilcock read all or part of the manuscript, and I profited from their comments and suggestions. Debbie Smith and Katherine Livas have helped with editorial skills.

Jon Snow in Washington, Gabrielle Krämer-Prein and Peter Ripken in Frankfurt, and Flavia Lambert and Jane Mills in London offered hospitality and friendship during periods of research. To Emma Letley I owe the idea of slowing down my normal hectic

mode of writing by doing a doctoral thesis at London University's
Birkbeck College, a remarkable institute of adult higher education
of which Britain should be proud.

It would be unfair to the reader not to indicate that I have been a
full-time trade-union official since 1977. Therefore personal experience with workers in negotiations, in organizing, in international
solidarity action, in political debate, in strikes, even (in Poland)
briefly in prison cells, as well as with trade-union officers from
many countries, informs the analysis and perspectives in this book.
One day perhaps the world's workers will have the international
labour movement their struggles, sacrifices, and needs deserve.

Finally I should like to dedicate this study to my wife Nathalie,
and my daughters Sarah and Laura. Without the sweetness of their
love and the joy of their company, it would have been finished
much sooner.

Contents

Abbreviations

ACWA	Amalgamated Clothing Workers of America
ADGB	Allgemeiner Deutscher Gewerkschaftsbund
AEU	Amalgamated Engineering Union
AFL	American Federation of Labor
AFP	Agence France Presse
AUCCTU	All Union Central Council of Trade Unions
CARE	Co-operative for American Relief to Everywhere
CDU	Christlich-Demokratische Union
CFTC	Confédération Française des Travailleurs Chrétiens
CGT	Confédération Générale du Travail
CGT-U	Confédération Générale du Travail Unitaire
CIO	Congress of Industrial Organizations
COMINFORM	Communist Information Bureau
COMINTERN	Communist International
CPGB	Communist Party of Great Britain
CPUSA	Communist Party of America
CSR	Comités syndicalistes révolutionnaires
CTAL	Confederación de Trabajadores de América Latina
CUA	Catholic University Archives
DGB	Deutscher Gewerkschaftsbund
DMDA	Dokumente und Materialen zur Geschichte der Deutschen Arbeiterbewegung
DMV	Deutsche Metallarbeiter-Verband
DSNA	Department of State National Archives
FDGB	Freier Deutscher Gewerkschaftsbund
FIOM	Federazione Impiegati Operai Metallurgici
FO	Force Ouvrière
FTUC	Free Trade Union Committee
IAM	International Association of Machinists
IFBW	International Federation of Building and Woodworkers' Unions

IFTU	International Federation of Trade Unions
IGMA	IG Metall Archives
ILGW	International Ladies' Garment Workers Union
IGS	International Graphical Federation
ILO	International Labour Office/Organization
IMF	International Metalworkers' Federation
IMFA	International Metalworkers' Federation Archives
IRIS	Industrial Research and Information Service
ISTC	Iron and Steel Trades Confederation
ITD	International Trade Department
ITF	International Transport Workers Federation
IUF	International Union of Foodworkers
IWMA	International Working Men's Association
IWW	Industrial Workers of the World
JPC	Joint Production Committee
KPD	Kommunistische Partei Deutschlands
LO	Landsorganisationen
LPCR	Labour Party Conference Report
MRP	Mouvement Républicain Populaire
NMM	National Minority Movement
OSS	Office of Strategic Services
NEP	New Economic Policy
NLRB	National Labor Relations Board
PCF	Parti Communiste Français
PROFINTERN	See RILU
RGO	Revolutionäre Gewerkschaftsopposition
RILU	Red International of Labour Unions
RPF	Rassemblement du Peuple Français
RPR	Rassemblement pour la République
SAP	Sozialistische Arbeiterpartei Deutschlands
SED	Sozialistische Einheitspartei Deutschlands
SFIO	Section Française de l'Internationale Ouvrière
SI	Socialist International
SPD	Sozialdemokratische Partei Deutschlands
SWOC	Steel Workers' Organizing Committee

TGWU	Transport and General Workers' Union
TP	Tanner Papers
TUC	Trades Union Congress
UAW	United Automobile Workers of America
UE	United Electrical, Radio and Machine Workers of America
UGO	Unabhängige Gewerkschaftsorganization
UGT	Unión General de Trabajadores
USWA	United Steelworkers of America
WFTU	World Federation of Trade Unions
WSA	Wayne State Archives

1

International Trade-Union Politics

THE end of 1945 was a good time to be a trade-unionist. In the preceding decade mass unemployment, employer opposition, and anti-union legislation had exacted its toll in Britain and France. In Germany and Italy, dictatorships had put an end to independent unions. In the 1920s and 1930s rivalry between socialist and communist trade-union organizations had weakened national unions and sundered the chances of unified international organization and action. In the United States, the founding of the Congress of Industrial Organizations (CIO) had boosted trade-unionism. But by 1940 unemployment stood at record heights. The CIO's president campaigned against Roosevelt. American labour's forward march appeared halted.

The picture was quite different at the end of the war. Unions had climbed into the saddle, or at least were able to hold on to the stirrups of state power. In Britain and France, trade-union officials held high government office. In the United States, Truman was president, in part because his nomination in 1944 as vice-president had been 'cleared' by Sydney Hillman, a leader of the Congress of Industrial Organizations.[1] Union membership was at a record high: there were 11 million union members in America, nearly 8 million in Britain, and 5 million in France. Workers in occupied Germany and Italy could rebuild and were rebuilding unions.[2] Socialists and communists were working together in the same unions.

Four factors explain the strong position of unions in 1945. Firstly, their contribution to the home front in America, Britain,

---

[1] Roosevelt is reported to have said 'Clear it with Sidney [Hillman]' when the question of Truman's possible vice-presidency came up at the Democratic Party convention in Chicago in 1944. As Nelson Lichtenstein points out, the decision was taken beforehand, but the widely reported remark suggested union influence close to the centre of American power which no previous labour leader possessed. See Nelson Lichtenstein, *Labor's War at Home: The CIO in World War II* (Cambridge, 1982), 176.

[2] For unions in Europe see Statistical Appendix in Walter Kendall, *The Labour Movement in Europe* (London, Allen Lane, 1975). For American unions see US Department of Labor, *Handbook of Labor Statistics* (US Government Printing Office, Washington DC, 1975).

and Russia had given them new status. The war was one of metal as much as of men. In the metal factories of the Allies, the unions were seen to have contributed to victory. Secondly, the unions in occupied Europe had provided the backbone of resistance movements. Thirdly, the new economic dispensations that became accepted as the basis for post-war policy were based on full employment, some public ownership, redistributive fiscal policies, planned resource allocation, and increased rights for employees. In all these areas, governments realized that trade unions, as social institutions, would be needed to act as brokers for the implementation of the new economic order.The final, more intangible factor was the sense that the war had not been a traditional one between nation-states but a struggle which engaged social forces, including organized labour, to defeat fascism. In exchange there was to be no return to the policies of the 1930s.

This new status of the unions in 1945 was underpinned by the belief that the post-war settlement should be based on the idea of a new world order. A global framework would link nations, social institutions, and economic relationships on an international basis so as to eliminate the causes of war. Both the United States and the Soviet Union sought international validation for their respective positions. Trade unions with their long-standing claim to internationalism appeared obvious institutions to benefit from the elevation of transnational relationships as a key to the post-war settlement.

Trade unions from the Soviet Union, the United States, Canada, Europe, Latin America, Africa, Australia, and Asia joined to launch the World Federation of Trade Unions (WFTU). For the first time, unions from the Soviet Union were members of the same international union federation as their counterparts from Europe and the United States. The founding conference of the WFTU in Paris took place between 25 September and 8 October 1945. Unions from fifty-six countries representing 67 million workers took part.[3] 'It was the supreme achievement of all trade-union history,' claimed one contemporary observer.[4] Such hopes were unjustified. By 1948 the WFTU was on the point of collapse. France's main union was split. The American unions were torn by

[3] Report of the 1945 Paris Conference of the WFTU, p. 232.
[4] Allen Hutt, *British Trade Unionism: A Short History* (London, Lawrence and Wishart, 1952), 169.

anticommunist purges and had been restrained by anti-union legislation. The British Trades Union Congress was still stolidly in place but the confidence and hopes of 1945 had been replaced by uncertainty over incomes control and other aspects of government policy.

Most historians who consider the evolution of unions in this period think that the Cold War is the key factor in the evaporation of the labour movement's elation of 1945. A leading tenet of historians in the 1950s and 1960s held that unions in the West had to respond to increasing Soviet and communist attempts to use unions and the World Federation of Trade Unions as a tool for communist destabilization and Soviet advance. Anticommunist policies, purges, and the creation of a Western-led trade-union international were therefore seen as a reaction to these threats.[5]

From the middle 1960s onwards, historians, especially in the United States and West Germany, drawing mainly on the archives of Western governments, their occupation forces, and advisers, as well as on statements made by union leaders, came to different conclusions. Their revisionist thesis was that the West's labour movement, led by the American Federation of Labor and the British Trades Union Congress, worked in collusion with government to develop a policy based on a secret agenda to destroy the radical policies, anticolonialism, and acceptance of the Soviet Union as embodied in the WFTU.[6] As against the traditional view, which has the Western unions acting autonomously in a defensive reaction to evidence of Soviet and communist onslaughts on democratic values, the revisionists believe that Western governments working through

[5] In the following chapters there will be detailed references to the orthodox view on world unions and the Cold War. Philip Taft, *The AFL from the Death of Gompers to the Merger* (New York, Harper, 1959), represents this strand among American labour historians while Henry Pelling, *A History of British Trade Unionism* (London, Penguin, 1976), takes a similar position for British unions. See also Lewis Lorwin, *The International Labor Movement* (New York, Harper, 1953).

[6] On the evolution of Cold-War historiography from orthodoxy to revisionism to post-revisionism see Martin McCauley, *The Origins of the Cold War* (London, Longman, 1983), 8–14. See also J. L. Gaddis, 'The Emerging Post-Revisionist Synthesis on the Origins of the Cold War', in *Diplomatic History*, 7 (Summer 1983), 171–90, and his *The Long Peace: Inquiries into the History of the Cold War* (Oxford, OUP, 1989). The present study, while focusing on trade unions, will attempt to show that the European roots of the Cold War are important in contrast to the influential American literature which, drawing generally from American sources, sees the Cold War, from an orthodox, revisionist, or post-revisionist perspective, very much through American eyes.

right-wing unionists embarked on a deliberate policy of weakening the WFTU and making co-operation with the Soviet Union internationally and communists domestically little short of impossible.[7]

Despite their differences both orthodox and revisionist historians tend to have the following points in common. They locate the problems forcing unions apart as deriving from the Soviet–American confrontation. Georges Lefranc, France's trade-union historian, writes: 'The creation of the World Federation of Trade Unions had been the result of the coming together of the governments who were allied against Hitler: its dissolution was the result of the alliance breaking up.'[8] Secondly, the key moment is seen as 1948, 'when the question of the attitude to the Marshall Plan split [the WFTU] wide open.'[9] Thirdly, the actors on the international union stage are seen as the national union confedera-

[7] The first major scholarly account of the revisionist case can be found in Ronald Radosh, *American Labor and United States Foreign Policy* (New York, Random House, 1969). A recent version grounded in much deeper work, especially in British archives, is Peter Weiler, *British Labour and the Cold War* (Stanford, Calif., Stanford University Press, 1988). Eberhardt Schmidt, *Die verhinderte Neuordnung 1945–1952* (Frankfurt, Europäische Verlag, 1970), and Sylvia Pfeifer, *Gewerkschaften und kalter Krieg, 1945 bis 1949* (Cologne, Pahl-Rugenstein Verlag, 1980), present the revisionist arguments from a German point of view. Annie Lacroix-Riz is the main French proponent of the revisionist position on unions and the origins of the Cold War. A good summary of her case is in her 'Autour d'Irving Brown: L'AFL, le Free Trade Union Committee, le Département d'État et la scission syndicale française 1944–1947', in *Le Mouvement social*, 190 (1990), 79–118. Unlike the traditional, revisionist, and post-revisionist trinity of political and diplomatic Cold War historiography, the labour history of the Cold War still tends to bifurcate between orthodoxy and revisionism. A tentative post-revisionist outline can be seen among German historians. See e.g. Siegfried Mielke's 'Die Neugründung der Gewerkschaften in den westlichen Besatzungzonen, 1945 bis 1949', in Hans-Otto Hemmer and Kurt Thomas Schmitz (eds.), *Geschichte der Gewerkschaften in der Bundesrepublik Deutschland* (Cologne, Bund Verlag, 1990), and in Siegfried Mielke's and Peter Rütters's introduction to *Quellen zur Geschichte der deutschen Gewerkschaftsbewegung im 20. Jahrhundert*, vii (Cologne, Bund Verlag, 1991). This study also hopes to push forward the post-revisionist, indeed post-Cold-War analysis of labour and the origins of the Cold War. New material and perspectives emerging from Eastern Europe and the Soviet Union, some of which were discussed at the Internationale Tagung der Historiker der Arbeiterbewegung in Linz, 1990, will modify the accounts of the traditional historians but are unlikely to offer much comfort to the certitudes of their revisionist opponents.

[8] Georges Lefranc, *Les Experiences syndicales internationales* (Paris, Aubier, 1952), 99.

[9] Pelling, *British Trades Unionism*, 230. Anthony Carew, *Labour Under the Marshall Plan* (Manchester, Manchester University Press, 1987), is a recent proponent of this position.

tions, national centres such as the TUC in Britain, the American Federation of Labor and Congress of Industrial Organizations in America, the Confédération Générale du Travail (CGT) in France.[10] Thus in the view of both orthodox and revisionist historians the cause of this fracturing of international labour unity was the Cold War which three years after the war's end forced national union centres into opposing camps.

This book sets out to question this position. It seeks to show that intra-left hostility in the trade-union movement was deep rooted, and it is wrong to argue that it was created, or even resurrected, by the Cold War. Anticommunism on the part of socialists and, equally important, antisocialism on the part of communists, were neither dead, nor even dormant in 1945. A legacy of Leninism, the international split of the trade-union movement in 1920 contributed significantly to the internal differences in the labour movement in the quarter-century that followed the second congress of the Communist International in 1920. It is, therefore, insufficient to argue that the Cold War was responsible for developments in the international trade-union movement. Indeed the confrontation within trade-unions domestically and internationally was one of the causes rather than a consequence of the Cold War.

When discussing the international labour movement, what exactly is meant? For the purposes of this book it is labour organized in trade unions that will be examined. The terms 'labour movement' or 'labour internationalism' can also cover a much wider spectrum including the political parties of the Left, or the organizations of the working class as a whole. The relationship between trade-unions and left-wing political parties is central to the arguments advanced. But this book will examine trade-unions as institutions and look at their international links, policies, and activities. Labour internationalism may be said to cover all the activities of organized labour-movement institutions such as unions and parties. Labour or trade-union internationals refer to the specific federations set up by unions while references to the Socialist or Communist Internationals

[10] John Windmuller, *American Labor and the International Labor Movement* (Ithaca, NY, Cornell University Press, 1954), and Gary Busch, *The Political Role of International Trade Unions* (London, Macmillan, 1983), are two examples of major studies which deal entirely in terms of national centres, but nearly all accounts of international union questions in this period take as given that national centres are the exclusive reference points for international policy and activities.

denote the international federations of the political parties of the working class.[11]

This study will concentrate on the thirty months between May 1945 and the split in the French CGT in December 1947. Most published studies in English on labour and the Cold War tend at best to skip over 1945 and 1946, preferring to start with the spring of 1947 when the Truman Doctrine and the Marshall Plan made clear America's break with Roosevelt's policy of co-operation with the Soviet Union.[12] The quarter of a century, a mere twenty-five years between 1920 and 1945, was one of intense political, industrial, and organizational upheaval for all trade-unions, with international points of reference emerging as never before. Therefore the attitudes of unions towards international questions prior to 1940 are important in order to see what light these throw on their policies and behaviour after 1945.

If the absence of a detailed examination of the prehistory of the Cold War is one problem to be overcome in trying to analyse labour's involvement in the Cold War, another factor that contributes to a limited understanding of unions and the origins of the Cold War is the focus that nearly all historians dealing with the subject have placed on trade-union national centres such as the TUC or AFL. One of the struggles that lay at the heart of the Cold War is that between doctrines of pluralism and centralism.[13] The political occasion that split the WFTU was the question of what attitude to adopt towards the Marshall Plan; but the underlying, preceding, and irreconcilable differences were already politicized as two world views—one centralist, one pluralist. It is remarkable then that most accounts, whether orthodox or revisionist, concentrate almost exclusively on national centres as the sole representatives and voices of organized labour in their respective countries.[14]

[11] Further helpful definitional discussion can be found in Peter Waterman, 'Some Reflections and Propositions on Workers and Internationalism', in *Newsletter of International Labour Studies* 30–1 (1986), 13–26.

[12] See e.g. Carew, *Labour under the Marshall Plan*. This, one of the richest and best-argued accounts of labour and the Cold War, skims through the political and economic events of 1945 and 1946 and barely refers to the divisions between 1920 and 1945.

[13] Discussion on centralist and pluralist concepts of trade unions will be developed in later Chapters.

[14] This needs to be modified in respect of German labour history of the period.

This essentialist rendering of labour history, while it is conveni-
ent, especially if one searches for patterns of state incorporation[15]
—national centres were the obvious partners for ministers, diplomats, and civil servants—downplays the institutional independence
and autonomy of powerful individual unions. In addition, the
written reports and minutes of the national centres which are
available for consultation tend to reinforce the centrality of their
interventions. But trade-union movements are more, far more, than
their national confederations.

This book, while not disregarding the national centres, looks at
how the unions of the metal manufacturing industries, which more
than any had emerged stronger from the war, developed their
international policies in this period. The metal unions which
organized workers in the steel, engineering, armaments, aeroplane,
shipbuilding, and other metal industries were at the peak of their
size and influence in 1945. In all countries they constituted the
largest single group of industrial workers. In the United States,
more than half the CIO's membership came from these industries.
A link that brought together metalworkers from different countries
and from different political systems was a commitment to increased
industrial production. Herman van der Wee has written that
economic growth in the post-war years 'became a *frontier*, even an
obsession.'[16] The cult of productionism in the metal unions had an
influence on their approach to international relations.

After examining one major international union federation and its
activity between 1945 and 1948, the book examines aspects of
these themes and their impact on union policy in the United States,
Great Britain, Germany, and France. This seems reasonable for an
account of international labour history, but in fact many of the
existing accounts of international trade-union developments in this
period are written from the standpoint of just one country's labour

Under the various zones of military occupation, no national centre existed before
1949, so German accounts concentrate on regional, zonal, and industrial organization and politics, including international contracts and activity.

[15] Peter Weiler expressly locates his study of British unions in the corporatist
tradition. 'One of the major characteristics of corporatism is the incorporation of the
trade union movement—or, more precisely, its leadership—into the workings of the
state.' Weiler, *British Labour and the Cold War*, 16.

[16] Herman van der Wee, *Prosperity and Upheaval: The World Economy 1945–
1980* (London, Pelican, 1987), 35.

movement. In particular, this tradition has over-emphasized the determining importance of the two major victors at the war's end— the United States and the Soviet Union. By contrast, this study argues that national traditions and, within them, domestic tensions and priorities in Britain, Germany, and France, stemming from a common European labour heritage, determined developments relating to international activity of the unions after 1945 as much if not more than interstate disagreements or political and financial interventions by the United States or the Soviet Union.[17]

The following discussion of international labour history therefore looks at various issues from the point of view of institutions— unions—and largely from the perspective of their leaders. Leaders believed they spoke for their members, and decisions were set or retrospectively validated by congresses. Obviously the subject matter here concerns the activity of a small élite of leaders. Rank-and-file union members showed particular concern over international questions such as the Russian Revolution, the rise of fascism, the Spanish Civil War, and the wartime alliance with the Soviet Union, but continuous participation in international labour organizations was reserved to a relatively small number of union officials with the position or means to participate in international work. After the founding congress of the WFTU in 1945, the leading participants in WFTU meetings were often fewer than a dozen. The cost of travel and the problems of translation and interpretation left international union work the preserve of a small group of union leaders. Inevitably a study such as this, of the policies of the national and international trade-union organizations, is a study of the institutional forms which produced these policies. It is outside the scope of this study to consider the wider sociological question of the extent to which these policies reflected the views of the broader mass of trade-unionists, whether activists or passive members.

[17] An important exception is Kendall's *The Labour Movement in Europe*, in which great attention is paid to the historical lineages of the post-war political orientation in major European trade unions. Kendall's research and publications on the impact of Lenin and the Communist International's divisive policies on the labour movement between the wars has been one of the guiding references for my own work. If finally all archives are opened in Moscow, Kendall's perspectives on trade-union internationalism *vis-à-vis* Leninism are likely to be more than vindicated.

In most of the accounts of what happened in the international labour movement after 1945, the same names recur: Walter Citrine, the general secretary of the TUC; Sydney Hillman, the CIO vice-president; and Léon Jouhaux, the general secretary of the CGT. Also active were a younger group of international union officials, such as the WFTU's general secretary, the Frenchman Louis Saillant, or his arch-rival, the AFL's European representative, Irving Brown. Both men were in their mid-thirties in 1945 with more than a decade of experience in the factional labour politics of their countries behind them. The older leaders had been embroiled in ideological and organizational battles for at least a quarter of a century, if not longer, prior to 1945.

This study will consider the leaders of the metal unions. They were important for two reasons. First, the metalworkers formed the biggest single industrial group in most national union federations in 1945. Secondly, the metal unions had been the locus of some of the most open political fights between communists and socialists between 1920 and 1945. Jack Tanner, the president of Britain's main metalworkers' union, the Amalgamated Engineering Union, was considered to be on the Left in 1945—he had been elected AEU president in 1939 with communist backing. Walter Reuther, elected president of the biggest American metal union, the United Auto Workers, in 1946, was seen as more radical than most other leaders of American unions. Unlike many of the older leaders who participated in international union activity after 1945, both Tanner and Reuther knew the Soviet Union from personal experience. Tanner had been a delegate at the second congress of the Communist International in 1920, and Reuther had worked in a car factory in Gorki in 1934.[18]

There was no homogeneity of union leaders controlling international labour-movement activity. Rather there was an older generation of long-established leaders of national federations, a younger group of activist specialists working as international union officials, and a layer of metal-union leaders. Tensions between these

---

[18] There is detailed discussion of the politics of Jack Tanner and Walter Reuther later in the Chapters on British and American unions. On 'élite', 'institutional', and 'rank-and-file' labour history see Eric Arnesen, 'Crusades against Crisis: A View from the United States on the "Rank and File" Critique and Other Catalogues of Labour History's Alleged Ills', in *International Review of Social History* 33 (1990), 106–27.

groups help explain the unfolding of the international labour movement's politics and policies in this period.

What were the goals of the international labour movement? Proclamations of internationalism had been a steady part of labour-movement discourse for a century. In the statutes of the International Working Men's Association (IWMA), Marx wrote: 'The emancipation of the workers is not a local, nor a national, but an international problem.'[19] This inspired the London Trades Council of the 1860s to help launch the IWMA on to a more universal plane. But at the same time London trade-union leaders were concerned by the importation of cheap labour and strike-breakers from the Continent, and they hoped through contact with fellow unionists across the Channel to regulate the problem.[20] Two roles of trade-union internationalism can be traced: firstly, the claim to be universal and inspirational; secondly, an instrumental purpose of being regulatory and functional. 'Trade unions will undertake international activities when such actions are perceived to be the most rational means to achieve members' goals,' is how one theoretician of international trade-unionism defines the regulatory-functional aspect.[21]

In addition to the *universal-inspirational* and *regulatory-functional* aspects of international trade-unionism there is a third, which developed strongly in the First World War, was enshrined by Lenin, and became general after 1945. This is the *diplomatic-national* representative role of unions operating internationally. Gary Busch sums up this aspect of international trade-union work thus: 'The international trade-union movement has been, and continues to be, a vital tool of governments in the shaping of the political destinies of foreign political parties and states and is an important part of most national foreign policy systems.'[22] Discussions of trade-union internationalism must take into account these three aspects: *universal-inspirational, regulatory-functional*, and

[19] Quoted in Ferdinand Claudin, *The Communist Movement from Comintern to Cominform, Part 1: The Crisis of the Communist International* (New York, Monthly Review Press, 1975), 16.

[20] See John Logue, *Towards a Theory of Trade Union Internationalism*, (Göteborg University, 1980), 32–3, and Knud Knudsen, 'The Strike History of the First International', in Frits van Holthoon and Marcel van der Linden, *Internationalism in the Labour Movement 1830–1940*, 2 vols. (Leiden, E. J. Brill, 1988), i. 304–23.

[21] Logue, *A Theory of Trade Union Internationalism*, 56.

[22] Busch, *Political Role of International Trades Unions*, 1.

diplomatic-national. Appeals to international solidarity mix with national interest, claims for democracy mix with domestic regulation of internal ideological conflict, and organizational questions hide irreconcilable political differences. Many accounts written in the 1950s and early 1960s, whether written from a Western or communist perspective, tended to underline the *universal-inspirational* aspects of first the WFTU and then the unions that left it to form the International Confederation of Free Trade Unions. The later revisionists saw the process much more as a struggle of *diplomatic-national* systems for supremacy in their respective spheres: a diplomatic power-play between the capitalist United States, helped by imperial Britain, against the totalitarian Soviet Union and its attendant Communist Parties. Less frequent was a recognition of the *regulatory-functional* aspect of trade-union internationalism which was a decisive cause of contestation between 1945 and 1947. This involved industrial unions and smaller countries to a much greater extent than has been allowed for in the accounts focusing on the major powers and their national centres.

Taking these three aspects of trade-union internationalism and testing them against the following account, what emerges is a picture of international activity by unions, irrespective of the proclaimed politics of the participants, which was used to bolster national positions. Unions engaged in international activity not only to promote or attain members' goals, but defensively to protect what they saw as the interests of the nations whence they came. This study does not directly address the debate about the linkages between the ideas of nation- and class-consciousness, but unions rarely, if ever, condemned their nation in an international forum. Once pro-union governments were in place (as was the case in 1945), the identification of trade-union and state interests became overwhelming. By 1945, of course, an important precedent had been set. One of the confusions that arises in treating the communist–socialist split after 1920 is that beneath the claims to universalism lay the specific interests of nation-states. As Fred Halliday has written: 'Under Stalin, proletarian internationalism was interpreted strictly as unwavering loyalty to the Soviet Union.'[23] The evidence suggests that internationalism as a means of defence of the interests of the Soviet state began with Lenin.

[23] Fred Halliday, 'Three Concepts of Internationalism', in *International Affairs*, 64/2 (1988).

In 1943, Adolf Sturmthal, a young Austrian socialist who had worked for the Labour and Socialist International (the federation of Labour and socialist political parties in the inter-war years), published an essay, *The Tragedy of European Labour*. In his preface he wrote:

Most of the European labour organizations were strongly committed to the defence of democracy. It had enabled them to grow into a powerful social force and to develop institutions that were amongst the highest achievements of European civilisation. But they failed in the decisive test. They were not able to stem the progressive disintegration of democracy and to offer a rallying point for the reconstruction of a democratic society. The defeat of democracy on the continent of Europe is due no less to this failure of labour than to the breakdown of democratic capitalism. Labour was strong enough seriously to interfere with the smooth working of the existing institutions of society, but it was neither sufficiently strong nor sufficiently constructive to rebuild society. It is this stalemate of conflicting social forces which, I believe, is the essence of democratic disintegration.[24]

Decades later, Sturmthal's 'stalemate of conflicting forces' is still a fair contemporary description of many countries, with governments of different political hues, in which workers and owners, managers and employees, unions and governments face off uneasily. The end of communist rule in Central and Eastern Europe in 1990 has emphasized, rather than lessened, the concern expressed by Sturmthal. On the other hand, Sturmthal's comment on the failure of unions after 1918 to 'offer a rallying point for the reconstruction of a democratic society' cannot be said to apply after 1945, at least in half of Europe. Indeed, since then the people of Western Europe, in Alan Milward's estimation, have never 'known so long a peace nor a life so prosperous and so humane'.[25] In the last years of the twentieth century, the entrenched unemployment, poverty, regional disparities, and racism in many parts of Western Europe call for some qualification of that judgement but, set in a longer historical context, Milward is right. Within their own countries, while unions

[24] Adolf Sturmthal, *The Tragedy of European Labour* (London, Gollancz, 1944), 5. Sturmthal worked for the Labour and Socialist International until 1938 when he emigrated to the United States. There he had a distinguished academic career as well as providing a link between American trade-unionists and democratic socialists in Europe. See Susan Russin (ed.), *Democracy Under Fire: Memoirs of a European Socialist. Adolf Sturmthal* (Durham, NC, Duke University Press, 1989).

[25] Alan Milward, *The Reconstruction of Western Europe 1945–1951* (London, Methuen, 1984), 502.

contributed after 1945 to the reconstruction of Western Europe, they failed to achieve the international goals they had proclaimed so often. What this means in terms of understanding the Cold War will be examined.

2

Metalworkers and Trade-Union Internationalism 1890–1920

To understand the approach of different labour movements to the problems and opportunities that presented themselves in 1945, it is necessary to consider international union activity in the preceding decades. Union leaders who took part in deciding international union policy in the 1940s belonged to a generation whose attitudes had been formed between the two world wars and even earlier. In Britain, Ernest Bevin, born in 1881, represented that generation. Although no longer head of the Transport and General Workers' Union after 1945, Bevin's hand can be seen everywhere in the elaboration of British international union policy in the post-war years. In France, Léon Jouhaux, born in 1879, had been general secretary of the Confédération Générale du Travail (CGT) since 1907. Hans Böckler, the leading German trade-union figure after 1945, was even older, born under Bismarck's rule in 1875.

In the United States, the two dominant figures in the Congress of Industrial Organizations, Philip Murray and Sidney Hillman, were born in 1886 and 1887 respectively. Their rivals, who headed the American Federation of Labor, were also of that generation. William Green, the AFL president, was born in 1870; George Meany, the AFL secretary-treasurer, who took a keen interest in international questions, was younger: he was born in 1894. He was closer in age to two other important British union leaders, Arthur Deakin (born 1891), whose position as Bevin's successor as TGWU general secretary was confirmed in 1945, and who succeeded Citrine as WFTU president in 1946, and Jack Tanner (born 1890), the president of Britain's main metalworkers' union, the Amalgamated Engineering Union. These latter, as leaders of the two biggest British unions had, in 1945, markedly different politics, but their views and experiences had been shaped and reshaped since first their union life began in the years before the First World War.

Finally, there is Konrad Ilg, who will play an important role in this account. He was head of the metalworkers' union in

Switzerland and secretary, from 1920, of the international federation of engineering, steel, and metal unions, the International
Metalworkers' Federation. Inside Switzerland, Ilg dominated the
trade-union scene much as Bevin had done in Britain. Like Bevin,
Ilg was born illegitimately and had only rudimentary schooling.
The union became his life, and Ilg persuaded several different Swiss
unions to merge to form one powerful industrial union for the
metal industry in 1917. He distrusted intellectuals, feared communists, and tolerated no challenge to his authority. Ilg was a Central
European Bevin, typical of many of the Continental union leaders
who held office in 1945.

The creation and accompanying problems of the World Federation of Trade Unions between 1945 and 1948, were thus events at
the end of the lives of a pioneering generation of trade-unionists—
men born in the nineteenth century, already active or even
established leaders before 1914. They had participated in the
growth of national trade-unions, whose size and influence had
become massive by 1945, and they had also witnessed and, in some
cases, taken direct part in the efforts to create enduring international union organizations in the half-century prior to the WFTU's
foundation.

The history of international trade-unionism falls into three
distinct phases: 1889 to 1914; 1919 to 1939; and the post-war era
up to 1990 and the fall of communist governments in Eastern
Europe. The two world wars were crucibles in which existing union
forms were melted down to be recast as wartime fractures mended
and passions cooled.[1] The initial push for the creation of

---

[1] There are many histories of labour internationalism, or rather labour
internationals, which is not quite the same thing. Hans Gottfurcht, *Die internationale Gewerkschaftsbewegung* (Cologne, Bund Verlag, 1966), and Georges
Lefranc, *Les Expériences syndicales internationales* (Paris, Aubier, 1952), are two
useful accounts. For a pre-*glasnost* Soviet account see Boris Ponomarev (ed.), *Die
internationale Arbeiterbewegung* 6 vols. (Moscow, Progress Publishers, and Berlin,
Dietz, 1978–85). The following provide useful background from a social-democratic
perspective: Julius Braunthal, *History of the International* (London, Nelson, 1957),
and John Price, *The International Labour Movement* (London, OUP, 1945). Franz
Borkenau, *The Communist International* (London, Faber, 1938), and James Joll,
The Second International 1889–1914 (London, Routledge, 1974), cover the politics
of the second and third Internationals. There is also considerable detail on the
politics, personalities, and activities of the political and trade-union internationals of
the late 19th and 20th centuries to be found in the respective multi-volume histories
of socialism by G. D. H. Cole, *A History of Socialist Thought* 5 vols. (London,
Macmillan, 1953–60) and of the Soviet Union by E. H. Carr, *A History of Soviet*

international trade-union federations came from union participants in the second (Socialist) International. To begin with, the union internationals of miners (founded in 1890) or metalworkers (founded in 1893) met at the same time as the Socialist International congresses, but within a decade the International Metalworkers' Federation (IMF) and the other industrial trade-union internationals had taken on an institutional life and organizational purpose of their own.

The international industrial federations found they could meet; exchange information; provide mutual support in strikes; compare developments on wages, working time, and training in various countries, proclaim internationalism; enjoy fraternal socializing; and do all this useful, uplifting, and agreeable work without ever having to cross the boundary into the arena of debates and action on class, theory, and revolution that were causing such problems in the Socialist International. From the start, this bifurcation between industrial and political internationalism, a split between the work of the union and the work of the party, was made into a tenet of labour-movement internationalism. This distinction has been helpfully defined by Susan Milner as the difference between 'labour internationalism, based on a desire for peace and freedom but measured in concrete, practical terms, and socialist internationalism, based on the central assumption of the primacy of class as an historical determinant'.[2] For one international industrial federation, the International Metalworkers' Federation, founded in 1893 and still in existence,[3] the focus of activity from its beginnings was seen by its affiliates to be industrial, not political.

The metal unions are important because the industries in which they organized—steel, arms, shipbuilding, electrical goods, machinery, rail and road vehicles, and general engineering—were the engine of economic growth, of national strength, and a symbol of

Russia, 14 vols. (London, Macmillan, 1950–78). Albert Lindemann, *A History of European Socialism* (New Haven, Conn., Yale University Press, 1983) is a good recent survey. Monographs on aspects of labour internationalism are usually reviewed or listed in the *International Review of Social History*, itself an invaluable source of articles and discussion in this field.

[2] Susan Milner, 'The International Labour Movement and the Limits of Internationalism: The International Secretariat of the National Trade Union Centres 1901–1913', in *International Review of Social History* 33 (1988), 10.

[3] An official history of the International Metalworkers' Federation exists. Fritz Opel and Deiter Schneider, *75 Years of the Iron International 1893–1968* (Geneva, IMF, 1968).

modernity and progress in the century that followed the first International in 1864. In addition, of course, the metal factories were where relations between capital and labour, between managers and managed, were in a state of contestation as new technologies and varying consumer demands confronted the evolving ideologies and managerial theories affecting both workers and employers.

The first period of international trade-union organization between 1890 and 1914 corresponded with a remarkable surge forward of growth and output in the metal manufacturing sector.[4] In Great Britain, metal-industry employment went up by 63 per cent between 1891 and 1911. In France, employment in the metal industries increased by 52 per cent between 1896 and 1913. In both countries, the metal industries overtook the textile industry as the major source of employment at the beginning of the twentieth century. Similarly in Germany, metal-industry employment increased by 53 per cent between 1900 and 1911.[5]

The metal unions increased in membership because they organized this dominant sector of employment in the most dynamic and growing sector of capitalism.[6] Yet they were relatively young organizations. The British Amalgamated Society of Engineers dated back to 1851; the continental metalworkers' unions were founded in the 1880s and 1890s. Their task according to Martin Segitz, a German metalworkers' leader, who addressed the International Metalworkers Federation Congress in 1896, was to 'pursue in all countries joint aims . . . to shorten working time, to raise wages, to acquire better protection for the workmen and strongly organize our particular industries'.[7] Involvement in international union

---

[4] See E. J. Hobsbawm, *The Age of Empire* (London, Weidenfeld, 1987), 34–55.

[5] Chris McGuffie, *Working in Metal: Management and Labour in the Metal Industries of Europe and the USA, 1890–1914* (London, Merlin Press, 1985), 115, 182, 204.

[6] Membership of unions affiliated to the IMF increased from 139,000 in 1896 to 1m. in 1913. Not all metal unions affiliated (especially from Britain), and some affiliated on a nominal figure to avoid paying full affiliation fees. Figures from IMF Congress reports 1896 and 1913. International Metalworkers Federation Archives (henceforth IMFA).

[7] Proceedings of IMF 1896 Congress, p. 160. The proceedings in English of the first 6 IMF congresses between 1896 and 1913 are to be found in a single volume, Charles Hobson, (ed.), *International Metalworkers' Federation*, (Birmingham, Hudson, 1915). References to IMF Congress proceedings up to 1914 are from this volume.

activity was a mechanism for providing facts and arguments in domestic negotiations and organization. The publications of the IMF between 1893 and 1914 focused on comparative wage and hour agreements and details of national legislation helpful to the unions. Money was collected for strikes in different countries, but no industrial action was organized on an international basis.

The existence and activities of the International Metalworkers' Federation, and the other international trade secretariats as they were called, did not lead between 1890 and 1914 to a weakening of nationalist trade-union sentiment to the profit of 'internationalism and the class struggle'.[8] If anything, the creation of the trade-union internationals strengthened the domestic institutional presence of unions by demonstrating that international working-class organization was possible other than on the apparently more combative terms laid down by the Socialist International. The idea of revolutionary action against any declaration of war, ambiguously endorsed at the Socialist International's Stuttgart congress in 1907,[9] was rejected by the International Metalworkers' congress the same year. For the first time, the International Metalworkers' Federation met separately—in Brussels—from the Socialist International. French metalworkers sought support for the principle of a revolutionary general strike, but the proposition was 'thrown out by a large majority' after British, German, Swiss, Dutch, Belgian, and Austrian delegates had spoken against it.[10]

The Socialist International and wider political questions do not feature large in the proceedings of the International Metalworkers' Federation up to 1914. The evidence of an attachment to a national self-assurance expressed especially by the representatives of the bigger countries is nevertheless overwhelming. It was a pride tinged with regret. Here, for example, is the lament of Charles Hobson, the Sheffield steel-trades official, who acted as secretary of the IMF in its first decade: 'The last thing a British trade-unionist will believe [in] is the necessity for international union,'[11] and a few years later in 1900, 'Men outside Britain cannot realise the great difficulty one meets in dealing with an ordinary French or German letter or newspaper, for as a rule an Englishman is as much averse

[8] George Lichtheim, *A Short History of Socialism* (London, Fontana, 1975), 246.
[9] See Joll, *The Second International*, 135–44.
[10] Proceedings IMF 1907 Congress, 360–371 (IMFA).
[11] Proceedings IMF 1896 Congress, 177 (IMFA).

to foreign languages as he is to the foreigner.'[12] Eric Hobsbawm has written that class consciousness 'neither excludes nor, usually, dominates national sentiments. The collapse of the Second International in 1914 into socialist parties and trade-union movements, is familiar. What is less familiar, since the internationalism of labour historians has not insisted on it, is the strong current of chauvinism which is found in some politically radical working classes.'[13] At the IMF Congress in Birmingham in 1910, the Berlin metalworkers' leader, Adolf Cohen, was cheered when he criticized the British metal unions for their inability to answer correspondence; when Alphonse Merrheim, the radical French metal-union leader, asserted that workers living under a monarchy were less likely to suffer violent repressions than those in a republic because 'the monarch would be afraid to get discredited by bloodshed', he provoked 'laughter and exclamations among the German delegates'.[14] The British blastfurnacemen's leader, Henry Walls, speaking in the same debate, criticized a German 'who has spoken twice during the same debate and who has thus grossly offended against an elementary principle of all parliamentary debate. [Cheers from the English delegates. The German and Austrian delegates called out: Only in England!]'[15]

It is not usual in looking at international meetings to record the noises off, as it were, but here is evidence of the strong national identity of the metal unions in the early part of the twentieth century. The decision then of the European socialist parties and trade-unions to line up behind their respective countries in 1914 cannot be seen as an unexpected betrayal of real existing internationalism. The principles and practice of international working-class organization did not suddenly tug in opposite directions in the summer of 1914; they had never been in harmony. As the anti-war Alphonse Merrheim said, 'The working class had been aroused by such nationalist passions that they would not have let the police shoot us [i.e. opponents of war]: they would have shot us themselves!'[16]

[12] Proceedings IMF 1900 Congress, 194 (IMFA).
[13] E. J. Hobsbawm, 'What is the Workers' Country?' in *Worlds of Labour* (London, Weidenfeld, 1984), 58.
[14] Proceedings IMF 1910 Congress, 423, 427 (IMFA).
[15] Ibid. 432.
[16] Quoted in Edouard Dolléans, *Histoire du mouvement ouvrier*, ii. *1871–1936* (Paris, Colin, 1939) 222 n.

Nor in fact did the outbreak of war in 1914 bring to an end all international contacts between the metal unions. The secretariat of the IMF had been in German hands since 1905 under Alexander Schlicke, president of the German metal union. During the war the IMF journal, the *International Metalworkers' Review*, continued to appear, printed in three parallel columns of English, German, and French. While troops died in the trenches, metal-union officials could read of British or German legislation and union initiatives to protect workers in the home factories. To a certain extent this was a tribute not so much to the force of internationalism but to this hybrid tradition of nationalist internationalism which had so quickly put down roots since the trade-union internationals were set up in the 1890s. Schlicke saw the outbreak of the war in 1914 thus: 'Although the working classes may regard the conflict as a blow to civilisation and therefore steadily set themselves in opposition, that does not prevent the organized workers from accepting a given situation, and even throwing themselves ardently into a struggle, because they recognize the preservation of nationality as indispensable.'[17] This tension between 'organized workers' (i.e. the trade-unions), with their interest in the 'preservation of nationality' and what Schlicke perceived to be the wider interests of the working class, was of course not new. As the two world wars dissolved existing patterns of power and thought in Europe, the energy and new outlook of the surges of working-class movement were channelled into that most sturdy institution—the trade-union. In turn, that institution was itself subordinate to, or confined within, the limits of the nation-state—its traditions, its language, its heritage of working-class organization, and, very often, was directly subject to command or heavy suggestions from government itself.

The more trade-union internationalism could focus on functional servicing tasks and steer away from the shoals of formal representation of national interests, the easier it was to survive. So the IMF, despite the obvious breakdown of communications between its major affiliates, the British and Germans, was able to maintain a tenuous existence during the war, with Schlicke putting out his IMF Review from Stuttgart and travelling to metal-union congresses in Switzerland, Denmark, and Hungary. The British metal unions sent

<hr>

[17] IMF Review, 9 (1914), 174.

fraternal messages to these meetings and sought, unsuccessfully, to have the headquarters of the IMF transferred to Britain.[18]

METALWORKERS AND THE IMPACT OF LENIN

The international effect of the overthrow of the Tsar, followed later in 1917 by the establishment of Bolshevik rule, lasted for many years. Revolutions always appeal beyond national frontiers, but the internationalist claims of the Bolsheviks and their setting up of the Communist International and its linked labour body, Profintern—the Red International of Labour Unions, institutionalized what otherwise might have been left to the workings of ideology and inspiration. The impact on working-class organization can still be felt today. Certainly in 1945, when the World Federation of Trade Unions was founded, the passions and personalities let loose by the fierceness of Lenin's revolution were still powerful forces to be reckoned with.

In 1902, in *What Is To Be Done*, Lenin wrote: 'Trade-unionism means the ideological enslavement of the workers by the bourgeoisie,'[19] and his hostility to the economism and the limited political goals of unions is well enough known. His language was vivid. 'British trade unions [were] insular, aristocratic, philistinely selfish and hostile to socialism,'[20] he wrote in 1908. Lenin's language is important. It set the tone of caustic denunciation that, when used by his followers in their abuse and polemics against their socialist rivals, soured the possibilities of co-operation and unity. The language of condemnation with its accusations of betrayal, servility, and class collaboration reverberates through the polemics of the 1920s and 1930s between socialist and communist trade-unionists. Here, in the contemporary translation, is how a German metal-union delegate listed the insults heaped upon his union by communists in the Ruhr in the early 1920s. 'Workingmen's Traitor . . . Servants of Capital . . . Handyman of Reaction . . . Full-Stuffed Trade Union Bonze . . . Chained Dog of the Bourgeoisie.'[21]

---

[18] Secretary's report to IMF Congress (1920), 11 (IMFA).
[19] V. I. Lenin, 'What Is To Be Done', in *Lenin on Trade Unions* (Moscow, Progress Publishers, 1970), 80.
[20] Ibid. 212.
[21] Report of National Organizations of the IMF (1921–24), 142 (IMFA).

Such insults may have roused supporters, but they alienated potential comrades and strengthened the latter's opposition. The language of trade-unionism was a language of agreements, constitutions, policies, and rules. What was said was meant. The meaning of Lenin's assault on existing unions was clear enough, as was that of his successors. When suddenly that language changed and friendship, co-operation, and unity became the watchwords—as they did especially between 1934 and 1938 and between 1942 and 1947—the memory of that harsher language could not be unmade.

The trade-union question was central for Lenin. After the split of the Russian Social Democratic Party into Bolshevik and Menshevik wings, there began a contest for control of the small unions existing in Russia. In 1907, Lenin urged Bolsheviks not to be swayed in their union activity by ideas that unions should be independent of party control but, instead, they 'should steadfastly promote acceptance by the trade-unions of the Social-Democrats' ideological leadership'.[22] This was in contrast to the Mensheviks who advocated 'mass-based democratic unions, organizationally independent from the Social Democratic party yet "organically" connected with Social Democracy through shared ideas and a common approach'.[23]

That simple distinction—between democratic centralist control of unions by a party organization on one hand and, on the other, an idea of independence, an autonomy limited by common politics, perhaps even formal union-party connections albeit blurred by bureaucratic leadership—is thus already evident in Lenin's writings before 1917. It was a political question, but the Bolsheviks also presented the problem as an organizational matter. Lenin's insistence on the creation of a new union international, the obligation of communists to work in secret cells within unions, the creation of 'red' or 'revolutionary' unions, meant the established unions were able to fend off communist attacks by organizational

[22] *Lenin, Lenin on Trade Unions*, 182. I have not in this book entered into a detailed discussion of Leninist concepts of trade-unionism, in particular, the theory of unions as a 'transmission belt', or indeed whether the trade-unions as they developed in the Soviet Union after 1917 had anything in common—apart from the name—with their counterparts in non-communist countries. As E. H. Carr has written, by 1921, 'The control of the party over the All-Russian Central Council of Trade Unions, as over the organs of the Soviet state, was absolute', thus leading to 'the fusion of the party, state and unions in a single complex of power'. Carr, *History of Soviet Russia*, ii. 326.

[23] V. Bonnell, 'Radical Politics and Organized Labor in Pre-Revolutionary Moscow 1905–1917', in *Journal of Social History*, 3 (1978), 287.

methods such as expulsions or bans on communists holding office and by organizational arguments against splitting and for unity. In this process, the role of the international union federations was important to reinforce a common anticommunist front after 1920.

Despite the appalling bloodshed, trade unions (and most especially metalworkers' unions) emerged from the First World War with a sense of significant increases in strength. In Germany the metalworkers, under the leadership of *revolutionäre Obleute* (revolutionary shop stewards), had organized strikes—to the disapproval of the official union leaders—in 1917 and 1918 that had contributed to the collapse of the Reich's will to wage the war. After the Kaiser's abdication, social democrats entered government. Schlicke, the German metal-union president—and still in 1919 the IMF secretary—became labour minister. The trade-union general strike in March 1920 that stopped the Kapp Putsch (an attempt by disaffected officers to restore authoritarian rule) appeared to show the strength of the unions.[24]

Similar signs of union power were to be seen in Britain. The vigour of the shop-stewards' movement, principally in the metal industries, had Churchill complaining to the cabinet in 1919 that 'the curse of trade-unionism was that there was not enough of it, and it was not highly enough developed to make its branch secretaries fall into line with the head office'.[25] In the summer of 1920, the Jolly George incident, followed by the creation of Councils of Action, which gave the impression that a united labour-movement action had stopped an attempt by the British government to intervene on the side of Poland against the Soviet Union, appeared to demonstrate union strength.[26]

[24] German working-class and union actions and politics in this period are well covered in Ben Fowkes, *Communism in Germany under the Weimar Republic* (London, Macmillan, 1984), and Chris Harman, *The Lost Revolution: Germany 1917–1923* (London, Bookmarks, 1982). On the metalworkers see Fritz Opel, *Der deutsche Metallarbeiter-Verband während des ersten Weltkrieges und der Revolution,* (Cologne, Bund Verlag, 1980).

[25] Quoted in Keith Middlemas, *Politics in Industrial Society* (London, Deutsch, 1979), 105.

[26] The Jolly George brought together such disparate figures as J. H. Thomas and Ernest Bevin and had them supporting Councils of Action and 'any and every form of withdrawal of labor' in order to prevent military intervention 'against the Soviet government of Russia'. On the day this motion was adopted (13 August 1920), hurriedly formed workers' battalions were leaving Warsaw to join with Polish peasants and soldiers to defeat the invading Red Army in the Battle of the Vistula. For from being invaded, by August 1920, the Soviet Union had become the invader.

In France, trade-union rights and the eight-hour day were now recognized in law though an attempt at a general strike launched by the CGT in May 1920 in support of striking railway workers failed, much as the TUC's effort did six years later. The French were the first to experience the effective counter-attack of capital and conservative governments that took place in the 1920s throughout Europe.

This changed status was reflected internationally. The International Federation of Trade Unions (IFTU)—the federation of national union centres—had been set up in 1919. Its affiliates organized twenty million workers in Europe. The IFTU was known as the Amsterdam international, from the city where its secretariat was located. In the same year the International Labour Organization was founded—proof of sorts that governments and employers now accepted the standing of unions to participate in tripartite negotiations and lay down international conventions, at least in the rarefied League-of-Nations atmosphere of remote Geneva.

When the first post-war congress of the International Metalworkers' Federation was held in August 1920, it counted 2.2 million members compared with fewer than 1 million before 1914. The key issue for delegates was the Soviet Union. In 1917 the IMF *Review*, still under German control, had welcomed the two Russian revolutions.[27] In 1918, it reported positively on the support of Petrograd metalworkers for the Bolshevik revolution, carried an enthusiastic description by the president of the Swedish metal union of conditions inside Petrograd after Lenin's takeover, and details of an agreement between Nordic metal unions and the Russian metalworkers' union for union membership reciprocity for members working outside their own country.[28]

But, as the full impact of Lenin's politics began to become clear, the tone changed. The IMF *Review* stopped celebrating the revolution and instead listed, under the heading 'Brilliant Success'

In any event, as E. H. Carr noted, the British government 'had never looked with favour on Polish military adventures', and the whole episode came at a moment when Lloyd George was responding positively to Soviet attempts to open up trade with Britain. (Carr, *History of Soviet Russia*, iii. 286.) None the less, the Jolly George incident has entered British labour-movement mythology as a moment when 'British workers stopped the war'. See James Klugman, *History of the Communist Party of Great Britain 1919–1924* (London, Gollancz, 1969), 81–6.

[27] IMF Review, 12 (1917), 111 (IMFA).
[28] Ibid. 2 and 3 (1918), 9–10, 20–2.

the rise in metal-union membership in different countries during the war. The most 'successful demonstrations of labour are . . . through . . . increasing membership by double or triple the former numbers'; readers were told not to be swayed by 'the Russian events of the last twelve months', and admonished not to treat 'the general strike . . . as the panacea for all which oppressed them'.[29] The CGT metalworkers in France had rejected a call for a revolutionary general strike in July 1918, and there had been an unsuccessful one in German-speaking Switzerland in November 1918. These had their impact on two important European metal-union leaders—Alphonse Merrheim of France, and the Swiss, Konrad Ilg, who henceforth definitively broke with their earlier syndicalist leanings and adopted reformist positions.[30]

If the European metal unions rejected Lenin's call for a revolutionary onslaught on their respective states, this did not diminish their enthusiasm for the Bolshevik revolution. It remained high at the time of the first post-war congress of the International Metalworkers' Federation, held in Copenhagen in August 1920, as the key resolution adopted suggests:

In close co-operation with the Trade Union International at Amsterdam, the Congress summons the metalworkers of all countries to . . . give to the Russian proletariat in its fight against international capitalism the most effective support by taking up with redoubled energy the fight against reaction and imperialist institutions in their own countries, which is the only means of saving the revolutionary results which the Russian comrades have gained, and of assuring the continued progress of the revolution.[31]

On the face of it, the Bolshevik leaders could not have wished for a stronger declaration of solidarity at a trying moment for the Soviet Union. But a closer look at the debates shows a different picture.

Merrheim had by 1920 abandoned his previous revolutionary zeal. He clashed with Richard Müller, leader of the Berlin revolutionary shop stewards, now the editor of the German metalworkers' journal—an important political post. For Müller, 'the trade-unions must proceed to direct their entire strength

[29]   Ibid. 4 (1918), 31.
[30]   On Merrheim, see Dolléans, *Histoire du mouvement ouvrier*, 274–7, and Paul Louis, *Histoire du mouvement syndical en France*, i. 1789–1917 (Paris, Valois, 1947) 316–8. On Ilg, see Philippe Garban and Jean Schmid, *Le Syndicalisme suisse* (Lausanne, Éditions d'en bas, 1980), 73–7.
[31]   Proceedings of IMF 1920 Congress, 45–7 (IMFA).

towards the downfall of capitalism'. Merrheim disagreed, stating that the application of Russian methods to France would provoke civil war leading to the 'annihilation of the proletariat'.[32] Merrheim also introduced a theme which would be developed over forth-coming years into a chorus heard repeatedly: 'In Russia, there is no trade-union movement, there the military method prevails. Every-one in the trade-union is to be a soldier and over the trade-unions are the courts martial. If anyone does not obey he is shot.'[33] No one at the IMF Congress referred to the recent second congress of the Communist International, held in July 1920 in Moscow, nor to its twenty-one conditions and its decision to launch a new revolution-ary trade-union international in direct opposition to the Interna-tional Federation of Trade Unions of Amsterdam.

The head of the Soviet metal union, Alexander Schlapnikof, did try to attend the IMF Congress from Norway where he had arrived after a tour of metal unions in North Europe. The Danish government refused him an entry visa, which occasioned a protest from several congress delegates. However Schlapnikof's non-appearance was not regretted by Anton Hansen, the Danish metal-union leader. Hansen complained to his fellow metal-union leaders that on a previous unspecified visit Schlapnikof had tried to organize internal opposition in the Danish metal union. 'Acts of agression were . . . directed against our Union as against me personally,' complained the Dane.[34] The Danish and Swedish metalworkers, although less polemical and more discreet than many of their comrades from unions to the south, showed themselves over the next quarter-century to be no less anticommun-ist than other European unions. Their support for the existing international federations is important as there was considerable respect in European trade-union circles for the achievements of the Scandinavian labour movement in the organizational, political, and social spheres.

LENIN SPLITS THE INTERNATIONAL TRADE-UNION MOVEMENT

From the second congress of the Communist International in mid–1920 stem the key decisions which dominate international union

---

[32] Proceedings of IMF 1920 Congress, 47–51.
[33] Ibid. 50.   [34] Ibid. 29.

relations for the next quarter of a century and after. The tensions inside unions between 1945 and 1948, the break-up of the WFTU, and their consequences for the Cold War are inexplicable without reference to the decisions on union activity taken in Moscow in July and August in 1920.

Two of the twenty-one conditions for membership of the Communist International adopted at the second congress concerned trade-union work. Clause 9 enjoined communist parties to form cells in trade-unions, and 'win the unions over to the communist cause . . . The cells must be completely subordinate to the party as a whole.' Clause 10 dealt with international union activity:

It is the duty of any party belonging to the Communist International to wage a determined struggle against the Amsterdam 'International' of yellow trade-unions. Its indefatigable propaganda should show the organized workers the need to break with the yellow Amsterdam International. It must give every support to the emerging international federation of Red trade-unions which are associated with the Communist International.[35]

Although it was independent, the International Metalworkers' Federation, like its sister trade secretariats, shared the same reformist, democratic-socialist outlook as the Amsterdam-based International Federation of Trade Unions. In declaring war on 'Amsterdam', Lenin and the Soviet leadership were also declaring war on the IMF. Arguably, communist work inside national unions could be justified as being parallel to the activity of the socialist parties within unions. But, divided as they were, the different socialist parties did not seek to promote divisions within unions nationally, nor openly promote a rupture in the international trade-union movement. Lenin's injunction to split the existing socialist union federation and to support the creation of a new rival Red labour international rebounded against communists everywhere. Only the preceding month, the International Confederation of Christian Unions, claiming 3.3 million members in Central, Western, and Mediterranean Europe, had been set up in the Hague as a rival to the IFTU.[36] At the end of 1920, workers had a choice

---

[35] *Proceedings of the Second Congress of the Communist International* (London, New Park, 1977), i. 307.

[36] See Georges Lefranc, *Le syndicalisme dans le monde* (Paris, Presses universitaires de France, 1977), 47.

between communist, Catholic, and socialist union internationals. The weight of evidence since 1918 was that existing unions held the loyalty of their members; in turn the existing unions were committed to the Amsterdam international. The end result of Profintern's creation was to play into the hands of the socialist leaders of the IFTU and the IMF, who could henceforth lay the charge of splitting and division against their communist rivals.

Lenin and other Russian leaders had lived long enough in the West not to underestimate the commitment of workers to their unions. He had implicitly recognized this in his tract, *Left-Wing Communism: An Infantile Disorder*, in which he criticized German communists who advocated setting up new unions in competition with established ones. Instead, communists should 'agree to make any sacrifice, and even—if need be—to resort to various strategems, artifices, and illegal methods, to evasions and subterfuges, as long as we get into the trade-unions, remain in them, and carry on the communist work within them at all costs'.[37]

This led to a twofold strategy of unity—with the goal of achieving communist control or influence within national unions—and disunity at the international level. As E. H. Carr observed, its application on an international stage had 'fatal consequences'[38] when the European revolution did not take place. Another argument possibly influenced the Soviet leaders and Lenin in their insistence on splitting the existing trade-union international. With the Western blockade now lifted and contact between Russian and Western trade-unions now normalized, there may have been the anxiety that Russian union activity in the existing internationals might be influenced in the direction of union independence, a position already being taken up by the Workers' Opposition inside Russia.[39] The best kind of shield against such ideas was to insist on a new communist-run trade-union international and make adherence to it a defining point of communist membership.

The Russians were told they were wrong to organize an international union split by Jack Tanner, a leading revolutionary shop steward from Britain. He was in the British delegation to the second congress of the Communist International, held in July 1920.

---

[37] Lenin, *Lenin on Trade Unions*, 357.
[38] Carr, *History of Soviet Russia*, iii. 357.
[39] See Leonard Schapiro, *The Communist Party of the Soviet Union* (London, Eyre and Spottiswoode, 1970), 201–5.

Later he became president of the Amalgamated Engineering Union from 1939 to 1954 and a member of the TUC general council during the birth, and then split, of the WFTU. [40] In Moscow in 1920 Tanner wanted any discussion about setting up a new trade-union international to take place outside Russia. In particular, he was alarmed at the assumption that the Bolshevik experience and tactics were universal norms:

What has now taken place in Russia cannot be a valid pattern for every country. In Britain, for example, the situation is completely different . . . The Second International collapsed because it was colourless and did not give clear instructions. I am afraid that the Communist International is falling into the opposite extreme and becoming too dogmatic. All organizations should be given freedom of movement in their own country,

declared Tanner in an exchange with Lenin.[41] But the Russians refused to heed his warning. They proceeded to make membership of the Communist International conditional on outright opposition to the IFTU and set in train the creation of the rival Red International of Labour Unions. At the end of July 1920, a schism opened in the world trade-union movement.

[40] Jack Tanner's life and politics are discussed more thoroughly in Ch. 9.
[41] *Proceedings of Second Congress of CI*, 61–2.

3

The Impact of Communism on the International Metalworkers' Federation 1920–1940

In the 1920s and 1930s the question of trade-union and other freedoms in the Soviet Union and the relationship between Soviet trade-unions and those elsewhere in Europe were themes that dominated the international debates of European unions, especially the metal unions and their international federation, the International Metalworkers' Federation. The secretariat of the International Metalworkers' Federation was now in Bern, in neutral Switzerland, by virtue of a decision of the 1920 IMF Congress. Konrad Ilg, head of the Swiss metalworkers' union, became the IMF secretary. The heart of the struggle between social democracy and communism in politics and in the unions was in Germany. Ilg, a German-speaking Swiss, was well suited to follow developments north of the Alps. He regularly attended and spoke at congresses of the German metalworkers' union. Meetings with representatives of the Russian metalworkers took place in Germany, where the Red International of Labour Unions, often known under its Russian acronym, Profintern, had an office in Berlin. Correspondence between the IMF and Profintern was also in German.

In his first act as IMF secretary, Ilg circulated two reports from Russian trade-unions in the autumn of 1920. In their different ways, both were far removed from the atmosphere of warm support for the Soviet cause contained in the resolution adopted a few weeks before at the IMF Congress. The first report came from the Bolshevik-controlled Russian metalworkers' union. Circulated in October 1920, it covered the historical background to the organization of metalworkers in Tsarist Russia and the role of the union in 1917. Details were given of economic reconstruction, factory committees, and wage systems. With capitalism overthrown, 'a new mentality of liberated work' had to be created. At its congress in April 1920, the Soviet metalworkers' union had

supported calls for the militarization of workers and the introduction of stronger regulations governing labour discipline.[1] As for
contact with metalworkers' unions in other countries, this 'could
only be on the basis of the guidelines' laid down by the Communist
International. The Executive Committee of the Communist International had already issued instructions to the Russian metalworkers
to seek 'at any cost to detach at least some of the yellow Amsterdam
unions at the International Metalworkers' Congress',[2] but the
refusal of a Danish visa for Schlapnikof had prevented any such
activity developing.

A very different report on trade-unionism in Soviet Russia was
circulated by the IMF secretariat in December 1920. This report
came from two small Menshevik-controlled metal unions. Their
representatives had met Ilg in London, where they offered to write a
'Report Regarding the Conditions of Labour in Soviet Russia'. The
document's criticisms of Bolshevik policies in the sphere of union
organization remained, for decades afterwards, at the heart of
democratic socialist or reformist objections to Soviet forms of
trade-unionism. The report must have carried additional authority
by coming from Russian trade-unionists rather than hostile
outsiders.

The report describes how the unions after 'the great Russian
revolution wiped out the Tsarist régime' struggled 'hand-in-hand
with the Socialist Parties, Councils of Workers' Deputies and Co-
operative Organisations against reaction', but after the second
revolution in November 1917 a

terrible fratricidal struggle got under way. Using the language and battle
cries of Socialism, the Communist government commenced its work of
destruction.

In order to clear their own way, the Communists declared that freedom
of speech, Unions, strikes and meetings were a 'superstition of the
bourgeoisie', and condemned all who demanded political rights as
'counter-revolutionaries.' Many comrades perished in prison, were sentenced to hard labour or even shot.[3]

[1] *Bericht des Vertreters des russischen Metallarbeiter an den am 20. August 1920
in Kopenhagen abgehaltenen internationalem Metallarbeiter-Kongress*, 28–35
(IMFA).
[2] Quoted in E. Dolléans, *Histoire du mouvement ouvrier* ii. *1871–1936* (Paris,
Colin, 1939), 338.
[3] *Report Regarding the Conditions of Labour in the Metal Industry in Soviet
Russia, December 1920*, 2–4 (IMFA).

Describing conditions in 1920, the report says that 'freedom of unions, freedom of meetings and freedom of speech' are all abolished and 'Strikes are declared counter-revolutionary acts': a communist worker in the August 1920 issue of the *Metallist* was quoted as stating:

Absolute submission to the director has been introduced at the works; neither interference nor contradictions on the part of the workmen are tolerated. At our Works absence without permission of the foreman means suspension of ration. Refusal to work overtime also means suspension of the ration. Whereas an obstinate refusal means arrest. For being late at work, a fine of two weeks' wages is imposed.[4]

In response to these conditions, 'strikes have been called in 77 per cent of the large and middle sized works', noted the report, adding, from an official report on Moscow prisons, 'In Bootursky Prison in Moscow 152 workmen from Briansky Works are detained; they were arrested for participating in a strike last March but have not yet been tried.'[5]

On international union relations, the Menshevik report put forward no policy of its own. Instead it included a lengthy extract from the speech of Zinoviev, as chairman of the Communist International, to the fifth All-Russian Congress of Trade Unions in November 1920. This extract read:

The question of the International Organisation of Trade Unions has become the key to the international movement and to the world revolution . . . Amsterdam is the last stronghold of the bourgeois régime and we must know how to put it down . . . In Germany and in the whole world it is not so much the bourgeoisie and the landowners or their military organizations, as the Trade Union reactionaries who are dangerous . . . We thought that our chief battle would be with the bourgeoisie, but it turns out in fact that the real obstacle to victory of the proletarian revolution is the presence of hardfisted ruling powers in the working trade-unions.[6]

In translating and circulating these two reports, especially the second, Ilg was preparing the ground for a rejection of communist influence or Soviet involvement in the IMF. In order to seal off the chances of institutional links between the European metal unions and their comrades in Soviet Russia, Ilg's anticommunism was, in

[4] *Report Regarding the Conditions of Labour in the Metal Industry in Soviet Russia, December 1920*, 13–14.
[5] Ibid. 14–15.   [6] Ibid. 16.

itself, insufficient. Another element was necessary to erect a barrier between Soviet and European trade-unions. This was the adoption of antisocialism as the guiding principle of Soviet relations with the non-communist left in Europe after 1920. In the autumn of 1920, the question of Russian participation in the IMF was still open. In a letter Ilg sent to Schlapnikof in October 1920, he invited the

Russian comrades [to] become members of our Federation . . . But as far as can be learned from the press, the Russian comrades have already decided not to join the present International Metalworkers Federation.

Likewise . . . the Russian Trade Unions have issued a call, according to which the International Federation of Trade Unions is to be abolished . . . The worst thing that could happen just now would be a disintegration and disruption of the existing trade-unions of the different countries of Europe. The Russian comrades would certainly be working in their best interests and approach more nearly to their aims if they join the present international associations and make their influence felt in them.[7]

Schlapnikof's reply, in January 1921, rejected Ilg's conditional offer. The IMF leader was 'following in the footsteps of the Danish haberdasher, Hansen, and the renegade Schlicke'. The Russian unions did not have to apply for membership of the IMF, argued Schlapnikof, as they were the successors of the pre–1914 Petrograd metal union which had been an IMF affiliate; furthermore, 'our determination to remain in the IMF does not however impose any obligations upon us in respect of the Amsterdam Trade Union Central. Its policy of going in hand in hand with the capitalists and adapting itself to the governments of the bourgeoisie we do not share.'[8]

The Russian's attempt to make a difference between the IMF, on one hand, and the IFTU, on the other, was superficially plausible, but Schlapnikof knew that the leaders of the big metalworkers' unions were also prominent in their national centres and thus committed to the Amsterdam IFTU. Moreover, by the time Schlapnikof's letter arrived in Bern, the political split between communism and socialism had been made permanent with the creation of communist parties adhering to the twenty-one conditions of the Communist International.

The attitudes of the European unions towards the newly created

---

[7] K. Ilg letter to A. Schlapnikof, 5 Oct. 1920 (IMFA).
[8] Schlapnikof to Ilg, 4 Jan. 1921 (IMFA).

communist parties hardened in the spring of 1921. In Germany, writes Ben Fowkes, the disastrous *Märzaktion*, an attempted communist uprising, was characterized by 'the great unwillingness of the proletariat, whether communist or not, to obey the [Communist] party's command'.[9] Robert Dissman, the 43-year-old leader of the 1.6-million-strong German metal union, Deutsche Metallarbeiter-Verband (DMV), who was a member of the Independent Social Democrats, the left-wing breakaway from the SPD, was alarmed at the fissures opened up in his union by the divisive row summed up by the slogan 'Moscow or Amsterdam?'[10]

In France, Merrheim had now thrown in his lot with the CGT leadership which in February 1921 declared that membership of the 'international trade-union section of Moscow's political international' was incompatible with membership of the CGT. This proscription was aimed at the Comités Syndicalistes Révolutionnaires (CSR), set up by sympathizers with the newly formed French Communist Party.[11]

Much had changed in less than a year since the IMF Congress in August 1920. The decisions of the second congress of the Communist International were being carried out with considerable effect. Everywhere, revolutionary communist parties were springing up. Local leaders translated into the vernacular the powerful appeals, radical analysis, and pungent denunciations of Lenin and Zinoviev; they enjoyed the notoriety and radical allure of being the authorized supporters of the only workers' state in the world. Unions were a principle area of contestation. As Lenin's intentions became clear, as they did by the beginning of 1921, the unions in Europe went on the defensive. The most important gain in the preceding thirty years had been organization. The unions, notably the larger, more self-confident ones like the metalworkers, defended themselves.

In March 1921, the Central Committee of the IMF assembled representatives from all its affiliates and adopted an important resolution on the communist question. Affirming that 'the prolet-

[9] B. Fowkes, *Communism in Germany under the Weimar Republic* (London, Macmillan, 1984), 67. See also Sigrid Koch-Baumgarten, *Die Märzaktion der KPD 1921* (Cologne, Bund Verlag, 1987).

[10] Quoted in Fritz Opel and Dieter Schneider, *90 Jahre Industriegewerkschaft, 1891 bis 1981* (Cologne, Bund Verlag, 1981), 233.

[11] Dolléans, *Mouvement ouvrier*, 345.

ariat of the whole world welcomes the Russian revolution enthusiastically and is inclined to assist the Russian proletariat . . . especially the trade-unions', the resolution went on to assert 'that the leaders of the Russian communist party . . . understand neither the economic nor political conditions of the proletariat and the bourgeoisie of Western Europe'; moreover, the Soviet leaders

> treat the endeavours of the Western European organizations with nothing but abuse, scorn and insult and [have] provoked discord and unpleasant conflicts among the organized working classes . . . They advise the workers of other lands to employ cunning and deceit and in their mighty arrogance and conceit they do not hesitate even to annihilate the organizations, which have required years of effort and sacrifices to create.[12]

Having established three enduring themes—a generalized welcome for the Russian revolution, accusations of lack of understanding of Western conditions on the part of the Soviet leaders, and reproaches over the promotion of internal conflict—the metal-workers' resolution went on to develop the concept of communist dictators leading Russian workers astray. This argument remained dear to Western socialists for years to come: 'This incomprehensible course cannot be the will of the Russian proletariat but is . . . the work of despotic leaders, who favour the principle of concealing the truth even towards the Russian working classes.'[13]

The defensive response to all these problems was laid down in the final sentence of the resolution, and from March 1921 onwards it governed relations between the IMF (and other Western trade-union internationals) and the Russian trade-unions, as well as communist unions elsewhere in Europe. 'Under the present conditions a co-operation in the same organization is . . . unproductive . . . Those organizations of metalworkers which join the Moscow International cannot be at the same time members of the International Metalworkers Federation.'[14]

Albert Lindemann has argued that 'by mid–1920, the Bolsheviks were more concerned about unity than the western Socialists; and . . . the Russians sought to limit the divisions of western revolutionary organizations',[15] but that is not how it appeared to

---

[12] Proceedings IMF Central Committee, 17 Mar. 1921 (IMF, Geneva).
[13] Ibid.
[14] Ibid.
[15] Albert Lindemann, *The Red Years: European Socialism versus Bolshevism 1919–1921* (Berkeley, University of California Press, 1974), 293.

socialist trade-union leaders in the West. The boom at the war's end was collapsing. By mid–1921, unemployment in the British shipbuilding, steel, and engineering industries had reached 36.1 per cent, 36.7 per cent, and 27.2 per cent respectively. This weakening of workers' strength encouraged employers to seek wage cuts and longer hours, reported Ilg.[16] There had been major strikes or lock-outs involving metalworkers in Czechoslovakia, Denmark, Finland, Italy, Luxembourg, and Norway. In Switzerland, wage reductions had been enforced.

In July 1921, the first congress of the Red International of Labour Unions, or Profintern as it was often called from its Russian acronym, institutionalized the proposals on trade-unions made at the second congress of the Communist International, and in the months afterwards. From now until its cessation of activity after the seventh congress of the Communist International in 1935, Profintern would serve two purposes. For communist trade-unionists in the West, membership of Profintern provided inter-national status and a formal union link to the revolutionary Soviet homeland. For their opponents, the very existence of Profintern, with its bureaux in Berlin, London, and Paris, its International Propaganda Committees, which functioned in parallel to the international trade secretariats, demonstrated the splitting tactics of Moscow and provided the justification for counter-measures against communists.[17] An example of the latter came in December 1921, when the Swiss metalworkers, under Ilg, adopted new rules banning communists from union membership.[18]

For the International Metalworkers' Federation, the issue of

---

[16] IMF Secretary's report to IMF 1921 Congress, Aug. 1921, p. 10 (IMFA).

[17] Profintern's origins, activities, and debates are well covered from Soviet sources in E. H. Carr, *A History of Soviet Russia* (London, Macmillan, 1950–78), iii. 398–401 and 459–62. Carr also covers Profintern thoroughly in vol. vii, ch. 36, and vol. xii, ch. 69. Details of Profintern's activities are also to be found in Carr's chapters on individual communist parties. The general secretary of Profintern, A. Losovsky, was a prolific writer. A Bolshevik from the earliest days (though he broke with Lenin between 1912 and 1917) Losovsky lived in Geneva and Paris in exile before the revolution. 'A cultivated, urbane, well-spoken man', according to Eddie Frow (in an interview with the author) who met him in 1930. Losovsky survived Stalin's purges up to 1949 when he was arrested and later died in a prison camp. See A. Losovksy ed. *Führer durch die Sowjetgewerkschaften für Arbeiterdelegationen* (Moscow, Verlagsgenossenschaft ausländischer Arbeiter in der UdSSR, 1937), and Losovsky, *Die rote Gewerkschafts-Internationale* (Frankfurt, ISP Verlag, 1978).

[18] P. Garban and J. Schmid, *Le Syndicalisme suisse* (Lausanne, Éditions d'en bas, 1980), 93.

relations with the Russian Metalworkers' Union, with Profintern, and with communist-led opposition unions remained a key one in the 1920s. Meetings between IMF representatives and the Russian metalworkers' union took place in Stockholm in September 1922 and Friedrichshafen in May 1923. Correspondence was exchanged in 1924 between the IMF and the Soviet metal union. At the IMF Congress in Vienna that year a delegation from the Russian metalworkers' union briefly attended and made a short presentation. On two key points the Russians appeared to be willing to make concessions to the IMF. At the discussions at Friedrichshafen, the Russians 'considered that a dissolution [of Profintern] was not out of the question', and they further declared themselves 'ready to co-operate in those countries in which there have been splits within the metalworkers' organizations, in order to clear away obstacles and to do their share towards bringing about again the unification of the metalworkers'.[19]

Whatever the hopes that statement entailed, they had disappeared by the time the IMF Congress considered the matter a year later in 1924. One of the problems of international trade-union activity was the time lapse between meetings, so that unforeseen developments could nullify commitments or statements made earlier. In Germany, the double impact of inflation and the German Communist Party's failed attempt at a general strike and uprising in October 1923 had robbed the unions of much of their confidence. In its weakened state, the German metal union blamed the communists. The Germans complained to the IMF that the 'contemptible agitation' of communists meant 'members cease paying their contributions'.[20]

Nearly all the twenty-two unions affiliated to the IMF in 1924 complained about the divisive activities of communists. The French, faced with the Confédération Générale du Travail Unitaire (CGT-U), set up in opposition to the CGT in 1922, demanded: 'How much time will be required in order to build up once more what was destroyed through the pernicious Moscow doctrine?'[21] In Czechoslovakia, which had the highest number of trade-union members after Britain and Germany, the IMF-affiliated union

[19] IMF Secretary report to IMF 1924 Congress, July 1924, p. 13 (IMFA).
[20] Reports of National Organizations of the IMF, 1921–4, p. 142 (IMFA).
[21] Ibid. 160.

complained of 'heavy losses through the industrial crisis and the destructive activities of the Communist Party'.[22]

Looked at from particular national perspectives, relations with the Russians and feelings towards communists varied over time according to national developments. In Britain, for example, the period between 1923 and 1926 saw considerable efforts to develop Anglo-Soviet trade-union links[23] at a time when bitterness against communists was high in France, Germany, and Czechoslovakia. The importance of the annual meetings and reports of the International Metalworkers' Federation lay in their provision of a wider international context for these national discussions; in general, the international exchanges at IMF meetings served to reinforce anticommunist tendencies in the European unions.

The last effort to integrate the Russian metalworkers with the IMF in the 1920s took place in Berlin in February 1927. There, Ilg, together with German, British, French, and Danish metal-union leaders, met three representatives of the Russian metalworkers. From the IMF side came the demand that 'dissident' groups be wound up as a condition for admitting the Soviet metalworkers, and Ilg reproached the Russians for the '21 conditions' of adherence to the Communist International.[24] The Russians proclaimed their complete willingness to abide loyally by IMF rules and protested that they had no influence over the communist metal unions in France and Czechoslovakia.[25]

A new element from the Russian side was a strong attack on the IMF leaders for a visit they had made to the United States in 1926 to seek recruits from amongst American metal unions. One of the Russians asked Ilg why he had not asked the Russians to join the IMF delegation to America. Ilg retorted that the Russians had not

[22] Reports of National Organizations of the IMF, 1921–4, 304. See also Jacques Rupnik, *Histoire du parti communiste tchécoslovaque* (Paris, Fondation nationale des sciences politiques, 1981), 41–4. In Czechoslovakia, the communists operated a double strategy of both creating a formal red union national centre, affiliated to Profintern, and also urging communist workers to stay in the socialist unions to push them leftwards. The unions were further split on linguistic and craft lines.
[23] See Daniel Calhoun, *The United Front, the TUC and the Russians 1923–1927* (Cambridge, CUP, 1976).
[24] The Russians felt sure enough of their arguments to print as a pamphlet the verbatim proceedings of the meeting, *Wer verhindert die Einheit der internationalen Metallarbeiterbewegung?* (Moscow, Verlag Internationales Propaganda-Komitee der revolutionären Metallarbeiter, 1927).
[25] Ibid.

invited the IMF to join their delegations to China.[26] The turn of the European metal unions towards America and of the Soviet unions towards Asia and the colonial world—themes of importance in the development of international labour politics after 1945—here entered the debate for the first time as a point of difference between communist and socialist metal unions.

This, however, was a side issue at the time. Centrally, Ilg insisted that the 'winding up of the dissident groups' was a pre-condition for unity. The Russian delegation replied that the problem of communist breakaway unions in individual countries could only be solved once there was international unity. This was a reversal of the position at the beginning of the decade when Lenin deplored national splits but supported the creation of a rival international union federation. The Russians ended the meeting by accusing the IMF of not wanting unity.[27]

Inevitably, the issue of unity died away during the 'third period' after 1928 with the attacks by Communists, nationally and internationally, on their 'social-fascist' rivals in other Left parties and unions. Profintern played its part in promoting still more separatist unions. In his closing address to the IMF Congress in 1930, the Danish metalworkers' president declared: 'Our comradeship and international solidarity will be stronger than the powers of the capitalistic, communistic and fascistic elements which are endeavouring to demolish the labour movement.'[28] Stalin's consolidation of power and the closer identification of Comintern and Profintern with the specific national interests of the Soviet Union justified, in the minds of the Western union leaders, the correctness of their rejectionist policies since 1921.[29]

The extent to which the refusal of the unions in Europe to cooperate with the Russians was a contributory factor to Stalin's withdrawal into the politics of the 'third period' is difficult to judge. As Donald Filtzer has shown, there was considerable worker resistance to Stalin's forced industrialization programmes, based as they were on a raised rate of exploitation.[30] The years 1928–33

---

[26] Ibid.   [27] Ibid.

[28] Proceedings of 1930 IMF Congress, 100 (IMFA).

[29] See Geoffrey Hosking, *A History of the Soviet Union* (London, Collins, 1985), 150–1, and E. H. Carr, *Twilight of the Comintern 1930–1935* (New York, Pantheon, 1982), 427.

[30] Donald Filtzer, *Soviet Workers and Stalinist Industrialization* (London, Pluto, 1986), 68–96.

cover a period of turmoil and change amongst Soviet workers. Links or involvement with European unions could have been counterproductive if the latter applied the same criteria about workers' rights and claims in Russia as they did in their own countries. None the less, when Stalin decided that unity with antifascist forces in Europe was needed, as he did in the Popular Front era, the order for Profintern to cease functioning was quickly given. At any stage in the 1920s, such a decision would have dramatically altered the debate about international trade-union unity. A few years later, positions were so entrenched that Profintern's disappearance had little impact.

Not all international union leaders shared Ilg's rigid hostility to communism. In contrast to the Swiss socialist's beliefs, the general secretary of the International Transport Workers' Federation (ITF), Edo Fimmen, remained an enthusiastic supporter of unity with the Russian unions throughout the 1920s. A Dutchman, Fimmen was general secretary of the ITF from 1919 to 1942. Between 1919 and 1923, he was also joint secretary of the International Federation of Trade Unions.[31] Fimmen had organized a transport workers' blockade of Hungary during the period of Horthy's suppression of socialists and trade-unionists and, during a visit to Moscow in 1919, had tried hard to persuade the Russian unions to join the IFTU.[32] He continued to preach unity at a time when most of the socialist-led unions in Europe were firmly anticommunist. As such, he was a favourite with the left-wing TUC leaders such as Albert Purcell and Alfonso Swales who, in 1925, had supported the setting up of the Anglo-Russian trade-union council.[33] Purcell wrote a foreword to Fimmen's book, *Labour's Alternative*, published in 1924, in which Fimmen stressed that it was 'vitally important that international unity should be established in the trade-union movement. Above all, collaboration with the Russian trade-unions and the incorporation of these into the international organizations is indispensable for the proper functioning of the Industrial Internationals.'[34]

---

[31] For an account of Fimmen see Lily Krier-Becker, unpublished manuscript biography in ITF archives, London, and *In Memoriam Edo Fimmen*, (ITF, London, 1952).

[32] Krier-Becker, 19.

[33] Hugh Clegg, *A History of British Trade Unions since 1889, ii. 1911–1933* (Oxford, OUP, 1985), 394. See also Calhoun, *The United Front*.

[34] Edo Fimmen, *Labour's Alternative* (London, Labour Publishing Company, 1924), 121–2.

One critic of Fimmen's attitude to the Russians was Ernest Bevin, the general secretary of the British Transport and General Workers' Union. Bevin's biographer, Alan Bullock, has argued that Bevin was more flexible to the Russian unions than other European union leaders. 'If there had to be a trade-union international, he thought it common sense that it should include the Russians and he was inclined to be critical of the implacable attitude of the Continental trade-unionists.'[35] But at ITF meetings Bevin showed himself no friend of the Soviet Union. In a discussion on the British General Strike at the ITF Congress in Paris in September 1926, Bevin declared: 'The British workers refuse to take advice and criticism from countries such as Russia, who believe they have a special monopoly of wisdom. The British workers say "Hands off Russia!", but they also say "Hands off England!" '[36]

At the ITF's next congress in Stockholm in 1928, Bevin clashed with Fimmen over a resolution calling for an extension of ITF activities to Africa and Asia. The use of the word 'imperialism' caused Bevin to bridle, and he urged the dropping of the offending paragraph because 'it refers to Imperialism but not to Sovietism'.[37] Later in the same debate, the contradictory nature of British trade-union attitudes towards the Soviet Union was clearly displayed. A motion submitted by the National Union of Railwaymen, also an ITF affiliate, called for an invitation to be extended to the Russian Transport Workers to become affiliated to the ITF. However, in moving the motion, the NUR delegate insisted that 'it is by no means the aim of the National Union of Railwaymen by this proposal to introduce Communism into the ITF. (Laughter) We are opposed to Communism and will have nothing to do with the Red Trade Union International. On the other hand we would like to see a reconciliation with the Russians and bring them into the ITF.'[38] Fimmen continued to call for unity. According to the undated draft of a speech found in his papers and which his biographer places around 1930, Fimmen argued that

The first step to unity must be some kind of agreement with the Russian trade-unions—unless it is hoped to crush the 'left-wing', a hope which, it is hardly necessary to say, no sane and practical man now shares whatever he

[35] Alan Bullock, *Life and Times of Ernest Bevin*, i (London, Heinemann, 1960), 384.
[36] Proceedings ITF 1928 Congress, 41 (ITF, London).
[37] Ibid.
[38] Ibid, 158.

may have thought in the past. Such an agreement is necessary because the Russian trade unions are the largest and most important body outside the IFTU, and, if I may be allowed to say so, still *kept* [Fimmen's emphasis] outside.[39]

By the 1932 ITF Congress, even the indefatigable Fimmen had to admit that he had changed his mind. Again the British railway union put up a resolution calling for an invitation to the Russian transport workers to join the ITF. Fimmen said such an affiliation was something he had 'hoped and worked for all the years I have been in the ITF'.[40] Fimmen went on to explain how, after the 1928 Congress, the invitation had been sent to the Russians to join. There had been no response. Indeed, continued Fimmen, the Russians had posed a direct challenge to the ITF:

The Russian trade-union movement has founded a new international for seamen and other transport workers. The one international organization of a sectional character founded by the Russians is directed against the ITF . . . In the circumstances, compelled as we are to defend ourselves against the so-called Red Opposition, I think it would be rather childish to approach the Russians and ask them to affiliate to the ITF.[41]

The British motion went down as did a call from the Czechoslovakian Motor Drivers' Union that the ITF send a fact-finding mission to the Soviet Union. This suggestion was supported by Bevin, a further example of what Bullock considers to be 'his open mind on the Communist experiment'.[42] Certainly, Bevin rejected what he described to the ITF Congress as 'an ostrich policy, a policy of self-delusion by not studying the situation in Russia and not trying to understand the new philosophy and its significance for the world',[43] but his 'open mind' on communism did not extend to endorsing anywhere the methods and values of Soviet trade-union organization. While he was prepared to go along with a visit to Russia, he was already a declared opponent of 'Sovietism' and had no time for Profintern. His treatment of communist opponents inside his own union, if not as blatantly discriminatory as in some other British unions, was none the less ruthless when he felt that the

[39] Krier-Becker, 206.
[40] Proceedings 1932 ITF Congress, 239 (ITF, London).
[41] Ibid.
[42] Bullock, *Bevin*, i, 508.
[43] Proceedings 1932 ITF Congress, 242.

union's authority (which he usually conflated with his own) was under challenge.[44]

As with the IMF, the issue of unity with the Russian trade-union within the framework of the industrial secretariats tailed off from 1930 onwards. Fimmen fell seriously ill in 1938 when fresh efforts were made to bring the Russians into the IFTU orbit. He died in 1942, shortly before the revival of East–West trade-union unity. As for Bevin, his position had been made clear at his union's Biennial Delegate Conference in 1935.

By God, I wish Russia could have seen that if she had never supported the Communist Party in England but allowed the British trade-union movement to help Russia she would have been in a much better position than today . . . The philosophy of the Red International cannot mix with our form of democracy. You had better accept this and try to do the best we can with the facts before us.[45]

The spread of fascism into German-speaking Europe robbed the Western internationals of their most important single affiliates, the German unions, and later the not insignificant Austrians and Czechs.[46] Unlike the late 1920s and early 1930s when there had been common international campaigns for the eight-hour day[47] and the first glimpses of common European-wide ideas of welfare capitalism and industrial democracy, after 1933 the unions tended to go their own ways. In Switzerland in 1937 and in Sweden in 1938, the metal unions signed agreements with metal-industry employer federations which, in both countries, inaugurated many decades of strike-free relations between unions and employers.[48]

[44] Bullock, *Bevin*, i, 609–14.

[45] Ibid. 559.

[46] IMF membership fluctuated in the 1920s and 1930s from a high of 3.2m. in 1921 at the peak of the post-war growth in trade-union membership down to 750,000 in 1933 when the Germans stopped being members. By 1938, membership had climbed back to 1.8m. from 22 unions in 17 European countries. The increase in membership at the end of the 1930s was due to the increase in organized metalworkers in France in the Popular Front era. See IMF Secretary's report (1938), 22 (IMFA).

[47] See Lex Heerma van Voss, 'The International Federation of Trade Unions and the attempt to maintain the eight-hour day (1919–1929)' in F. van Holthoon and M. van der Linden (eds.), *Internationalism in the Labour Movement* (Leiden, E. J. Brill, 1988), ii. 518–43.

[48] On the Swiss 'Peace Treaty', as it is called, which was signed by Ilg in 1937, against strong left-wing opposition, see *The Peace Agreement in the Swiss Engineering and Metalworking Industries* (Zürich, Association for Historical

The turn towards what Göran Therborn has called 'popularly organized Capitalism' was most marked in Sweden;[49] in Britain there grew up 'structures of co-operation', an 'equilibrium' consisting of a 'corporate triangle between government, employers and unions'.[50] Although the TUC general secretary, Walter Citrine, tried to argue that Roosevelt's New Deal was a kind of action programme such as had been put forward by the IFTU, the turn towards domestic introspection and the search for national solutions for economic and social problems was marked after 1933.[51]

The Popular Front era between 1934 and 1938 had less of an impact on the international trade-union organizations than might have been expected, given its effect on some national labour movements, notably in France and the United States. Arguments about Profintern became irrelevant as the Red trade-union international ceased functioning in 1937. There were no more 'dissident' unions to complain about. In France, the CGT merged with its communist rival, the CGT-U, in 1935.

International unity had now come down to a simple question: When would the Russians join the International Federation of Trade Unions? The IFTU sent a delegation to Moscow in 1937 to negotiate the affiliation of the Russians, but the talks broke down. There was foot-dragging on both sides. The Russians wanted various commitments from the IFTU, including a reorganization of the international trade secretariats such as the IMF, while the IFTU leaders insisted on a simple affiliation of the Russians to the IFTU

Research in Economics, 1967), 29–75. On the Saltsjöbaden Agreement signed in Sweden in 1938, see Leif Lewin, *Governing Trade Unions in Sweden* (Cambridge, Mass. Harvard University Press, 1980), 31.

[49] Goran Therborn, 'The Coming of Swedish Social Democracy', in E. Collotti (ed.), *L'Internazionale Operaia e Socialista tra le due guerre* (Milan, Feltrinelli, 1985), 586. Therborn emphasizes that Swedish arrangements did not entail state intervention, (nor did those of the Swiss) and therefore, he writes, the term corporatism 'whatever this notion means' does not apply to Sweden.

[50] Keith Middlemas, *Politics in Industrial Society: The Experience of the British System since 1911* (London, Deutsch, 1979), 243.

[51] According to Citrine, 'President Roosevelt's . . . conversion to . . . measures long advocated by the trade-union and labour movement in our own country, and by the IFTU, are a convincing proof that our policy is the only one . . . adequate to deal with the present solution.' Quoted in Robert Shackleton, 'Trade Unions in the Slump', in Ben Pimlott and Chris Cook (eds.), *Trade Unions in British Politics*, (London, Longman, 1982), 135.

as presently constituted.[52] Léon Jouhaux, the French CGT leader, had a surprise call for a night-time meeting with Stalin, who dismissed the differences between socialists and communists as an 'unavoidable family quarrel'; in Jouhaux's estimation, Stalin showed little idea of the reality of French trade-unionism, in particular the CGT's rejection of control by political parties.[53]

The affiliation of the American Federation of Labor in 1937 strengthened the anti-Russian majority in the IFTU executive, and the conditions the Russians set for affiliation provided a bureaucratic excuse to do nothing. It would need a greater shock before either side would shift its position. A similar attempt by the French metalworkers, now 750,000 strong and under communist leadership, to get the IMF to seek affiliation from the Russian metal unions was deflected at the 1938 Congress by a wording that insisted that unions 'wishing to join up must recognise the rules and abide by the decisions of' the IMF.[54]

Despite the menacing presence of fascism in power to the south, east, and north of Switzerland, Ilg was still not prepared to make common cause with the Russians. He recognized that war was coming, writing to the Swedish metal-union leader in June 1939: 'Two thirds of German industry are today working exclusively on war material and the greater part of Germany's wealth is invested in war material or goods that increase the capacity for making war . . . All the ways back to a normal economy are cut off.'[55] But despite this analysis of the German drive towards war, his anticommunism prevailed over his antifascism. In his report to the

---

[52] The Russians wanted a second general secretary designated by themselves, and a three-person presidium, one of which would be a Russian. They also wanted a guarantee that their dues payments would not be used for propaganda against the Soviet government. Details from an IFTU perspective can be found in W. Schevenels, *45 Years IFTU*, (Brussels, International Confederation of Free Trade Unions, 1955), 263–7, and in Bernard Georges, Denise Tintant, and Marie-Anne Renauld, *Léon Jouhaux dans le mouvement syndical français* (Paris, Presses universitaires de France, 1979), 217.

[53] 'Rencontre avec Staline, Novembre 28, 1937', Jouhaux archives. Reprinted in Georges *et al.*, *Léon Jouhaux*, 411–14. Whether deliberately or not, Stalin was repeating Léon Blum's formula pronounced at the French Socialists' Congress of Tours in 1920 when the French Left broke into its socialist and communist wings. Blum appealed to the breakaway supporters of the Third International, 'Let us remain brothers, brothers that have been separated by a cruel quarrel, but a family quarrel, and that a common home will one day bring us together again.'

[54] Proceedings IMF 1938 Congress, 68 (IMFA).

[55] Ilg to A. Svenson, 26 June 1939 (IMFA).

IMF Congress in 1938, he attributed to 'the rulers of Soviet Russia' the arousal of 'passions [and] general chaos' in Germany which eased the way for Hitler's takeover.[56] Further evidence for Ilg's anticommunism can be seen in a 1939 IMF pamphlet on the Spanish civil war. This, the last pre-war publication of the IMF, was written by Wenceslas Carrillo, leader of the UGT, the (socialist) metalworkers' union, and a socialist minister in the republican government. *The Truth about the Events in Spain: An Open Letter to Joseph Stalin* is a bitter attack on the role of the Spanish Communist Party and the Communist International and their hounding of socialist opponents during the civil war.[57] It is also partly a justification of Wenceslas Carrillo's role in the final days before Franco took over and a reproach to Stalin for having politically seduced Carrillo's son, Santiago, later the general secretary of the Spanish Communist Party.[58]

Its significance lies not so much in its precise argument but as evidence of Ilg's continuing hard-line anticommunism and his belief that the other metal unions of Europe would consider Carrillo's *Open Letter* a proper document for the IMF to translate, print, and distribute. This suggests that by the summer of 1939, therefore, there had been no major shift in the long-standing hostility to Communism and the Soviet Union in the IMF.

The pact between the Soviet Union and Nazi Germany in August 1939 was taken as proof by many union leaders that their suspicions of Stalin's honesty and intentions during the popular front years had been justified, and it reinforced the general distrust of the Soviet Union and communist activity evident since the early 1920s. Metal-union leaders from Britain (the AEU and the Iron and Steel Confederation), France, Belgium, the Netherlands, and Switzerland met in January 1940 and announced that Europe was 'threatened by a general war due to the attitude of German Nazism and Soviet Russia . . . War is the inevitable result of a totalitarian system of government.'[59]

Before 1914, war had been blamed on capitalism; now totalitari-

[56] IMF Secretary's report 1938, 13 (IMFA).

[57] Wenceslas Carrillo, *The Truth About the Events in Spain: An Open Letter to Joseph Stalin* (Berne, IMF, 1939).

[58] In 1990, Santiago Carrillo, who had stopped being general secretary of the Spanish Communist Party in 1985, applied to join the Partido Socialista Obrera de España, his father's party.

[59] Resolution at IMF Central Committee, 29 Jan. 1940 (IMFA).

anism was to blame. Internationalism in the labour movement had been unable to move beyond the exchange of information and a reinforcement of national union identities. Unions looked increasingly towards the state as the source of economic and social protection. When communist parties sought to take up international labour questions, it was with a view to establishing their differences and separate identity in respect of their socialist rivals. German communist attempts to develop support for British miners in 1926 or British communist work for Indian trade-unionists served as causes to promote the internal profile of the national communist party.[60] Each aspect of internationalism was linked to national specificities. No one argued for a return to Marx's universalist principles as he elaborated them for the first international. Far from the workers having no country, that was almost all they had, including the transferred allegiance to another country, claimed as the workers' state, the Soviet Union.

The continuing strength of nationalism was one major reason for the failure of the international labour movement to make much impact after 1918. Equally important was the political division on the Left. For Lenin to build communism it was necessary to smash social democracy, but democratic socialism proved a sturdy beast. Extending that anaylsis into the trade-union movement was an error and transformed European trade-unions into bastions of anticommunism from 1921 onwards. International trade-union federations, such as the IMF, acted politically, in addition to their ostensible purpose as industrial federations, to keep at bay communist involvement. Communist antisocialism, in turn, ensured that unity became impossible. The enthusiasm of activists and militant union officials inspired by the Soviet revolution, who might have transformed the existing unions and their internationals, was not felt. Lenin's conditions for adherence to the Communist International saw to that. By the time Stalin had changed policy towards popular frontism, the inherited suspicions and divisions were too deep-rooted. Even the national shift in the direction of unity, such as in France after 1935, failed to transform

[60] See Larry Peterson, 'Internationalism and the British Coal Miner's Strike of 1926: The Solidarity Campaign of the KPD among Ruhr Coal Miners' in Holthoon and Linden (eds.), *Internationalism in the Labour Movement*, ii. 459–89, and John Saville, 'Britain: Internationalism and the Labour Movement Between the Wars' ibid. 565–83.

anything in the international organizational sphere because the old enmities dominated. The war would transform the perspective for international trade-unionism. But the views and positions of Ilg or Jouhaux, of Citrine or Bevin, had been forged over two decades and would not be changed by the future.

4

Metalworkers and the Creation of the World Federation of Trade Unions

THE World Federation of Trade Unions was launched in Paris, in September 1945. Unions from fifty-four countries representing 67 million workers took part. For the first time, the trade-unions from Russia were in the same world body as British and American unions. Despite the array of countries represented, the WFTU remained firmly in the hands of the heavyweight unions of the victorious powers—the Soviet Union, Great Britain, the United States, and France. The WFTU constitution was carefully balanced to give no one union or country predominance. A right-wing president, Britain's Walter Citrine, followed by another right-winger, Arthur Deakin, was balanced by the left-wing general secretary, Louis Saillant, from France.

Once in place, what exactly was the WFTU to do? International labour unity was a remarkable achievement in itself, but a union organization, national or international, accommodationist or anti-capitalist, must sustain variable processes of regulation, mobilization, and presence in order to command loyalty and justify continuing support.[1] The WFTU constitution committed the new

[1] There is considerable literature on the origins and short life of the united WFTU, 1945–8. Two recent revisionist accounts are P. Weiler, *British Labour and the Cold War* (Stanford, Calif., Stanford University Press, 1988), and A. Carew, *Labour Under the Marshall Plan*, (Manchester, Manchester University Press, 1987). The introduction to the collection of documents on the WFTU and the international trade secretariat edited by Sigrid Kock-Baumgarten and Peter Rütters, *Zwischen Integration und Autonomie: Der Konflikt zwischen den internationalen Berufsse-kretariaten und dem Weltgewerkschaftsbewegung 1945 bis 1949* (Cologne, Bund Verlag, 1991), offers a post-revisionist German account of the events leading up to the WFTU's rupture. John Windmuller, *American Labor and the International Labor Movement 1940 to 1953* (Ithaca, NY, Cornell University, 1954), is an older but reliable account which provides a good narrative of the WFTU. Schevenels, *45 years IFTU* (Brussels, International Confederation of Free Trade Unions, 1955), tells the story from an official side. He is hostile to the WFTU. L. Lorwin, *The International Labor Movement* (New York, Harper, 1954), has clear chapters on the WFTU, though he draws on Windmuller. Morton Schwartz, 'Soviet Policy and the World Federation of Trade Unions, 1945–1949', Ph.D. thesis (Columbia University, 1963), is a thorough account of WFTU debates and decisions illuminated

body to 'the struggle for the extermination of all fascist forms of government'.[2] With the exception of Franco's Spain, that goal had already been achieved. There were no calls to replace capitalism or for even mildly reformist aims such as the nationalization of key industries already under way in Britain and France. The WFTU was 'for the full exercise of the democratic rights and liberties of all peoples'.[3] Yet during its first two years of existence, when faced with demands for support from Greeks, Spaniards, or Tunisians struggling for their democratic rights, the WFTU leaders, including the Russians, endorsed do-nothing policies.[4]

If the WFTU was not to support political upheaval, what was its purpose? Its constitution gives some clues. It was in favour of full employment, better wages, and fewer hours, adequate social security, and the organization of workers into unions throughout the world.[5] Such were the ends of the WFTU. What were the means? How could the WFTU develop a functional purpose that would give it stable roots and an enduring *raison d'être* able to transcend possible political differences?

The answer lay in the relationship between the WFTU and the international trade secretariats, such as the International Metalworkers' Federation. These were the organizations representing unions carrying out basic industrial activities. Linking the secretariats to the WFTU would further unify world labour and give the new body an effective industrial and servicing role below the level of the national centre. As Jack Tanner, the AEU president, put it in August 1945, when addressing representives of the seventeen metal unions grouped in the British section of the IMF, the meetings of the IMF 'bring many of us together who would not otherwise meet in the ordinary course of our trade-union duties . . . If the results are

---

by the author's reading of contemporary Soviet commentaries on international union issues. To this writer's knowledge, the account by Schwartz is the only one in the West which extensively cites Russian sources, mainly Moscow journals, which mentioned the WFTU or related labour issues. *The World Federation of Trade Unions 1945–1985* (Prague, World Federation of Trade Unions, 1985) is an official communist history. Later chapters on national unions will examine the WFTU in some detail and give reference to other sources.

[2] *Report of the World Trade Union Conference Congress* (Paris, WFTU, 1945), 262.
[3] Ibid.
[4] This is discussed more fully in Ch. 8.
[5] Report of WFTU Congress, Paris, 1945, 261.

beneficial on national basis, [they] will certainly be so on an international plane'.[6]

The need to link the international trade secretariats to the WFTU was universally acknowledged, but the failure of the WFTU to move from being a political-diplomatic expression of world trade-union unity to developing an organizational or service-functional role was the rock on which the WFTU first foundered. For some of those drafters of the WFTU constitution the answer was simple. The existing international trade secretariats should dissolve and new industrial departments of the WFTU would undertake their previous activities. At the end of the Paris Congress, the relevant clause on the secretariats' Article 13 of the constitution, read:

> The General Council [of the WFTU] will establish within the WFTU trade departments for such trades and industries as determined by the WFTU. The trade departments will concern themselves with technical problems relating to their trades. In this regard they will enjoy complete autonomy within the WFTU. But they will have no power and may not be active in matters relating to general policy which shall remain exclusively for the Congress, the Executive Committee and the Bureau. The trade departments are ultimately responsible for their activities to the General Council and the Executive Committee. The aims, working methods, duties, rights and financial arrangements pertaining to the trade departments will be determined by a special regulation which will be adopted by the Executive Committee and approved by the General Council.[7]

This convoluted language sought to reconcile two sets of aims. The Russians wanted the new trade departments merely to have an advisory status within the WFTU concentrating on the problems of working hours, wages, and social legislation. Saillant endorsed this view, dismissing the existing secretariats as European organizations no longer relevant for global labour activities. On the other hand the TUC leader, Citrine, warned that the secretariats would 'liquidate themselves [only] under proper conditions' and insisted that British acceptance of the WFTU constitution 'depends upon the satisfactory outcome of negotiations . . . with the international secretariats . . . Let that be clearly understood'.[8]

This then was the earliest test for the WFTU set before its leaders in October 1945. How could they find a mechanism that would

---

[6] IMF British Section Annual General Meeting, 11 Aug. 1945 (IMFA).
[7] Report of WFTU Congress, Paris, 122.
[8] Ibid. 22, 33.

integrate the secretariats into the new world body? This was not, as Anthony Carew points out, 'a mere technical issue of how to merge separate institutions [but] a profound philosophical conflict over the nature of trade-union organizations—their aims and methods'.[9] In his view, British insistence on a satisfactory settlement with the international trade secretariats amounted to 'an escape route from the WFTU' reflecting the TUC's 'natural wariness over too close a link-up with the inscrutable Russians'.[10] Carew also stresses the role of the American Federation of Labor (AFL) which Peter Weiler argues 'correctly identified the [international trade secretariats] as the Achilles' heel of the new international and set out to capture them [and] used them to strengthen opposition to the WFTU at the individual trade-union level'.[11]

Both historians, and it is a view shared by others writing on this question, consider the AFL's interventions to be the key to the development of effective anti-WFTU policies by the secretariats. Yet most of the direct AFL interventions touching upon the relationship between the WFTU and the secretariats are seen to unfold only from early 1947 onwards. Well before this, hostilities between the secretariats and the WFTU had become obvious, and other important factors were determining international trade-union relations. The eighteen months between the WFTU's Paris Congress in September 1945 and the announcement of the Truman Doctrine in March 1947 is an important but underconsidered period in international labour history which provides important clues in the search for the causes of the split in the WFTU.

The IMF had enjoyed an attenuated existence during the war. Many continental union leaders found themselves in Britain, but there was no support for a call to transfer the IMF's secretariat to London for the war's duration; to be dependent on and grateful for British hospitality was one thing; to place the international secretariat in the hands of the powerful, domineering British unions was another.[12] Isolated in Switzerland, Ilg could do little save to correspond with, send packages to, or try to arrange Swiss visas for metal-union leaders in the rest of Europe.[13] Within two months of

---

[9] Carew, *Labour under the Marshall Plan*, 71.
[10] Ibid.
[11] Weiler, *British Labour and the Cold War*, 92–3.
[12] IMF British Section, 19 Sept. 1942.
[13] See 'Emigranten 1935–1945' file in IMF archives.

the war's end, Ilg was in correspondence with British, French, Austrian, Swedish, Dutch, Spanish, Belgian, Czechoslovakian, and Hungarian metal-unionists. Karl Maisel, president of the newly-created Austrian metal union, wrote in August 1945 to resume contact with the IMF, while the Dutch metal union asked if the IMF could provide a car, as transport in the Netherlands was badly disrupted.[14]

For Ilg, the five years of the war had changed little. His two obsessions, the Soviet Union and communism, continued to dominate his thinking. A week after European hostilities ceased, Ilg expressed concern over what was happening in 'Soviet-occupied territory . . . It seems as if an iron curtain has fallen . . . behind which developments are taking place about which we know hardly anything'.[15] Ilg received the documentation on the WFTU, including the proposal to merge the IMF into a newly created trade department, but also a warning from a former colleague, the Spanish metalworkers' leader, Carrillo, in exile in London. The Spaniard wrote in June 1945: 'I am not enthusiastic about the creation of the new world federation . . . I see no loyalty forthcoming from the Communists. They look only after their own interests.'[16]

These doubts about relations with communists inside the WFTU or within the metal unions themselves surfaced at the first meeting of the IMF's Central Committee held in October 1945, in Switzerland. The AEU's Jack Tanner had just taken part as a TUC delegate at the WFTU and had come from the bustle of Paris to the placid calm of a lake near Lucerne where the Swiss metalworkers had a holiday home to which Ilg invited Central Committee delegates. There was a great difference between the expressions of unity in Paris at the WFTU's launch and the fears and hostility about communism at the IMF's gathering. Tanner, from the proud, confident British metal unions, was alone in proclaiming satisfaction about relations with the communists. 'They collaborate willingly and, even in the Amalgamated Engineering Union, two Communists are on the Executive Committee. Various local groups and districts are under communist leadership. As long as they follow the policy of the British trade-union movement, we make

[14] K. Maisel to Ilg, 29 Aug. 1945; N. van den Born to Ilg, 9 July 1945 (IMFA).
[15] *Schweizerische Metalarbeiter Zeitung*, 16 May 1945.
[16] W. Carrillo to Ilg, 6 June 1945.

no opposition against them,' he explained to his Continental comrades.[17]

From other countries there were complaints about the relations between the socialists in the metal unions, represented at the IMF meeting, and communists. The Belgian delegate reported that disputes with the communists were hampering trade-union activity. The socialists had just managed to retain control of the metal union and had beaten back an attempt by communists to disaffiliate from the IMF.[18] Neighbouring Luxembourg also reported difficulties in re-establishing the union under socialist control. 'The main danger for us is Communism. Once strong enough, it will certainly seek to render our existence impossible . . . We only fear that the British comrades do not sufficiently realize the communist danger.'[19] The three Scandinavian metal unions, whose achievements for workers— and in Norway's case, her wartime resistance—had been admired everywhere, also reported serious problems with communists. For Norway and Denmark, the 'tactical manœuvres' of the Communist Party had caused problems, while in Sweden a major strike by metalworkers—the biggest in Swedish history—had been 'promoted mainly by the Communists'. The strike, which began in the winter of 1945, came to an end when the leadership of the metal union, against the balloted wishes of the members, ordered a return to work in July 1945. It was a major test of power between Swedish social democrats and communists, ending in a decisive victory for the former. Shortly afterwards, in Norway, the communists were expelled from the governing coalition—a Nordic forerunner to what happened in France two years later.[20]

The speakers presented their own national perspectives, but the general impression was clear enough. Communist activity in the metal unions in several West European countries was seen as a threat, except in Britain where communists were tolerated as long

---

[17] Proceedings IMF 1945 Central Committee.
[18] Ibid. 25.
[19] Ibid. 11.
[20] Ibid. 32–8. See also Pär-Erik Back, *Svenska Metallindustriarbetareförbundets historia 1940–1956* (Stockholm, Tiden Verlag, 1977), 278–303 and Einhart Lorenz, 'Scandinavische Arbeiterbewegung und Marshall Plan: Reaktionen der Arbeiterparteien und der sozialdemokratischen Regierungen Dänemarks, Norwegens und Schwedens', in Othmar Nikola Haberl and Lutz Niethammer (eds.), *Der Marshall-Plan und die europäische Linke* (Frankfurt, Europäische Verlagsanstalt, 1986), 424.

as they did not directly oppose the existing leadership. Naturally, in turn, these attitudes had an effect on the question of the metal unions' relationship with the WFTU. For Ilg, the main purpose of the meeting was to decide 'whether the international professional secretariats should be built into the new World Organisation and how far their independence and autonomy can be safeguarded'.[21] Opinions were divided between hard-line anticommunists, such as the Belgian Keuwet, who argued that the WFTU would be 'in favour of Communism and . . . will be used by Russia in its foreign policy', and the Swedish Svensson, who supported the creation of 'a strong international trade-union organization . . . which is built up on socialist and democratic principles'; the Swede supported the draft statutes of the WFTU, arguing that once the international trade secretariats 'are built into the new World Organisation they will play a more important part'.[22] The middle ground was defined by Lincoln Evans, the able right-wing leader of Britain's Iron and Steel Trades Confederation and secretary of the British Section of IMF affiliates. He expressed himself 'in favour of the creation of the [WFTU] but the autonomy of the [international trade secretariat] must be safeguarded'.[23]

The policy of folding the IMF into the WFTU, but only on certain conditions, proved impossible to implement as events in 1946 and 1947 were to show, but here, in the early autumn of 1945, is clear enough evidence on two important issues which would determine the course of attitudes and decisions over the next two years. Firstly, the metal unions of Europe were not ready at this stage, and unconditionally, to liquidate their international as the price for joining a world body. Secondly, hostility between socialists and communists in the trade-unions had not dissolved as a result of the common struggle against Hitlerism. The first was dependent on the second, and in this continuing hostility dating back to the 1920s and 1930s lie the roots of this early major organizational—though in reality political—failure of the WFTU.

There were other factors which also determined the fate of the WFTU and the IMF (and other secretariats) and which are not considered in those accounts of the WFTU in which it is seen purely as a locus of Anglo-American confrontation with Russia. Four of these are worth considering in detail: the role of the International

[21] Ibid. 7.   [22] Ibid. 6–7.   [23] Ibid. 5.

Labour Organization; the antisocialism of communist unions and their policy of self-exclusion from the secretariats; the position of unions from small countries faced with the super-power politics of the WFTU, and, finally, the personalities of Ilg and the other international secretaries.

Meanwhile, the meeting of the IMF in 1945 took another important decision which was to renew payment of affiliation fees to the secretariat in Bern. These had been suspended during the war, save in Switzerland, Sweden, and Britain, and it was agreed to spend these dues on relief work for the war-ravaged metal unions on the Continent. This, a seemingly minor aspect of financial bureaucracy, was organizationally important. It meant the IMF was back in business as an international union organization with income and expenditure. One of the key advantages that the WFTU might have had, that of being the sole channel for receiving and allocating funds for international trade-union work, was thus nullified, at least for the metalworking field.

While the WFTU had nothing to offer industrial or craft unions below the level of national centres so long as the question of the transformation of the international secretariats into trade departments remained unresolved, another established international body was waiting and anxious to step into the partial vacuum thus created. This was the International Labour Organization, which between the wars had been an important international forum for union activity. At its general conference in Philadelphia in 1944, the ILO had sought to redefine its role so as to be one of the arbiters of labour questions in the post-war world. The ILO constitution was rewritten to make full employment a post-war international goal.[24]

Government, employer, and worker representatives from all over the world, including representatives in exile of the occupied European countries, took part in the ILO conference in April and May 1944. The noteworthy exception was the Soviet Union which had refused to join the ILO when it was set up and only became a not-very-active member during the Popular Front era. Although the ILO director-general expressed a hope that the Soviet Union would rejoin, the Russians stayed out of the ILO until 1954. Apart from its tripartite character which admitted the complementary role of

---

[24] See *A New Era: The Philadelphia Conference and the Future of the ILO* (Montreal, ILO, 1944). The ILO secretariat had moved from Geneva to Montreal for the war's duration.

employers alongside unions and governments, the philosophy of the existing unions active in the ILO was far from Soviet or communist ideas on trade-unions. J. H. Oldenbroek, general secretary of the International Transport Workers' Federation, speaking as a Dutch delegate, put forward the classic Western position on union independence at the Philadelphia conference: 'The right of free association and the existence of free trade-unions are the very foundations of this organization. Free trade-unions means no interference by Governments or employers or others.'[25]

Once the war ended, the ILO swiftly established industrial committees for the iron and steel industry and the metal trades industry.[26] These two committees of direct interest to metal unions affiliated to the IMF organized separate conferences in the United States in April and May, 1946. They provided a forum for leaders of the metal unions from different countries to discuss industrial problems and to have political consultations other than at an IMF meeting. Ilg made use of his participation at the ILO Metal Trades Committee in the United States for contacts with American unions. AFL unions took part in ILO meetings, while the Russians did not. The ILO, operating with a more progressive mandate than had been the case before the war, quickly became a functioning, purposeful world body dealing with industrial matters of concern to the metal unions. Twelve months after the war's end, the WFTU had provided no services of interest to the metal unions, while the ILO had organized two world conferences which, in the view of the British steelworkers' leader, Lincoln Evans, offered: 'wide opportunities for metalworkers to discuss their problems and seek solutions on a higher international level than has been possible in the past . . . One can see [the committees] playing an increasingly important part in world metal affairs and in the development of a closer understanding between the workers engaged in metal industries in the various countries.'[27]

---

[25] Ibid. 67.
[26] See 'The International Labour Organisation Since the War', in *International Labour Review*, 107: 2, (1953), 17.
[27] Proceedings IMF British Section AGM, 28 Sept. 1946.

ANTISOCIALISM, SMALL UNIONS AND KONRAD ILG

Conventional usage describes those hostile to communism as anticommunists, terminology perfectly accurate in itself though its implied negation involves a sleight of tongue or of pen not applied in the other direction.[28] Yet antisocialism of a very specific kind can be seen in the post-war behaviour of some metal unions, previously affiliated to the IMF. The refusal of metal unions now under communist influence to join again in IMF activities, as well as the lack of interest by the Soviet metalworkers' union, was doubtless meant to put pressure on the Federation by showing it up to be a small rump of some West European organizations. Yet this expression of antisocialism, the shunning of the IMF by the communist unions, paradoxically served mainly to strengthen those keen to renew their public, declamatory anticommunism which had been suspended during the war.

The French CGT metalworkers' federation politely turned down Ilg's invitation to take part in the Vitznau Central Committee of 1945, stating that any such meeting should await the 'reconstitution of a real world trade-union'.[29] A year later the tone had hardened, with Raymond Semat, the new communist general secretary of the French metalworkers' union, rejecting the invitation of what he called the 'ex-International Federation of Metalworkers' to the 1946 Central Committee which 'cannot take any proper decisions because its existence does not conform to the WFTU constitution'.[30] Up to the outbreak of the war, the French CGT metalworkers' union had been a key IMF affiliate. So, too, had been the Czechoslovak metal union, whose president, general

[28] William Graf discusses some of these points in 'Anti-Communism in the Federal Republic of Germany', in *The Socialist Register 1984* (London, Merlin Press, 1984), 164–214. He cites the following helpful distinction: 'Whereas the anticommunism of the bourgeoisie is based on its interest in defending its political and economic power positions, the anticommunism of the wage-dependent classes has a different motivation. For them it is a matter of maintaining their higher standard of living, their freedom of opinion, their freedom of movement, in short all those things that are the result of the struggles of the . . . labour movement.' (p. 182).

[29] R. Semat to Ilg, 8 Aug. 1945.

[30] R. Semat to Ilg, 20 Sept. 1946. Semat was only the acting general secretary of the CGT metalworkers' union while Abroise Croizat was a minister in the French government. A communist since 1920, Croizat had been secretary of the CGT-U metal union and active in Profintern before taking over as head of the unified CGT metal union in 1936. He returned to lead the CGT metalworkers after the communists left the French government in May 1947.

secretary, and treasurer had all died at Nazi hands during the war. After the Red Army had liberated most of Czechoslovakia, 'a single centralized Union without special unions for the various trades' was set up under the leadership of Anton Zapotocky, a former communist deputy; its daily paper was also edited by a communist.[31] Ilg had this information from Josef Bělina, an official of the pre-war Czechoslovak union, now in exile in London. Bělina went back to Czechoslovakia in 1945, and again in 1946, but found no welcome from the communists who now controlled the trade-unions. Traditionally, the progressive thrust of Marxist thinking on union organization had been in the direction of industrial unionism. Now, reported Bělina, there was a new concept, borrowed clearly enough from the Soviet Union. According to Bělina, by October 1945,

in Eastern Europe no individual trade-unions exist as all are represented in one single state trade-union centre . . . In Czechoslovakia, for example, we have a unified trade-union secretariat. At present they are discussing the creation of 21 professional committees in order to replace the old federations. Nevertheless, the general questions of wages, prices and contract policy would be decided by the [central] trade-union secretariat, while the individual committees or groups would only be charged with administrative work.[32]

In saying this at the 1945 IMF Central Committee, Bělina may well have been tailoring his description of what was happening in his own country to fit the fears of his friend Ilg about the WFTU's proposals for industrial activity, but his accounts do accord with later investigations of the development of Czechoslovak unions after 1945.[33] Bělina reported to Ilg that factory works' councils were elected on the basis of a single list being presented to workers for approval without competition between opposing slates, and that once a metal union had been set up within the framework of the centralized confederation, its leaders were pre-war communists.[34]

[31] J. Bělina to Ilg, 18 June 1945.

[32] Proceedings IMF 1945 Central Committee, 10.

[33] See Jon Bloomfield, *Passive Revolution: Politics and the Czechoslovak Working Class 1945–1948* (London, Allison and Busby, 1979), 135, which details communist domination in the unions. In 1946, 94 of the 120 members of the union's central council were communists. See also J. Rupnik, *Histoire du parti communiste tchécoslovaque*, (Paris, Fondation nationale des sciences politiques, 1981), 148–88, on the communist takeover of unions. Works councils were seen as key institutions to be brought under communist control. No independent workers' activities outside the communist-dominated unions were permitted.

[34] Bělina to Ilg, 18 Nov. 1945.

According to Bělina, fighting against communist control of the union was 'hopeless', and pre-war socialist trade-union organizers were isolated; some who returned from exile upon the liberation of the country, hoping to rebuild a democratic socialist Czechoslovakia, only stayed a few months before emigrating.[35]

Living in neutral Switzerland, with his eyes anxiously fixed on developments in Central Europe, Ilg sought to make contact with former comrades in the pre-war metal unions. In 1945 and 1946, he corresponded with the metalworkers' union in Hungary and, in 1946, offered to send them 10,000 Swiss francs to help buy a car, but he pointed out that as far as he knew the unions in Czechoslovakia, Hungary, Romania, and Poland had all formed centralized organizations affiliated to the WFTU, and the metalworkers within these new unions did not want to be members of the IMF.[36]

The policy of non-participation in the IMF by unions which were either in Soviet-liberated areas of Europe or which were dominated by communists, as in France and in Italy, backfired. Had the French, Italian, or East European metal unions, let alone the Russian, entered the IMF in 1945, they would have been in a position to attempt to force a vote on its dissolution or incorporation into the WFTU on the WFTU's terms, or, at the very least, alter its constitution and secretariat—Ilg was 68 in 1945 and talked openly of retirement. Instead, the IMF remained a grouping of West European metal unions. At its various meetings between 1945 and 1947, the communist position was not heard. The French, with 800,000 members, could have outvoted all the other Continental IMF affiliates combined. The East European unions, especially the Czechoslovaks with whom there were ties of respect and attachment dating back many years, could have made their voices heard. But the refusal to continue with their pre-war membership of the

[35] Bělina to Ilg, 25 Nov. 1946. Many social democrats did seek to work with the Czech communists to build a united union movement in place of the politically divided pre-war unions, but the communists ensured that they secured dominance, reflecting the genuine orientation of a significant section of the Czech working class that looked to communism and the Soviet Union as better defenders of their interests than the pre-war politics which had led to the betrayal of Czechoslovakia by Britain and France at Munich. See Pavla Vošahlíková, 'Tschechoslowakische Gewerkschaftsbewegung nach dem zweiten Weltkrieg und die Teilnahme der Sozialdemokraten daran' (Paper presented at the Internationale Tagung der Historiker der Arbeiterbewegung, Linz 1990).

[36] Ilg to Magyarországi Vas-És Fémmunkások, 19 June 1946.

IMF, even on a temporary basis, until the position with the WFTU was clarified, combined with the Soviet self-exclusion, meant that the European industrial unions remained disunited even if the national centres were joined in the WFTU.

Another explanation for the IMF's survival at a time when it appeared on the brink of being swallowed up by the WFTU was that it provided a voice for the smaller unions and little countries. The WFTU was very much the creation of the victorious powers, especially Britain, the Soviet Union, and the United States. As Ilg told the British metal unions: 'The WFTU deals mainly with purely political questions, the consequence being that only the big [unions] would have a say in the meetings while no notice would be taken of small countries like Switzerland at all.'[37] The meetings of the WFTU that took place after the founding conferences of 1945 involved representatives of the national centres of the big powers. The voices of smaller organizations are barely to be noted in WFTU minutes. The key unions in the IMF were British and, to a lesser extent, Swedish, but the IMF allowed the Belgians, Dutch, Danes, and Swiss—small countries perhaps but each with a well-rooted trade-union movement—to have a say.

Finally, there was Ilg himself. He had been secretary of the IMF since 1920. Like his contemporary, Ernest Bevin, his life corresponded with the growth of trade-unions to the important place they occupied in 1945. He was a powerful figure in Switzerland, president of his union, a member of the Federal Assembly, with an honorary doctorate in a society that attaches importance to titles and such marks of distinction. About to enter his eighth decade, he threw himself with a vigour and a passion unusual when judged by the cautious, discreet norms of his countrymen, into a fight to revive his IMF and keep it free from communist taint. A close colleague described Ilg's anticommunism: 'He was utterly opposed to agreement with the Communists. Half a century's knowledge of the world's labour movement led him instinctively to consider that any coalition with the Communists was a fool's paradise for those who remained attached to the principles of workers' rights and who opposed the use of violence to resolve social conflicts.'[38] The

[37] Ilg speaking to British Section of the IMF, 27 Sept. 1946.
[38] Adolphe Graedel in *Hommage à Conrad Ilg* (Berne, Swiss Metalworkers' Union, 1954), 30. Horst Lademacher stresses what he calls the 'egoism of industrial and craft unions' and their international trade secretariats, as well as the personal

question of the WFTU was the greatest single issue for Ilg between 1945 and 1947. He corresponded in English, French, and German; organized the publication and translation of reports in a more thorough and professional way than the large WFTU secretariat in Paris, and travelled to the United States, Britain, and other countries in Europe to argue his case. As he looked at the metalworkers' organizations in France, Czechoslovakia, and the Soviet zone in Germany, he saw his old enemies in control. But significant as was his position as IMF secretary, he alone could not determine IMF policy on the WFTU. That would be decided by the Central Committee of the IMF in which the British metal unions, by dint of their 1-million-strong membership, which was five times that of the next biggest union from Sweden, played the key role.

'desire for power' of a principal secretariat leader, Oldenbroek, as a reason preventing the incorporation of the secretariats into the WFTU. This may over-anthropomorphize political institutions—after all the TUC had let the IFTU die, and had relegated its high-profile secretary, Walter Schevenels, to a secondary post in the WFTU. See Horst Lademacher, 'Die Spaltung des Weltgewerkschaftsbundes als Folge des beginnenden Ost-West-Konflikts', in Haberl and Niethammer (eds.), *Der Marshall-Plan*, 527.

5

Centralism or Diversity: Two World Views

BY the autumn of 1945, the metal unions in the IMF had taken no decision on merging their international federation into the newly created WFTU. This position appeared to be reversed at the end of the year when Lincoln Evans, on behalf of the British metal unions, wrote to Ilg. His letter stated that as the national centres in most countries had agreed to join the WFTU, it was now 'a matter of liquidating the IMF', and if it came to 'a choice between being attached to a [WFTU] trade department or the IMF, the British Section would have no alternative but to belong to the trade department'.[1] Yet twelve months later, at the end of 1946, the IMF was not liquidated, and the British metal unions were not involved in the WFTU. The new world federation had thus failed to make the key advance of incorporating the industrial internationals, which was essential for its success. Already, early in 1946, there were external factors such as the deteriorating relations between the Allies, simultaneously symbolized and exacerbated by Churchill's speech at Fulton, Missouri.[2] For Eddie Frow, a communist member of the AEU's National Committee, reading about the speech was 'the moment when I realized that the alliance and friendship between Britain and the Soviet Union was at an end'.[3]

On the Continent, attempts to merge socialist and communist parties had come to nothing by the winter of 1946—a sign of the deterioration of intra-left relations.[4] An important political quarrel in Britain over the British Communist Party's bid to affiliate to the

[1] L. Evans to K. Ilg, 31 Dec. 1945.

[2] On the importance of Fulton see Fraser Harbutt, *The Iron Curtain: Churchill, America and the Origins of the Cold War* (New York, OUP, 1986). This account is firmly in the tradition of Cold-War history as a political-diplomatic contest disconnected from social and economic questions.

[3] Eddie Frow interview, Manchester, 16 Apr. 1986.

[4] See the Chapters on France and Germany for details. An exception of course was the Soviet Zone of Germany where socialists and communists fused to form the Socialist Unity Party, but the nature of that merger was so controversial it added to socialist-communist rivalry elsewhere in Germany and in Europe.

Labour Party also opened up in the winter of 1946.[5] Some, early
that year, had little faith in the WFTU's ability to survive.
Wenceslas Carrillo, the socialist trade-union leader from Spain,
revealed his doubts in a letter to Ilg: 'Who can be certain that the
new world federation will have a long life? Personally, I doubt if the
alliance between the Communists and Socialists can last long. The
Communists, sooner or later, will apply their usual dishonest
methods with the aim of following Moscow's orders.'[6] The
external omens then, so early in the WFTU's life, were not good.
But a detailed examination of the efforts to merge the IMF with the
WFTU shows that the differences, even at a trade-union level, were
substantial and unbridgeable, irrespective of the state of relations
between governments or between the two parties of the Left.

Following the WFTU Congress and the IMF Central Committee
in the autumn of 1945, negotiations were to take place to arrange
the terms upon which the IMF and the other trade secretariats
would come into the WFTU. The WFTU appointed Walter
Schevenels, an assistant general secretary, to conduct the negotiations. It was an ambiguous choice. Schevenels was the former
general secretary of the defunct IFTU. Despite the TUC's support,
Schevenels had lost to Saillant in competition for the post of WFTU
general secretary.[7] On the surface, his appointment as the mediator
to bring the international trade secretariats into the WFTU was
logical. Their secretaries were old colleagues. Unlike Saillant, the
WFTU general secretary, Schevenels spoke languages other than his
mother tongue, and he appreciated the organizational sensibility
and traditions of the secretariats. Yet, given Schevenels' anticommunist inclinations, he was unlikely to seek an incorporation of the
secretariats on terms that would have weakened the Western and
social democratic trade-union tradition from which he stemmed.
Perhaps he hoped to string out negotiations so that the independence of the socialist-controlled secretariats could be preserved.[8]

---

[5] See Ch. 10.
[6] W. Carrillo to Ilg, 23 Jan. 1946.
[7] See J. Windmuller, *American Labor and the International Labour Movement*
(Ithaca, NY, Cornell University Press, 1954), 59–60.
[8] Schevenels accuses Saillant of ensuring that 'the negotiations [between the
WFTU and the secretariats] were protracted to such a length of time as to paralyse
the activities of the [secretariats] but adduces no evidence for his charge. See W.
Schevenels, *45 Years IFTU* (Brussels, 1955), 352. If anything, delay benefited the
secretariats, not the WFTU.

But in fact he had no plenipotentiary powers, and his own political views were irrelevant since the leadership of the WFTU themselves decided the issue of international trade secretariats.

The question of terms was quite crucial. Evans had made clear to Ilg that the British unions wanted no misunderstanding on the basic principle of joining the WFTU. He reaffirmed that position in February 1946. The British metal unions, he reminded Ilg, 'are committed to work in the trade departments of the new federations', but 'the conditions under which the trade departments are going to operate and the statutes which are going to govern their activities are equally important as the fact of being attached to the WFTU itself'.[9] This was a relief for Ilg. The British provided him with a lifeline by stressing the question of conditions. But the IMF would now only retain its separate existence, detached and independent from the WFTU, if the negotiations failed to come up with suitable terms.

Schevenels offered his solution in a set of draft regulations for the setting up of WFTU international trade departments which would incorporate and replace the existing secretariats. The draft regulations were relatively centralist. The WFTU would have the right to approve the secretary of a new International Trade Department (ITD), to place the ITD office at the WFTU headquarters in Paris; further, the WFTU would allocate only 25 per cent of the affiliation fees paid by an ITD member via its national centre to the WFTU for ITD work.[10] Such terms were unacceptable to another major secretariat, the International Transport Workers' Federation, whose full Congress met in Zürich in May 1946. It adopted the double-headed position of being in favour of joining the ITF with the WFTU, but at the same time the two bodies should 'continue the negotiations . . . in order to reach acceptable conditions'.[11]

If the international trade secretariats were proving difficult, so was the Executive Committee of the WFTU. At its meeting in Moscow in June 1946, the WFTU leaders told Schevenels that he had made too many concessions and not moved fast enough. Instead, a joint conference between the WFTU leaders and trade

---

[9] Evans to Ilg, 28 Feb. 1946.
[10] Draft General Regulations for the ITDs of the WFTU, IMF circular, 8 Apr. 1946, (IMFA).
[11] Proceedings, International Transport Workers' Federation Congress, May 1946.

secretariat representatives should be held to clear up the matter once and for all.[12] The whole problem was lying like a shadow over the future work of the WFTU. In a valedictory speech at the 1946 TUC Congress, Citrine stressed that the WFTU 'must be a Trade Union Federation. If an attempt is made to make it into a political international, it will surely fail . . . The sooner the international trade secretariats are integrated, then the more durable will the Federation be'.[13]

When the IMF Central Committee met in London in October 1946 the position was unchanged. Support for the WFTU came from the British and the Swedes. Jack Tanner, the AEU president, urged his fellow union leaders 'to realise the great importance of the fusion of the metalworkers of the whole world' within the framework of the WFTU. But he was confronted by Ilg who stuck to his demand for autonomy of decision by metal unions relating to their industrial activities, their choice of secretary, and the location of the secretariat as well as for sufficient funding to carry out their activities.[14] Ilg's position was accepted by other delegates. Even Tanner agreed that the key decisions about the future International Trade Department lay with the metal unions themselves 'and not with the Executive Committee of the WFTU'.[15]

The meeting between the WFTU leaders and the representatives of the secretariats, held in Paris in December 1946, was the crucial moment to see if the WFTU could incorporate the secretariats and become an effective labour international. Ilg was accompanied by Evans from Britain and the vice-president of the Swedish metal union, Axel Svensson. They were representatives from the two countries whose national confederations were publicly committed to the WFTU. Whatever the feelings of anticommunist Ilg, or the equally anti-Soviet Oldenbroek, general secretary of the International Transport Workers, the presence of these two leading members of Britain's TUC and Sweden's LO would ensure that the case for incorporation into the WFTU would be given a fair hearing.

The first two days of the meeting were spent searching for agreement. The Russian delegation was absent because of travel

---

[12] See Windmuller, *American Labor*, 108.
[13] TUC Annual Report 1946, 272.
[14] Proceedings IMF 1946 Central Committee, 5–10.
[15] Ibid. 14.

difficulties. But on the third day appeared Mikhail Tarasov, the Soviet Union's representative on the WFTU's Executive Bureau, and the tone changed abruptly. He was precise and clear about the Soviet position on the issue of changing the secretariats into trade departments of the WFTU. To begin with, declared Tarasov, there should be only four ITDs—for metal, transport, coal and textiles— and they should be created immediately. It would not be necessary for them to have their own constitutions, executives, or general secretaries; their offices 'should be in the same building as the WFTU', and their budgets would have to be 'approved' by the WFTU.[16] His intervention left the rest of the conference 'dumb-founded', as one participant described it.[17] In his report for IMF affiliates on the Paris meeting, Ilg wrote that following Tarasov's statement, the discussion 'increased the apprehension, that with the integration of the Professional Secretariats into the WFTU other intentions are [being] pursued', and added that the secretariats had to be 'very watchful' against being transformed into 'lifeless technical bodies'.[18]

In effect, the Russian undermined all Schevenels' negotiating work since the autumn of 1945 and put an end to the possible integration of the secretariats into the WFTU. Although the question would remain on the agenda into 1948, the opportunity that presented itself in the course of 1946, when the major affiliates of the IMF, the British and the Swedes, were urging integrative co-operation with the WFTU, would not come again. It has been argued that the WFTU was 'ready for compromise' but could not prevail over the secretariats' demands for autonomy in the two years between the WFTU's founding and the divisions over the Marshall Plan.[19] Yet as the evidence from 1945 and 1946 indicates, the majority of unions inside the IMF expressed a willingness to join the WFTU. It was the WFTU itself which was unwilling to come to terms that even the pro-WFTU British metal unions

[16] *Report on the Creation of International Trade Departments within the WFTU* (presented to the WFTU Executive Council in Prague, June 1947).

[17] M. Bolle, *Vereinbarung zwischen dem Weltgewerkschaftsbund und den internationalen Gewerkschaftssekretariaten zur Errichtung von Gewerkschafts-verbanden*, (report prepared for meeting of international trade secretariats' general secretaries. (No date, presumably early 1947, IMFA.)

[18] Ilg to IMF affiliates, 20 Dec. 1946.

[19] See K. van Oene, 'Der Weltgewerkschaftsbund: zwischen Einheit und Spaltung 1945–1949', in W. Olle (ed.), *Einführung in die internationale Gewerkschaftspolitik* (Berlin, Olle und Walter, 1978), 164.

considered the absolute minimum. The meeting in Paris in December 1946 put in sharp relief the division between Soviet concepts of centralized trade-union direction and the older traditions pre-dating 1920 which—while seeking unity—acknowledged diversity and allowed some separation between the different unions that might come together to form a national or international confederation.

The demise of the WFTU's potential to become an effective international labour body can be dated from that moment in December 1946 when Tarasov came into the Paris meeting and made clear that the secretariats would have to be incorporated into the WFTU on Soviet terms or not at all. From now on the secretariats, individually and collectively, would function as a kind of alternative world union grouping. This had never been the intention of the British and Swedes, who made clear publicly and privately in their communications with Ilg, their whole-hearted commitment to the WFTU. But instead of playing on that engagement, by allowing the limited autonomy the secretariats sought, the Russians demanded full incorporation and the effective dissolution of the IMF and other secretariats. While on the surface there appeared still to be political agreement on the need to work with the Soviet Union and to bring socialist and communist unions into one international body, the organizational difficulties were now insurmountable. Of course these apparent organizational questions represented real political differences. On one side stood democratic centralism and control from the top down; on the other, pluralist ideas about autonomy, diversity, and diffused control. When the moment to decide arrived, as it did at the end of 1946, neither side was prepared to give up what lay at the core of two visions of social organization.

THE INFLUENCE OF AMERICAN UNIONS

Some historians have insisted that it was the American unions, particularly the AFL, who were largely to blame for the break-up of the WFTU. As a British labour historian writing in the 1950s put it: 'Since 1945 the AFL had been spending money like water on disruptive intrigues in Europe'.[20] This refrain was picked up twenty

[20] A. Hutt, *British Trade Unionism* (London, Lawrence and Wishart, 1952), 79.

years later by a Dutch historian who asserted that the AFL 'played an important role in several international trade secretariats' in organizing opposition to the secretariats being integrated into the WFTU.[21] More recently, an American historian of international trade-unionism has argued that the AFL 'used the [international trade secretariats] to strengthen opposition to the WFTU at the local level'[22] and that the '[international trade secretariats] failed to affiliate [to the WFTU] not because of Soviet intransigence but because of the successful delaying tactics of the AFL'.[23] Finally, the British author of a recent, thorough account of the impact of the Marshall Plan on European labour has written: 'In the years 1945 to 1948 much of [the AFL's] energy was devoted to gaining influence within the trade secretariats and steeling them to pursue a hard line against the WFTU.'[24]

But, in fact, considering the attitude of the metal unions and the IMF towards the WFTU between the founding conferences in 1945 and the disastrous meeting in Paris at the end of 1946, the most outstanding feature is the absence of American involvement in the IMF decision-making processes. American unionists were present in Europe of course. At the WFTU conferences, representatives of the CIO would have talked with people like Tanner and Evans. Other American labour representatives attached to embassies, to the occupying forces in Germany, as well as the AFL's represent-ative in Europe, Irving Brown, most certainly met with different European leaders. But such meetings, such discussions do not constitute a formal intervention in the affairs of the metalworkers' trade secretariat. As the record shows, the IMF unions took their decisions on what attitude to take towards the WFTU without any involvement or prodding from the AFL.

Indeed, many historians have been casual in their precise dating of the AFL's involvement with the trade secretariats. They tend to put American union statements about using the secretariats against the WFTU into an earlier period as if this policy had been in

---

[21] Van Oene, 'Der Weltgewerkschaftsbund', 164.
[22] Peter Weiler, 'The United States, International Labor and the Cold War: The Break-up of the World Federation of Trade Unions', in *Diplomatic History* (Winter 1981), 8.
[23] Ibid. 21.
[24] A. Carew, *Labour under the Marshall Plan* (Manchester, Manchester University Press, 1987), 71–2. In his monograph, *Britain and the Marshall Plan* (London, Macmillan, 1989), Henry Pelling cites Weiler and Carew in regard to AFL attempts to secure a 'breach with the WFTU' (p. 62).

operation since the war's end, and that consequently, without the AFL's intervention, the secretariats would have been smoothly integrated into a durable and vigorous WFTU.

From his first contacts with Oldenbroek, the ITF secretary Irving Brown was made aware of the hostile uncertainty amongst secretariats about being incorporated into the WFTU, yet the first written document from Brown, the AFL's European representative, in which he encourages the involvement of American unions in the secretariats is dated 23 December 1946. In it he urged the affiliation of American unions to the appropriate secretariat in order to 'constitute an impregnable fortress against the WFTU'.[25] Yet by that date European metal unions had resisted incorporation into the WFTU. Indeed, the key meeting in Paris in December 1946, the last serious moment for bringing the industrial unions represented by the trade secretariats into a structural relationship within the WFTU, slipped by because of Soviet behaviour, without any direct intervention by the AFL. Far from the AFL trying to embrace or use the IMF, it was to begin with, if anything, the other way round. It was Ilg who took the initiative in contacting American metal unions. With the support of his European colleagues, including the pro-WFTU British and Swedes, the IMF secretary sought to get American unions fully involved in IMF affairs. Even before the war ended, Ilg was acting as an intermediary for US officials in order to obtain permission for the use of relief funds to buy typewriters and office equipment for the metalworkers' union in Luxembourg.[26] Ilg was also informing himself on American labour affairs in correspondence with Adolf Sturmthal, an Austrian socialist, who had worked in Switzerland for the Labour and Socialist International between 1926 and 1938. Sturmthal, in 1945 a university researcher into labour questions in New York, 'knew Ilg very well' and offered to send the IMF secretary reports on developments in American unions, an offer which Ilg accepted.[27]

[25] Brown report to AFL, 23 Dec. 1946, quoted in Weiler, 'The United States, International Labor and the Cold War', 8. On Brown's earlier contacts with Oldenbroek see Lademacher, 'Die Spaltung des Weltgewerkschaftsbundes', in O. Habert and L. Niethammer (eds.), *Der Marshall Plan und die europäische Linke* (Frankfurt, Europäische Verlagsanstalt, 1986), 508.

[26] A. Krier (general secretary of the Luxembourg metal unions) to R. Mac-Cleland, US Embassy, Berne, 26 Apr. 1945. Krier to Ilg, 28 Apr. 1945 (IMFA).

[27] Information from Adolf Sturmthal in letter to author, 10 Feb. 1986, and Sturmthal to Ilg, 3 May 1945.

The hostility of the AFL to the WFTU was no secret to Ilg. The American Federation sent a letter to all secretariats in May 1945 explaining their refusal to join the new body. 'We believe it is an attempt to establish a world bureau for the propaganda and infiltration of a world order . . . [which does] not conceal [its] expectations of controlling the trade-unions of democratic countries for their own undemocratic goals'.[28] That however is the only communication from the AFL to be found in IMF files for 1945 and 1946.

Instead, it was Ilg who took the initiative in the spring of 1946 after participating in the ILO metal-trades committee meeting in Ohio. Sturmthal had alerted Ilg to the importance of Walter Reuther, the rising radical but non-communist star of the Congress of Industrial Organizations who was poised to become president of the important automobile workers' union, the UAW. Ilg tried to meet the autoworkers' leader, but this was prevented by bad weather. Reuther wrote to Ilg urging the 'closest possible relationship between European and American labor movements'.[29] At this stage, the CIO was firmly in the WFTU. Despite this, Ilg decided to write to the young CIO leader, unburdening himself (he asked Reuther to keep the letter confidential) in a long letter to a fellow metal-union leader whom he had never met, and who, thirty years younger than the Swiss unionist, came from a different generation and background.

Ilg described his past as a socialist activist, a Swiss MP, leader of the Swiss metalworkers, and secretary of the IMF since 1920. For Ilg, the unity that existed in the early part of the century was spoilt by the 'quarrel between the bolshevist-communist and socialist tendencies' and, in particular, the German unions were undermined by this political 'civil war, brought about by communist-socialist' disagreements.[30] Ilg told Reuther that 'the WFTU will remain a political instrument' and would reflect the policies of the great powers 'with the inevitable consequence that their quarrels will be carried into the Trade Unions'. He concluded with his belief that it would not be 'possible to bring Eastern democracy into harmony with Western democracy'.[31] Ilg appealed to Reuther to join the

[28] R. J. Watt to Ilg, 3 May 1945.
[29] W. Reuther to Ilg, 25 May 1946.
[30] Ilg to Reuther, 12 Aug. 1946.
[31] Ibid.

IMF, an appeal he also directed to the AFL's Metal Trades
Department, which grouped the metal unions affiliated to the AFL,
in August 1946.[32] The following month he reported these contacts
to the British unions: 'Something important is missing and that is
co-operation with America. We have got to get this under way. It
is only by co-operation and . . . by solidarity that the working class
can be freed from the yoke of capitalism.'[33] Ilg must have trusted to
the ignorance of his British audience if he thought they, or anyone
else, believed that the AFL or even the CIO was opposed to
capitalism, but he went on to make clear his purpose in seeking
American union participation which if it 'could be achieved before
the adherence [of the IMF] to the WFTU would very much
strengthen the position of the Western federations and a counter-
balance would be created against hostile organizations in the
WFTU'.[34]

In October 1946, at the IMF Central Committee in London, Ilg
again stressed his belief that the American metal unions in the AFL
and the CIO must be brought into IMF membership. His initiative
was endorsed, and it was agreed to send a delegation to the United
States to make personal contacts. Another of Ilg's correspondents
in the United States was Martin Plettl, the former head of the pre–
1933 German textile workers' union and a former president of the
textile trade secretariat. He wrote to Ilg in the autumn of 1946,
discussing different tendencies in the American labour movement
and encouraging Ilg to contact the AFL.[35]

Ilg needed no urging. As soon as American affiliation had been
formally approved by the IMF Central Committee, he wrote to the
AFL urging the affiliation of the AFL's metal unions before the full
IMF Congress took place in 1947: 'By such an affiliation the
autonomy of the IMF would be safeguarded', he argued.[36] In
seeking the involvement of the AFL metal unions, Ilg played up the
need to form an anti-Russian front. The unions in the countries

[32] Ilg to J. Brownlow, 8 Aug. 1946.
[33] Ilg to IMF British Section, 26 Sept. 1946.
[34] Ilg to IMF British Section, 27 Sept. 1946. Although this portion of Ilg's speech
is printed in the minutes of the meeting, it is crossed out in the original text in
German—the language in which he would have delivered the speech. Did someone
tell Ilg, or did he sense himself that such a crude invocation of American help against
the WFTU would not go down well with British trade-unionists? In any event, the
printed record with Ilg's hostile remarks was distributed to all British metal unions.
[35] M. Plettl to Ilg, 24 Oct. 1946.
[36] Ilg to Brownlow, 5 Nov. 1946.

occupied by Soviet troops 'are already under direct Russian influence as free trade-unions no longer exist'; in France and Italy, the metal unions were dominated by 'communist leaders'; in Germany, 'the communist direction of the WFTU is trying to bring the German unions under their control'.[37] In Ilg's view the contest for influence or control in the metal unions of Europe reflected the conflicts between the big powers 'for political and economic predominance in which struggle Russia plays an important part as she is making every effort to conquer Europe ideologically'.[38] Ilg concluded with the urgent appeal of the West Europeans to the Americans: 'We are extraordinarily anxious to get into close relationships with the American metalworkers' organizations.'[39]

By the autumn of 1946, Ilg's American policy had three components. Firstly, he had his own German-speaking, reliable sources of information in America. Secondly, he had begun a process of personal contacts with American unions urging them to get involved as IMF affiliates explicitly to counter the communists in the WFTU. Thirdly, he had the approval of the IMF leadership for the turn to the United States. It was only at this stage that Irving Brown, representing the AFL, made contact with Ilg and began to act as a middle-man. From 1947 onwards, Brown and the highly politicized labour attachés in the US State Department, together with British Foreign Office officials, sought actively to encourage Western trade-unions and the trade secretariats to move against the WFTU. But they arrived to find their work already largely achieved.[40] Ilg, without dissent from his colleagues in the IMF, had begun the process of seeking the participation of American unions and was doing so explicitly as a policy to bolster the IMF against the WFTU. American union involvement in post-war European affairs, at least as far as the IMF is concerned, was in the first instance in response to pleas from Europe, and was not conceived and did not originate in Washington.

The only American union to join the IMF while the WFTU question remained important was the International Association of Machinists (IAM) which was renewing its sporadic membership of an earlier period. Ilg punctiliously informed all IMF affiliates about

[37] Ibid.
[40] See Weiler, *British Labour and the Cold War* (Stanford, Calif., Stanford University Press, 1988), 90–6 on American union-diplomatic efforts to use the secretariats against the WFTU.

the IAM's application. He persuaded the Machinists to drop a
condition that their participation was contingent upon the IMF
remaining 'a free trade-union organization, having no connection
with the WFTU'.[41] Having achieved that, he did not seek to hide his
satisfaction, telling the British that the adherence of the IAM was
'of the greatest importance. A close collaboration with the
American organizations will certainly be of much greater use than
the integration of our international into the WFTU.'[42]

Apart from discussions at the ILO Metal Trades Committee
meeting in the United States in May 1946, Ilg's contacts with
American unions had been in writing. From the beginning of 1947,
he was in touch with Irving Brown whom he met in Geneva and
Paris. The IAM appointed Brown to be their delegate to the IMF
Congress in July 1947. Brown was a political ambassador from the
AFL rather than a metal-union delegate seeking greater co-
operation on metal-industry issues. His interventions at the
Congress, and later on, were far from decisive.

When the IMF held its first full Congress in the Danish parliament
building in Copenhagen at the end of July 1947, the question of the
international trade secretariats and, in particular, the IMF's
relationship with the WFTU, continued to dominate the agenda.
The Congress was, under the IMF's rule, the body that could make
a final decision about incorporating the federation into the WFTU.
The reaction of both the Central Committee meetings in 1945 and
1946 had been to refuse the WFTU's terms. Ever since the end of
the war, Ilg had used his authority and guile to keep the IMF at
arm's length from the WFTU. Yet the respect that existed for his
three decades of service as IMF secretary would not have prevented
the British metal unions from liquidating the IMF if they had so
wished. The TUC had pulled out from the International Federation
of Trade Unions and accepted the demotion of Citrine's close
colleague, Schevenels, to a subordinate position in the WFTU.

The WFTU had softened its position a little after its general
council meeting in Prague in June 1947, but the world body was
still not ready to meet the three IMF conditions of autonomy in
choice of headquarters, in control over the IMF secretary, and in
provision of sufficient funding. To underline the point that

---

[41] E. Peterson, secretary-treasurer of the IAM, to Ilg, 19 Feb. 1947.
[42] Ilg to Evans, 21 May 1947.

opposition to the WFTU and suspicion about the communist attitude to the secretariats were not his personal hobby-horse, Ilg circulated to all delegates a copy of a letter sent to the WFTU by the International Federation of Building and Woodworkers' Unions (IFBW), the secretariat representing construction industry unions.

Unlike the metalworkers in the French CGT, who had refused to participate in IMF activities, the construction industry federation of the CGT had reactivated its membership of the IFBW in 1945. At the IFBW Congress in 1946, the French had proposed the incorporation of the IFBW into the WFTU as a trade department. This had been rejected by a majority of delegates whereupon the French union announced it would have nothing further to do with the IFBW. What was worse, complained the IFBW in its letter to the WFTU, the French union had acted against the line agreed by other worker representatives—mainly IFBW delegates—at an ILO's tripartite committee for the construction industry in November 1946. The CGT construction workers voted with the employers against a proposal endorsing the forty-hour week. The IFBW appealed to the WFTU's general council to tell the CGT that it 'was not permissible to place obstacles in the way of the International Trade Secretariats' and, further, that WFTU unions 'should support [trade secretariat] activities energetically'.[43]

Ilg placed his letter in the material distributed to the delegates and observers from thirteen countries taking part in the Congress, in order to stiffen their anti-WFTU resolve. If he hoped to obtain from the Congress a clear rejection of the WFTU, in formal political as well as organizational terms, he left Copenhagen empty-handed. For Ilg, the IMF should 'not go down bowing and scraping before its adversary', but he was rebuked for such open hostility to the WFTU by British, Swedish, and Danish delegates.[44] Instead, the previous double-headed policy of support for the aims of world union unity combined with demands for IMF autonomy was reaffirmed.

From the first moments of discussion, the tensions were apparent. As leaders of the British TUC or Sweden's LO, Tanner and Svensson endorsed WFTU positions. As leaders of the IMF,

[43] Letter of International Federation of Building and Woodworkers to the WFTU (Amsterdam, 30 May 1947) reproduced in English, French and German as an IMF Congress document, July 1947.
[44] Proceedings IMF 1947 Congress, 38 (IMFA).

they erected obstacles to the full implementation of the WFTU's organizational goals. A minor, and in terms of Western trade-union practice, not an unusual contradiction perhaps, but one that allowed some of the major Western unions to be inside the WFTU but not wholeheartedly committed to the new body. As Jack Tanner, the AEU president, declared in Copenhagen: 'What we are aiming at is the greatest unity possible amongst the working classes of all countries', but in the same breath he added that the time was not yet ripe to dissolve the IMF into the WFTU: 'Before we give our consent to the Prague General Regulations' which the WFTU had proposed in June 1947, 'the IMF must try to obtain better conditions concerning the autonomy of the Professional Departments . . . A new Congress [will] take a final decision.'[45]

More significantly, Tanner proposed that Ilg be confirmed as IMF secretary and that a representative of the American metalworkers be placed on the four-strong IMF Executive Committee. Some delegates were unhappy about giving the AFL's Irving Brown a role in the IMF leadership, but the weight of the IAM's 850,000 members—the second biggest IMF affiliate after the 1.1 million members from Britain—gave the American union the right to nominate a representative on the Executive Committee. Brown had made no bones about his opposition to the WFTU: unions in the AFL, he told the European metal-union delegates, would 'not be party to any trade-union organization based upon big power politics in which one of the big powers is immune from all criticism or investigation [and] controls the trade-unions in its orbit'.[46]

Brown's election illustrated the weakness of the pro-WFTU position inside the IMF. The world body's supporters were neither numerous, nor determined enough to prevent the election to the IMF executive of the notoriously anti-WFTU Brown. His election highlights the ambiguities and contradictions in the participation of the Western unions below the national centre level in the WFTU in the two years after 1945. In political principle they were for the WFTU. In organizational practice they kept a distance. As a TUC leader, Tanner approved the regulations for turning the international trade secretariats into trade departments agreed by the WFTU at Prague in June 1947. As chief spokesperson of British

[45] Minutes of IMF Central Committee, 25 July 1947, 19. A short Central Committee meeting took place prior to the full Congress.
[46] Proceedings IMF 1947 Congress, 69 (IMFA).

metalworkers, Tanner upheld the autonomy of the IMF. Was this pragmatism in the light of the uncertain East–West relations between governments, or cynical double-dealing which from the beginning was aimed at destroying world union unity? Answers to this question, as has been seen from the various historians already cited, tend to depend on the political starting-point of the writer. An interesting exception is the West German printworkers' union leader, Leonhard Mahlein, who was president of the printworkers' secretariat, the International Graphical Federation, between 1976 and 1983. Mahlein advocated contacts and co-operation with the Soviet Union and welcomed communist unions into his international federation. He was an exception to the generally anticommunist, anti-Soviet position of Western international trade-union leaders in the 1970s and 1980s. In a book written after his retirement, *Trade Union Internationalism: An Area of Tension between East and West*, Mahlein examined the history of the WFTU. He is sympathetic to the motives that led to the WFTU's creation but, as an experienced trade-union official, after reading the background documents and the minutes of the relevant meetings, he concluded that 'the incorporation of the trade secretariats was a key question. The original agreement on the full autonomy of the secretariats in respect of their particular industrial activities broke down over the realities of the post-war situation as well as the delaying tactics of the WFTU.'[47]

The delaying tactics Mahlein mentions are to be attributed to both sides, but they serve to underline the suspicion and mutual hostility that existed once the wish for world trade-union unity had to be turned from conference resolutions into durable organizational form. Not long after the IMF Congress in Copenhagen in August 1947, inter-government hostility was to break out in a manner that spelt the complete end to lingering remnants of wartime unity, the definitive burial of what might be called the spirit of Tehran and Yalta. World union unity disappeared at the same time, but as far as the key industrial unions of the world were concerned it is doubtful whether in any meaningful sense such unity can be said ever to have existed after 1945.

After the Copenhagen Congress of the IMF, the question of what

---

[47] Leonhard Mahlein, *Gewerkschaften international im Spannungsfeld zwischen Ost und West*, (Frankfurt, Nachrichten-Verlag, 1984), 17.

attitude to adopt towards the Marshall Plan became the issue that divided the WFTU and rendered co-operation between communist-led and socialist-orientated unions impossible. Already by July 1947, Tarasov, one of the Soviet representatives on the WFTU executive, had denounced the Marshall Plan as the 'weapon [of] the transatlantic republic of the dollar and atom bomb . . . to split Europe, to create reactionary adventurist blocs'.[48] Attempts to form a rival metalworkers' international which would incorporate communist metal unions were announced by the Italians in September 1947 but rebuffed by the British who refused to attend an international metalworkers' conference organized by the communist-led metalworkers' union in Italy: 'If there is desire amongst the Italian metalworkers to renew their international contacts and obtain information as to the situation in other countries, they could easily do this by re-associating with the IMF', Evans wrote to the Italians on behalf of the British metal unions.[49] His rebuke to the Italians in September 1947 is one of the last expressions of the organizational question. Three months later, Evans analysed the problem in much graver terms:

The failure of the WFTU at the Paris meeting (in November 1947) to reach any sort of agreement on the Marshall Plan does throw the issue of the Professional Secretariats into the background because the Marshall Plan discussion will show very clearly for the first time the deep division of opinion between ourselves and those who are following the Russian line. . . . The question that is now in balance is not whether the secretariats shall become Trade Departments but whether the WFTU is likely to continue. This issue has got to be cleared up before there can be any question of the Professional Secretariats being converted into Trades Departments.[50]

By the end of 1947, the WFTU's fate had been settled. The letter from Evans posed the key, irresolvable questions.

[48] Quoted in M. Schwartz, 'Soviet Policy and the WFTU, 1945–1949', Ph.D thesis (Columbia University 1963) 287.
[49] Evans to G. Roveda, general secretary of FIOM (Italian Metalworkers' Federation) 20 Sept. 1947.
[50] Evans to Ilg, 11 Dec. 1947.

6

The American Federation of Labor and the International Labour Movement After the Second World War

THE entry of the United States into the Second World War transformed the position of trade-unions in American society. In 1933, there were 3.5 million American workers, one-tenth of the work force, who belonged to trade-unions. In 1946, more than one third of American workers were in unions: 7.8 million belonged to the American Federation of Labor and 4 million to the Congress of Industrial Organizations. In December 1941, unemployment stood at 15 per cent. Six months later, it was down to 2 per cent. For the United States, the war was a war of production capacity which demanded the maximum involvement of American workers. Union leaders were put on the War Production Board and other tripartite committees. In return for a no-strike pledge and wage protection, the unions were guaranteed their membership and given check-off facilities for payment of dues which enhanced their financial security.[1] Union officials were subordinate to the business interests that dominated in wartime Washington. Roosevelt never accorded the same role to the AFL or the CIO that Churchill had to offer to Bevin and British union leaders, but the rise in membership, recognition by companies, and political influence in the Democratic Party did amount to a transformation of organized labour's place in American society compared with pre-war days.

Trade-union contacts and personnel had formed part of the Office of Strategic Services (OSS), the wartime forerunner of the Central Intelligence Agency. In 1942, the War Department was telling the Labor Desk of the OSS that 'every fact bearing on labor morale, labor activities and contact and co-operation between labor groups, especially any such international relationships is of

[1] See N. Lichtenstein, *Labor's War at Home: The CIO in World War II*, and P. Taft, *The AFL from the Death of Gompers to the Merger* (New York, Harper, 1959), for the growth in numbers and influence of the two federations.

importance'.[2] Arthur Goldberg, later the CIO's chief lawyer, was head of the OSS Labor Desk and regularly crossed the Atlantic to keep in touch with British and exiled trade-unionists.[3] With the war over, the American military governments in Germany and Japan had large labour departments. Trade-union policy was an important consideration in Allied ideas on what to do with the defeated countries. By 1946, the US State Department had twenty-two labour attachés, mainly former union officials, covering thirty countries, and the US Labor Department set up a parallel bureaucracy of its own covering international affairs.

These links between American unions and the government, and the active interest of the administration and its agencies in overseas labour affairs, have given rise to much critical discussion. For one historian, critical of US labour's foreign activities, 'American presidents have come to depend on the co-operateion of the organized labor movement in the carrying out of United States foreign policy.'[4] Another historian, also a revisionist, has written: 'The United States emerged from the Second World War with the greatest accumulation of power in modern history, but its leaders had no clear ideas about how to use it.'[5] Perhaps the two comments can be brought together in the argument that while there was confusion in Washington about what policies to adopt after the summer of 1945, there was an extremely clear set of ideas available from the American Federation of Labor. Over the next three years, it was not that American labour followed US foreign policy, but rather that the US administration came round to endorse the AFL's view, as expressed by its secretary-treasurer, George Meany, a few weeks before the end of the war, that post-war co-operation with the Soviet Union entailed 'grovelling in the dust of a false unity which would simply replace one form of totalitarianism with another'.[6]

The military and diplomatic representatives of the United States

---

[2] Military Intelligence Dept. of War Dept. to OSS Labor Desk, 3 Sept. 1942, in OSS History Files 99/62–271, Box 37, Defense Dept., NA.

[3] Ibid. 106/37.

[4] R. Radosh, *American Labor and United States Foreign Policy* (New York, Random House, 1969), 434.

[5] Richard Barnett, *The Alliance: America-Europe-Japan, Makers of the Postwar World* (New York, Simon and Schuster, 1983), 99.

[6] George Meany speaking at the New York Central Trades and Labor Council, 5 Apr. 1945, quoted in Joseph Goulden, *Meany* (New York, Atheneum, 1972), 125.

overseas needed American labour's involvement for technical reasons, as post-war planners agreed that the organization of unions in the liberated and occupied countries in Europe, as well as in Japan, would be important in the post-war settlement. Army officers and foreign-service officials were not, on the whole, much skilled in union questions. The American unions, however, had a role that went beyond that of expert adviser. Walter Laqueur, contrasting the behaviour of America and Russia in post-war Europe, has written: 'America was unprepared for political warfare; it lacked the experience and the organizational weapons. There were "Russian" parties, some big, some smaller, in all European countries, but there was no corresponding "American" party.'[7] It was this void that American trade-unionists served to fill after 1945. They formed the 'American Party', functioning politically and organizationally. Their prime task was to counter communism, but they also acted with generosity in arguing for trade-union rights, especially in Germany, and in making the case for labour to military authorities and the US administration. They came with American ideas on trade-union organization, though the pattern of trade-unionism such as developed in Western Europe after 1945 owed nearly everything to national peculiarities.

The trade unions served America better than a formal political party might have done. In particular, the American unions could operate a dual-track involvement with the workers of Europe. The AFL stayed faithful to its anticommunist line and did all in its power to damage, restrict, and ridicule communist activity in the European unions and the idea of any co-operation with the Soviet Union. For its part, the Congress of Industrial Organizations was an active participant member of the WFTU.

In the months after the war's end, the United States had to decide what policies to adopt in order to be able to integrate and discharge its new responsibilities. Two alternatives stood out. One was to continue the wartime co-operation with the Soviet Union. Many hoped and believed that the wartime spirit of alliance could be maintained, and one major democrat, Henry Wallace, a leading member of both Roosevelt's and Truman's cabinet until 1946, fought a presidential campaign on such a programme. The alternative was to strike out to achieve a *Pax Americana* in which

---

[7] Walter Laqueur, *Europe Since Hitler* (London, Penguin, 1985), 120.

the principal enemies, (essential to mobilize the domestic population and tighten up the ranks in other countries) would be the Soviet Union and communism. In the immediate aftermath of the war, the CIO in the WFTU represented the first strand of opinion; the AFL and its aggressive anticommunism, the second.

ANTI-ANTI-CAPITALISM: THE AFL'S INTERNATIONAL POLICY

In March 1919, a few months before the opening of the AFL convention, due to be held that year in Chicago, one of the convention organizers wrote to a powerful local industrialist, saying that the AFL convention

will mark the most momentous period in the history of the relationship between capital and labor, which has [sic] been drawn infinitely closer together through the forceful action of Samuel Gompers and the executive council of the American Federation of Labor in stamping out Bolshevik and other radical movements in America and the leading countries of Europe, demonstrating clearly that the organized labor movement in America will not countenance the disruption of business and financial enterprise created through individual initiative. May we ask you to contribute $100 to the expenses of the Convention?[8]

The description of the AFL's hostility to anticapitalism, or Soviet communism, in 1919 can hardly be bettered and with only minor changes represented the AFL's policy over many decades. The AFL's attachment to business unionism, which has been defined as 'the permanent expression of organized workers seeking remedies for the evils of problems arising in the place of employment. Business unionism stresses limited objectives, immediate improvements and eschews broader programmes of social and political change,'[9] was reflected in its international policy.[10]

[8] B. Walker to C. Dawes, 7 Mar. 1919. Letter reproduced in Proceedings of 1919 AFL Convention, 161.
[9] Philip Taft, *Organized Labor in American History* (New York, Harper, 1964) p. xv.
[10] David Montgomery, *The Fall of the House of Labour* (Cambridge CUP, 1987), is the best recent account of the American labour movement from 1865 to 1925. He stresses the vitality and radicalism of many local movements, and different sections of workers at different times, but these never coalesced into an ideologically coherent, united, class-based union organization linked to a similar party. Ethnic, geographical, institutional, language, gender, and racial differences were too great to be overcome and all the time the labour movement faced unremitting hostility from

As far as Russia was concerned, the hostility of the AFL predated 1917. For Samuel Gompers, the AFL's forceful president between 1886 and 1924, 'the greatest tyrant upon the face of the earth [was] the Russian Tsar', and he protested American attempts to draw up an extradition treaty with the Tsarist government in the 1890s.[11] Other influences on the AFL's foreign outlook were important. A strong pride in Americanism permeated all aspects of AFL activities overseas. This nationalist internationalism was reflected in Gompers and his successors. In the first two decades of the century, Gompers travelled to Europe several times. He concluded his book, *Labor in Europe and America*, thus:

The Old World is not our world. Its social problems, its economic philosophies, its current political questions are not linked up with America. All the people of the globe may be on the broad highway to social justice, peace amongst men of all tongues, and universal brotherhood, but all the nations and governments have not reached the same points on the road. In the procession, America is first.[12]

In 1919, Gompers had taken part in the deliberations leading to the creation of the ILO, but America's retreat into isolationism was mirrored by the AFL which took no part in the Europe-based international trade-union institutions in the 1920s. Hitler's onslaught on German trade unions and violent anti-Jewish attacks shifted some AFL unions, particularly the garment unions in New York with their predominately Jewish membership, into a more energetic engagement with European labour, but there was no *rapprochement* with the old enemy, Russia. The AFL became a member of the International Federation of Trade Unions in 1937,

the state, judicial apparatus, and the security forces, public and private. For an institutional history of the AFL see Philip Taft's 2 vols., *The AFL in the Time of Gompers* and *The AFL from the Death of Gompers to the Merger* (New York, Harper, 1954–59). Philip Foner's 6-vol. *History of the Labor Movement* (New York, International Publishers, 1956–82) offers a critical account. On the theoretical background see Mark Perlman, *Labor Union Theories in America* (New York, Row, Peterson, 1958), and Mike Davis, 'Why the US Working Class is Different', *New Left Review*, 127 (1980) Kim Scipes, 'Trade Union Imperialism in the US Yesterday: Business Unionism, Samuel Gompers and AFL Foreign Policy', in *Newsletter of International Labour Studies*, 40–1 (1989) stresses that AFL foreign policy was 'a natural outgrowth of business unionism' and was made within the AFL and not by the US government or corporate interests.

[11] Taft, *The AFL in the Time of Gompers*, 443.
[12] Samuel Gompers, *Labor in Europe and America* (New York, Harper, 1910), 286–7.

but nothing altered the AFL's implacable hostility to the Soviet Union and communism. Internationally, the AFL opposed the admission of the 'governmentally directed, controlled and dictated'[13] trade-unions from Russia. Inside America, the AFL was battling with its rival, launched in 1935, the Congress of Industrial Organizations, some of whose most effective organizers were communists. 'Every time I hear the words "international industrial unions", I know where it comes from. It comes straight from Moscow!' shouted one AFL official at a young activist trying to persuade Detroit car-workers to form an industrial union in the mid–1930s.[14]

AFL hopes of maintaining anticommunism and anti-Sovietism as the guiding lines for international trade-union work appeared on the surface to become more and more irrelevant as the war, at least from 1942 onwards, changed previous ideas and policies. Despite the willingness of all other IFTU members to join the WFTU, the AFL was unmoved. The Americans set out their opposition shortly before VE day.

We decline to associate ourselves with this alleged World Trade Union Congress because it is composed of an irreconcilable grouping of organizations rival in character, raiding in action and in conflict with each other on the home field and in hopeless disagreement on international lines . . .

We have declined to identify ourselves with a world trade-union movement that is inspired by a political philosophy which is designed to subordinate and subjugate man and property to the exclusive will of the state.[15]

AFL enmity towards the Tsar's Russia and, after 1917, to Lenin's and Stalin's Soviet Union was thus part of its heritage pre-dating US hostility to the Soviet Union after 1945. At another level, the AFL's antagonism towards the WFTU was a continuation of its domestic opposition to the CIO. The AFL warned the TUC in 1942 that 'if the British Trades Union Congress did open negotiations with the Congress of Industrial Organizations they would imperil their relationship with the American Federation of Labor'.[16]

---

[13] W. Green to W. Citrine, 16 June 1939, quoted in Taft, *The AFL from the Death of Gompers to the Merger*, 240.
[14] Quoted in Wyndham Mortimer, *Organize: My Life as a Union Man* (Boston, Beacon, 1971), 71.
[15] AFL Executive Council statement, 4 May 1945.
[16] W. Citrine, TUC Report 1942, 242.

Up to the Second World War, apart from forays into Latin America, the AFL's hostility to left-wing ideas and its anticommunism had been restricted chiefly to domestic labour politics. After 1945, an important change took place. Under a generation of leaders who would lead the AFL into its post-war world, an international policy was developed that transformed the AFL into a major permanent participant on the international trade-union scene. What Lenin and Zinoviev had intended Profintern to become —a decisive actor in labour affairs all over the world—the AFL actually became. Of all the aftermath of the Russian revolution, the two most internationally feared and condemned institutions had been Comintern and its trade-union offshoot, Profintern. Men and money had been sent all over the world to help spread the word of proletarian revolution, to split old socialist unions, and finance new communist ones, to agitate, and make propaganda about the values and vision said to be inherent in Soviet Russia. Both bodies had met opposition from foreign governments, from socialist parties west of Russia, and from established trade-unions everywhere. Comintern and Profintern representatives had been denounced as meddlers owing allegiance to a foreign power. By any reasonable yardstick, their mission had not been successful. In deference to the objections of putative allies, Stalin shut down Profintern in 1937 at the height of Popular Frontism, and Comintern in 1943 when the anti-Hitler coalition was at its mightiest.

Yet, the idea of sending abroad envoys to act in the name of the values and vision of the American Federation of Labor, envoys with the mission and money to do from their perspective what the emissaries of Profintern had done on behalf of the Soviet Union, would now take hold. As the war ended, the AFL sent off its representatives to France and Germany, to Britain, to Italy and to Japan, and into Latin America. They propagated the values of the AFL—anticommunism, non-political trade-unionism, partnership with free enterprise; above all that, liberal democracy in the form of private property, free elections, and a free judiciary were the necessary conditions for free trade unions to exist. The principal enemy of liberal democracy was communism—its parties, its unions, its supporters in every guise: these had to be extirpated like weeds as a minimum condition for the flowers of democracy and trade-unionism to survive. To put into practice this interventionist policy, two conditions had to be met. The policy had to be accepted by the AFL leadership, and it had to be put into effect with precision and competence. George Meany discharged the first task; Jay Lovestone, the second.

Meany had been secretary-treasurer of the AFL, the number-two position, since 1941. A vigorous, articulate New Yorker, not yet 50 in 1945, he took hold of the AFL's international activities, partly to give himself an increased role within the Federation, partly because he sensed international questions would give the AFL openings to the government that would be useful for domestic lobbying. There was also a sheer political pleasure that Meany got from no-holds-barred anticommunism. This gave him a high profile inside the AFL and helped ensure his election as president in 1952, his accession after the AFL and CIO merged in 1954 to the presidency of the AFL-CIO, where he remained in office until 1979.[17] In the 1930s, Meany had headed the AFL's state federation in New York where he supported the activities of New York trade-unionists on behalf of European refugees. Like the president of the AFL, William Green, Meany was deeply religious. Green was a Baptist; Meany, the son of Irish immigrants, a Catholic. His hostility to Russia had no limits. In 1944, he had voted for Roosevelt's opponent in the 1944 presidential election because he 'was convinced that we would have real problems with the Russians after the war . . . I just felt that in dealing with the Russians after the war, we would be better off with Dewey [Roosevelt's Republican opponent]'.[18] As the AFL's fraternal delegate to the TUC Congress in 1945, Meany was ready to take his views into hostile territory and was shouted down as he attacked Soviet trade-unions 'as instruments of the state . . . and its ruling dictatorial policies'.[19]

Meany's was not the only voice articulating the AFL's determination to thwart communism and the WFTU. With David Dubinsky, the energetic leader of the International Ladies Garment Workers' Union, who had taken the lead in the 1930s on supporting refugee unionists, and Matthew Woll, an immigrant from Luxembourg who headed a print union, Meany secured endorsement for the

---

[17] In addition to biographies of Meany cited elsewhere, there is a useful analysis by Ronald Ziegler in Melvyn Dubofsky and Warren van Tine, *Labor Leaders in America* (Urbana, University of Illinois Press, 1987).

[18] Quoted in Archie Robinson, *George Meany and his Times* (New York, Simon and Schuster, 1981), 21.

[19] TUC Annual Report 1945, 172.

AFL's international policies from the Federation's executive. The man who put the policies into effect was Jay Lovestone.

Lovestone became the executive secretary of the Free Trade Union Committee (FTUC), set up by the AFL leaders in 1944 to act as an operational foreign-policy institute. The FTUC had its offices in the headquarters of Dubinsky's union in New York. The location was significant. If Washington was a city of government and policy, New York was the centre of left-wing politics in America where sectarianism and factional hatreds rose to new heights. There may be street corners in Washington, but no socialist orator has ever stood at them to argue a case. By contrast, New York was home to America's most engaged ideologues; it was the capital of American Popular Frontism in the 1930s and 1940s, and the AFL principals mentioned in this chapter had grown up in New York labour politics. The headquarters of the socialist, communist, and Trotskyist organizations were in New York. It was to New York that labour-movement refugees from fascist Europe gravitated. It was in New York that the OSS set up its labour desk. To have run the AFL's foreign affairs from Washington would have been to sanitize them, dull them with the bureaucracy of the AFL headquarters. In New York, Meany's city, Jay Lovestone was in his element.

Lovestone became secretary of the American Communist Party (then called the Workers' Party) in 1927, aged 29. An immigrant, who arrived from Lithuania aged 9, Lovestone was a founder member of the American Communist Party. As well as being a skilled propagandist and prolific writer, his rise to the top owed much to his ability to play internal politics 'more ferociously and indefatigably than anyone else'. [20] He acted as a conduit for money for Comintern and was privy to the financial allocation made by Profintern to William Foster, the party's trade-union organizer and Lovestone's rival inside the party leadership. The internal rivalries were usually settled by appeals to Moscow, and on his trips there Lovestone met the leaders of world communism.

In Moscow, Lovestone misread the shifting constellation, allying himself closely with Bukharin at a time when the latter was falling from grace. In 1928 Lovestone applied the 'class against class' politics of the 'third period', with its call to build separate

[20] Theodore Draper, *American Communism and Soviet Russia* (New York, Viking, 1960), 248.

communist unions, with considerable reluctance, thus leaving his party opponents room to offer themselves as more loyal implementers of policy decided in Moscow. At the Comintern Congress in 1928, he openly attacked Losovsky, the general secretary of the Red International of Labour Unions, Profintern. 'The tragedy of Profintern consists in the fact that it is led by Lozovsky, who hopelessly muddles almost any affair that he touches . . . Let him take his hands out of American factional affairs, or we will do it for him,' Lovestone declared.[21] In 1929, Comintern ordered Lovestone to stand down as party secretary and remove himself to Moscow to work for Comintern. Instead, Lovestone led a protest delegation to Moscow to confront Stalin. The latter was unmoved. 'Who do you think you are? Trotsky defied me. Where is he? Bukharin defied me. Where is he? And you? When you get back to America, nobody will stay with you except your wives.'[22]

Upon Lovestone's return, he found that the party preferred loyalty to Comintern. He was expelled. The virus of political factionalism remained present. Still a Marxist, he formed the Communist Party (Opposition), which in 1936 was attacking the Popular Front strategy and had set itself 'the task of helping the Comintern to return to communist principles'.[23] An ambition easier to realize was to warn trade-union leaders about pro-Stalin communists in their own ranks, a task for which Lovestone was equipped.[24] By 1940, Lovestone had made a complete break with his communist past. He became the international director of Dubinsky's union and from 1944 onwards was an AFL official.

Writers have depicted Lovestone in a lurid light. For Ronald Radosh, he was the 'somewhat mysterious architect of labor's foreign policy. No other non-governmental figure . . . wields as much power in the making of foreign policy.'[25] For Victor Reuther, one of the founders of the UAW, who grappled with Lovestone in

[21] Quoted in E. H. Carr, *A History of Soviet Russia* (London, Macmillan, 1950–78), xiii. 604.

[22] Draper, *American Communism*, 422. Carr notes that the source for Stalin's onslaught was the abused American delegation. His insults were not recorded in the official minutes.

[23] Jay Lovestone, *People's Front Illusion* (New York, Workers' Age Publishers, 1936), 84.

[24] See Harvey Klehr, *The Heyday of American Communism: The Depression Decade* (New York, Basic Books, 1984), 245–6.

[25] Radosh, *American Labor and Foreign Policy*, 308.

the 1930s, Lovestone was one of the 'most Machiavellian union-splitters ever to prey on the American labor movement'.[26] An opposite view comes from Philip Taft who believes that 'after shedding his communistic views' Lovestone became 'a dedicated believer in the merits of trade-unionism' and that under his leadership, the FTUC 'provided the intellectual capacity and drive for a free world labour movement'.[27] To a certain extent, these views telescope backwards the charges and counter-charges made about the activities of the AFL, and then the AFL-CIO, in the 1950s and 1960s. In the 1940s Lovestone was a well-known figure with twenty years of high-profile activity in the American labour movement behind him. He took all the techniques developed by American communists in the 1920s and used them against American communists in the 1930s. Humiliated by Stalin and Losovsky in 1929, he had his revenge applying the Comintern's and Profintern's tactics against communist unions and parties overseas after 1945. This required little 'intellectual capacity' but rather the shrewdness, organizational ability, energy, and experience to spot and denounce enemies for which Lovestone's ten years as a communist factionalist and functionary had been the most perfect training. Lovestone was no idealist for whom the god failed. He was not a Koestler, a Strachey, or a Malraux. He was a keeper of files, a lister of names, an organizer of field agents. As Meany put it, Lovestone 'had more documents and more material on Communists and their activities in various parts of the world than any other American'.[28] Lovestone was a creation of communism such as it was in the first decade after Comintern's founding. He found a new master after the first one spurned him, but his tactics did not change, and he set out to inflict as much damage on post–1945 communism as the communists had inflicted on post–1918 socialism and trade-unionism.

AFL OFFICIALS IN EUROPE AFTER 1945

Irving Brown, who had worked for Lovestone in anticommunist drives in the United Auto Workers' Union, the principal CIO

[26] Victor Reuther, *The Brothers Reuther* (Boston, Houghton Mifflin, 1976), 308.
[27] Taft, *The AFL from the Death of Gompers*, 342–4.
[28] Quoted in Robinson, *George Meany and his Times*, 128.

affiliate, in the 1930s, became the FTUC's, hence the AFL's, representative in Europe in 1946. He felt he was contributing to the 'struggle between democracy and Communism' as he told the AFL Convention in 1946.[29] According to Brown, the French Communist Party had 'captured' the French trade-union movement and 'through the control of the economic center of France, the Communist Party can and has prevented any French government from taking an all-out stand for democracy as against totalitarianism in foreign policy'.[30] In letters back to America, Brown urged financial support for groups inside France's CGT union opposed to the communists controlling the confederation.[31] At meetings with American diplomats, he insisted upon the importance of 'the consolidation of the non-Communist labor leaders . . . into a bona-fide trade-union center'.[32] Such meetings, of course, were private; but for the most part, Brown acted openly, not as a secret conspirator. He wrote articles for union newspapers attacking the WFTU.[33] In turn, Benoît Frachon, the communist secretary of the CGT, attacked him in the CGT newspaper as a 'pilgrim of American reactionaries . . . ready to do anything against trade-union unity in the name of anticommunism.'[34]

Brown was the employed representative of the AFL in Europe, but equally important were the American union officials, detached from their unions, who worked for the US military government in Germany. The senior of these was Joe Keenan. Keenan had a background in the AFL's construction union and had helped run the AFL's operation in Chicago. Called to Washington during the war, Keenan became, in 1943, vice chairman of the War Production Board.[35] In Washington, the army general with whom Keenan had most contact was Lucius Clay, the military engineer who headed the War Department's production operation. In 1945, Clay was chosen to run the military government in the US zone in occupied Germany. He asked Keenan to join him as his labour

[29] *The Machinist*, 24 Oct. 1946.
[30] Ibid.
[31] See Radosh, *American Labor and US Foreign Policy*, 311–22.
[32] Brown at a meeting in the US Embassy in London, 27 Nov. 1947, 841.5041/11–2747 (DSNA).
[33] *The Machinist*, 23 May 1946.
[34] *La Vie ouvrière*, 25 Oct. 1946.
[35] Details of Keenan's wartime activities are in Francis Gannon, *Joseph D. Keenan: Labor's Ambassador in War and Peace* (Lanham, Md., University Press of America, 1984), 35–62.

adviser, and Keenan stayed in Germany with the temporary rank of brigadier-general until 1947. Trade-union policy had been laid down in the Joint Chiefs of Staff Directive 1067. Clay was told to 'permit the self-organization of employees along democratic lines', and to 'permit free collective bargaining between employees and employers'.[36]

Keenan's contribution was twofold. Firstly, he reinforced the anticommunism, inherent in any case in the US military government. Secondly, he stood for a rebirth of German industry. In these two areas he was at one with Clay. His status and rank provided some cover for those German trade-unionists he approved of, but it is not possible to see any major decision or act on his part that significantly altered the overall development of trade-unionism in Germany after 1945. Keenan was opposed to the activities of some officials in the US military government who were too supportive of radical elements in the German trade-union movement. In Washington, the AFL protested publicly about the alleged communist leanings of some of the labour staff in Germany.[37] Keenan, however, could find little evidence of communism. In 1946 he wrote, 'Communists are not a serious menace in Germany. On the basis of my observation, I can positively say that the Communists exercise less influence in Germany than in any other continental European country.'[38]

Such views were not to the liking of the AFL, whose representative in Europe sought to develop the theme of a titanic contest between two great forces, using the kind of language and imagery that Lovestone had deployed from an opposite perspective in the

---

[36] JCS 1067, paragraphs 23 and 24 in *Occupation of Germany: Policy and Progress 1945–1946* (Washington DC, US Government Printing Office, 1947), 205. For military directives on trade-union questions to May 1945 see H. Weber and S. Mielke (eds.), *Quellen . . .* (Cologne, Bund Verlag, 1987), vi. 125–30.

[37] See e.g. the speech in the House of Representatives by G. Dondero (Rep. Mich.) in which he attacked Clay's staff 'whose loyalty record is highly questionable'. This speech was reprinted by the AFL and widely circulated in Europe. A copy ended up in Ilg's hands at the IMF. A major source for the allegations of pro-communist leanings amongst civilians working for the US military government was a former AFL union official, Paul Porter, who worked for the US military government in Germany. He wrote to Meany in Sept. 1945 to complain of the 'infiltration into both the policy making and operations branches of Military Government of persons who, when working for Federal agencies in Washington, were known as followers of the Party line'. P. Porter to G. Meany, 21 Sept. 1945, in Weber and Mielke (eds.), *Quellen*, vi. 1002–7.

[38] Quoted in Gannon, *Joseph D. Keenan*, 76.

1920s. According to Brown, 'the Communists have developed a tremendous campaign to capture control of the works councils . . . Communist demagogues . . . attempt to pit the works councils, which contain many non-union members as well as unionists, against the trade-union movement in order to destroy the influence of the more moderate, rational leaders'.[39] Brown's analysis was rebutted in the secret report made by the official in charge of the US military government's section covering works' councils. In 1947, he wrote, the communists 'received an important set-back in the attempt to expand control of the Works Councils'.[40] At several factories in the Hanau district, a stronghold of pre–1933 communists, the SDP had overturned communist majorities in the 1946 works-council elections. At the large Opel car works in Rüsselsheim, a 10–6 majority in favour of the KPD in 1946 became a 10–6 SPD majority in 1947. In the metal industry in Wiesbaden, of 298 works' councillors, 175 were socialists and 41 were communists. In the Frankfurt chemical industry, the SPD had 70 per cent of the workers' vote against 5 per cent for the communists.[41]

These factory elections matched what was happening in other polls. In October 1946, in Berlin, the SPD won 48.7 per cent of the votes against 19.8 for the communist-dominated Socialist Unity Party (Sozialistische Einheitspartei Deutschlands (SED)) in the poll for the city government; even in the Soviet sector of Berlin, the social democrats outpolled the communists by nearly two to one. In Austria, the parliamentary elections of November 1945 gave 76 seats to the social democrats and 4 to the communists.[42]

Thus whatever they were saying back in America, the AFL could not point to a rising tide of communism threatening to subvert the German trade-unions, nor, despite their fulminations against the behaviour of some US military government officials, was there any evidence that American policy was helping the communists. But to narrow down the AFL's role in foreign policy after 1945 to a series of the anticommunist interventions or statements is to miss the major impact of the Federation in this period. This was in throwing

[39] Irving Brown, 'Report on Situation in Germany', 15 May 1947 (IMFA).

[40] OMGUS (Office of Military Govt., US), 'Communist Influence in Hesse Labor Organizations', 1 Nov. 1947, 862. 504 11–1347 (DSNA).

[41] Ibid. More details of the preference of German workers for socialists rather than communists in works' councils and union elections are given in Ch. 12.

[42] See Martin McCauley, 'East Germany' in McCauley (ed.), *Communist Power in Europe 1944–1949* (London, Macmillan, 1977), 64–6.

its influence and weight behind the swiftest possible reconstruction of German industry and the clear economic, political, and social separation of the three Western zones from the one occupied by the Soviet Union.

In the debate over the future of Germany that took place continuously after 1945, the AFL argued for a functioning democratic capitalist Germany and accepted the consequence that this would mean a partition. Who persuaded whom is difficult to say but General Clay, for one, was arguing against the dismantling of German industry even before the war ended.[43] Clay argued that the allied military occupation of Germany would prevent the revival of German militarism. The rebirth of German industry geared to peaceful production would, through internal trading and exports, help pay for food imports. The Soviet zone and the areas transferred to Poland included two-thirds of the food-growing areas of pre-war Germany. Alternatives, such as a pastoralized Germany along the lines of the Morgenthau plan, or a Germany whose industrial capacity was reduced by reparations based on dismantling and transfer of plant and equipment, would lead to starvation and social chaos. For the Americans and British, the burden of feeding the German population, at a time when there were food shortages in Britain (not even President Truman could obtain roast beef in much-better-fed America), became a source of domestic political discontent in the two countries.[44]

A team of AFL dignitaries visited Germany in the autumn of 1946. Back in the United States, its leader, William Doherty, a vice-president of the AFL, told a radio audience: 'The future of German trade-unions depended on the development of political liberty and

[43] See Clay to J. McCloy, Asst. Sec. of War, 26 Apr. 1945, in Joan Smith (ed.), *The Papers of General Lucius D. Clay 1945–1949* (Bloomington, Indiana University Press, 1974), 8. Many of the government officials in Washington responsible for the elaboration of policy in Germany, as well as advisers to Clay in Germany itself, were industrialists, bankers, or corporate lawyers. Some had pre-war interests in Germany. There was no experience or belief visible in the American occupiers in other than privately owned and managed capitalism. For a highly personalized account of the makers of US policy in Europe after 1945 see W. Isaacson and E. Thomas, *The Wise Men* (New York, Simon and Schuster, 1986), and for a critical contemporary observation see I. F. Stone, 'American Big Business and the Future of the Reich' (19 Mar. 1945), and 'It Begins to Happen Again' (17 July 1946, in Stone, *The Truman Era 1945–1952* (Boston, Little Brown, 1972).

[44] On food shortages in Britain see Paul Addison, *Now the War Is Over* (London, Cape, 1985), 29–44. On the United States see Roger Donovan, *Conflict and Crisis: The Presidency of Harry S. Truman 1945–1948* (New York, Norton, 1977), 124–5.

on what is done to encourage production and relieve misery. The United States economy would eventually suffer should the Germans continue to be ill-fed, ill-housed and denied the bare necessities of life'.[45] The crippling winter of 1946–7 in Europe added to the misery. Climate can emphasize or reorder priorities. Writing in the spring of 1947, Irving Brown presented a bleak picture. The official ration of 1,550 calories a day had fallen in the larger industrial cities to 800. Industrial output in 1946 in the Anglo-American zone was 35 per cent of 1938 figures, and industrial activity for the first three months of 1947 'would be 25 per cent less than in the previous quarter due to the shortage of coal, steel, electricity and transport'.[46] More than Germans were thus affected. Ports and farms in the Netherlands and Belgium were idle, denied trade and markets. An 'inflationary spiral has robbed the masses of the incentive to work since the monetary values have become meaningless in an economy where a carton of cigarettes can bring more Marks or goods than several months of hard work in the mines and factories'.[47]

In such conditions, argued Brown, 'instruments of democracy—trade unions, works councils, political parties—are also inherently the media of revolutionary or rebellious action'.[48] There was a need for a 'democratic economic policy', and it was 'necessary to plan Germany's future in terms of European and world economic ties. Assuming the reality of the present Eastern European political situation, there should be no hesitation about the creation of an integrated Western European economy'.[49] In conclusion, Brown recommended the integration of the West German economy into the 'rest of Europe and the world', support for the industrialization of Western Germany, and monetary stabilization to restore 'incentive in Germany's economic life'.[50]

A month after Brown circulated these recommendations to the AFL in America, the Marshall Plan was announced, and the United States formally changed its policy toward Germany in almost precisely the way Brown had suggested. The changing course in American policy towards Germany and the Soviet Union between 1945 and 1947 was affected by many outside factors and relentless

---

[45] *The Machinist*, 14 Nov. 1946.
[46] Irving Brown, 'Report on Germany', May 1947 (IMFA).
[47] Ibid.   [48] Ibid.
[49] Ibid.   [50] Ibid.

political struggle in Washington. The AFL's steady drip of propaganda—anti-Soviet, anti-WFTU, pro-German economic restoration—was its contribution to that process.

The AFL and its affiliates carried out an unceasing attack on the Soviet Union. In April 1946, the journal of the AFL's major metalworkers' union, the International Association of Machinists, accused the Soviet Union of 'imperialism' and listed annexations by Russia amounting to '273,947 square miles of territory with 23,355,500 people'.[51] AFL union journals carried digests of FTUC reports from Brown. In May 1946, Brown told American trade-unionists that in Berlin 'there is being crystallized the coming fight between democratic forces and Communism. On the trade-union front, the Russian-inspired super-centralized organizations are controlled by the Communists while the Social Democrats and Christians are their prisoner.'[52]

AFL editors made use of Clement Attlee to attack communism. *The Machinist* quoted the British premier telling a Labour Party rally in Newcastle early in 1946 that 'the Communist Party gives lip service to democracy but is essentially undemocratic. The methods by which it seeks power disregard altogether the obligation to maintain the standards of conduct which make life possible in a civilized society.'[53] The use of the Labour Attlee to make the case against the Soviet Union was repeated in October 1946 in a report on the TUC Congress which was headlined, 'British Labor Hears Attlee Blast Russia'.

If in any part of the world the Communist Party, by no matter what means, is in power—that is democracy. If anywhere the Communists fail—however fair the conditions—it is regarded as fascism. . . . It is one of the tragedies of the world situation that the Soviet government appears deliberately to prevent intercourse between the Russian people and the rest of the world. . . . The Russian newspapers give fantastic misrepresentations of the world outside Russia. A wall of ignorance and suspicion is being built up between nations.[54]

Writing of the change in American public opinion towards the Soviet Union, Daniel Yergin has argued that 'the post-war anticommunist consensus existed first in the center, in the policy

[51] *The Machinist*, 11 Apr. 1946.
[52] Ibid. 3 May 1946.
[53] Ibid.
[54] Ibid. 1 Oct.1946.

elite, before it spread out to the nation'.[55] Even if one assumes that the mass of the AFL's 8 million members were relatively uninterested in foreign affairs, the position taken by the officers of AFL unions, the articles in the widely circulated journals, the speeches made at their conventions, add up to more than the private views of a policy élite.

In February 1946, George Kennan, in his famous 'long telegram' from Moscow, underlined his belief that the Kremlin attached 'vital importance . . . to [the] international labor movement. In this, Moscow sees [the] possibility of sidetracking Western governments in world affairs and building up an international lobby capable of compelling governments to take actions favourable to Soviet interests in various countries and of paralyzing actions disagreeable to the USSR.'[56] For the AFL, who had been making the same point since before the end of the war, Kennan's observation was most welcome. The 'long telegram' was read by President Truman; Secretary of State James Byrnes congratulated its author on a 'splendid document' and distributed it to US missions all over the world; the Navy Secretary, James Forrestal, had hundreds of copies made for senior military personnel, and it was widely leaked to the press.[57]

How many of the recipients of what officially was a highly confidential diplomatic despatch paused over Kennan's animadversions on Russia's international labour policy is hard to say. From the spring of 1946 onwards, American policy towards the Soviet Union hardened.[58] In July 1946, Meany was confident enough about the overall direction of US attitudes towards the Soviet Union and other international questions to write in the AFL's *Federationist*, 'There cannot be a special foreign policy for the American labor movement and another for American society.'[59]

---

[55] Daniel Yergin, *Shattered Peace: The Origins of the Cold War and the National Security State* (London, Penguin, 1980), 171.

[56] G. Kennan, telegram to State Department, 3 Feb. 1946, in George Kennan, *Memoirs 1925–1950* (Boston, Little Brown, 1967), 547–65.

[57] On the impact of the 'long telegram' see Yergin, *Shattered Peace*, 234.

[58] See Fraser Harbutt, *The Iron Curtain: Churchill, America and the Origins of the Cold War* (New York, OUP, 1986).

[59] *Federationist*, July 1946.

7

Internationalism and the Congress of Industrial Organizations

WHILE the AFL remained aloof, and campaigned against the WFTU, its rival trade-union confederation, the Congress of Industrial Organizations, was a founder member of the new international. The WFTU is often considered as a product of the war. The CIO is usually described as a child of Roosevelt's New Deal. It may also be helpful to see both as part of the Popular Front tradition, whereby the inheritors of Lenin's testament sought to reintegrate themselves with other social forces, notably the non-communist parties of the Left, as well as with liberals, progressive conservatives, and, most especially, with the trade-unions. There is a continuing historical discussion about whether these *rapprochements* reflected a push from the base or were a function of the decisions arising from the seventh congress of Comintern in 1935. The likely answer is a mixture of both, though that does not satisfy those who want to see the Popular Front as a Moscow-directed manipulation, or, alternatively, a genuine demand for unity coming from below in response to the impact of economic depression and fascism of the 1930s.[1]

In terms of the political goals set by its supporters, Popular Front politics were not successful. They failed to sustain a government in France, failed similarly in Spain, and failed in the task of preventing Hitler's war. Popular Front politics also failed to reconnect communism and socialism. The Hitler–Stalin pact marked the formal end of Popular Frontism. Yet in a broader sense, the political outlook associated with the Popular Front had an enduring impact. It energized new waves of workers, young activists, students, and intellectuals. In W. H. Auden's words, it made a virtue out of 'the expending of powers on the flat ephemeral

---

[1] There is a useful discussion of this in *International Labor and Working Class History, Special Issue: The Popular Front*, 30 [1986]. See also Theodore Draper, 'American Communism Revisited' (New York Review of Books, 9 and 25 May 1985). On Britain see Ben Pimlott, *Labour and the Left in the 1930s* (London, Allen and Unwin, 1986), 143 ff.

pamphlet and the boring meeting', an osmotic process that hugely changed ideas and contributed significantly to the manifold revolution of 1945. In the United States, the era which in Europe is thought of as the Popular Front is called the New Deal, while the term 'Popular Front' is often reserved as an epithet for Henry Wallace's third party campaign in 1948.[2] America's New Deal and Europe's Popular Front were not the same but they shared one important quality: the incorporation, for a while, of communism into mainstream political life. Communists and communism were central to the birth of the CIO, to its political profile in the 1930s and 1940s, and to its international policy after 1945.

Categorizations reserved for European political discussion are also helpful in considering the CIO's outlook. The principal architect of the WFTU for the CIO was the garment-union leader, Sidney Hillman. According to Steven Fraser, the CIO leader sought to create 'a world labor organization committed to a global version of the New Deal . . . social democratic in orientation'.[3] The CIO's social democracy was limited. If Hillman believed in 'the advantages of state intervention on labor's behalf and . . . the regulation of the economy more generally',[4] the CIO president, Philip Murray, regarded advocates of nationalization as 'nuts'[5] and stayed within the adversarial traditions of American collective bargaining. The CIO shared one social democratic premise, that of a commitment to growth and an acceptance that industrial democracy in the sense of rights for workers depended on 'the always fragile economic health of . . . industry'.[6] To oppose economic growth in general, and in

---

[2] 'I was a Popular Fronter, I supported Henry Wallace,' I. F. Stone told the author (interview, Washington, DC, 5 Oct. 1985).

[3] Steven Fraser, 'Sidney Hillman', in M. Dubofsky and W. van Tine, *Labor Leaders in America* (Urbana, University of Illinois Press, 1987).

[4] Ibid. 213.

[5] Murray to John L. Lewis in 1933 quoted in Dubofsky, 'Labor's Odd Couple: Philip Murray and John L. Lewis', in Paul Clarke, Peter Gottlieb, and Donald Kennedy (eds.), *Forging a Union of Steel: Philip Murray, SWOC, and the United Steelworkers* (Ithaca, NY, Cornell University Press, 1987), 35.

[6] Nelson Lichtenstein, 'Great Expectations: The Promise of Collective Bargaining and its Demise, 1935–1965', in Howell Harris and Nelson Lichtenstein, (eds.), *Industrial Democracy, Past and Present* (New York, CUP, 1991). Lichtenstein is referring here to regulatory efforts developed by progressive union leaders in the US textile industry in the 1930s, but his observation holds true for CIO positions generally. The attractiveness of Walter Reuther to radicals in the 1940s lay in his vision of combining economic growth, fairer distribution, and more rights for workers.

particular as it was offered under the Marshall Plan, for both American and European industry, was to cut at the heart of all CIO economic thinking.

If dependence on the state—in itself highly problematic given the WFTU's partial reflection of interstate diplomatic relations—was one aspect of the CIO's social-democratic profile, and commitment to economic growth a second, then the third way in which the CIO resembled European social democracy of the era was in a tortuous relationship with communism. When they made the break with the AFL in 1935, the founders of the CIO accepted communist activists into their ranks.

The CIO was adept at using the media and finding legal formulas to promote its causes. The CIO editor, Len de Caux, was an English public-school-educated radical who arrived in America in the 1920s and joined the Communist Party. The CIO's legal counsel, Lee Pressman, who drafted many of Murray's speeches and letters as well as giving legal advice, was close to the Communist Party and had briefly been a member in the 1930s. Although John L. Lewis and Philip Murray, who succeeded him as CIO president in 1940, were long-time anticommunists, they worked with left-wing intellectuals and accepted communist leaderships in some CIO unions. The relationship between communists and non-communists in the CIO was never an easy one, and by the time the WFTU had begun operating the tension was marked.[7] At the core of the CIO lay giant metalworkers' unions, for automobile, steel, and electrical industry workers.[8] A brief examination of one of these unions, that of the

[7] See Irving Bernstein, *Turbulent Years: A History of the American Workers 1933–1941* (Boston, Houghton Mifflin, 1971); Bert Cochran, *Labor and Communism: The Conflict that Shaped American Unions* (Princeton, NJ Princeton University Press, 1977); Art Preis, *Labor's Giant Step: Twenty Years of the CIO* (New York, Pathfinder Press, 1964); Len de Caux, *Labor Radical: From the Wobblies to the CIO* (Boston, Beacon Press 1970). On communism see Harvey Klehr, *The Heyday of American Communism: The Depression Decade*, (New York, Basic Books, 1984); Max Kampelman, *The Communist Party versus the CIO* (New York, Praeger, 1957), and Maurice Isserman, *Which Side Were You On? The American Communist Party in the Second World War* (Middletown, Conn., Wesleyan University Press, 1982).

[8] In the United States the term 'industrial union' is used loosely. According to 19th c. social democratic (i.e. Marxist) definitions, an industrial union organizes all workers in a general industrial branch such as metalworking, chemical, transport, textiles, and so forth. Thus, steel, automobile, and electrical industry workers would all be in one industrial metalworkers' union as they are in Germany or Sweden. In America, by contrast, workers in various sectors of one industrial branch were

autoworkers, who by 1945 made up a quarter of the CIO's membership, will help explain the CIO's relationship with the WFTU as it passed from enthusiastic begetting in 1945 to hostile rejection in 1948.

From its founding in 1935 onwards, international events played a considerable part in the United Automobile Workers, the largest and politically the most lively and interesting of the CIO unions. Understandably, this is not always reflected in the standard accounts of the union which focus on domestic issues of sit-down strikes, the first agreements with General Motors and Chrysler, the establishment of the union in the component and aircraft industries, the creative and well-publicized initiatives of its dominant personality, Walter Reuther, and the non-stop highly politicized struggle for control which only ended in 1947 when Reuther, elected president the previous year, established full authority.[9]

John L. Lewis, the CIO's first president, was an isolationist. He took a limited interest in Latin-American trade-unionism but believed the CIO should restrict its international contacts and activity to the Western hemisphere.[10] While the AFL rejoined the IFTU in the late 1930s, and organized support for labour refugees from Hitlerism, the CIO focused on American problems. This was

organized in separate CIO unions. Their bargaining and representative relationship were with individual or groups of companies, rather than with a wide range of employers organized in a regional or national industrial employers' federation. Further, CIO unions organized different groups of workers in the same industry: both the United Automobile Workers and the United Electrical Workers had members and sought recognition in the automobile industry, and organizational rivalries could be acute. In the textile industry, there were three major CIO unions. I have preferred to use the term 'industry union' to distinguish American industry unions from the European industrial ones.

[9] There are many books and articles on the UAW. The massive UAW files at Wayne State University in Detroit provide source material unmatched by any other union. In addition to works already cited—and the UAW takes up considerable space in the histories of the CIO—the following were useful: Irving Howe and B. J. Widdick, *The UAW and Walter Reuther* (New York, Random House, 1949); Victor Reuther, *The Brothers Reuther and the UAW* (Boston, Houghton Mifflin, 1976); Roger Keeran, *The Communist Party and the Autoworkers' Union* (Bloomington, Indiana University Press, 1980); John Barnard, *Walter Reuther and the Rise of the Autoworkers* (Boston, Little Brown, 1983); and Peter W. Schulze, *Gewerkschaftskampf von unten: Amerikanische Automobilarbeiter im New Deal* (Frankfurt, Campus, 1987).

[10] See Melvyn Dubofsky and Warren van Tine, *John L. Lewis: A Biography* (New York, Quadrangle Books, 1977), 330–2.

reciprocated. Little effort was made by European unions to express support for the achievements of the CIO in expanding trade-unionism in the United States or the major struggles with employers in the 1930s. The International Metalworkers' Federation, to take one example, reported on the economics of the New Deal in 1938 but referred only to 'the two rival trade-union organizations'[11] and made no effort to establish links with the CIO.

Against this background, it is surprising that Victor Reuther, who played a leading part in the establishment of the UAW and was a close aide to his brother throughout this period, should assert that as far as the Reuthers and their followers were concerned, foreign policy was 'the main bone of contention in the union' in its first years.[12] However an examination of the internal politics of the UAW supports this view. While the union was not affiliated internationally or active abroad in any way, it was obliged, year after year in the late 1930s and the 1940s to take positions on international questions. This process exposed the differences between opposing camps in the union, and international questions were used as a rallying point in the bitter factionalism inside the UAW. In that sense internationalism was internalized, but it did mean that the UAW and the CIO arrived at 1945 and events connected with the WFTU with considerable baggage on international issues in their train.

The Reuthers themselves had wide international experience. Walter Reuther was born in 1907; Victor, his brother, in 1911. They were sons of a German immigrant who was a leading trade-unionist in Ohio and active in the American Socialist Party, for whose leader, Eugene Debs, he campaigned in three presidential elections. Thus he brought up his sons in an atmosphere of political engagement. Walter and Victor campaigned for Norman Thomas, the socialist candidate in the 1932 presidential election. Both became qualified tool-makers and spent a year in Europe in 1933, arriving in Berlin at the moment of Hitler's take-over. In England they met Fenner Brockway and Jennie Lee, contacts in Britain arranged, as elsewhere in Europe, through the American Socialist Party. In 1934 and 1935, the Reuthers were in the Soviet Union, working in Gorky at the automobile plant set up with Henry Ford's

[11] IMF Secretary's report, July 1938, 30 (IMFA).
[12] Interview with Victor Reuther, Washington. DC, 4 Oct. 1985.

help, which employed hundreds of American technicians and skilled workers. Upon their return to the United States, the Reuthers plunged into the newly created CIO union for auto-workers and this work dominated the rest of their lives. They brought with them not only international experience which few other American union leaders could match—how many had worked as toolmakers in a Soviet factory?—but a set of democratic socialist values to guide them through the ideological fights that lay ahead.

Although part of the loose left-wing alliance of socialists and communists in the UAW in 1935 and 1936 and, as such, the target for Jay Lovestone's anticommunist campaigning, Reuther had parted company with the communists by 1938. One dispute leading to the break was that of collective security, supported by communists and opposed by many socialists who considered any future European war to involve a defence of British and French capitalism and imperialism and, therefore, to be shunned. Left-wing, pacifist isolationism had a powerful hold. The Hitler–Stalin pact widened the split between communists, who supported the view that America should keep out of the European conflict, and their opponents who argued for support for the nations fighting Nazism. At the UAW convention in August 1940, Reuther taunted the communists, reminding them of their support only twelve months previously for Roosevelt, the man they now denounced as supporting an imperialist war. Resolutions condemning 'the brutal dictatorships and wars of aggression of the totalitarian govern-ments of Germany, Italy, Russia and Japan', and supporting the re-election of Roosevelt, 'the greatest friend of labor ever to hold the office of President', were overwhelmingly adopted despite com-munist opposition.[13]

One question needs to be considered. Did the expressions of anticommunism in the period of the Hitler–Stalin pact represent a fundamental cleavage, or were they simply practical propaganda ploys which were used by one faction against its rivals in the struggle for organizational control? If the latter were the case, the question of communism and the Soviet Union might be expected to fade away, especially after America's entry into the war. Instead any reading of the politics and organizational development of the

---

[13] Proceedings UAW 1940 Convention, 292–303, and 431–40.

UAW, the major CIO union in the war, shows that these remained glowing, divisive questions that resurfaced continually in the union's wartime history.

Even in 1940, the CIO was faced with its first great crisis when its leader, John L. Lewis, resigned. Lewis had stirred millions of workers. He was the inspiration of the CIO breakaway from the AFL. He had provided the national leadership to exploit the changed atmosphere of the New Deal. Yet Lewis was never at ease with Roosevelt, a rival in seeking the affection of American workers— in thousands of miners' homes in America two pictures would hang on the wall, those of Lewis and Roosevelt—and believed the president had betrayed labour's cause in the late 1930s. This, coupled with his isolationism, led Lewis to endorse Wendell Wilkie, Roosevelt's Republican opponent in the 1940 election. To stress his opposition and to encourage labour votes for Wilkie, Lewis promised to stand down as CIO president if Roosevelt defeated his candidate. When this happened, he was replaced as CIO president by his chief aide and fellow miner, the Scottish-born Philip Murray, who had become leader of the CIO steelworkers' organization. [14]

Murray was cautious, conciliatory, and 'as a devout Roman Catholic', writes Ronald Filippelli, 'drew his labor ideology from the papal encyclicals *Quadragesimo Anno* and *Rerum Novarum* . . . the religious dimension of Murray's social and labour theory was evident in his support for the moral rearmament movement, a Protestant variant on Catholic social theory based on class love and global co-operation as an answer to Communism'.[15] Anticommunist in the 1920s and early 1930s, this aspect of his beliefs was kept guarded from public view in the first decade of the CIO's existence but reappeared from 1946 onwards. Murray may have kept anticommunist denunciations suppressed, but communism and the Soviet Union remained the most animated political questions for the CIO unions between 1940 and 1945. In 1940, the CIO convention unanimously adopted a resolution which, pre-echoing the language of 1947 and 1948, rejected 'any policies

[14] On Lewis, see Dubofsky and van Tine, *John L. Lewis: A Biography*. There is a good sketch of Murray by Ronald Schatz in Dubofsky and van Tine, (eds.), *Labor Leaders*.
[15] Ronald Filippelli, 'The History is Missing, Almost: Philip Murray, the Steelworkers, and the Historians', in Clark, *et al.* (eds.), *Forging a Union of Steel*, 26–9.

emanating from totalitarianism, dictatorships, and foreign ideologies such as nazism, communism and fascism'.[16] The resolution
was moved by Lee Pressman. His friend Len de Caux, the CIO
editor, later wrote that in trying to keep in with the CIO leadership
by endorsing resolutions so clearly aimed at the communist
position, 'the Lefts seemed to lack strength, principle, or guts'.[17]

As American industry moved on to a war production footing in
1941, wage demands, which had been frozen since 1938, burst
through in the form of strikes, notably in defence-related industries.
Anticommunist union organizers accused communists of sabotaging
war production efforts in the period up to Russia's entry into the
war, and this charge would linger and be used as an anticommunist
reproach in years ahead. Yet in the judgement of Harvey Klehr, a
historian not sympathetic to communist perspectives, 'in virtually
all instances there were good and sufficient trade-union reasons for
striking'.[18]

Despite the changed attitudes of the communists after Hitler's
attack on the Soviet Union, the Reuther-led group secured a
resolution at the UAW convention in August 1941, barring from
office anyone 'who is a member of or subservient to any political
organization such as Communist, Nazi or Fascist which owes its
allegiance to any foreign government'.[19] It was a political and
organizational fight to the finish in a major trade-union, not a
decade old, with neither settled institutional structures, nor a
permanent bureaucracy, nor even a dominant political line. The
abrupt change in position of the communists in the UAW and CIO,
from anti-war denunciations to exaggerated pro-war enthusiasm,
once the Soviet Union was attacked provided easy excuses for scorn
on the part of their opponents. The policy of the CIO unions, after
America's entry into the war, was explicit. Murray's call, as
expressed in the CIO newspaper headline was 'WORK! WORK! WORK!
PRODUCE! PRODUCE! PRODUCE!',[20] and the CIO gave the government a
no-strike pledge and endorsed wage controls. The communist
leader, Earl Browder, half of whose 44,000 members in 1942 were
in CIO unions, enthusiastically backed this whole-hearted com-

[16] Proceedings CIO 1940 Convention, 233.
[17] De Caux, *Labor Radical*, 241.
[18] Klehr, *Heyday*, 404.
[19] Proceedings UAW 1941 Convention, 178.
[20] *CIO News*, 9 Mar. 1942.

mitment to the war effort. One contribution he made was his offer to shake hands with Wall Street's most representative figure, J. P. Morgan, if it would help the anti-Nazi fight.[21]

POLICY AND POLITICS IN THE CIO

The CIO's policy of complete, unquestioning support for the war effort appeared to unite the CIO leadership with the communist activists, but policy is not the same as politics.[22] The history of the CIO unions in the war and, by extension, of the WFTU after 1945 is one of policy and politics coming into continual and ever sharper conflict. In 1942, the enmities of the preceding two years were not to be forgotten. In the United Electrical Workers (UE), another major CIO union, the fight between its 30-year-old leader, James Carey, and his communist opponents had been narrowly contested. The leaders of the Communist Party instructed their members in the union to make their peace with Carey. He refused the offer, writing in the *UE News* of the communist

back flip with a full twist and presto—Great Britain is purged of all her sins. Hitler is to be hated even more than Roosevelt. The 'imperialist blood bath' becomes a people's war for freedom . . . Political acrobats in pink tights posing as labor leaders are a disgrace to the union and an insult to the intelligence of the membership.[23]

Carey's anticommunism did not carry the day inside his own union. He was replaced as president as much because of his indifference to union administration and lack of skill in building up a base.[24] His loss of office in the UE did not affect his status as CIO secretary-treasurer (like Murray, whose paid job was president of the steelworkers' union, Carey's position at the CIO was unpaid), and he played an important role as the main CIO representative at the WFTU in 1947 and 1948.

Inside the UAW, the politics of wartime policy erupted in 1943 in a struggle over pay systems. To increase war production, the communists backed proposals to return to piece-rates and incentive

---

[21] Isserman, *Which Side Were You On?*, 247.
[22] On the difference between policy and politics see David Marquand, *The Unprincipled Society* (London, Fontana, 1988), 59–61.
[23] Quoted in Isserman, *Which Side Were You On?*, 116.
[24] Ibid. 117.

pay to replace the hard-won hourly rates which the CIO unions had fought for. The call for incentive pay was unpopular with the rank and file, and opposed by Walter Reuther, now clearly identified as the leader of the anticommunist wing of the UAW. At the UAW's convention in 1943, supporters of piece-rates were said to 'take their orders straight from the office of Joe Staleen [sic] . . . to make the workers a machine' and the proposal was rejected.[25]

Reuther also lent his support to a rally in March 1943 in New York, called to denounce Stalin's execution of two Polish Jewish socialist politicians, Henryk Erlich and Victor Alter, who had fled eastwards to what they thought was safety in Russia after the German invasion in 1939. The two Reuther brothers, Walter and Victor, had met Alter during their European tour, and although the CIO kept its distance from what was an emotional anti-Soviet event, the Reuther faction portrayed the putting to death of Erlich and Alter as a further example of communist misbehaviour.[26]

More important, however, were developments in workplaces and the tensions spilling over from the strains of war production. While profits in the corporate sector soared—General Motors' net profits went up 50 per cent in 1943—workers had their wages frozen and were living in crowded, dirty conditions as the industrial cities coped with the huge influx of new labour needed to cope with expanded war production. Major race riots had broken out in Detroit in 1943 partly as a result of the inability of the city's housing infrastructure to cope with the new arrivals. A rash of 'quickie' strikes (so called because they rarely lasted more than a day) broke out in 1943, turning into a wave of strikes in 1944, each lasting no more than two or three days. In the automobile and aircraft industries, the centres of war production, one worker in two took part in a 'quickie' strike in 1944. In the plants, reported one UAW official, 'the workers were so tired from long hours and no vacations, and provoked by endless petty management mal-practices, that they wanted to walk out just for a rest'.[27]

Under these conditions the UAW increased its membership from 165,000 in 1939 to 1,065,000 in 1944. It was also potentially

[25] See Barnard, *Walter Reuther*, 83.

[26] Interview with Victor Reuther. See also Samuel Portnoy, *Henryk Erlich and Victor Alter: Two Heroes and Martyrs for Jewish Socialism*, (New York, Jewish Labor Bund, 1990).

[27] Quoted in Keeran, *The Communist Party and the Autoworkers*, 242.

fertile ground for anti-employer, anticapitalist agitation. Yet the communists in the UAW and other CIO unions, so agile in previous years in building on such justified grievances, now urged workers to accept their lot. While the 1943 UAW convention had called for public ownership of key industries and a thirty-hour week to maintain full employment after the war's end, the Communist Party's leader, Browder, wrote: 'In the United States, we have to win the war under the capitalist system . . . we have to help the capitalists.'[28] In 1944, Browder arguing that American communists were ready to make 'capitalism work effectively in the post-war period',[29] dissolved the Communist Party, replacing it with the Communist Political Association, a 'non-party organization of Americans which carries forward the traditions of Washington, Jefferson, Paine, Jackson and Lincoln, under the changed conditions of modern industrial society'.[30]

This unusual political manœuvre was matched by increased communist discipline to maintain production in the factories. The communist *Daily Worker*, denouncing a walk-out by Dodge workers in Chicago in June 1944, said that to go on 'strike is to scab, and scabs should be treated as scabs'.[31] *Business Week* believed that, by 1944, in the CIO unions in which communists held control, 'the leadership . . . has moved from the extreme left-wing to the extreme right-wing position in the American labor movement'.[32]

It was not a question of a CIO leadership keen on strikes against communist trade-unions willing to hold the line. Murray and Hillman, as much as communist union leaders, sought a consensually run post-war world based on full employment, a balance between union and managerial powers, a corporate equilibrium linked to economic and social progress, all presided over by a benevolent president. In March 1945 the CIO endorsed a Labor–Management charter which the CIO welcomed with the headline, 'It's Industrial Peace for the Postwar Period'.[33]

Yet missing was the social or political pressure needed to convert

[28] Quoted in Lichtenstein, *Labor's War*, 145.
[29] Isserman, *Which Side Were You On?*, 188–9.
[30] Preamble to Constitution of Communist Political Association, May 1944.
[31] Quoted in Keeran, *The Communist Party and the Autoworkers*, 243.
[32] *Business Week*, 18 Mar. 1944.
[33] *CIO News*, 23 Mar. 1945.

this amorphous programme into governmental or legislative reality. Unlike the countries across the Atlantic where the war had obliged conservatives such as Churchill and de Gaulle to give real governmental power to the representatives of the labour movement, and where pre-war political, financial, and industrial castes such as the appeasers in Britain, or the *Munichois* leaders in France had been discredited, the American experience had been, if anything, a vindication of New Deal policies and the 'can-do' techniques of American management. None the less, although tripartite structures were set up, American labour leaders had nothing like the position and power of their equivalents in Britain. If power at the top was missing, there was very great social pressure from the base. In 1944 there were 4,956 reported work stoppages involving 1.98 million workers, and in 1945, 4,750 strikes involving 2.12 million workers.[34] Yet this pressure was more a problem to the CIO and especially to the communists, than it was a force able to be used to change social or economic relations in a radical way.

Calls for a more socialized economy were heard. In 1944, Walter Reuther, for example, put forward a plan for a 'Peace Production Board' and for government control of key monopolies. Later he suggested that 'Government authorities similar to the Tennessee Valley Authority . . . be set up in housing and transportation. Throughout industry,' he wrote, 'the issue is the same: back to monopoly, to operation of a fraction of capacity . . . or forward to full use of resources, full employment, and an equitable distribution of the products of our labor.'[35]

For any of these aims to be put into practice, a very broad coalition of forces was necessary. Instead, at the time Reuther made his appeal—September 1945—the American labour movement was in the process of disuniting. Several reasons explain why. There was mounting concern about the post-war economy. Billions of dollars of wartime contracts had been cancelled, unemployment rose to 2 million by October 1945, and there were 8 million in the US forces to be reintegrated into civilian life. Murray and the CIO leadership confronted a new president, Harry Truman, who was less beholden to labour than Roosevelt. The AFL, which had also

[34] US Dept. of Labor, *Handbook of Labor Statistics*, 1974.
[35] *New York Times Magazine*, 16 Sept. 1945.

greatly expanded in size, was back firmly in its adversarial business-unionism tradition. John L. Lewis, now back in the AFL fold, but still head of the mighty miners' union, had denounced what he described as the CIO pleas for a 'corporate state, wherein the activities of the people are regulated and constrained by a dictatorial government'.[36]

Another factor that contributed to the turbulence in the unions' ranks in late 1945 and early 1946 was the decision of the communists to change towards a more militant posture. Browder's decision to dissolve the party in 1944 and form a Communist Association had been attacked as 'revisionism' by Jacques Duclos, the number two in the French Communist Party. Duclos's attack was printed in the communist press in many countries in the summer of 1945 and was read as a coded message, taken to emanate from Moscow, of disavowal of Browder. In July 1945, the Communist Party was refounded as a party, and Browder was replaced by William Foster at its head. The new Communist Party leader had headed Profintern's operations in America in the 1920s and applied Stalin's 'Third Period' policies with loyalty. By August 1945, the Communist Party was denouncing 'Browderism' and, by inference, the now-disgraced leader's no-strike policy and support for industrial co-operation. Instead they endorsed a more militant industrial policy.[37]

The communists were following rather than leading as the end of price and wage-controls in autumn 1945 came with a major strike-wave in the automobile, steel, rubber, and coal industries. One UAW member employed by General Motors in Chicago recalls

how the Communists tried to get us to go on strike only a few days before the big strike vote was due to take place. My local was split 50–50 between the Reutherites and the CPers. They called a meeting on a night shift to get us to go on strike but I stood up and said 'Why? What's the reason, when we are going to vote next week anyway?' And everyone knew the vote would be for a strike. It was just the Communists trying to show themselves more militant than Reuther.[38]

So again, as in 1939 and then in 1941, there was a change in communist policy and practice. Roger Keeran considers that 'the

[36] Dubofsky and van Tine, *John L. Lewis*, 456–7.
[37] See Isserman, *Which Side Were You On?*, 221–31.
[38] Herman Rebhan interview, 22 Feb. 1986.

Cold War, rather than the Second World War' was the determining factor for the communists in the UAW and, by extension, the CIO.[39] This however de-emphasizes the extraordinary politicized atmosphere of the UAW during the ten years of its existence since 1935. The American Communist Party's industrial, domestic-political, and foreign-political positions had changed so violently, so many times, that irrespective of the standard American academic anticommunist charge that communists were distinguished by 'unconditional and unwavering loyalty to the dictates of Soviet policy, both foreign and domestic',[40] the only certain thing about the communists at the war's end was the complete uncertainty about who or what they would be supporting in six, twelve, or twenty-four months' time. Trade-union movements prefer a settled sense of direction and prize 'stability and regularity'[41] above all else. For UAW members interested, active, or leading in union affairs, the communists since 1935 had oscillated too sharply and, it seemed clear, too obviously in response not to their own estimation of what should be done, but to external considerations linked to policies decided in Moscow. This is not to imply the UAW communists were puppets with no minds of their own, but their political oscillations, linked to international questions, were not helpful to their attempts to secure power in the union.

Walter Reuther, by contrast, owed his success, not just as Keeran asserts to a 'combination of . . . political sagacity and personal ambition'[42] but to a reasonable consistency. UAW members knew where he stood on Roosevelt, on Hitler, and on Stalin, both before and after August 1939, as well as on the need for a substantial modification of employer–union relations in manufacturing industry and on the need to defend workers' rights and living standards when either were being threatened in the name of wartime patriotism. Reuther's success, as Nelson Lichtenstein points out, 'did not rest on the kind of reactionary and demogogic red-baiting that would soon characterize cold war political culture. Reuther did not ally himself with conservative anticommunist forces; in fact, he surrounded himself with radicals and Social-

[39] Keeran, *The Communist Party and the Autoworkers*, 248.
[40] Klehr, *Heyday*, 415–16.
[41] Michael Poole, *Theories of Trade Unionism: A Sociology of Industrial Relations*, (London, Routledge, 1981), 101.
[42] Keeran, *The Communist Party and the Autoworkers*, 248.

ists.'[43] Although the United States in 1945 had no equivalents to the labour and socialist parties of Europe, and certainly nothing like the communist presence that existed in France or Germany, it is possible to discern the outline of a European-style contest between socialism and communism inside the trade-union movement that gathered speed once the war was over.

From 1945 onwards, the CIO had a new horizon to contemplate —its participation in the WFTU and its broader involvement in overseas activities in collaboration with the US government and its agencies. If, between 1935 and 1945, foreign questions had impinged on the CIO's internal politics, now the reverse would be the case. The domestic politics of the CIO and labour relations generally in the immediate post-war period had a direct bearing on CIO activities overseas. In its key union, the UAW, the internal struggle between communists and their opponents, headed by Reuther, continued unabated in 1945, 1946, and 1947.

Linked to this widely publicized battle for control of the UAW, and by extension the CIO, was an onslaught by the anti-union Republican Congress elected in 1946 aimed at the New Deal labour legislation. Employers and their Republican allies focused on the labour–Democratic Party link. Labour had been central to the Roosevelt coalition that had won four consecutive presidential elections for the Democrats. Weaken the unions, draw their radical sting, and the Democrats' hegemony in American politics might be reversed. Anti-unionism and anticommunism came together in the Taft-Hartley Act of 1947. The new law compelled trade-union officials to sign affidavits that they were not communists in order to have access to the National Labor Relations Board (NLRB). Unions whose officials refused to comply would find—as indeed they did—that the NLRB refused to protect their union membership agreements (a form of closed shop) against employer-encouraged raids from anticommunist unions. What the law had given, the law could take away.

Then there was President Truman. He did not enjoy Roosevelt's *noblesse-oblige* sureness of touch with labour and, during his first eighteen insecure months in office, was confronted with many labour problems. Like most small-town businessmen (he had run a draper's shop before moving into politics) his instinct was to blame

[43] Nelson Lichtenstein in Dubofsky and van Tine (eds.), *Labor Leaders*, 29.

unions first. In the summer of 1946 when he faced strikes in the railways and coal mines after the rail-union leaders and the ever-combative Lewis had refused to accept a presidential settlement, Truman wrote out his own draft for a radio broadcast on the disputes. It was far from Rooseveltian in tone. After attacking the wartime activities of union leaders, especially Lewis who 'called two strikes in War Time to satisfy his ego', Truman criticized 'Mr. Murray and his Communist friends . . . strikers and their demagog [sic] leaders who have been living in luxury'. His longhand draft finished with this appeal:

I am tired of government's being flouted, vilified and now I want you men who are my comrades in arms you men who fought the battles to save the nation just as I did twenty-five years ago to . . . eliminate the Lewises, the Whitneys, the Johnstones [rail union leaders], the Communist Bridges [dockers' leader] and the Russian Senators and Representatives and really make this a government of, by and for the people . . . Let's put transportation and production back to work, hang a few traitors make our own country safe for democracy, tell Russia where to get off . . . Come on boys lets do the job.[44]

The broadcast was never made as White House advisers substituted a more measured text in dignified (and grammatical) language. Truman valued labour's support, as did any elected democrat, and the two strikes he had to deal with were sectional and economistic; but the language of his draft expressed not only his private feelings but also the extent to which the national mood had drifted from the pro-unionism of the New Deal in the 1930s. The president broke the rail strike by threatening to draft all railway workers and stopped a miners' strike by using the courts to fine Lewis's union 3.5 million dollars.

Congress came in where the president had been so willing to tread. In the Taft-Hartley Act of spring 1947, the political-industrial era inaugurated with the birth of the CIO came to an end. In addition to demanding the non-communist affadavits, the Act banned secondary boycotts, states were allowed to ban union membership agreements or closed shops, and many state legislatures, especially in the as yet unorganized South, promptly did so. Furthermore, supervisors and foremen, the key brokers of mana-

---

[44] Quoted in Roger Donovan, *Conflict and Crisis. The Presidency of Harry S. Truman 1945–1948* (New York, Norton, 1977), 212–13.

gerial authority (and, in Europe, an important group of organizable labour), were not allowed to join unions. The passage of the Taft-Hartley Act froze US labour where it had reached by 1947. The 35 per cent of American workers in unions in 1947 had shrunk to 15 per cent forty years later.

Two responses were possible in opposition to the Taft-Hartley Act. One was to reject some or all of its provisions and attempt to render it unworkable. This was suggested by Lewis, who pointed out that if all union officials simply refused to sign the non-communist affidavits they would render ineffectual that section of the Act, the most explicit attempt to divide the unions politically. A third response was to seek the Act's repeal. Truman had unsuccessfully sought to veto the Taft-Hartley Act, thus beginning a reconciliation of the presidency with the labour movement (though as late as 1948 Reuther and some CIO associates were hoping that a replacement might be found for Truman as presidential candidate). Nevertheless, and despite grumblings, the CIO remained committed to the Democratic Party, while the passage of Taft-Hartley pushed the AFL into a much closer relationship with the democrats. Joe Keenan, for example, was called back from Germany to head a powerful new AFL political committee to campaign for Truman's election.

The tabling, controversy, debates, and passage of Taft-Hartley occurred at the same time as the announcement of the Truman Doctrine and the Marshall Plan. To repeal or amend Taft-Hartley, the American unions needed Truman's re-election and a resurgence of democrats into Congress. A successful foreign policy for Truman, which showed him saving Europe from chaos and standing up to the Soviet Union, would pay dividends in the elections of 1948. And if, thanks to Taft-Hartley, labour had temporarily lost the benevolent protection of the state, the unions could regain that desired condition through displaying their worth and usefulness by supporting and even helping implement America's new international role.

Yet the drafters of Taft-Hartley had been subtle in making the anticommunist affidavit one of the elements of the package. They thus sought to remove the CIO's most committed left-wingers at a time when such indeed were the intentions of the CIO leaders themselves. To have endorsed Lewis's proposal of mass non-compliance or to have launched a major civil liberties campaign in defence of communist trade-union officials would have been to run counter to the CIO's own drive against the communists in the unions.

In the UAW, for example, the Reuther faction blamed the communists for the unsatisfactory result in the 1946 General Motors strike. The strike lasted for 113 days and involved much hardship. A fact-finding commission established by Truman had recommended an increase of 19½ cents an hour, less than the UAW claim but more than the company would concede. In separate talks with General Motors, the communist-led United Electrical Workers Union (UE) accepted 18½ cents for the 30,000 GM employees it represented against the 150,000 UAW members under Reuther's leadership in the strike. This was 'a double-cross by a sister union', wrote Victor Reuther. 'It was not only an attack against Walter; it was a sellout of 150,000 GM auto workers.'[45] In fact, Philip Murray had accepted 18½ cents for his steelworkers who were on strike at the same time, but in his subsequent successful campaign to become president of the UAW in 1946, Reuther made much of the UE-communist 'double-cross', linking it to the wartime communist support for incentive pay and the no-strike pledge. Reuther's success in winning the presidency of the UAW in 1946 was a clear defeat for the communist group inside the CIO's largest union. Reuther only captured the presidency, and the rest of the executive board remained in the hands of his opponents. It was not until November 1947, after further months of internal union conflict, that the Reuther forces secured an outright victory by winning control of the top offices and a clear majority on the executive board.

Every participant or later historian who has analysed the struggle in the UAW between 1945 and 1947 agrees that it was an open, political fight. Supporters were openly rallied, debates were publicly held, votes were secretly counted. As Victor Reuther recalls, foreign affairs played little part. The UAW, like the CIO, loyally supported the post-war policy of international co-operation with the Soviet Union as expressed in membership of the WFTU. Although Reuther was in touch with the IMF's Ilg, there was no time in the relentless turmoil of electioneering in 1946 and 1947 to get involved deeply in international questions. The CIO's member-

[45] Reuther, *The Brothers Reuther*, 255.

ship of the WFTU foreclosed open public criticism of the Soviet Union but it did not prevent the continuation of the anticommunist campaigns inside the CIO unions. But how long could friendly fraternity with communists abroad coexist with anticommunism at home?

Taft-Hartley and the strains the Marshall Plan imposed on the WFTU came at the end of a period in which the CIO gradually shifted into a clear anticommunist gear. This was expressed politically to begin with before it turned into administrative actions against communists in the CIO, but in trade-unions, organizational and personnel consequences tend to follow hard on the heels of political pronouncements. Three main causes can be identified in this rising anticommunism in the CIO. Firstly, there was the inherent, traditional anticommunism of the majority of CIO leaders and officials. Although Murray in 1946 resisted attempts by members of the United Steelworkers' executive to write into the union's constitution a ban on communists holding union office,[46] he told the CIO convention in November 1946 that 'the CIO must never be communistically controlled or inspired'.[47] A policy statement adopted at the CIO convention in 1946 began: 'The Congress of Industrial Organizations is an American institution [with only] one national allegiance and that is allegiance to our own country, the United States of America'; furthermore, the CIO as 'an American organization has no interest apart from the interests of our people and our country . . . We stand unswerving in our loyalty to these principles which America symbolizes'; the main thrust of this patriotic sentiment came at the end of the statement when it declared that delegates 'resent and reject efforts of the Communist Party . . . to interfere in the affairs of the CIO'.[48]

Secondly, the mood of the country had turned more hostile against the Soviet Union as a result of the revelations of a Soviet spy-ring in Canada and difficulties in Germany and Iran; Molotov's *Nyet*s when the foreign ministers met and Gromyko's televised walk-out from the United Nations in March 1946 also helped fuel American public opinion against the Soviet Union. The large number of Polish workers in the UAW and other CIO unions based in Chicago, Detroit, and Pittsburgh, who had enthusiastically

---

[46] USWA Executive Board Minutes, 12 May 1946.
[47] CIO 1946 Convention, 18 Nov. 1946.
[48] CIO statement on communists, CIO Convention, Nov. 1946.

embraced the New Deal and who had been effective CIO organizers, often in harness with communists in the 1930s, now started becoming more hostile to anything linked to the Soviet Union, particularly as Stalin made clear that Poland would fall within a communist and Soviet orbit. The role of the Catholic Church in influencing the ideological reorientation of this strategic group of ethnic CIO members was important.[49]

A third problem was the activity of FBI agents who investigated communist activities and let it be known locally that such-and-such a union activist or official was a communist. The effect of this rising anticommunist tide can be seen in the discussion in the United Steel Workers' Executive Board, presided over by Murray, in April 1946. One regional director, Frank Bourke, wanted communists barred from holding office:

The international situation I don't claim to know much about only those things I read in the papers. But I certainly don't think this organization should have anybody point or even think that we feel like some of those people who are representing a certain country in the UNO . . . I am sick and tired of the FBI nosing around my district and telling you in an indirect way that this guy in our outfit [is] a Communist and that this one lends support to the CP and what are we going to do about it.[50]

A fellow executive-board member, Bill Doherty, announced he would 'quit the USWA' if it came under communist control and then gave vent to his feelings.

I don't consider this is a great problem. Hell, I think one white man can whip a dozen damn Communists anywhere . . . It is no time to handle this with silk gloves. It is true that it might not be expedient or proper to bar a man from membership . . . but at the very least we can debar him from either national office or local union office.[51]

At this stage, in 1946, Murray was not yet ready to call for such a ban but to keep control of his executive he had to show himself as much an anti-communist as they. In his analysis, the Communist Party had changed since Browder had been removed. Now the Party wanted 'to

[49] On East European left-wing immigrant support for the UAW in the 1930s see Schulze, *Gewerkschaftskampf*, 141–3. I am grateful to Professor Nelson Lichtenstein for drawing my attention to the importance of the swelling anticommunism amongst Polish workers in CIO unions in the mid–1940s.
[50] USWA Executive Board, 11 Apr. 1946.
[51] Ibid.

take over American labor unions . . . I am going to fight them . . . I say to them: keep your damn nose out of our business'.[52]

So at home, in 1946, anticommunism was on the rise in the unions but internationally co-operation with the communists in the WFTU was still pursued. Walter Citrine, the TUC leader who was visiting America in the summer of 1946, sought to justify this apparent contradiction. He told the steelworkers' convention in June 1946 that 'if we are to wait until every one of us believes in precisely the same form of political organization, or economic conception . . . we will wait a long time before we have succeeded in developing the organizations that are so badly needed'.[53] At one level, the admonition of the British union leader was well taken, and the CIO convention in November 1946 endorsed co-operation with the WFTU. But the main foreign-policy resolution was introduced from the platform with the affirmation that 'the resolution, from end to end, backs up every action of the United States of America'.[54] To ensure central control over foreign-policy questions, the CIO prohibited its state or city councils from expressing an opinion on foreign affairs. At the same time state councils were given the green light to move against communists locally. The Massachusetts CIO banned communists in 1946, the New Jersey CIO declared communism to be 'alien to the philosophy and desires of the American people', and anticommunists won control of the Milwaukee and Wisconsin state councils of the CIO.[55]

While the CIO journal, which remained under de Caux's editorship until June 1947, continued to support the WFTU and printed nothing critical about the Soviet Union, the same could not be said for other papers read by workers. The left-wing and widely read *Labor Action*, under a headline 'Stalinism—Worldwide Menace to Labor', made the connection between domestic Communism and foreign policy in January 1947: 'It is in the interests of the ruling class of this land of labor's enslavement [i.e. Russia] that the Communist-Stalinist parties in various countries operate. Their policies shift with every turn of foreign policy of the Russian state.'[56] A month later, the *Pittsburgh Press*, not a left-wing paper

---

[52] Ibid.
[53] *Steel Labor*, June 1946.
[54] *New York Times*, 20 Nov. 1946.
[55] See Kampelman, *The Communist Party versus the CIO*, 63.
[56] *Labor Action*, 20 Jan. 1947.

but one read by steelworkers, published an article under the heading 'Labor Under Communism'.

Under a new law approved by the totalitarian regime in Czechoslovakia, the government can assign workers to jobs and punish them if their performance is not satisfactory. Concentration camps are provided for the habitual laggards. The camps were requested by the Czechoslovakian Confederation of Trade Unions, communist-dominated, on the theory that a man who will not do the work assigned to him is sabotaging the work of others . . . It is easy to see why American labor organizations should seek to purge themselves of communist influences.[57]

Thus by the beginning of 1947, before the key detonators of the Truman Doctrine and the Marshall Plan, the anticommunist pressure in American labour was rising hard.

The communist union leaders in the CIO had used the three and a half years of the war in the United States to help push upwards the CIO to new heights of strength by emphasizing two aspects of CIO philosophy and policy. These were the CIO's identification with and reliance upon the administration to change government policy, laws, or institutions in favour of trade-unions; secondly, the communists sought to promote the CIO by insisting upon the patriotism and pro-American nationalism of the CIO.

Once American nationalism and government in Washington turned away from friendship with the Soviet Union, the CIO, bound as it was in chains so strongly fashioned by the forgers of wartime American communism, was unlikely to break away and strike out in new directions. Communism, Browder once remarked, is twentieth-century Americanism. When twentieth-century Americans decided they wanted nothing to do with communism—and that, if ever it had been doubted, was certainly the case of the CIO leaders by the end of 1946—a formalized break between the CIO and the communists was only a matter of time. This implied one fundamental consequence. The identification of communism with the Soviet Union was so strong that following the endorsement of anticommunism as CIO policy at its 1946 convention, anti-Sovietism could not be far away. This had important implications for the CIO in the WFTU. If the latter was strong and purposeful enough in its own right, then perhaps it might withstand this swelling tide of anticommunism. But was this the case?

[57] *Pittsburgh Press*, 14 Feb. 1947.

8

The Congress of Industrial Organizations, the World Federation of Trade Unions, and the Marshall Plan

THE three years 1945–8, in which American unions in the Congress of Industrial Organizations were linked with their Soviet equivalents in the World Federation of Trade Unions, were an important, if short, period in international labour history. Never before, never since, have the mass workers' organizations of the two principal contestants for global dominance for much of the twentieth century shared participation in a single world union federation. Trade unions were the expression, in part, of the economic and social systems in the countries where they existed. No one in 1945 expected the United States to become communist, or the Soviet Union to move to capitalism, but if the unions of the two countries could work together, an important bridge would be created. Moreover, between Standard Oil and Stalin lay a variety of different ideas of economic and social organization. The examples of nationalization and the welfare state in Europe were one alternative model. Hovering was the question of decolonialization which had been so strongly raised at the 1945 conferences of the WFTU. If trade-unions were now essential components in national development, did it not therefore follow that they would play an important role internationally?

Nationally, unions operated at two main levels: those of mobilization and regulation. Regulating workplace relationships, the establishment of what the Webbs called the 'Common Rule', was an end in itself as well as a means of obliging a fairer economic balance between capital and labour. In different countries, whether by law, through collective agreement, or custom and practice, via joint or tripartite bodies, unions had incessantly sought to regulate, to draw up rules, to govern the role of citizens as workers. Unions also sought social regulation in the form of common welfare provision and influence in the running of the economy.

To do so they first had to mobilize: mobilize into unions, form bigger unions or confederations, mobilize electorally in alliance with political parties, mobilize as well by use of strikes, demonstrations, pressure on governments, and even revolutionary upheavals. Mobilization is the begetter of regulation, though both advance in parallel—the securing of new rights helping to promote organization, and such mobilization in turn providing the springboard for further promotion of rules, particularly in the payment of wages or control of working time.

Regulation and mobilization were clearly applicable at the national level, but in 1945, as in the past decades, finding a meaningful regulatory and mobilizing purpose and course of action internationally was not so easy. It was one thing to set up the WFTU, but what actually was it to do? Efforts were made to integrate the international trade secretariats so that the WFTU would have a defined industrial role, but this did not come about. The ILO remained in active existence and was quickly adopted as the United Nations' agency for labour affairs. Apart from exhortations or demands, the WFTU was thus unable to interject itself as a regulatory body in the unfolding of new relationships between unions, employers, and governments after 1945. The American and British governments refused to support calls from the WFTU to be given special status at the UN. The question then arose, how was the WFTU to mobilize sufficient support for its claim? How could it achieve some standing that would justify its existence as a functioning trade-union body and not merely as a labour-movement reflection of the diplomatic togetherness of the Allies?

The triumphant cry that the great achievement of the WFTU was that it brought communist and non-communist unions together proclaimed what was in practice highly problematic, as one of the main regulatory purposes of preceding internationals had been to rule on the political bona fides of affiliated organizations or, more importantly, would-be affiliates. Exclusionary regulation based on ideological differences was certainly a negative reason for international union activity but, in the pre-war internationals, it had provided an important area of actual decision-making, as opposed to declamatory statements and information exchange. The AFL, after all, had joined the union internationals twice before, in 1911 and 1937. Each time, the AFL's first activity had been to demand the exclusion of what it considered hostile unions; firstly, the syndicalist Industrial Workers of the World (the Wobblies), and then the Soviet All Union Central Council of Trade Unions.

On the surface, the WFTU sought to de-ideologize the relations between trade-unions coming from countries with different political and economic systems. Far from excluding organizations, the WFTU sought to be all-inclusive. It was an attempt to create, at an international level, an institution functioning along Popular Front lines. In parallel with the emerging corporatism to be seen in capitalist states (a corporatism taken to its ultimate end in the Soviet Union), the WFTU offered itself as a corporate partner at a global level. But global corporatism in a world of differing national priorities, of nation-state rivalries, of fading but economically still important European empires, of two hostile economic systems, was likely to be difficult to implement. So if a global corporate role was unavailable and ideological sharpness was to be avoided, what was the WFTU's purpose?

For the CIO, perhaps unwittingly, the American concept of the WFTU contained its own contradictions from the very beginning. Lee Pressman, outlining the CIO's idea of the task of the new international federation, wrote that the WFTU's objective was the establishment of 'basic freedom of press, speech, assembly, religion, political association and [the right] to organize labor unions'.[1] The emphasis on such liberal democratic rights, none of which existed in the Soviet Union, was curious in laying down criteria for what was to be a working-class, trade-union organization. Pressman was reflecting the Rooseveltian justification—that of defending democracy—for America's involvement in the war. Stalin once observed that trying to introduce communism into Poland was like trying to saddle a cow, and the simile could be extended to the proposition that American and Soviet trade-unions could work in harness for any length of time. To begin with, the diplomatic niceties were maintained. Philip Murray, even in the relative privacy of the steel union's executive, declared: 'I shall never attempt to criticise Russia or her form of government.'[2]

But, under the surface of these politenesses, the picture of co-

---

[1] P. Murray to W. Citrine, 5 Apr. 1944. Box 116, CIO Secretary-Treasurer (Carey) Papers, Wayne State University, Detroit (henceforth WSA). That Pressman wrote the letter for Murray's signature can be seen in Pressman's letter to J. Carey, same date. Lee Pressman was the CIO's chief counsel. Briefly a member of the American Communist Party in the 1930s, he was considered to be pro-Soviet.

[2] Murray at USWA Executive Board, 1 Apr. 1946.

operation between the CIO and the Soviet trade-unions looks a lot more ragged from the very outset of the WFTU's existence. Murray never went to Europe to participate in WFTU meetings. Another architect of the CIO, its vice-president, Sydney Hillman, died in 1946 having helped give birth to the WFTU but disappearing at the moment when difficulties began to appear. The CIO took almost two years to fill one of the three assistant-general-secretaryships reserved for an American. John Brophy, one of Murray's key aides, was nominated but, after a 'disagreeable conversation' with Louis Saillant, he refused to take up the post.[3] 'You might as well be in the Communist Party as in that sort of operation,' he told Murray upon his return to the United States.[4]

Such early suspicion or unease about the WFTU on the CIO's part can also be seen in the dispute over the report of the CIO delegation that went to the Soviet Union in October 1945. Publicly there was no row. The CIO editor, Len de Caux, wrote that the CIO delegation was 'enthusiastic about the Soviet people we'd met —their human, friendly warmth, their grit, their likenesses to the United States unionists, the hope for the future they saw in the CIO's attitude'.[5] The delegation report was drafted by James Carey, the CIO secretary-treasurer, who circulated it to his fellow delegates for comments prior to publication. John Green, president of a CIO shipbuilders' union, wanted Carey to mention that US Embassy attachés 'are not given the freedom of movement, which I believe is so highly necessary for free understanding between the Soviet government and our own', and 'another matter that should be pointed out is the great fear American newspapermen have of being expelled from Russia if they incur the enmity of one of the officials there'.[6] Another CIO delegate, Emil Rieve, head of the textile workers' union, complained that the report did not mention the special access to shops enjoyed by government officials nor that Soviet payment systems were dominated by piece-rates and incentive payments.[7]

Lee Pressman, on the other hand, proposed amendments to

[3] John Brophy diary, 16 Oct. 1945. Brophy papers, Catholic University Archives (CUA).

[4] Brophy Oral History, 980, Brophy papers, CUA.

[5] L. De Caux, *Labor Radical* (Boston, Beacon Press, 1970), 460.

[6] J. Green to Carey, no date but in response to Carey's draft report circulated 29 Dec. 1945, Box 117, Carey papers, WSA.

[7] Emil Rieve to Carey, 3 Jan. 1946, Carey papers, CUA.

Carey's draft which cast the Soviet Union in an even more favourable light. He sought the removal of a comment that the CIO delegation was ushered in to see Lenin's tomb in front of the queue of ordinary people. He also wanted to delete a reference to the 'abjectly low' living standards of the Soviet people; instead, Pressman wanted to have inserted a statement underlining the democratic nature of the Soviet trade-unions.[8] The final report came down in the direction urged by Pressman, and concluded with high praise for the Soviet trade-unions and a pledge to promote 'understanding and friendship . . . between the working and common people of all nations'.[9] Amongst Carey's papers and notes on the trip, there is a short and pathetic letter from an American engineer, who had worked in Russia in the 1930s and there married a Russian woman. He had to leave his wife behind on returning to the United States at the war's outbreak, and now the Russian authorities refused to let her join him. He begged Carey to intervene in Moscow.

These otherwise minor and insignificant details left their trace on those union leaders who went, open-eyed, to the Soviet Union in the period immediately after the war's end. The British steel-workers' leader, Lincoln Evans, had also been worried about the 'rigid censorship' and fear of speaking out that he noticed on his trip there in July 1945.[10] Under the supreme pressure of war, such differences mattered little. Yet in the CIO's own estimation, the WFTU had been set up to promote freedom of assembly, speech, and press. At the base of nineteenth-century concepts of working-class organization—whether the Marxian social democracy of Germany, or Gompers' business unionism in America—lay the concept of assembly, public dissent, and collective withdrawal of labour. Supporters of the Soviet Union would argue that such rights had been superseded in a state where workers owned the means of production and managed their own industries. Yet if this were so, what did the Soviet unions have in common with those still existing under capitalism? Was it not a case of two fundamentally different types of organization sharing the same title—trade-unions—but utterly different in function, purpose, and outlook? Hillman and

[8] Pressman to Carey, no date, Carey papers, WSA.
[9] *Report of CIO Delegation to the Soviet Union, October 1945* (Washington DC, CIO Publication 128, 1945).
[10] See Ch. 10.

Murray said they did not wish to comment on the Soviet Union's internal affairs. But if the WFTU had been established to promote freedom, in the sense that the CIO understood the concept, how long could such diplomatic aloofness be maintained?

In its internal memorandum, 'Why We Have Left the WFTU', written in 1949, the CIO could find little concrete with which to reproach the WFTU in the first two years of its existence save that 'the Communist trade-unionists were deliberately pressing demands of a political character': in the CIO's view what counted more than 'agreements and conventions' was the need for 'good faith in the relationships, sincerity in expressions of fraternity and mutual respect for the various conceptions of trade-unionism'.[11] The reason why the CIO had to resort to such generalizations lies in the fact that, until the dividing moment of the Marshall Plan in late 1947, the CIO had little to complain of in the work or political decisions of the WFTU. The Soviet members of the WFTU sought to accommodate American and West-European desires in the first two years of the WFTU's existence. Voting was arranged so that the Soviet Union with 40 per cent of the WFTU's claimed 64 million members could not dominate. Britain and America with a combined total of 12.5 million members had five seats on the executive committee compared with three for the Soviet Union's 27 million trade-union members. Article 4 of the WFTU constitution provided for the autonomy of each organization: the WFTU could not impose its will on any affiliate.

Writing of the period 1945–7, John Windmuller has argued that the WFTU's activities were directed 'into political channels where they could be used effectively to support Soviet foreign policy', a view also advanced by Morton Schwartz, who asserts that after 1945 'the Russians cautiously began to explore the possibilities of transforming the WFTU into an instrument of Soviet policy'.[12] Yet between 1945 and 1947, WFTU decisions reflected not only accommodation on the part of Soviet delegates with the wishes of American or British representatives but a further Russian willing-

---

[11] 'Why We Have Left the WFTU' (CIO, 2 May 1949) Box 118, Carey papers, WSA.

[12] J. Windmuller, *American Labor and the International Labor Movement* (Ithaca, NY, Cornell University Press, 1954), 88. Schwartz, 'Soviet Policy and the WFTU 1945–1949' (Ph.D thesis, Columbia University, 1963), 139.

ness to use the WFTU to damp down any suggestion that globally organized labour might strike out in its own name and, in words or deeds, urge workers to go beyond the limits laid down by their governments.

An early example of the Soviet commitment to quiescence on the WFTU's part was over the organization of German trade-unions. The Russians in the WFTU supported the British view that separate, financially autonomous industrial unions were to be preferred to the idea of a centrally run, commonly financed union covering all workers. The WFTU report, based on a delegation sent to Germany at the beginning of 1946, endorsed the attitudes on union organization held by the British and American occupying forces and was in opposition to communist ideas of centralization already being implemented in the Soviet occupied zone in Germany.[13]

Another potentially divisive issue was Spain. The WFTU was pledged to extirpate all vestiges of fascism. What greater test for international labour action than Spain, so vulnerable to a blockade and other union boycott actions? France had given refuge to the exiled labour movement from Franco's Spain and had closed her frontiers to Spain in March 1946 as domestic pressure grew for action against Franco. Saillant, the WFTU general secretary, and Jouhaux, the CGT leader and WFTU vice-president, had called for action against Spain. The opposition at the WFTU to Saillant's proposal for a quarantine came from the TUC and the CIO. The arguments were conservative and traditional—that the WFTU could not invoke action over the heads of national federations, and that it was an area to be left to government or diplomatic pressure.[14] The Russians, who along with communists in many countries had called for action on Spain between the WFTU's founding and the meeting in June 1946 of its executive organs which had to take decisions, dropped the issue and left Saillant isolated. Instead, their representative, Tarasov, proposed propaganda activity but no action, a compromise which preserved WFTU unity and left Franco undisturbed.[15] At the same meeting, the Russians dropped their demand that the CIO's Philip Murray

[13] This is more fully discussed in Ch. 12.
[14] WFTU Executive Bureau and Executive Committee Minutes, Moscow, June 1946. The executive bureau first discussed the matter (EB minutes, 57–60), and then the larger executive committee went over the ground again. (EC minutes, 38–54).
[15] Ibid.

should replace Walter Citrine as WFTU president upon the latter's resignation from the TUC. Instead, they accepted as WFTU president the transport workers' leader from Britain, Arthur Deakin, whose political and organizational hostility towards communists inside his own union and country knew few limits.

Greece was yet a further example of the Russians carefully avoiding confrontation with the British and the Americans, to the extent of badly letting down a WFTU affiliate and snubbing Saillant and Jouhaux. The situation in Greece had been bitter and complex since the German withdrawal and Churchill's sending of troops to crush a communist uprising in December 1944. Trying to find some way of controlling, or at least bringing together, the warring elements in the Greek trade unions, within the overall British policy of maintaining pro-Western conservative rule in the country, the TUC sent a mission to Greece in January 1945. This was followed at the end of 1945 by a mission in the name of the WFTU consisting of Saillant and a TUC official, Vic Feather. In February 1946, another WFTU mission supervised elections to the executive of the Greek trade-union confederation. They produced a majority for the communist group. The response of the right-wing Greek government was to dissolve the executive and declare all its local union leaderships illegal.

This assault on a WFTU affiliate in a key European country after elections supervised by a WFTU team including a TUC representative was a serious challenge to the WFTU's authority. Jouhaux left in July 1946 at the head of the third WFTU mission to Greece in little more than six months. In his report he described the attacks on Greek workers by the government: 'The Greek Confederation of Labour is dissolved, our comrades have been arrested and terror is widespread. The World Federation must protest this state of affairs which denies trade-union legality, flouts the workers' will and outrageously violates individual liberties.'[16] In the short life of the WFTU, the treatment of the Greek confederation by the Greek government was the first and worst attack on a WFTU affiliate. The TUC was embarrassed because Greece clearly fell within the British sphere of influence, indeed had been placed there under the notorious Stalin–Churchill percentage agreements. The Labour Foreign Secretary, Ernest Bevin, was vigorously continuing the

[16] Report of Léon Jouhaux presented to WFTU Executive Bureau, Sept. 1946.

British policy inherited from Churchill which, while it searched for some democratic middle way, was chiefly motivated by the desire to keep Greece free of communist influence. Unlike France or Italy, where communist dominance in the trade-unions had to be lived with, the right-wing Greek governments were not prevented by their British sponsors from openly repressing left-wing trade-unionism.

Faced with the choice between strongly and publicly backing the WFTU and the cause of trade-union rights in Greece or not, the TUC preferred to avoid any embarrassment with its government. At the WFTU executive in September 1946, the TUC delegates opposed Saillant's suggestions for WFTU-organized demonstrations on behalf of Greek trade-unionists. Instead, the TUC, backed by other WFTU executive members including the Russians, was only prepared to endorse a resolution which recommended that WFTU affiliates 'take appropriate steps to bring the situation in Greece to the attention of their members'.[17]

The nadir of Greek left-wing trade-union hopes came in December 1946 when the deposed executive arrived in Paris for a meeting with the WFTU leadership. During the autumn, the British labour attaché in Athens had drawn up a formula for representation of differing tendencies in the Greek Confederation of Labour, which, if it had been accepted, would have left the communists in a permanent minority. Instead of backing their fellow communists, who after all had been duly and democratically elected earlier in the year, the Russians in the WFTU leadership told them to accept the British formula, and they sided with Deakin in agreeing that the WFTU should not take up the repression of Greek unions as an issue at the United Nations.[18]

The story of Greek trade-unionism takes a different tone after March 1947 when the Americans replaced the British as the dominant power, and later in this chapter the experiences of an important CIO official in Greece in 1947 are examined. What is significant in this case is not the conciliatory attitude of the Soviet delegates in the WFTU towards the political requirements of their British colleagues, but rather the overall failure of the WFTU to undertake any useful effort to protect its affiliate in Greece. The

---

[17] WFTU, *Information Bulletin*, 15 Oct. 1946.
[18] WFTU Executive Bureau Minutes, Dec. 1946.

Greeks may have been infuriating to deal with; Deakin said 'they refused to accept their own responsibilities',[19] but the WFTU's refusal to take up the Greek issue—its first major test on behalf of an affiliate—suggested that as a body just twelve months old it would not be able effectively to raise the defence of trade-union rights above the niceties of government needs. The indignation of Jouhaux and Saillant over union rights in Greece was not extended to supporting claims by Tunisian workers for admission of their union to the WFTU. Instead, the CGT extended its organization to French possessions in Africa.[20] At each moment of division, the Soviet trade-union opted for the status quo. For Greeks struggling to assert trade-union independence, the Russians were hardly better defenders of trade-unionism than their Western partners in the WFTU.

One of the reasons why the WFTU was unable to withstand the pressures placed on it by divisions over the Marshall Plan was precisely because it had not established a strong identity for itself as an effective, independent trade-union body. The executive bureau complained that the American and British governments stopped the WFTU from having a major role at the United Nations, awarding it only consultative status with the Economic and Social Committee on a par with dozens of other international bodies. That was a humiliation but trade-union bodies had overcome worse. Yet where it could have acted on its own account over Spain and Greece, the WFTU—under the guidance of the Russians as much as the CIO and the TUC—was able to do nothing. By the end of 1946 it had mishandled relations with the international trade secretariats so badly that the prospects of the WFTU intervening in the industrial sphere were at a standstill. The WFTU had failed by the end of 1946 to establish its own institutional *raison d'être*, transcending its component members, by providing services or organizing interventions with effect. It neither mobilized nor regulated. At the beginning of 1947, WFTU unity was only on paper, its power was limited to rhetoric, and it had provided no positive help for repressed trade-unionists.

---

[19] WFTU Executive Bureau Minutes, Dec. 1946.
[20] Resolution on Tunisia adopted at WFTU General Council, Prague, June 1947. See also J. Meynaud and A. Salah Bey, *Le Syndicalisme africain*, (Paris, Payot, 1963), 62–4.

THE CIO GOES OVERSEAS

While the CIO had concentrated on the WFTU, the AFL had made the running in having its own representatives in key locations overseas. This changed when Clint Golden, an influential official in the CIO, went to Greece in 1947. He went as head of the labour section in the American mission sent there following the announcement of the Truman Doctrine. In December 1946, the US Labor Department had set up a Trade Union Advisory Committee on International Relations on which sat AFL and CIO representatives. It was to this committee that Dean Acheson, number two in the State Department, turned as he sought to mobilize support for the Truman Doctrine. Acheson told the American trade-unionists that if US military, economic, and administrative help were not given to Greece, 'the Communists would emerge in control. If Greece falls into the Soviet orbit, Turkey must follow. If Greece and Turkey go, the whole Middle East and on to the Far East will be endangered.'[21] The domino-theorizing Acheson was seeking the endorsement of the trade-unions for two reasons. Firstly, labour was an important domestic constituency to be courted. Secondly, as America embarked on a policy of sending military and administrative echelons into countries other than the defeated Axis powers, the orientation and control of the trade-unions in countries which President Truman claimed were resisting subjugation would, from now on, be of the highest importance to Washington.

Reacting to Acheson's remarks, the AFL representatives at the meeting 'expressed unqualified approval, basing themselves on the need to oppose Soviet Russia and suppress Communists' while 'the CIO representatives agreed that speedy help should be extended to Greece . . . such as to encourage democratic freedom, including the reconstruction of the free Greek Trade Union movement, as Greek economic recovery takes place'.[22]

In choosing Golden, Washington was sending out a different figure from the combative ideologues associated with Jay Lovestone's Free Trade Union Committee. A skilled metalworker, Golden was a self-taught intellectual. He was a lecturer at the

---

[21] D. Acheson quoted in M. Ross (CIO official), Report on Labor Dept's Trade Union Advisory Committee on International Affairs, no date, Box 116, Carey papers, WSA.
[22] Ibid.

socialist Brookwood College in the 1920s where hundreds of trade-unionists had the chance to think and assemble their thoughts. As well as economics and labour theory, students attended classes in English literature. Len de Caux, for example, the left-wing CIO editor, was a Brookwood graduate.

Within the CIO, Golden became vice-president of the steel-workers' union, to which he brought a belief that a reasoned case and willingness to compromise were as important in a union's armoury as militancy and industrial action. In an influential book, *The Dynamics of Industrial Democracy*, published in 1942, Golden argued that it was the job of senior union leaders 'to show to their followers, on the union staff and in the mines, mills and factories, the way towards industrial peace and fruitful union–management relations.'[23] Like Joe Keenan, Golden had been a vice-chairman of the War Production Board and his conciliatory, co-operative manner helped oil wartime industrial production. He was a close aide of Philip Murray and, like Murray, was a strong advocate of the idea 'that the way for industrial unions to survive and advance in North America was to bond themselves with government'.[24] For Golden, by 1946 the United Steelworkers had become 'a firm, united, stable force . . . a permanent institution in American industrial life'.[25] In the post-war world, Golden saw an integrated trade-union movement, able through collective bargaining and joint regulation to put an end forever to the unilateral managerial authoritarianism which he blamed for the poverty of workers and strife in American industry of his earlier years. The Brookwood socialist now placed all his hopes on regulation—not mobilization.

For the 59-year-old Golden, the purpose in accepting a difficult mission to Greece at a time when he had already announced his retirement was not primarily to thwart communism. Instead it was to try and transfer his vision that advice on the precepts and practice of productivity-driven industrial growth, underpinned by joint regulation between employers and unions, was the best contribution that the American labour movement could offer to

---

[23] Clint Golden and Harold Ruttenburg, *Dynamics of Industrial Democracy*, (New York, Harper, 1942), 67.
[24] Ronald Schatz, 'Battling Over Goverment's Role: Philip Murray, the USWA and the Steel Companies 1946–52', in P. Clark *et al.* (eds.), *Forging a Union of Steel* (Ithaca, NY, Cornell University Press, 1987), 87.
[25] Golden at USWA Executive Board, 21 Feb. 1946.

workers overseas. Increased output, properly paid jobs, and employer acceptance of union rights would weave their own tissue of integrated relationships in which the starker, confrontationary message of communists would fade away.

However, when he arrived in Athens, Golden quickly and depressingly found out that American notions of collective bargaining, joint industrial regulation, and democratic trade-union practices were simply irrelevant when applied to Greece. His bewilderment can be seen from his many letters home. In the first, he summed up the Greek union leaders he had met as 'pretty slippery politicians' and noted with despair that Greek laws permitted 2,200 autonomous unions to function.[26]

In the autumn months of 1947, Golden tried to establish some joint bargaining machinery between unions, employers, and the government, but the arcane and politically motivated functioning of Greek labour legislation as well as the differing practices and expectations of union and employers defeated him. Despairing over efforts to reform the tangled social-security system, Golden wanted to send for a team

of experts from the US to come over and examine the situation separately with a view to improving and rationalising the administration of the system. What will happen? I'll be damned if I know. But it illustrates what happens when Americans get into a foreign country without any background or experience and with a determination to 'clean things up' and 'show foreigners how to run their affairs efficiently'.[27]

Golden's unease deepened in December 1947, when the government suddenly announced new laws bringing in the death penalty for unauthorized strikes. The move was part of a complicated political battle between different right-wing factions in the Greek Confederation of Labour and their respective political allies. But Golden was unhappy advising and, therefore, implicitly endorsing a government that could so casually propose to execute workers who went on strike. He outlined his perplexity in a letter to a businessman friend in the United States.

We talk about 'recovery' in a way at least here in Greece that conveys the idea we are trying to recreate an old order that no one particularly wants.

[26] C. Golden to M. Bernstein, 5 Sept. 1947, in Robert Brooks, *Clint: A Biography of a Labor Intellectual* (New York, Atheneum, 1978), 255.
[27] Golden to Bernstein, 30 Nov. 1947, ibid. 277.

We are not talking about the possibility of making Greece anything but what she has always been—a poor country where most of the people grub a precarious living from the barren hillsides and narrow valleys.[28]

Golden's answer was to show the Greeks 'how their country could become an industrial workshop . . . in which our American technology could be utilized and at the same time impart, through a vision of a possible future, new hope and courage and a reason to work and strive for something other than a restoration of an old and meaningless social order'.[29]

Golden left Greece in March 1948. Over the same period, as Ronald Radosh has shown, Irving Brown of the AFL was busy manœuvering support for the fanatical anticommunists in the Greek Confederation of Labour, moves that almost went too far when a pre-war minister in the proto-fascist Metaxas dictatorship nearly emerged as president of the Greek confederation in March 1948.[30] Golden raised no objections. He was no friend of the communists, writing to a colleague in the Steelworkers that '135 of the more promising younger leaders of the Union here were executed by the Communists in the early days of liberation when the Communists were in positions of authority. You can evidently subject the Greeks to a lot of abuse and pushing around but when you kill one it is never forgotten or forgiven.'[31]

Yet while he achieved little for Greek trade-unionists, Golden's mission to Greece created an important precedent for CIO participation in administering trade-union aspects of American intervention overseas under the Truman Doctrine and the Marshall Plan. Golden himself became chief labour adviser to the latter.[32] Golden's mission to Greece, as a leading CIO representative, was an effort to promote economic reconstruction through industrial growth based on an American vision of democratic trade-unionism. But the CIO's industrial unionism, even if it offered a wider social-democratic vision than that of the AFL, required industries to reconstruct and union leaders to be willing to combine under some

---

[28] Golden to W. L. Batt, 5 Jan. 1948, ibid. 307–8.
[29] Ibid.
[30] R. Radosh, *American Labor and United States Foreign Policy* (New York, Random House, 1969), 340–5.
[31] Golden to Bernstein, 30 Nov. 1947, in Brooks, *Clint*, 275.
[32] A. Carew, *Labour Under the Marshall Plan* (Manchester, Manchester University Press, 1987), gives details of Golden's involvement with the Marshall Plan as well as providing a shrewd assessment of his character and ideology.

minimal banner of unity. When, as in Greece, industrial production played little part in the economy, or the most effective working-class leaders were communists, then the only role left was to play power politics. In December 1947, Golden wrote to his friend, Tom Holland, acting head of the State Department's International Labor Division: 'My experience [in Greece] has impressed me with the importance of enlisting the active interest and practical assistance of the labor movement in international affairs. The need for this is especially urgent if the so-called "cold war" of ideologies is to continue as now seems likely.'[33]

THE MARSHALL PLAN AND AMERICAN UNIONS

From the moment of its inception the Marshall Plan divided different representative groups and commentators, and has done so ever since.[34] Its success lay in the fact that it was responsible for most of the things that both its supporters and critics, then and later, would claim. It helped ease an economic crisis that America faced because of Europe's inability to pay for imports from the United States, but it also contributed—psychologically, as much as in terms of dollars—to the economic development of post-war Europe. It began the process of forming a Western bloc under American leadership but showed up Soviet hegemonic designs when Moscow displayed its contempt for the sovereignty of Poland and Czechoslovakia by vetoing those governments' participation in the Paris talks following the Marshall Plan's announcement.

The creation of Cominform in September 1947 made clear that Moscow would not allow the East European nations to exercise control over the political, economic, and social development of their countries and that Stalin expected the Communist Parties of Western Europe to be active in supporting policies laid down by the Kremlin. Capitalism in Western Europe was given a boost, but the

[33] Golden to T. Holland, 6 Dec. 1947 in Brooks, *Clint*, 280.

[34] There is extensive literature on the Marshall Plan. In addition to works already cited, two recent studies are Henry Pelling, *Britain and the Marshall Plan* (London, Macmillan, 1989) and Annie Lacroix-Riz, *Le Choix de Marianne: Les Relations franco-américaines de la Libération aux débuts du Plan Marshall 1944–1948* (Paris, Éditions sociales, 1985). From a labour movement perspective, the collection of studies in O. Heberl and L. Niethammer, *Der Marshall-Plan und die europäische Linke* (Frankfurt, Europäische Verlagsanstalt, 1986), is invaluable.

revived Western European economy before too many years was posing serious competitive problems to sectors of the US economy, especially in manufacturing. France, a major beneficiary of Marshall Aid, was before long, under de Gaulle, to strike out with its own foreign policy, often openly at odds with that of Washington, and was to leave the military alliance of NATO. Moreover, the dollars that came with Marshall Aid helped make successful economies with large-scale state ownership in Britain, France, Italy, and Austria as well as collectivist public welfare schemes. This economic-social model was at odds with American insistence on maximum private ownership and a minimal state role in the economic and social sphere.

One of the most scornful left-wing critics of many of the Truman administration's policies, especially in foreign affairs, was I. F. Stone. Yet, in 1947, he was in no doubt that 'Men of good will will have no choice but to try and work out something like the Marshall Plan for the financing of European reconstruction by American capital.'[35] In Stone's analysis there were three ways of raising capital; imperial plunder—the method of Europe in previous centuries; Stalinist accumulation with its 'harsh, ruthless' methods; or by borrowing, as America had done in the nineteenth century. The Marshall Plan belonged to the third category.

Stone's contemporary judgement has stood the test of time. Critics who count only the rising statistics of industrial output and suggest that Europe had no need of Marshall Aid[36] miss the social pressure caused by the fuel and food shortages or the tensions arising out of the bitter winter of 1947. Even communist discipline over workers was cracking as Renault workers showed when they refused to obey Communist Party instructions not to strike in April 1947. Those who argue that Marshall Aid should have been rejected agree that in Britain, for example, there would have had to have been 'something approaching a siege economy . . . involving a

[35] I. F. Stone, 'From Marshall Plan to Military Aid', 29 Sept. 1947, in Stone, *The Truman Era 1945–1952* (Boston, Little Brown, 1972), 71.

[36] See e.g. Andrew Glynn, 'Opening the Cold Front', in *New Statesman*, 17 May 1985: 'By early 1947 . . . industrial output had practically regained its pre-war level.' For a more detailed discussion on the limited extent to which Marshall Aid contributed to the rebuilding of post-war Europe see Alan Milward, *The Reconstruction of Western Europe, 1945–1951*, (London, Methuen, 1984), 90–113.

much greater degree of austerity'[37] but do not explain how this policy would have found support amongst the people. As the historians, Northedge and Wells, pointed out:

It would have been a strange way of rewarding the British voters, who fancied in 1945 that they were opting for a better future, to condemn them to live indefinitely in siege conditions, ration book in hand, while the American horn of plenty was full to overflowing and the Americans were only too willing to share it.[38]

In the United States the CIO and the AFL (the latter after some initial hesitancy) competed with each other to be the more fervent supporter of the Marshall Plan. The way forward, suggested the AFL, was for the trade-unions of the sixteen countries that had agreed to participate in the Marshall Aid programme to hold their own joint conference to develop a trade-union response.[39] Thus the kernel of an alternative to the WFTU was placed on display.

The administration in Washington was well aware that union reaction to the Marshall Plan would condition its effectiveness. 'The success or failure of European reconstruction efforts will depend in great part on the attitude of European labour movements,' wrote one State Department official.[40] The CIO leadership had endorsed Marshall Aid, and Murray invited the secretary of state to be a guest speaker at the CIO convention in October 1947. There was one obvious alternative to the AFL's proposal for a union conference of the Marshall Aid recipient countries, and that was to enlist the support of the world federation. After all, the CIO's foreign-policy statement adopted at the same convention had praised the WFTU for demonstrating 'that the workers of the world can agree upon a common programme for the preservation of peace, the full enjoyment of democracy and economic security and abundance for the peoples of all the world'.[41]

So the CIO sent its envoys off to Europe with a new mission for the WFTU, that the latter should become the channel for trade-union participation in the administration of Marshall Aid. Were

[37] John Saville in 'Ernest Bevin and the Cold War 1945–1950', in *The Socialist Register 1984* (London, Merlin Press, 1984), 97.
[38] F. Northedge and A. Wells, *Britain and Soviet Communism: The Impact of a Revolution* (London, Macmillan, 1982), 109–10.
[39] Proceedings 1947 AFL Convention, 474.
[40] C. Swayzee to P. Nitze, 23 July 1947, 851.504/7–2347 (DSNA).
[41] CIO Convention report in *Steelabor*, Nov. 1947.

they being disingenuous? Certainly, by the time the WFTU executive met in Paris in November, Moscow's position left little room for manœuvre. The day before the WFTU leaders were due to meet, Moscow Radio described the Marshall Plan as 'a clear programme of colonial policy' while the AFL endorsement of Marshall Aid was 'a farce in which overalls are supposed to camouflage a ruse against the working people of other countries'.[42] The *New York Times* also carried a report from Trud, the Russian trade-union paper, quoting the head of the Russian unions, V. Kuznetsov, calling for the elimination of 'reformist and conciliatory influences' from the WFTU, whose 'most important shortcoming is the presence of old reformist tendencies which remained as the heritage of the Amsterdam International'.[43]

For the first time in the WFTU's history, there was a divided vote, 4–3, on whether the CIO secretary-treasurer, James Carey, should be allowed to make a CIO presentation seeking WFTU support for the Marshall Plan. In the end, he was allowed to make a statement in which he argued that the Marshall Plan was in conformity with WFTU policies on post-war relief and reconstruction.[44] According to Carey, conservative groups in the United States, such as the Chamber of Commerce and the *Wall Street Journal*, were against the Marshall Plan, whereas 'the more liberal groups are, the more they favour Marshall Aid'.[45]

Despite being obliged to hear Carey's statement, the communists on the WFTU executive bureau remained opposed to any consideration by the WFTU of the Marshall Plan. They refused to debate the issue and argued against Carey's remarks being printed in the WFTU bulletin. Deakin sided with them on that point. It was clear that the Marshall Plan was an issue that, given the attitudes being adopted, would divide the WFTU if it was forced to a vote. The Soviet representatives had been accommodating in the past about American and British sensitivities over Spain and Greece. Surely Western union leaders could acknowledge the obligations of the

---

[42] *New York Times*, 17 Nov. 1947.

[43] Ibid. According to G. Ra'anan in *International Policy Formation in the USSR: Factional 'Debates' during the Zhadanovschina* (Hamden, Conn., Archon Books, 1983), Kuznetsov was associated with Andreii Zhadanov who was leading the faction in the Soviet Union calling for increased confrontation with the United States.

[44] WFTU Executive Bureau Minutes, Nov. 1947.

[45] Ibid.

Russians to keep in line with the policy emanating from the Kremlin.

The Russians' refusal to discuss Marshall Aid within the WFTU, which extended in February 1948 to the claim that Soviet union leaders could not find the time to meet their WFTU colleagues to discuss the issue because of 'important collective bargaining'[46] in Russia, provided the opening that the anti-WFTU elements in the American and British governments, the AFL, and elsewhere had been looking for.[47] Their efforts to split apart the WFTU were made even easier by the nature of the Federation. Although it claimed to speak in the name of 70 million workers, it is doubtful if many were aware of its existence. The debates were within a small coterie of leaders of national trade-union centres. Kuznetsov, the head of the Russian unions and their spokesman at the WFTU, was a skilled diplomat, trained as an engineer in America, an urbane, friendly figure, fluent in English. Carey was unable to win a leadership position in his own union; at Murray's pleasure he held the number two position in the CIO, which allowed him to speak for American workers in the WFTU. No WFTU congress was held between 1945 and the final split in 1949. No wider debates involving more than the top leadership took place. The differences over the Marshall Plan showed the extent to which the trade-union leaders when operating on an international plane could not argue beyond the policies of their respective governments. From autumn 1947 onwards, the communist-dominated unions in France and Italy argued against their governments. Yet, they did not move towards an independent position. Instead, they threw in their lot with another government, that of the Soviet Union.

In an editorial commenting on the growing cleavage inside the WFTU, the London Times observed,

The Russians undoubtedly use the WFTU as a sounding board for their propaganda. Yet, although they and their supporters command a large majority of votes, they have not yet taken characteristic advantage of this, and the WFTU is the one international body on which representatives of

[46] V. Kuznetsov to A. Deakin, 29 Jan. 1948, quoted in Carew, *Labour Under the Marshall Plan*, 76.

[47] The anti-WFTU campaign by the American and British government is fully discussed in P. Weiler, *British Labour and the Cold War* (Stanford University Press, 1988), and Carew, *Labour Under the Marshall Plan*. See also Alan Bullock, *Ernest Bevin: Foreign Secretary* (London, Heinemann, 1983), 550.

Eastern Europe and the Western democracies have been able to reach some sort of agreement. The choice before the TUC, if events leave any choice, will not be easy to make.[48]

Events left very little choice. The non-communist Left in Britain endorsed the Marshall Plan. 'In left-wing periodicals such as Tribune and the *New Statesman*, the sagacity and moderation of George Marshall were acclaimed.'[49] There was no question that the TUC and the non-communist unions in Europe would back it and insist on full trade-union participation in its implementation.

Formally, the CIO leaders had not yet given up on the WFTU. In February 1948, Murray described the split in the WFTU as 'extremely bad' but not 'hopeless', and said he was 'hopeful that the whole problem could be thrashed out in the councils of the WFTU'.[50] On the other hand, in the United Automobile Workers (the CIO's largest affiliate), one of the union's key policy advisers, Guy Nunn, a Rhodes scholar and former OSS operative in Europe, was urging UAW involvement in Europe to offset the power of communists in European unions. American aid, wrote Nunn, 'can best be developed and administered by American labor represent-atives . . . if the confidence of European labor is to be retained and the consequences of seemingly "political interference" avoided'; a first step, in his view, was the establishment of an 'international trade-union federation to replace the bankrupt and Communist-ridden WFTU. This federation should admit all unions free of Communist control.'[51] The exclusionary role of international trade-union organization, the erection of an ideological purity test which Lenin had laid down a quarter of a century earlier in his twenty-one conditions, was thus re-established as a criterion for international labour organization and activity.

So by 1948, CIO thinking on the WFTU was converging with that of the AFL. The WFTU continued an attenuated existence for a further year against the background of deepening East–West tension, including the communist takeover in Czechoslovakia, the Berlin blockade, mounting anticommunism in Western countries and further Stalinization in Eastern Europe. Philip Murray's language changed. He denounced the 'Soviet . . . murder of

[48] *The Times*, 17 Nov. 1947.
[49] Kenneth Morgan, *Labour in Power 1945–1951* (OUP, 1984), 277.
[50] USWA Executive Board, 16 Feb. 1948.
[51] G. Nunn to W. Reuther, 6 Jan. 1948. Box 438 Walter P. Reuther papers, WSA.

innocent citizens without trial' in Eastern Europe and 'the four or five million people now in concentration and slave camps' in Russia.[52]

The nucleus of a non-communist international trade-union federation had already been created in London in March 1948 when sixteen national union centres, including the AFL and the CIO, met to discuss and endorse the Marshall Plan. Arthur Goldberg, the former head of the Labor Desk at the OSS, replaced Lee Pressman as chief legal officer of the CIO. Goldberg's advice, recalls Victor Reuther, brother of the UAW president, Walter Reuther, was that the CIO could not stay in the WFTU. 'If we had stayed we would have created serious difficulties with US government agencies.'[53] Victor Reuther also supported his UAW colleague, Guy Nunn, in the view that the CIO should leave the WFTU. In a memo to his brother Walter, he urged the CIO to step up its work in Europe and station permanent representatives there. Moreover, argued Victor Reuther,

several top CIO people should meet with Truman and ask that federal funds . . . be made available to the CIO and AFL . . . I mean at least five million dollars . . . I cannot over-emphasize the importance [that] whatever funds are sent in the name of Labor being channeled through trade-union groups. Under no circumstances should there ever be any indication that funds other than trade-union contributions are being sent to these trade-union groups overseas.[54]

The WFTU split in January 1949 when Western representatives walked out after the Soviets and European communist unions refused to accept a proposal from the TUC to suspend the WFTU's activities for a twelve-month period. In Britain, Ernest Bevin was 'delighted [that] all links with the WFTU were broken'.[55]

The immediate post-war history of the WFTU was not exclusively an affair that concerned only America, Russia, and Britain, as well as continental European states, although the first three were the most important countries involved. The practices of the American military government in Japan and General MacArthur's breaking of a general strike in February 1947 gave an indication, prior to both the enunciation of the Truman Doctrine and the

[52] *CIO News*, Nov. 1948.
[53] V. Reuther interview.
[54] V. Reuther to W. Reuther, 9 Dec. 1948. Box 439, Reuther papers, WSA.
[55] Bullock, *Ernest Bevin: Foreign Secretary*, 742.

Marshall Plan, that the United States, in so far as it controlled a local situation, or where it sought to exercise influence as in Latin America, would seek to restrict trade-union activity to that which was the norm in America.[56] Similarly, the Russians permitted no trade-unionism in their zones of control other than on traditional Leninist terms.

In the background lay the colonial question. At the founding congress of the WFTU, delegates from India and Jamaica had called for support in their independence struggles. In 1946, the British were reproached with the arrest of the trade-union organizers in Cyprus, while in France the metalworkers' union, a bulwark of communist presence in the CGT, changed its title in 1946 and renamed itself the Federation of Metalworkers in France and the Colonies.[57] Had not the split come over the Marshall Plan, the question of colonial freedom would have proved an extremely divisive issue, not least for the Americans who were uncomfortable with the colonial policies of the European imperial powers.

Yet to focus on the Marshall Plan or the potential for rupture over the colonies is to confuse occasions or moments of schism with causes. The hostile behind-the-scenes manœuvering of American and British government officials played its part, but it is wrong to see an external force—government or the state—imposing its brute will on trade unions. It had been the CIO in 1943 which had suggested to the government that 'labor men [should] be attached to the State Dept, both at home and abroad.'[58] The closer relationships between unions and the state was a complex process, and to reduce the WFTU's collapse to a function of Western government hostility is unsatisfactory as an explanation. The

[56] See J. Moore, *Japanese Workers and the Struggle for Power 1945–1947* (Madison, University of Wisconsin Press, 1983), 233–5, and M. and S. Harries, *Sheathing the Sword: The Demilitarisation of Japan* (London, Heinemann, 1989), 194–196 and 200–2. On US activities in Latin America see Victor Alba, *Politics and the Labor Movement in Latin America* (Stanford, Calif., Stanford University Press, 1968), 329–30, and Henry Berger, 'American Foreign Policy and the Cold War in Latin America, 1945–1950' (Paper presented at the Linz conference of international labour movement historians, Sept. 1990).

[57] The Prague WFTU executive in June 1946 heard complaints about the British in Cyprus. In Aug. 1945 the French metal union was called Fédération des Ouvriers des Métaux et Similaires de France. In Sept. 1946, the letterhead proclaimed the union's affiliation to the WFTU and the name was now Fédération des Travailleurs de la Métallurgie de France et des Colonies (IMFA).

[58] J. Carey to E. Stettinus, 11 Nov. 1943. Box 116, Carey papers, WSA.

crudeness with which Stalin called for obedience after the launch of Cominform is also amongst the contributory factors rather than the overarching reason for the WFTU's demise.

Where is the cause to be found? A lead was offered by Harold Laski who was invited in 1949 to give a series of lectures in New York in honour of the CIO's Sidney Hillman, the principal American architect of the WFTU. Laski used the occasion to tell his hosts that 'an important weakness in the American trade-unions [is] that they get their political results by acting as a pressure group', and that while 'the trade unions in the United States obviously exercise great influence, they do not exercise responsible political power'.[59] This refrain is also to be found in other English left-wing intellectuals, notably R. H. Tawney, who were fond of comparing the superior effectiveness of British trade-unions, linked to a Labour Party, to their more simple American cousins.[60] But the WFTU did not founder because the hostility of American business unionism triumphed over the more political labour movements of Europe. If anything, many of the European unions were in the van of anti-WFTU hostility, and, in the international trade secretariats, the socialist, government-linked trade-unions of the Benelux and Nordic countries were determined to preserve autonomy in the face of the WFTU's claims for control of industrial activity.

It was not that the unions of what would soon be called the West were so utterly different from those in the Soviet Union, but that in one important way they had come to resemble them. The whole drift of trade-unionism since 1920 had been in the direction of seeking a closer co-operation, reliance, corporate relationship, even partial integration with the state. This is not to suggest a theory of equivalence, because the trade-unions under socialist or labour control in Europe, as well as the American unions, remained distinct from their communist or Soviet counterparts by adhering to liberal values of representative democracy with its freedoms of assembly, speech, and press. Yet, for the CIO, its future strength lay to a great extent in securing friendly attitudes from the administration. In theory it was possible but in practice it was extremely

---

[59] Harold Laski, *Trade Unions in the New Society* (New York, Viking, 1949), 41.

[60] The condescending tone of British left-wing intellectuals towards American labour is well represented in R. H. Tawney, *The American Labour Movement and Other Essays* (London, Macmillan, 1955).

unlikely that the CIO could break with Washington on the fundamental lines of US foreign policy any more than the Soviet trade-unions could take up a position at odds with Stalin's policy.

For the American trade-unionists, this did not represent an automatic obedience to State Department dictates. Indeed, the American unionists believed, with some justice, that their support for the Marshall Plan gave it a social dimension. As I. F. Stone's contemporary endorsement of the Marshall Plan suggests, the support for American economic and political activity overseas was seen as a progressive cause. According to Alan Wolfe: 'The most critical opponents of isolationism were global humanitarians who saw themselves at the left end of the political spectrum. [They] argued that America must take the lead in reconstructing the world along idealistic lines . . . Foreign aid would bring the New Deal to the world.'[61] The unfolding of the Marshall Plan brought with it considerable political conditions, but in 1947 it was seen in positive terms as economic help.[62] 'How could any Frenchman not accept with satisfaction the aid of our American friends?' asked Maurice Thorez, the French communist leader, in July 1947.[63] If left to itself, the WFTU would probably have welcomed Marshall Aid and insisted on trade-union involvement in its administration, in such a way to be discomfiting for those in Washington, for whom Marshall Aid was principally aimed against the Soviet Union and the presence of strong communist institutions in Western Europe. For Stalin, however, the Marshall Plan, with its seductive appeal for Poles and Czechs as well as for some Western communists, was too threatening to his political control. Certainly, he wanted the military security guaranteed by Russian domination in Eastern and Central Europe, but equally important was an ideological *cordon sanitaire* to prevent the bacillus of democratic-socialist ideas spreading eastwards, and, if all these contacts between Russian and Western labour movements continued, perhaps even penetrating the Soviet Union? Instead of trying to finesse the Marshall Plan's implementation, it had to be opposed utterly. If the WFTU had to be sacrificed to maintain discipline, so be it. It was the opening the AFL and all those ideologically at odds with the WFTU needed. The

---

[61] Alan Wolfe, *America's Impasse*, (Boston, South End Press, 1981), 111.

[62] Carew, *Labour under the Marshall Plan*.

[63] M. Thorez, quoted in Georgette Elgey, *La République des illusions* (Paris, Fayard, 1965), 320.

only way the WFTU might have stood up to these pressures would have been if it had some firm independent existence and achievements of its own. This, however, was not the case.

Finally, it is impossible to understand the split in the WFTU without acknowledging the centrality of domestic politics. The fights between communists and their opponents for control of major CIO unions, especially the UAW, continued between 1945 and 1948. Many CIO members, activists, and leaders were Catholic or of East European origin and not well disposed to 'godless' communism or Soviet domination in Eastern Europe. Yet, within the CIO, membership of the WFTU meant dropping anti-Sovietism as part of the public discourse in internal struggles for union control. The key contest—inside the CIO's biggest affiliate, the UAW—was settled before the post-Truman-Doctrine Cold War got under way. It was a fight that had begun in the 1930s and had continued since the founding of the CIO.

It was not the Cold War that created or deepened the split between communists and their opponents in the CIO, but a decade-long struggle that moved from a national to an international plane from 1948 onwards. As in the European unions, there was no easy coexistence between communists and non-communists in the CIO. Either one or the other had to be dominant.

9

British Metalworkers and the Origins of the Cold War

A PRINCIPAL argument of this book is that it is not enough to explain the political split in trade-unions at all levels—national and international—which occurred by the middle of 1948 by the external factor of the Cold War. In the International Metalworkers' Federation the roots of that split are to be found in the enmity between communism and social democracy, and the heritage of the splits in trade-unions in the 1920s and 1930s. In Britain, at first sight, these factors were absent. The British trade-union movement was united around one national centre, the TUC. The Communist Party of Great Britain, although its membership had increased to 50,000 during the war, was weaker than sister parties in most Continental countries. But a closer examination of the politics of trade-unionism in the immediate post-war period shows that many of the political themes and arguments animating the Continental labour movement are to be found in Britain.

Three strands in the international policies of British trade-unions before 1945 are worth examining in this light—the Soviet Union, the colonies, and the importance of Ernest Bevin. The question in 1945 of the relations that British trade-unions should have with the Soviet Union was one which had been on the agenda since the 1920s. Walter Citrine, the TUC general secretary, had written two books on the Soviet Union, one critical, *I Search for Truth in Russia*, which appeared in 1936 and the other a friendlier wartime account, *In Russia Now*, published in 1942. Ernest Bevin, still the general secretary of the Transport and General Workers' Union, on leave of absence since 1940 (he officially stood down from the TGWU only in 1946), had been grappling with the question of British labour and the Soviet Union since the 'Jolly George' incident in 1920.

In 1925 the TUC Congress had welcomed the creation of the Anglo-Russian Joint Advisory Council but few tears were shed when it was wound up in 1927 in a storm of mutual recriminations over the General Strike.[1] The following year, the Amalgamated Engineering Union's National Committee 'denounced the attempts of the Communist Party and its chief subsidiary body the National Minority Movement to form rival bodies to the Labour Party and the TUC': it went on to authorize the AEU executive to take 'such steps as may be appropriate',[2] coded language for expulsions.[3] The TUC's 'Black Circular' of 1934 banned communist delegates from TUC-recognized trades' councils and urged unions 'to exclude Communists from posts of responsibility'.[4]

The timing of the TUC proscription was unfortunate since the tide was turning in favour of Popular Front unity in opposition to Nazism. The winding-up of Profintern, the communist trade-union international, after the Seventh Communist International Congress, opened the way in 1937 for talks about the Russian trade-unions' affiliation to the International Federation of Trade Unions, whose president was Walter Citrine, the TUC general secretary, and whose dominant affiliate was the TUC. But the revulsion over the Moscow trials as well as Soviet disagreements over terms for entry into the IFTU cooled support for a Russian affiliation.[5] Stalin's participation in the invasion of Poland in 1939 reawakened anti-Russian and anticommunist hostility on the TUC's part. Citrine told the TUC Congress in 1939 there was 'a dictatorship in Russia as severe and cruel as anything that has happened in Germany'.[6] The Russian invasion of Finland in 1940 was condemned by TUC and Labour Party leaders. Citrine was a member of a labour-movement delegation that visited Finland and urged British support for the Finns.[7] Abroad, Russia; at home, the communists were the enemy. In 1941 the TUC opposed the People's Convention on the

---

[1] See D. Calhoun, *The United Front, the TUC and the Russians, 1923–1927* (Cambridge, Cambridge University Press, 1976).

[2] AEU Journal, June 1928.

[3] See Roderick Martin, *Communism and the British Trade Unions 1924–1933* (Oxford, Clarendon Press, 1969), 135.

[4] H. Pelling, *A History of British Trade Unionism* (London, Penguin, 1976), 198.

[5] In addition to the references in other chapters a concise summary of the pre–1939 politics of the IFTU, including the question of Soviet admission in the late 1930s can be found in John Windmuller, 'International Trade Union Movement', in R. Blancpain (ed.), *International Encyclopaedia for Labour Law and Industrial Relations*, (Deventer, Kluwer, 1987), 36.

[6] TUC Report 1939, 198.

[7] Bill Jones, *The Russia Complex: The British Labour Party and the Soviet Union* (Manchester, Manchester University Press, 1977), 36.

grounds that it was communist-backed, and dissolved or 'reorganized' trades' councils which supported communist positions.[8]

The first twenty-two months of the war was a period of open anticommunism on the TUC's part. British communists tended to respond in kind. Wal Hannington, a communist long active in the AEU, wrote in 1941, 'Trade union and labour leaders who have been given seats in the government have made it easier for the ruling class to carry out its attacks upon the workers' conditions by using those leaders to do their work and at the same time silence the rank and file in the Labour movement.'[9] The Soviet entry into the war on the side of Great Britain changed all this. The 'Black Circular' was withdrawn, a Joint Committee of British and Soviet Unions was set up, Citrine was given orders by the TUC Congress to bring the Russians into a unified trade-union international and the WFTU was set up in 1945.

By 1945, the TUC had become institutionally enmeshed in international affairs at several levels. After the failure of the 1926 General Strike, the TUC sought to extend its influence incrementally with employers and the government.[10] As far as the latter was concerned, one opportunity lay in the rise of trade-unions in India and the colonies. These unions turned to the TUC for help. Gradually during the 1930s the TUC was drawn into discussion of government and Labour Party policy on the colonies. The Colonial Office hoped that the TUC would help develop 'moderate' and 'responsible' trade-unions[11] and the TUC's anticommunism, as well as its rivalry with the Profintern, shaped its attitudes towards nascent unions in India and the West Indies.

Yet the support for the creation of trade-unions as independent institutions within the colonies was a double-edged process. Early in 1945, the TUC invited various colonial trade-unions to London for the preparatory conference leading to the WFTU's founding.

---

[8] TUC Report 1940, 108 and 320–2. On the Peoples' Convention see Noreen Branson, *History of the Communist Party of Great Britain 1927–1941* (London, Lawrence and Wishart, 1985), 308–10.

[9] Wal Hannington, *Labour Monthly*, Feb. 1941.

[10] See Martin Jacques, 'The Emergence of "Responsible" trade-unionism: A Study of the "New Direction" in TUC Policy 1926–1935' (Ph.D. thesis, Cambridge, 1977).

[11] See Marjorie Nicholson, *The TUC Overseas: The Roots of Policy* (London, Allen and Unwin, 1986) and P. Weiler, *British Labour and the Cold War* (Stanford, Calif., Stanford University Press, 1988), for contrasting views on the development of TUC colonial policy.

Far from being grateful for the TUC's patronage and obediently accepting their colonial status, the leaders of the Gold Coast, Nigerian, British Guianan, and Gambian TUC's jointly signed a manifesto calling for 'full self-government'.[12] No matter what the Colonial Office wanted, the unions, once established and sanctioned by the TUC, would develop a life of their own: indeed, in due course the unions in the colonies formed the core of independence movements.[13]

Already by 1940, the TUC was nominating labour advisers in the colonies. Ernest Bevin, once in government as Minister of Labour, went a step further by appointing labour attachés in key embassies. By 1945, when he moved to the Foreign Office, there were labour attachés in place in Washington, Paris, Rome, Brussels, Stockholm, and Cairo. Bevin personally 'approved the appointment of these various Labour attachés' and took 'a keen interest in their work'.[14]

As wartime Minister of Labour, Bevin retained his interest in international trade-union developments while, as Foreign Secretary, he met regularly with 'his' labour attachés (technically they were seconded from the Ministry of Labour to embassies), and took a continuing interest in the problems of the WFTU. Nearly every year between 1920 and 1939, Bevin travelled abroad either to an ILO conference or to take part in meetings of the International Transport Workers' Federation in which he played a prominent part. He first went as the TUC's fraternal delegate to the United States in 1916. After 1945, when visiting the United States as Foreign Secretary, Bevin met with AFL leaders to exchange views.[15]

In any consideration of British trade-unions and international affairs following 1945 the presence of Bevin has to be kept in mind. V. L. Allen has written that Bevin 'was an exception' to the rule that 'trade union leaders normally lose their influence with unions when they lose their union posts . . . Right until his death he carried some influence over union behaviour.'[16] His interventions at the

---

[12] *Labour Monthly*, May 1945, 154–5.
[13] See Michael Manley, *A Voice at the Workplace: Reflections on Colonialism and the Jamaican Worker* (London, Deutsch, 1975), 24–41.
[14] PRO Lab. 13/191.
[15] On Bevin and wartime labour attachés see G. H. Hall to Bevin, 13 Nov. 1943, PRO Lab. 13; on contacts with the AFL see A. Bullock, *Ernest Bevin. Foreign Secretary* (London, Heinemann, 1983), 108.
[16] V. L. Allen, *Trade Unions and Government* (London, Longman, 1960), 289. A detailed study of Bevin's foreign policy and the hostility of the Foreign Office to co-

post-war Labour Party and TUC conferences, aimed at trade-union delegates, invariably swung debates on foreign affairs. His influence on union affairs especially in the international field and on the relations of the TUC and the Labour government were all the more marked with Citrine's retirement from the TUC in 1946. Rivals and colleagues over two decades, linked by mutual jealousy and respect, Bevin and Citrine none the less agreed on most international questions and shared hostility to the Soviet Union and communism. However Citrine insisted that the TUC should keep some independence from government. Indeed during the war the government had been uneasy about Citrine's active international policy. MI6 reports on the left-wing leanings of North American trade-unionists that Citrine proposed to invite to London were circulated between the Foreign Office, Home Office, and Ministry of Labour.[17] An anxious Anthony Eden wrote, as Home Secretary, warning Citrine that the government might exclude on 'security grounds' overseas delegates invited by the TUC.[18] But with the emergence in mid–1946 of Arthur Deakin, Bevin's protégé and successor at the TGWU, as the key TUC leader after Citrine's departure as well as being Citrine's successor as president of the WFTU, the government-TUC nexus was even more firmly established. Before presiding for the first time over a WFTU meeting in New York in the autumn of 1946, Deakin met with government representatives and promised to keep 'in close touch' with the Foreign Office minister attending the UN gathering in New York 'so as to keep the discussion at the WFTU as far as possible on proper lines'.[19]

The presence of twenty-nine trade-union officials in the Labour government, six of them in the cabinet, reinforced a joint union–government outlook. The hostility of the Foreign Office to the Soviet Union complemented Bevin's anticommunism. Only a few weeks after the WFTU's launch, Bevin received a report from the British Embassy in Moscow about Soviet satisfaction with the WFTU 'because the authorities believe [it] can be used to advance the interests of Soviet foreign policy'.[20] The hostility of Bevin and

operation with the Soviet Union can be found in Anne Deighton, *The Impossible Peace: Britain, the Division of Germany, and the Origins of the Cold War*, (Oxford, Clarendon Press, 1990).

[17] SC/6298, 10 May 1944 in PRO Lab. 13.
[18] Eden to Citrine, 23 Mar. 1944, ibid.
[19] 13 Aug. 1946 in PRO Lab. 13/596.
[20] A. Clark Kerr to Bevin, 26 Nov. 1945, PRO Lab. 13.

his officials towards the Soviet Union and the WFTU of course had great influence. But there were other, equally if not more decisive, factors which contributed to the formation of international policy. Some of them can be examined through the eyes of Jack Tanner, in 1945 president of the Amalgamated Engineering Union, Britain's principal metal union.

JACK TANNER

Jack Tanner's views were shaped by the two forces of mass industrial production and class-conscious trade-unionism. Born in 1890 and raised in London, he was president of Britain's principal metalworkers' union, the AEU, from 1939 to 1954. Just as Ernest Bevin had far more international experience from his travel and contacts within the international labour movement than a superficial reading of him as a bulldog English labour leader might indicate, so did Jack Tanner. He spent two years at sea after training as a fitter, and in his twenties spent considerable time in France, Belgium, and Spain. He worked for eighteen months in France in 1915–16 and joined the French metalworkers' union.[21]

A syndicalist before 1914 and a leader of the shop stewards' movement during the First World War, the most important international event in Tanner's life, which shaped his later views, was his participation as a delegate from the Shop Stewards' and Workers' Committee in the Second Congress of the Communist International in Moscow in 1920. In the 1940s and 1950s he would be the only member of the TUC General Council to have participated in the founding moment of the world communist movement. Elected AEU president in 1939 with communist backing, Tanner ended his days very much in the anticommunist camp. Tanner's leftism seemed marked enough during and after the Second World War. For more than half his fifteen years in office as AEU president he was considered to be of the Left, an ally of the communists. In 1945, he did not have the same anticommunist background of other TUC leaders like Citrine, Deakin, Ebby Edwards (of the Miners), or Charles Dukes (of the General and

---

[21] Eddie Frow prepared a sketch of Tanner which he kindly showed me. There is a brief mention of him in Richard Croucher, *Engineers at War*, (London, Merlin Press, 1982), 65.

Municipal Workers). Tanner represents a strand in British trade-unionism that is not easily categorized into the tidy division of pro-Soviet Left versus reformist, comfortable-with-capitalism Right. In psephological terms, Tanner and others like him would be called floating voters. In the prehistory of the Cold War, in the search for its causes, this group has been largely ignored but their attitudes in the three years after 1945 helped transform the pro-Sovietism that underpinned the creation of the WFTU into the anti-Sovietism that led to its collapse. Tanner's views and their evolution thus stand as an exemplar.

Four aspects of his views can be seen to be at work at different times and with different emphasis in his life as an active trade-unionist. One was syndicalism, the idea of workers controlling their own industries. The second was a belief in productionism, mass industrial production linked to full employment. The third is the idea of trade-unions guarding some autonomy and independence in their relations with other sources of power and authority in society. The fourth was a commitment to some form of internationalism, a residual belief in the pre–1914 rhetoric of the Second International. Although like so many skilled, qualified metalworkers he was widely read, 'fond of poetry, and very well-read especially Morris, Ruskin and Kropotkin',[22] Tanner never articulated his views into anything longer than a speech or an article but during his visit to Russia in 1920 to take part in the Second Congress of the Communist International, he kept a fairly detailed diary of the events surrounding the birth of Profintern—the Red International of Labour Unions.

Zinoviev's announcement at the plenary of the Communist International on 16 June 1920 that the 'Russian, English and Italian' delegations had agreed to the formation of 'a Red Industrial International in opposition to the Int[ernational] Fed[eration] of T[rade] U[nion]s in Amsterdam'[23] came as a shock to Tanner who knew nothing of any such agreement. Consultations with Scandinavian and Italian trade-unionists, as well as with John Reed, one of the American delegates, confirmed his fears that Zinoviev was imposing a Russian proposal to set up a separate and rival body—

---

[22] Eddie Frow interview, Manchester, 16 Apr. 1986.
[23] Tanner's Moscow diary is in Box 1, Tanner papers (henceforth TP), Nuffield College, Oxford.

'which would be subject to the 3rd'[24] International on the European trade-unionists, many of whom preferred to work within the existing international federations.

Tanner, and most of the other European union delegates, argued that in any event a conference even to discuss a new international should be 'held outside of Russia'[25] so as to remove the issue of revolutionary trade-union internationalism from the physical control of the Communist International. Discussion continued over the next month. Tanner expressed anger about the 'double-dealing' of Losovsky, the future Profintern general secretary, and recorded his dismay at the refusal of the Russians to acknowledge the danger of 'leaving the ranks of the existing trade unions'.[26] Tanner's opposition to splitting existing trade-unions or creating a rival international was ignored by the Russians who were determined to set up their own trade-union international under Comintern's control.[27]

Although he was angry at Lenin's and Zinoviev's insistence on the split in the trade-union movement, Tanner did not reject his commitment to the Soviet revolution. He returned to Britain a committed revolutionary shop steward. He chaired the meeting in Leeds which fused the various British left-wing groups into the CPGB.[28] Walter Kendall suggests that Tanner tried to keep some distance between the shop-stewards' movement and the Communist Party; furthermore, by stressing the shop-stewards' orientation to the British bureau of the Profintern, he sought to preserve some room for trade-union autonomy from the Communist International and its British section.[29]

This was a hopeless task as the discipline of Moscow ruled over both political and industrial wings of the communist movement in Britain as elsewhere. Indeed Tanner accepted a subvention from Comintern for *Solidarity*, the syndicalist journal he edited.[30] Tanner loyally served the communist-dominated National Minor-

[24] Ibid.   [25] Ibid.   [26] Ibid.

[27] A detailed discussion of the negotiations between the British shop stewards and the Russians is to be found in Martin, *Communism in British Trade Unions*, 6–10.

[28] James Klugman, *History of the Communist Party of Great Britain, 1919–1924* (London, Lawrence and Wishart, 1969), 68.

[29] Walter Kendall, *The Revolutionary Movement in Britain 1900–1921* (London, Weidenfeld and Nicolson, 1969), 262.

[30] Ibid. 255.

ity Movement (NMM) in the 1920s. But he never joined the Communist Party. It made no difference to his political identification since his high-profile activity in the National Minority Movement located him firmly in the communist camp. In 1930, he moved a resolution at the national conference of the Friends of Soviet Russia which accused the Labour Foreign Secretary, Arthur Henderson, of encouraging 'every kind of anti-Soviet propaganda' in obedience 'to the imperialist campaign' against the Soviet Union.[31]

Tanner belonged to those trade-unionists who were unhappy with the Comintern's new policy after 1928, calling for the creation of separate revolutionary trade-unions. He approved of the warnings given by Harry Pollit, the Communist leader, and Arthur Horner, the miners' leader, about the damaging effects this would have on left-wing agitation in British trade-unions. Arguing against Profintern policy in 1929, Tanner had appealed in vain for the Russians 'to recognise the need for a flexible policy . . . without falling into the error of overlooking national circumstances and traditions'.[32] This was the plea of many in those years, and it was an issue that became live again after 1945 as Tanner observed the problems between the International Metalworkers' Federation and the Russians with their insistence on the need for the international trade secretariats to bend to Soviet views of world trade-union organization. In Tanner can be seen the contradiction summed up by Roderick Martin in his study of the NMM, the main trade-union vehicle for the communists between the wars. As Martin wrote, 'The Minority Movement's main plea was for working class unity against capitalism: yet the very existence of the Movement posed a threat to that unity . . . Moreover, the Movement simultaneously denied that the working class could improve its situation under capitalism, and sought to win support by agitation for immediate improvements in wages and working conditions.'[33]

Tanner faced a number of critical choices in his career. He chose to stay with his shop-stewards' movement rather than join the Communist Party, to stay with his union rather than with external rank-and-file groups and, after 1945, to go with the industrial IMF rather than the political WFTU. His commitment to staying in the

---

[31] Friends of Soviet Russia National Conference, 16 Feb. 1930 (TP).
[32] Quoted in Martin, *Communism in British Trade Unions*, 113.
[33] Ibid. 179.

mainstream union movement rather than ploughing a separate revolutionary furrow outside was already made clear in 1931 when, unlike other NMM shop stewards, he chose to submit to the discipline of the AEU executive. They were expelled. He was elected a full-time official and in 1939 was elected president of the union.

Eddie Frow, the chronicler of shop-steward activity in the engineering industry, notes that Tanner 'made his peace'[34] with the AEU executive, but for all that Tanner remained on the Left in the 1930s and was associated with initiatives such as the Unity Campaign which was supported by the Communist Party, the Independent Labour Party, and the Socialist League.[35] He hankered for unity or at least mutually supportive work between the various strands of the Left, and this longing remained with him for years afterwards. He remained true to his syndicalist commitment to rank-and-file action, backing strikes at Ford's Dagenham works in 1938,[36] and endorsing shop-floor action in opposition to the speed-up methods associated with the Bedaux system.[37]

By 1945, Tanner was no novice in international labour questions. In addition to his forays into Europe and the Soviet Union, Tanner travelled to the United States in 1921 where he was an official fraternal delegate from the British shop-stewards' movement to the convention of the syndicalist labour organization, the Industrial Workers of the World—the 'Wobblies'. In his papers are to be found the minutes of the meeting between the International Metalworkers' Federation delegates and the Russian metal-union representatives in 1927, as well as the proceedings of the 'Conference of Revolutionary Metalworkers' in Moscow in 1930. Tanner campaigned actively on behalf of the defendants in the Meerut trial, and saw copies of Jawaharlal Nehru's correspondence as president of the Indian trade-union congress with the TUC's Walter Citrine.[38] He was also the NMM's delegate to the League Against Imperialism.

From 1945 onwards, Tanner travelled widely as a TUC or AEU delegate. In September and October 1945 he was in Paris and then

[34] Eddie and Ruth Frow, *Engineering Struggles: Episodes in the Story of the Shop Stewards' Movement* (Manchester, Working Class Movement Library, 1982), 93.
[35] See Ben Pimlott, *Labour and the Left in the 1930s* (London, Allen and Unwin, 1986), 77.
[36] Frow, *Engineering Struggles*, 95–6.
[37] Ibid. 100.
[38] TP.

Switzerland for the first post-war meetings of the WFTU and the IMF. He travelled through Germany, Austria, and Czechoslovakia later that year as a TUC delegate, and afterwards participated actively in IMF meetings. For the two years after the war's end Tanner's role in the IMF expressed his wish to maintain friendly relations with the Soviet Union by actively supporting the WFTU, a continuation of his political philosophy which had not much changed since 1920. But at the same time he never wavered from the position that an integration of the international industrial union secretariat should be on terms that maintained its autonomy, and accountable control by its member unions—a position, of course, which was unacceptable to the Russians. He expressed face-to-face with Lenin and Zinoviev in Moscow in 1920 that to place, by political or administrative statute, all trade-union organization under centralized authority was quite wrong.

In themselves, these two impulses in Tanner's political make-up —an anticapitalist support for friendship with the Soviet Union[39] while maintaining trade-union autonomy—need not have come into conflict. But Tanner was also a productionist and this aspect of British trade-unionism, which he exemplified, has to be considered if the sources of the Cold War as it relates to the labour movement are to be revealed.

PRODUCTIONISM

Addressing, as AEU president, his union's National Committee in June 1947, Jack Tanner outlined a key difference between the United States and Britain: 'Unlike the American problem of distribution, the problem for the rest of the world is production. For us production transcends all. It is the focal point to which all effort must be directed,' he told his union activists.[40] The problem of production was far more than a question of industrial output. Around the issue of production revolved much wider questions about the nature and direction of society, about the role of workers

---

[39] See, for example, Tanner's address to the 1946 AEU National Committee, in which he hails Labour's election victory as 'an important stage in the fight to end capitalism' and calls upon the AEU to 'fight for our solidarity with the Soviet Union'. Amalgamated Engineering Union National Committee report (henceforth AEU NC) 1946, 207–9.

[40] AEU NC 1947, 265.

and the power of their union, and about the ability of differently constructed political systems to deliver the necessities as well as some of the pleasures of life for all.

The question of what and how to produce had not been greatly addressed in 1945. The Left demanded nationalization of the basic resource and service industries (coal, road and rail transport) but manufacturing industry was to be left in private hands. Of all engineering firms, 90 per cent employed fewer than 100 workers, so nationalization in the manufacturing sector presented quite different administrative problems from taking over the mines and railways. Still, it was a lacuna in the British vision of public ownership that no modern, profitable firms were considered for public ownership. There would be no equivalent of the confiscated and state-owned Renault in France or Volkswagen in Germany to offer to workers in the manufacturing sector a sense that they now produced for other than private profit.

While for some, nationalization was the key to increasing output, Keynesians, gathered around Hugh Dalton and Evan Durbin, looked to fiscal, regional, and resource allocation policies, usually lumped together as 'controls', to increase output in a guided and socially desirable fashion.[41] Stafford Cripps dismissed arguments for industrial democracy or workers' control as syndicalism, the very idea was 'almost impossible . . . even if it were on the whole desirable'.[42] The TUC came down against workers' control at its Congress in 1945, stressing that unions had to avoid 'dual responsibility'.[43]

The discussion about how the relations of production should be organized came a long way behind the overwhelming urge to produce as such. Increased production, especially for export, became a mythic goal in itself. It embraced all. For the Chancellor, Hugh Dalton, 'finding a way to pay for imports to prevent mass unemployment and starvation' was his most 'immediate and difficult' task upon entering office.[44] For one AEU activist, the communist Reg Birch, 'maximum production must be achieved . . .

[41] See Elizabeth Durbin, *New Jerusalems* (London, Routledge, 1985), and Alec Cairncross, *Years of Recovery: British Economic Policy 1945–1951* (London, Methuen, 1985), 299–310.
[42] Quoted in Ken Coates, 'The Vagaries of Participation', in B. Pimlott and C. Cook (eds.), *Trade Unions in British Politics* (London, Longman, 1982), 182.
[43] Pelling, *History of British Trade Unionism*, 222.
[44] Ben Pimlott, *Hugh Dalton* (London, Jonathan Cape, 1985), 427.

years and years of necessary work stare us in the face'.[45] Productionism was endorsed by the TUC. *The Economist* summed up the 1946 TUC Congress thus:

Lord Citrine, making his farewell speech, observed that in the past any speaker who called for increased production and higher productivity would have been howled down. It is significant that 'increased production' should have been the recurrent theme of nearly all the speakers at the 1946 conference. Mr Charles Dukes [head of the powerful General and Municipal Workers Union] its chairman, told the conference bluntly that the unions would not fulfil the requirements of the post-war situation, and would not play their full part in industry, unless they radically revised their traditional attitudes and abandoned the restrictive practices which grew up in periods of unemployment and under-employment.[46]

The left-wing press was just as keen on increased production at all costs. The communist *Labour Monthly* filled its columns, as did the *Daily Herald*, *Tribune*, and the *New Statesman* with appeals for more production and higher productivity. 'There has to be a plan for an increased production drive and a scientific plan for the increase in productivity of all engaged in the [engineering] industry,' declared *Labour Monthly* in February 1946. A few months later communist members of the AEU were told: 'More must be done by the unions to impress on workers that we are in the midst of the real economic crisis . . . Increased production is a means to an end, namely, the overcoming of the crisis of the British economy and the guaranteeing of a rising standard of life for all workers.'[47]

The dollar shortage and the need for exports to pay for vital imports were the economic reasons behind this drive for higher production that united all political tendencies active in the labour movement. There was continuous government exhortation to export which was transformed into policies. Car firms, for example, which needed to import raw materials could only get them if the majority of the finished cars were exported.[48] This, too, was one way in which the links between Britain's economic future and international conditions were driven home.

[45] Reg Birch, *A Wage Based on Human Needs* (London, Communist Party, 1946), 15.
[46] *The Economist*, 26 Oct. 1946.
[47] J. R. Campbell, 'Where is That Production Drive?', *Labour Monthly*, June 1946.
[48] See P. Addison, *Now the War is Over* (London, Jonathan Cape, 1985), 190.

In itself, the call to export orientated production, even if British economic survival was held to be at stake, was not enough to motivate unions and left-wing political organizations. Later attempts to engage support for such drives such as the 1968 'I'm Backing Britain' campaign turned into embarrassing farce. The difference is that in the 1940s productionism was perceived as a key element in the construction of socialism. As Tanner wrote in 1945 in the introduction to a pamphlet, *Engineering and Reconstruction*:

During the war, the working class for the first time in its history, has had to show the employers how to overcome their narrow sectional outlook and learn to produce for an urgent need . . . We have seen how the productive forces can, through conscious planning, be multiplied and used not only to win a war but also to transform the life of every worker in the country.[49]

Once the war was over capacity production was the goal of trade-union and left-wing endeavour. There was a quiet moral satisfaction drawn from the passage of heroic arms production and the 'Britain Can Take It' of the war to the 1946 Exhibition, 'Britain Can Make It' in which progressive designers showed off their new functional and socially purposeful designs.

Barely a decade before, the world had appeared locked in a compound of mass unemployment, poverty, and rising fascism. The exception seemed to be the Soviet Union, where Stalin, after turning his back on the market-orientated New Economic Policy, had made a fetish out of industrial production. As John Strachey wrote in 1936, 'the towering achievement of the first socialist system has been the simultaneous abolition of glut and unemployment'.[50] Scores of thousands of copies of Strachey's book as well as of other Left Book Club editions, many of them extolling the Soviet Union's abolition of unemployment through industrial production, lay on the shelves of trade-unionists in the 1940s. Between 1934 and 1938, wrote Jürgen Kuczynski, the exiled German communist, in a Left Book Club edition, workers in the Soviet Union had seen an improvement in their conditions 'which has no parallel in the history of labour'.[51] The later revulsion from the Moscow trials,

[49] Labour Research Department pamphlet, 1945.
[50] John Strachey, *The Theory and Practice of Socialism* (London, Gollancz, 1936), 62.
[51] Jürgen Kuczynski, *The Condition of Workers in Great Britain, Germany and the Soviet Union 1932–1938* (London, Gollancz, 1939), 90.

the Stalin–Hitler pact, and the terror of the secret police did not, in the eyes of many trade-unionists, detract from the Soviet Union's accomplishment in using mass industrialization and productionism to abolish unemployment.

If the second half of the 1930s had shown how Soviet productionism solved capitalism's most notorious negative feature —mass unemployment—the first half of the 1940s produced an equal economic feat in Britain and the United States. The war changed many factors in the equation but here were two industrial states committing themselves to full production and with it came full employment. Complete commitment to production was, it seemed, quite possible without the political form of the USSR. The decade between 1935 and 1945 led trade-unionists not just to hope but to believe that unemployment could be abolished.

This was not just a moral issue, for full employment enhanced the institutional power of the unions. But maintenance of full employment needed constant effort, and was always relatively precarious. The cold winter of 1947 caused a shutdown of industry that within a fortnight had nearly 2 million workers registering as unemployed. The impact of those terrible three weeks on the outlook of British trade-unionists cannot be underestimated. As V. L. Allen pointed out:

This transitory break in the state of full employment reminded union leaders how quickly and easily the economic strength of their unions could be swept away. The high membership of the unions was in part a product of full employment . . . Union leaders saw clearly that the size and power of their organizations and the state of the economy bore a direct relationship to each other.[52]

In their discussions at the ILO metal and steel industrial committees in the summer of 1946, the union representatives, mainly from IMF affiliated unions, had emphasized the need for full employment; this was declared to be one of the principal aims of metal unions at the IMF's annual central committee meeting in 1946.[53] After the war's end, Tanner and other British metal-union representatives participated in these international union meetings, in the context of either the IMF or the ILO, and some of what foreign trade-unionists had to say stuck in their minds. In particular, the alarming

---

[52] V. L. Allen, *Trade Unions and Government* (London, Longman, 1960), 283.
[53] IMF Central Committee Proceedings 1946, 21–3.

economic situation in Germany, and the immense financial drag a non-productive Germany was on the British exchequer, combined with the apparently illogical exclusion of German productive capacity from the overall European need to produce, was pressed home.

So Britain joined in the world-wide chorus from the unions to produce. This productionist frenzy aimed at supporting the domestic policies of a Labour government and especially full employment silenced those voices which questioned the way in which the workplaces themselves were run. As Tanner told the 1946 AEU National Committee:

We must not allow the employers' rising profits to provoke us into slackening our production drive . . . Rather does more output mean higher standards for the working class. The Labour Government, which is the instrument of progress, stands or falls on its economic programme. It *must* [Tanner's emphasis] achieve full employment . . . it *must* restore devastated Europe and industrialise the colonial countries; it *must* provide exports.[54]

Every factor that could be used to maintain productionism was brought into play. During the war, the TUC had re-established its relations with the Soviet All Union Central Council of Trade Unions once Hitler invaded Russia. But the main practical purpose of the joint statements between the British and Russian trade-unions and the delegation visits from the Soviet Union was to increase productivity. Citrine urged the Soviets, from foreign minister Molotov down to individual union leaders, to encourage increased work and production in the factories of Britain. British workers, he told the Russians, had 'a casual attitude to production' which could be put right by the Russians sending 'as quickly as possible comrades from the Soviet Trade Unions who can talk to our workers direct and show them the need for their doing everything they can to work and to do everything for production'.[55]

Production did increase in the war but productivity did not. In 1944, for example, it took 63,502 Daimler-Benz workers, operating under great difficulties in heavily bombed Germany, to produce 28,669 aeroplane engines. Rolls Royce's 56,000 employees produced 18,100 engines, a productivity rate of 71 per cent in comparison to German output.[56] The comparison with America

---

[54] AEU NC 1946, 210.
[55] Anglo-Soviet Trade Union Committee, 13–15 Oct. 1941 (TUC).
[56] Correlli Barnett, *Audit of War* (London, Macmillan, 1986), 158.

was even worse. In terms of weight American aircraft workers were producing nearly three times as many aircraft as their British equivalents. Tanner visited the United States during the war and returned impressed by American methods of aircraft production predicting to left-wing friends that air transport would become important after the war.[57]

Productivity—increasing output using the same amount of labour—was not simply an academic or managerial question. Some of the aims of British workers, especially a shorter working week after the enforced six-day week and compulsory overtime of the war, as well as higher wages, could only be achieved if productivity rose. 'Our job', Tanner announced in June 1946, 'is to see that there is more output for less effort' so that 'the real wages of the mass of the people can be increased and hours reduced'.[58] This shift of emphasis from production to productivity was gradual; the words were casually, almost interchangeably, used. But the difference was important in terms of international labour politics because whereas production was something that the Russians appeared expert at, productivity was supremely an American art. Once the war was over Russia could no longer serve either as an example of the only society which had abolished unemployment nor as a model of how to organize production. The reports of visitors to the Soviet Union could not gloss over the poverty of Russian life while Russian Stakhanovism—in due course to be exported to other East European countries[59]—was unattractive to trade-unionists whose whole life had been devoted to resistance to such methods.

The switch of focus from Russia to the United States as the problematic catalyst to maintain high levels of production and hence full employment came gradually, and, at first, was not centred on the question of productivity. Initially, America was important as a source of capital. Much of the Labour Left as well as the communists approved the American loan negotiated by Keynes

---

[57] Ibid. See David Edgerton, 'Liberal Militarism and the British State', *New Left Review* 185 (1991). 158–9, for a correction of Barnett's assessment of inefficiency in wartime British industry *vis-à-vis* Germany. However, a wartime Ministry of Aircraft Production report did find that US production was 75% more efficient than British.

[58] AEU NC 1946.

[59] See François Fejtö, *Histoire des démocraties populaires* (Paris, Seuil, 1952), 315–22.

at the end of 1945. The capital from America was seen as a way of shoring up the socialized state the Labour government was creating. Far from tying Britain more closely to the United States, Michael Foot believed that the American loan both permitted, and required 'a terrific, unexampled burst of productive energy' if Britain was 'not to become the bondslave of Wall Street'.[60]

The emphasis of the Labour Left, amongst whom on the trade-union side was counted Jack Tanner (though there is no evidence that he worked with parliamentary left-wingers associated in the Keep Left group) on production was maintained in their response to the fuel crisis of February 1947. The pamphlet, *Keep Left*, urged an increase in exports to 65 per cent above their pre-war level. The pamphlet listed a set of proposals—increased controls, enforced management efficiency, stronger joint production committees, and nationalization of the motor-vehicle and some electrical manufacturing firms—which the authors felt were necessary to increase output.

The chances of implementation of such a radical programme—more radical than communist demands of the time—were not robust.[61] The heterogeneity of the Left after 1945 was its single most marked characteristic. The various personalities and groups in parliament, in the unions, or in the opinion-forming journals never seem to have co-ordinated their activities, publications, or policies, nor did they seek to ally with non-Labour forces in any organized fashion. In any event, the economic programme of the Keep Left group fell victim to the political battering the pamphlet and its authors received at the hands of Bevin whose ferocious opposition was mainly to the foreign-policy section.

Embracing America to secure the dollars to maintain output was underlined by the convertibility crisis in the summer of 1947 and by the announcement of Marshall Aid. For the Labour Left, Jonathan

---

[60] *Daily Herald*, 14 Dec. 1945. Productionism as a purely capitalist concept of 'producing the largest volume of specialized goods for sale in the widest possible market' based on a free market economy seeking to 'maximize profits' is discussed in T. J. McCormick's *America's Half Century: United States Foreign Policy in the Cold War* (Baltimore, Johns Hopkins University Press, 1989), 50–3. See also Charles Maier, 'The Politics of Productivity: Foundations of American International Economic Policy after World War II', in *International Organization*, 31 (Autumn, 1977), 607–33.

[61] See Jonathan Schneer, *Labour's Conscience: The Labour Left 1945–1951* (London, Unwin, 1987), 80–90, for a discussion of the Labour Left's economic programme as it developed between 1945 and 1948.

Schneer has written, 'the Secretary of State seemed to be offering . . . funds for reconstruction without imperiling British socialism'.[62] Representatives of the Left, like Michael Foot and Fenner Brockway, welcomed Marshall's offer no less eagerly than did Bevin and Attlee.

In Anthony Carew's estimation, the trade-unions approached the Marshall Plan as a collective-bargaining exercise 'in which labour would have to make some concessions, but through which there were also gains to be made if they played their cards carefully'.[63] Carew also believes that the split in the WFTU 'was, arguably, the first achievement of the Marshall Plan'.[64] The problem with this argument is that it negates the history of the two years between the war's end and Marshall's speech. The British unions' embrace of Marshall Aid and their later involvement in productivity tours of the United States was the result of two powerful and linked strands in trade-union thinking which encompassed Left and Right.

The first was the productionist–full employment impulse allied to the objective of a strong economy to help the Labour government achieve its social programme. The *New Statesman* was clear enough in the immediate aftermath of Marshall's speech: 'Our very survival depends on the extent to which the Marshall offer is made a reality.'[65] The second was a sense that Britain could accept help in this area from other countries. Before 1939 it had been the Soviet Union that apparently provided an almost scientifically precise example of full employment through productionism and during the war the Russians, at the TUC's behest, had sent productionist cheer-leaders over to stir workers to greater efforts. But after the war, the United States replaced the Soviet Union as the model to be followed as well as being a source of dollars. The political implications of this became evident in the following years as Britain fell more and more into the US orbit. But what mattered to the manufacturing unions, in particular the AEU, in the months after Marshall's Harvard speech, was the economic lifeline and the promise that productionism—in the twin sense of full employment production to maintain unions' strength and increasing produc-

---

[62] See Jonathan Schneer, *Labour's Conscience: The Labour Left 1945–1951*.

[63] A. Carew, *Labour Under the Marshall Plan* (Manchester, Manchester University Press, 1987), 16.

[64] Ibid. 17.

[65] *New Statesman*, 5 July 1947.

tivity to improve the material base of Labour's welfare state—could be sustained.

'Increased production, increased productivity, is the only means by which we can hope to escape economic disaster, and to maintain our living standards,' Tanner told the AEU leadership in 1948, stressing that 'the Government and our movement, must succeed in devising methods of maintaining full employment'.[66] In Tanner's eyes the union's longstanding commitment to production was now linked to the flow of dollars under the Marshall Plan. The conference of European trade unions in March that year had endorsed the European Recovery Programme and the IMF was also in favour. Tanner spelt out the alternative: 'To refuse European Aid in the present situation, would be to condemn our people to an immediate drastic cut in their present living standards, and the prospect of growing unemployment, which must further reduce their standards to an unprecedented low level.'[67] For Tanner, acceptance of Marshall Aid did not automatically mean 'acceptance of a joint anticommunist alliance with the US' as has been asserted.[68] In the same speech, made in June 1948 with the Prague coup and the first confrontations in the Berlin blockade much in the headlines, he repeated his previous belief that 'the inclusion of Russia, as of Germany, in any plan for European development is necessary for its success'.[69]

There was no question of rejecting the Marshall Plan 'except if the terms of such aid prevented our recovery, or robbed us of our independence', Tanner declared.[70] The Marshall Plan delivered the economic part of the deal and even the later historian critics of the Marshall Plan note that in Britain, between 1948 and 1950, 'Full employment was sustained, domestic capital formation increased from £2.1 billion in 1948 to £2.5 billion in 1950, the balance of payments was in comfortable surplus by that year, and industrial production increased by 7–8 per cent each year.'[71]

Tanner and British productionists could hardly ask for more. The

---

[66] AEU NC 1948, 222.

[67] Ibid. 215.

[68] T. Brett, S. Gilliat, and A. Pope, 'Planned Trade, Labour Party Policy and US Intervention: The Successes and Failures of Post-War Reconstruction', in *History Workshop*, 13, (1982), 139.

[69] AEU NC 1948, 218.

[70] Ibid.

[71] Brett *et al.*, 'Planned Trade', 136.

political and economic crisis that followed from the decision of the fading Attlee government to double military expenditure to pursue the Korean war followed upon the political miscalculations of a group of exhausted ministers, thereby producing cabinet resignations, and the subsequent general election threw away the benefits of the Marshall Plan to the electoral profit of the Conservatives. Marshall Aid certainly brought with it an implied obligation to support US policy in its generalized confrontation with communism, of which the North Korean attack seemed an example. But the Labour Cabinet's enthusiastic response with its negative implications for the economic and social advances achieved since 1945 reflected Labour's illusion that Britain was still a global power whose status would be undermined if it failed to discharge what were perceived as far-flung responsibilities alongside the United States. Marshall Aid can be blamed for many things but English self-delusion about Britain's place in the world is not one of them.

Nor, given the productionist ethos of Tanner and most other trade-unionists, can the Marshall Plan be held exclusively responsible for the anticommunism that Tanner embraced by 1949 when he helped to found IRIS—the Industrial Research and Information Service, a small organization which tracked communist activities inside trade-unions. The move was a response to the open hostility of the Communist Party to the Labour government. In the communist view, by the autumn of 1947 Labour had become 'an active partner in the imperialist camp, carrying through a capitalist solution to the crisis'.[72] The Communist Party's general secretary, Harry Pollit, directly challenged trade-union leaders like Tanner and announced 'that the mass of organized workers should refuse to accept class-collaboration leadership and should go into action for their demands'.[73] From 1948 onwards, communist endorsement and encouragement of industrial action validated rank-and-file protests that had been simmering ever since the war—strikes of dockers in 1946, of lorry drivers, bus workers, and miners in 1947, and several small-scale strikes in the engineering industry mainly over the victimization of shop stewards.[74] The wage-restraint

---

[72] Pollit quoted in John Mahon, *Harry Pollit* (London, Lawrence and Wishart, 1976), 325.
[73] Ibid. 326.
[74] Frow, *Engineering Struggles*, 314–20.

policies agreed by the TUC in March 1948 provoked further grumblings and resentment at the base.

The Communist Party, however, called for more than economistic action. Pollit argued that 'the disorganizing role of social democracy, which at every decisive moment throws its weight on the side of the capitalists was insufficient. The main danger now is to underestimate the workers' readiness to fight for their demands.'[75] This return to almost Leninist invocations dating from the founding era of the Communist International was not just a serious misreading of the extent of support for the Labour government amongst organized labour; it was a declaration of political war that would be answered in kind.

Pollit defended the previous communist policy of calling for increased production, but now the Marshall Plan together with 'US imperialism had become the central driving force of world reaction'.[76] The global call to a political and industrial struggle against the Labour government across all fronts meant that the issue of productionism and the dollar-gap problem was lost within an analysis in which every aspect of Labour policy was negative and to be opposed. Had the communists offered a more differentiated assessment, and had they been able to turn away from Moscow's call to spurn Marshall Aid, they might have succeeded in keeping some allies, as well as finding terrain where they would not have been so isolated. The government's lack of policy, for example, for harnessing the productionist energy at the base was one such area. The *New Statesman*, recognizing the complaints of, among others, the AEU, had urged earlier in 1947

a recasting of Trade Unionism that will make the shop stewards and other factory groups the real driving power . . . as members of workshop teams upon whom devolves the responsibility of making a success or failure of the experiment in democracy for which they voted in 1945 . . . In the vast majority of factories this knowledge and power which the workers do possess, is simply not being used . . . Only the harnessing of this power will make the workers feel that the nature of their jobs and of their relation to industry and to the community have really been changed.[77]

If that had been the reason for communists switching their policy to

[75] Mahon, *Harry Pollit*, 325.
[76] Ibid.
[77] *New Statesman*, 15 Feb. 1947.

one of endorsement of workers' involvement in the running of their factories then, perhaps, it might have engaged the support of Tanner the syndicalist and productionist. But by making opposition to the Marshall Plan one of the main justifications for supporting militant rank-and-file activity, the communists lost the support and sympathy of the AEU president, their former friend, and, up to the beginning of 1948, their political ally. Political opposition to the Marshall Plan required a political response, Tanner told the AEU National Committee: 'In a Social Democracy the attacks come not only from without, not only from one quarter but from a number of quarters . . . Anybody who suggests that the workers should hold up production . . . is giving very wrong and very dangerous advice.'[78]

The Marshall Plan, whatever its other intended or unforeseen results, was able to tap the productionist–full employment ethos which lay at the heart of the social vision of metalworkers like Tanner. The productivity propagandists and advocates of depoliticized labour–management harmony who arrived with the Marshall Plan had fertile ground in which to work: ground that had been seeded with ideas of syndicalist productionism, watered with the example of the Soviet Union in the 1930s, fertilized with the full-employment economics of the Labour government after 1945, but whose fruit was threatened when the Communist Party, which had been pro-production between 1941 and 1947, suddenly turned into a malignant, anti-production pest from 1948 onwards.

This switch of line had important implications in the developing Cold War. But the relationship of the Communist Party to the wider trade-union movement and especially to the main metalworkers' union, the AEU, was already deeply problematic, with international relations being a principal area of contention well before the Marshall Plan acted as the catalyst for a final rupture.

[78] AEU NC 1948, 225.

10

British Metalworkers, Communism, and the Soviet Union After 1945

As Britain's principal metalworkers' union, the Amalgamated Engineering Union emerged from the war transformed in many ways. Its membership had risen from 413,000 in 1939 to a wartime peak of over 900,000 before settling down to 704,000 in 1945. It was the second biggest union in the TUC. It ceased being exclusively a craft union and became a general metalworkers' union. The rules were changed to allow women to join, and 139,000 women were enrolled. A new youth section was set up: in 1945 there were 111,000 young workers enrolled. Membership of the semi-skilled and unskilled sections of the AEU went up from 146,000 to 335,000.[1]

These changes in the sociological composition of the union made the AEU quite different from the pre-war union of highly skilled, craft, male workers. Politically, the pre-war AEU was divided into a right-wing majority which dominated the executive and the policy-making National Committee and a minority of activist shop stewards amongst whom were many active communists. By 1945, although never holding a majority of seats, left-wingers and two communists were on the executive, and a solid group of communists was elected to the National Committee. The AEU communists, as Raphael Samuel points out, 'were drawn exclusively from the "Class 1" members, the "time-served" [i.e. apprenticed] men'.[2] How did this elite relate to lesser-skilled AEU members, now one third of the union's strength, who, under the union's constitution, were firmly placed in separate and implicitly inferior membership categories? What was the attitude of women to the leadership style of AEU communist men?[3]

---

[1] James Jefferys, *The Story of the Engineers* (London, Lawrence and Wishart, 1945). I am grateful to Dr Jefferys for additional comments on the AEU in this period.

[2] Raphael Samuel, 'Class Politics: The Lost World of British Communism', in *New Left Review*, 165 (Sept. 1987), 75.

[3] This aspect of the AEU's transformation is discussed thoroughly in Richard

The expansion of young workers brought vitality to the union which was a contested recruiting ground for different political allegiances. But during the war the militancy of young workers chafed against communist insistence on industrial discipline. An important strike by Tyneside engineering apprentices in 1944 was seized upon by Trotskyists who then felt the combined wrath of the Communist Party and Bevin who sought to imprison the Trotskyist leader, Jock Haston.[4] Aneurin Bevan took up the case from a civil-libertarian perspective, and found himself on the edge of being expelled from the Labour Party, while AEU committees in several cities came to the defence of the Trotskyists.[5]

The rise in membership and the desperate need for workers in the war industries had produced a new confidence and aggressiveness. More than a million days were lost in strikes in the engineering industry in 1944.[6] Shop stewards, like their predecessors in the First World War, were back in the saddle. A total of 1,800 shop stewards from 450 factories and shipyards, attended an engineering industry shop-stewards' conference in London in March 1944. But unlike their militant, strike-orientated, production-disrupting brothers of 1917 and 1918, the shop stewards of 1944 boasted of 'increased production . . . due to the working class' and they demanded 'an end to inefficiency and muddle in the factories'.[7] For communist shop stewards, as Richard Croucher has pointed out, their wartime activities were 'anti-fascist *and* anti-managerial'.[8]

Croucher, *Engineers at War 1939–1945*, (London, Merlin Press, 1982). The most important women's pay strike, at a Rolls Royce factory near Glasgow in 1943, was actively supported by the Catholic Workers' Guild and criticized by communists. The number of Irish workers who came to work in Britain during the war and after 1945, and were influenced by the Catholic Church in the direction of anti-Sovietism and anticommunism is a factor to be considered in the development of post–1945 union politics. Terry Duffy (AEU president 1978–86), who was a young AEU activist in the West Midlands after 1945, was a staunch Catholic. In Scotland, the AEU activist, John Boyd (AEU general secretary 1969–80), was a member of the Salvation Army.

[4] See Angus Calder, *The People's War* (London, Granada, 1971), 509–10.
[5] See S. Bornstein and A. Richardson, *War and the International: A History of the Trotskyist Movement in Britain 1937–1949* (London, Socialist Platform, 1986), 116–37. There was a parallel between the language and calls for action by the Communist Party against their Trotskyist rivals ('A Vote for Haston is a vote for Hitler' was one of their kinder slogans) and the later attacks by the Labour Party and the TUC against the communists.
[6] Calder, *People's War*, 456.
[7] Ibid. The most detailed account of shop stewards in the metal industries in the war is to be found in Croucher, *Engineers at War*.
[8] Croucher, *Engineers at War*, 375.

The term 'little Hitler' was coined to describe the bossy foreman or authoritarian manager, but the anti-fascist struggle, or more accurately, the fight to help the Soviet Union's battle against fascism (since the communists had taken little interest in Britain's fight against Nazism between 1939 and 1941), took precedence over anti-employer activity. So along with rank-and-file militancy expressing itself in short, sharp strikes there was a commitment by shop stewards to maintain production to help the war effort.

As with the major metal unions of continental Europe and the United States in the immediate post-war period, the AEU was a union in which political activity was the norm. Its almost *communard* constitution encouraged constant political campaigning. Full-time officials faced election every three years. There was a careful separation of powers between the chief officers. Jack Tanner, the president, was considered to be on the Left, while the general secretary, Ben Gardner, who edited the union journal, was a right-winger. Further democratic checks and balances included a lay appeal court which could overturn executive decisions and a fifty-two-man national committee consisting of elected lay members, not full-time officials, which met annually to lay down policy. This was a tiny annual conference by the standards of other unions but its debates and debaters were of high quality.[9]

The Communist Party in the 1940s has been described as an 'engineers' party', with AEU members accounting for approximately a third of the delegates to Party congresses between 1942 and 1945.[10] But it does not follow that the AEU was a communists' union despite their presence and activism within the union. The exact number and strength of communists inside the AEU in 1945 and the years immediately following is not known. The communist-edited rank-and-file paper, the *New Propellor*, had a circulation of 94,000. A communist, Len Powell, was full-time secretary of the Engineering and Allied Trades' Shop Stewards Council. The Left in the AEU was strong, but it was an extremely heterogeneous Left which sometimes adopted positions that were initiated or supported by the communists but which refused blanket endorsement of all communist demands and was not under communist control.

The AEU National Committee, for example, supported the affiliation of the Communist Party to the Labour Party in 1946 but

[9] See V. Allen, *Power in Trade Unions* (Lonson, Longman, 1960).
[10] Samuel, 'Class Politics', 75.

refused in the same year to buy shares in the communist newspaper, the *Daily Worker*.[11] Two years later the National Committee reaffirmed 'its allegiance to the World Federation of Trade Unions' but refused to put through a motion instructing the 'Executive Council to take steps immediately to use the influence of the AEU to secure the entry of the IMF into the WFTU on the conditions laid down by the WFTU'.[12] The National Committee repeatedly passed resolutions critical of the Labour government's policy on Greece or Spain, but as with much of the Labour Left it welcomed the Marshall Plan.

The simple division into Labour right-wing loyalists and communist or crypto-communist opposition is no longer a satisfactory description of the politics of the time. In Jonathan Schneer's assessment, 'there existed among trade-unionists an identifiable non-communist left-wing tendency which was particularly strong inside the . . . AEU'.[13] Schneer has also argued that 'the Left in the TUC . . . during 1945–51 cannot be understood outside the context of the developing Cold War'.[14] From this perspective the Cold War is something external to the trade-unions which forces its way into their sphere of activities, an inter-governmental conflict, or a new systematic ideological conflict, the 'Great Contest' in Isaac Deutscher's expression,[15] which stamps its divisions on the labour movement. In the context of the British labour movement, as elsewhere, external factors should not be given priority over internal ones. The split between communist and non-communist Left in the British labour movement was intensified by the Cold War but the reason remained the fundamental incompatibility between two concepts of socialism, one ready to accept dictatorship if it was carried out in the name of the Soviet Union, the other more confused but unwilling to forsake civil liberties. This had been glossed over between 1941 and 1945 but resurfaced soon enough after VE day.

[11] AEU NC 1946, 247.

[12] Ibid. 1948, 274.

[13] J. Schneer, *Labour's Conscience: The Labour Left 1945–1951* (London, Unwin, 1987), 134. B. Jones, *The Russia Complex* (Manchester, Manchester University Press, 1977), and Mark Jenkins, *Bevanism, Labour's High Tide* (Nottingham, Spokesman, 1979), are also important discussions of the underestimated importance of non-communist left-wing ideas and organization in this period.

[14] Schneer, *Labour's Conscience*, 135.

[15] Quoted in F. Halliday, *The Making of the Second Cold War* (London, Verso, 1983), 30.

It would help the process of classification if one could describe these two tendencies as revolutionary or reformist, but by 1945 the communists had given up any claims to form a revolutionary party such as they would have considered themselves up to the end of the so-called 'third period' prior to the change to Popular Frontism visible from around 1934 onwards. This was particularly evident in the AEU where communists had risen to positions of influence because they were the champions of productionism and increased output. By 1945, there were over 4,000 Joint Production Committees (JPC) in the engineering industry. The AEU and the communists hailed these, correctly, as a major inroad on managerial authority. The *New Propellor* in August 1945 urged shop stewards to work 'through the JPC machinery to supervise the controller and make full use of workers' initiatives on the job.'[16]

At the same time, the JPCs were a major incorporation of activist shop stewards into responsibilities that were distant from Leninist evocations of class confrontation. As the AEU's official historian noted, 'greater responsibility fell on the shoulders of the workshop representatives and district officials' who found themselves sitting on all manner of joint committees with employer and government representatives.[17]

Thus communist shop stewards had to transform themselves into advocates of incremental progress within an existing if changeable system. This process began on the shop floor, and extended into political analysis with the Communist Party calling in 1945 for a continuation of the wartime coalition government, including Churchill and Eden, but under socialist leadership. This confused at least one old-time communist militant engineering worker, Harry McShane, the Glasgow secretary of the Communist Party in the war: 'Some members saw no point in working inside the Communist Party when the Party was no longer distinguishable from the Labour movement; they might as well be in the trade-unions as officials, or inside the Labour Party.'[18] The election result of 1945 showed that the Communist Party was unlikely ever to make an electoral breakthrough. The Labour Party was the only vehicle for those trade-union activists looking for parliamentary or local-government careers. One could be a communist in the union but

---

16 *New Propellor*, Aug. 1945.
17 Jeffereys, *The Story of the Engineers*, 259.
18 Harry McShane, *No Mean Fighter* (London, Pluto, 1978), 241.

that meant working within the limits of constitutional trade-unionism.

Noreen Branson, the historian of the British Communist Party, writes that 'the workplace had been regarded by the Party as the chief focal point—the place where spreading Party influence was not just possible, but crucial'.[19] She lists three tasks for communist trade-unionists—recruiting members for the union, negotiating with management over factory pay and conditions and then, finally, Communist Party activity—the selling of the *Daily Worker* and attempts 'to recruit people into the Party'.[20] The first two tasks—union building and shop-floor representation—were activities endorsed by the trade-unions, and in themselves satisfying and rewarding to most working-class militants. However the third, Communist Party recruitment, represented an organizational challenge to the Labour Party's position within the unions.

The AEU had launched a campaign during the war to increase the number of members paying the political levy and 'induce all branches of the Union to affiliate to the appropriate local Labour Party'.[21] Despite these efforts the National Committee was told that in 1944 only 11 per cent of AEU members were paying the Labour Party levy.[22] 'The engineering industry', writes Noreen Branson, 'remained an important recruiting ground for the Party'[23] but that was precisely the problem. The more effective the communists were inside workplaces and the unions, the more of a threat they would become to the Labour Party's hegemonic dominance within the working class. The wartime partner could become a potent rival and a challenger on the organizational level. The more successful the communists were, the more likely that Labour would have to find a way of repressing them. The political differences over aspects of domestic and foreign policy, which later within the context of Cold War became marked and virulent, followed on from this fundamental organizational rivalry in which the trade-unions were deeply implicated.

One way of resolving such rivalry, for both unions and the two

[19] I am grateful to Ms Branson for sending me a draft of the first section of her chapter on Communist Party industrial work between 1945 and 1949 which will form part of her next volume of CPGB history. The quotes are taken from that draft.
[20] Ibid.
[21] Jefferys, *The Story of the Engineers*, 251.
[22] Ibid.
[23] Branson, see n. 19.

parties, was to affiliate the Communist Party with the Labour Party, a form of fusion that would allow the Communist Party to maintain an existence as a Marxist grouping within the Labour Party. Calls for mergers or formal alliances became the standard appeal within Europe immediately after the war's end. In France, Italy, Germany, Denmark, Norway, and Sweden communist parties sought mergers with their socialist rivals. This was a significant extension of Popular Front politics. In Britain after 1935 there had been several futile attempts by communists to form common fronts with other left-wing parties, especially the Labour Party, and other antifascist forces. The call for affiliation which arose after 1945 was a new development, and required a distinct response from the Labour Party in Britain and socialist parties on the Continent.[24] By the end of 1945, socialists in most European countries had rejected such mergers. *Labour Monthly* itself attacked the Labour Party's role in arguing against such mergers, and complained about the activities of the party chairman Harold Laski, and general secretary Morgan Phillips, at the French, Danish, and Norwegian Socialist or Labour Party congresses in the autumn of 1945.[25]

Despite the evidence that such mergers were unacceptable to their social democratic or Labour *confrères* on the Continent, the Communist Party in Britain persisted in formally applying for affiliation to the Labour Party in January 1946. The affiliation call was endorsed by the AEU's National Committee. At the 1945 Labour Party conference, Tanner had called for co-operation between the two parties in the general election. Support for 'co-operation' was narrowly defeated by 1,314,000 to 1,219,000 votes.[26] Instead of treating this vote for limited co-operation in an election campaign as the high-water mark of Labour enthusiasm for unity with communism, the Communist Party leadership saw it as the opening wide of a door to full entry into the Labour Party. This was a mistake, because whatever logic lay behind the affiliation request, the move reopened many of the pre-June 1941 fissures between Labour and the communists.

The campaign for rejection of communist affiliation, although supported by the government was also backed by left-wingers in the

---

[24] See Paolo Spriano, *Stalin and the European Communists*, (London, Verso, 1985), 261–9.
[25] *Labour Monthly*, Sept. 1945.
[26] Labour Party Conference Report (henceforth LPCR) 1945, 182.

Party, such as Michael Foot, and especially Harold Laski, the left-wing Labour chairman. The application was overwhelmingly defeated and the rejection of communist affiliation was supported by rank-and-file Labour Party members in both the constituencies and the unions. The 1946 campaign over Communist Party affiliation receives only cursory treatment in most histories of the period. Kenneth Morgan gives the issue one erroneous line in his magisterial account of the 1945–51 Labour governments.[27] Perhaps because the defeat was so overwhelming, and the Communist Party's electoral strength in comparison to that of Labour so meagre, historians have tended to relegate the issue to the status of a passing mention. Yet in many ways the campaign in the first five months of 1946 is an important part of the prehistory of the Cold War. It forced every constituent voting body in the Labour Party and its affiliated trade-unions to take a simple 'yes' or 'no' decision on the communist question, and implicitly on the Soviet Union.

At the beginning of 1946, the Labour Party and the unions were being bombarded with anticommunist arguments, and material that would have done justice to the early 1930s, or to the propaganda of the Cold War a short while later. And when the affiliation issue was settled the communist leadership openly turned from co-operation with the Labour Party to seeking increased influence in the unions. Every gun the Labour Party had to fire was called into action against the affiliation proposal. In January 1946, the Labour Party NEC rejected affiliation 'from another political party which has a separate philosophy, programme, leadership and organization' and followed this with a statement in March 1946: 'It is clear that the temporary Communist talk of working-class unity is merely a clumsy camouflage for their real aim of breaking up the Labour Movement so as to increase their own chances of establishing a party dictatorship.'[28]

Speakers' notes were distributed widely inside the Labour Party to argue the case against affiliation. Harold Laski, the left-wing *bête noire* of the Labour Party, weighed in with a pamphlet entitled *The Secret Battalion*. This accused communists of seeking to 'penetrate and . . . to control all working class organizations, the trade-unions,

---

[27] Morgan, *Labour in Power 1945–1951* (Oxford, OUP, 1984), 77. Morgan writes that Tanner 'led the opposition to the affiliation of the Communists in 1946' but the opposite was the case.

[28] Labour NEC statements in LPCR 1946.

the Labour Party [in order to] break the hold of their social democratic leaders upon the rank and file'.[29] Laski went further. Evidence about communist techniques had been 'built upon the experience of Russia, and the habits of states, especially the Nazi and Fascist states', he wrote.[30] Although he peppered his pamphlet with praise for Soviet heroism in the Second World War, Laski's linking of Soviet communism with Nazism and fascism as political systems committed to the 'suppression of freedom' re-established the terms of anticommunist, anti-Soviet discourse as an integral part of Labour Party public statements from the beginning of 1946.

In a crudely sardonic pamphlet that was nominally published by a London constituency Labour Party, though it was written anonymously by the TUC official, Vic Feather, who lived in the constituency, those who stayed in the Communist Party had to be 'capable of stifling their own thoughts in a bale of dogma [and had to] develop a sheep-like adherence to the Party "line" shaped by the Executive Committee'.[31] The cartoons showed comfortable university teachers, upper-class women selling the *Daily Worker*, and a chain-smoking Claud Cockburn (Frank Pitcairn) as typical communists. 'If Labour were to accept the affiliation of the Communist Party, would Labour be strengthened?' asked the pamphlet's author. 'On the contrary . . . Because the Labour Party wants unity, it must keep the Communists excluded. Because the Labour Party wants a strong Labour Government to build up Socialism in Britain, the Communists must be kept out.'[32]

Labour's campaign extended to the unions. Morgan Phillips, the Labour Party secretary, denounced 'Communist Intrigue', and insisted that 'the working people of this country distrust the Communist Party' whose 'well-organized minorities attempt to dominate trade-union branches and thereby to achieve some measure of control over the general policy of the Trade Union Movement and the Labour Party'.[33] Phillips called upon Labour Party members in the unions to do 'their utmost to combat Communist Party manœuvrings and intrigue'.[34] Prior to the

---

[29] Harold Laski, *The Secret Battalion*, (London, Labour Party, 1946), 9.
[30] Ibid. 10.
[31] *Communist Circus* (Labour Party, 1946), 13.
[32] Ibid.
[33] *Man and Metal* (Journal of the Iron and Steel Trades' Confederation, ISTC), May 1946.
[34] Ibid.

Labour Party conference only one branch of the iron and steelworkers' union urged the union's executive to support communist affiliation to the Labour Party. The executive rejected the call.[35]

The lack of support for Communist Party affiliation was even more marked at the Labour Party conference held in June 1946 in Bournemouth. It was the first conference after Labour's victory. The motion calling for Communist Party affiliation to the Labour Party was debated immediately after the foreign affairs debate, placed at that point in the agenda by skilful managers of conference business. Bevin's reply to the many criticisms of his foreign policies was overwhelmingly successful, producing a standing ovation at the end of his speech. The motions opposing his policy were withdrawn or defeated on a show of hands.[36]

In this atmosphere, Herbert Morrison moved rejection of the Communist Party's bid for affiliation. It was a lengthy exposition of classic Labour Party hostility to the Communist Party. The communists, said Morrison, believed 'neither in constitutional government nor in Parliamentary democracy [nor] in the principles of civil liberty'.[37] The Communist Party was 'a conspiracy' issuing 'secret instructions to members and to "fellow-travellers"'.[38] Morrison scorned as 'defeatism' Pollit's call in 1945 for a continuation of the national government. Although Morrison never referred to the Soviet Union in his speech he accused the Communists of 'seeking . . . steadily to subordinate British interests to external interests', and 'of espionage against the security of this country'.[39] Turning his attention to the engineers, Morrison taunted the AEU with not having had a 'ballot', or a more recent 'democratic decision' on the issue of Communist Party affiliation, pointing out that unions in which communist influence was also marked, such as those of the electricians and the miners, had decided to support the Labour leadership's rejection of affiliation.[40]

When Jack Tanner, the AEU president, rose to move the affiliation motion, he did so against the clear mood of the conference and, consequently, spent the first third of his speech

---

[35] ISTC Executive Council Minutes, Mar. 1946.

[36] A. Bullock, *Ernest Bevin: Foreign Secretary* (London, Heinemann, 1983), 278–9; LPCR 1946, 169.

[37] LPCR 1946, 169.

[38] Ibid.   [39] Ibid. 170.   [40] Ibid. 172.

defending the AEU's democracy, and right to move such a motion. His main positive argument in favour of Communist Party affiliation was that this would engage the 'enthusiasm' of 'the very large proportion of the leading shop stewards in the engineering industry [who] are Communists' in securing 'increased production'.[41]

After making that argument, Tanner veered off into a rambling defence of communist relations with Russia, his own ups and downs with the Communist Party, and a suggestion that 'some form of dictatorship' would have to be imposed on employers who refused 'to carry out decisions made by the government'.[42] His speech ended with an admission that the vote would go against him, and a final appeal from the man who had begged Lenin and Zinoviev not to create a rival trade-union international or encourage splits in existing unions: 'The question of unity of the working-class is still going to be a very urgent one indeed, and until we can achieve that unity, and until we can reach some compromise, then Socialism is going to be longer out of our grasp than it would be if we could only achieve that unity.'[43]

Tanner had made the best case possible. Since 1920, he had been an advocate of joint work with communists, and had been their close ally in the Minority Movement and in the Popular Front politics of the 1930s and wartime. He refused as a trade-unionist to separate communist chaff from Labour wheat. But the core of his argument was the need to embrace communist shop stewards to increase production. Tanner at least, as president of the second biggest union in the country, was heard in respectful silence. But his seconder from the fire brigades' union could not even get well into his speech before that ultimate humiliation for a Labour Party conference speaker took place: calls for a vote were made from the floor and the chairman cut off the speaker to move to the vote. The Communist Party bid for affiliation was defeated by 2,678,000 to 468,000 with only the engineers and railwayworkers amongst the major unions voting in favour.[44]

The rejection of the Communist Party bid for affiliation in June 1946 was a decisive turning-point in the internal relations of different currents inside the labour movement. Reinforced by the overwhelming majority at the Bournemouth conference the Labour

[41] Ibid.
[43] Ibid.
[42] Ibid.
[44] Ibid. 173.

Party moved more openly on to the offensive against the British communists. Attlee openly denounced them at the TUC Congress in October. On the whole, a division, at least in public, was made between communists on one hand and the Soviet Union on the other. Stalin's name was rarely mentioned. But like Banquo, he was present at the feast of anticommunism that was taking shape.

Stung by their rejection, the Communist Party reverted to traditional insults. 'The smug self-satisfied complacency of the Labour Party leader will be shattered sooner than is yet realised,' proclaimed Harry Pollit after the Bournemouth conference.[45] The Communist Party's theoretician, Palme Dutt, invited readers to consider the 'irony that at the very moment when Social Democracy is going down in discredit in Europe, its tattered record of bankruptcy is being held up as a new gospel of wisdom here'.[46]

Although Pollit was angry with Attlee's 'vicious attack upon the Communist Parties of every country in Europe' made at the TUC Congress in October 1946, he nevertheless contrasted the 'illusionary atmosphere' at the Bournemouth Labour Party conference to the 'sober and serious' TUC.[47] This turn from seeking co-operation with Labour to building up support through activities in the trade-unions was congenial to a boilermaker with a solid trade-union background like Pollit, all the more so as he could rely on the support of well-implanted communists in major TUC-affiliated unions.

Yet any hopes he might have had of finding support in the trade-unions where none existed in the Labour Party were soon dashed. They were in fact completely unrealistic. Trying to play the TUC against the Labour government was unlikely to work given that it would be seen as a communist tactic to damage the Labour Party which had so soundly rejected its bid for affiliation. By the autumn of 1946, the communists in Britain had put down their only effective card, a merger with Labour on their terms based on their war-created growth in numbers and prestige. The card was not picked up, indeed it was vigorously spurned. The language used thereafter, as indeed the terms in which Labour had campaigned against the affiliation in the first six months of 1946, suggests that the two parties of the Left were still at odds, not so virulently, but

[45] *Labour Monthly*, July 1946.
[46] Ibid. Dec. 1946.
[47] Ibid.

no less determinedly, as in the 1920s and 1930s. Here then is one major reason why the events of 1947 such as the Marshall Plan or the founding of Cominform worked to create the Cold War atmosphere inside the unions as quickly as they did. They merely opened further a door which was already well ajar.

In June 1946, a fortnight after his Bournemouth defeat over Communist Party affiliation, Tanner spoke to the AEU National Committee and stressed: 'Never was it more vital to reiterate and fight for our policy of solidarity with the Soviet Union. It is at once a bread-and-butter issue and a question of life and death. Without it the future prospect is black indeed.'[48] Yet why exactly was it that this close relationship with Russia was so desperately needed? According to Tanner, 'Britain needs exports, yet trade with the Soviet Union and the rising democracies of South-East Europe is at a standstill. It is in the interests of Britain as a whole, and of engineering workers in particular, to develop long-term stable markets for engineering products. The Soviet Union offers such a market on a vast scale.'[49] To reduce twenty-five years of urging solidarity with the Soviet Union, the purveyor of anticapitalist revolution, to the banal exigencies of an export drive was not Tanner's purpose but it was the strongest argument he could muster. Because well before the Labour Party conference in 1946, the lustre of Stalin's Russia was wearing thin in the labour movement.

Take, for example, *Tribune*, which 'was required reading for left-of-center Labour Party activists', and which together with the *New Statesman* 'enjoyed a virtual monopoly in the distribution of opinion in the [Labour] party on foreign affairs.'[50] In many respects, *Tribune* was sharply critical of the Attlee government, especially on foreign issues. 'Bevin was frequently condemned,' observes Kenneth Morgan.[51]

But a reading of *Tribune* for the first twelve months after the war's end produces a considerable amount of material on Central and East Europe, and on the activities of communists in Germany and France. Nearly all the writing is critical, even hostile. People

---

[48] AEU NC 1946, 209.
[49] Ibid.
[50] Schneer, *Labour's Conscience*, 32; Morgan, *Labour in Power*, 238.
[51] Ibid.

were 'living in a dreamworld about conditions in Eastern Europe', noted *Tribune* on 20 July 1945.[52] On 10 August 1945 the paper gave up a whole page to three maps of Europe—a rare sacrifice of space in print-rationed, word-hungry days. The first showed the French *cordon sanitaire* against the Soviet Union in the 1920s, the second showed German expansion the following decade, and the last—by far the biggest and most detailed—was headed 'Domination from the East: The Advance of the USSR into Central Europe.'[53] Words were not needed to make the historical comparison. The next week *Tribune* published a letter from a Pole who wrote: 'The position of the Polish Left is that of Austrian socialists . . . who refuse to bow to the idol of Moscow.'[54] The paper defended closer co-operation between Western governments:

We make no apology for advocating as socialists, the closest possible political and economic co-operation between progressive democratic governments of Western Europe . . . If the Soviet commentators cannot see in this co-operation any purpose but the forming of a *glacis* of Anglo-American anti-Soviet policies, let them brush up on their Marxist economics and study the economic position of Europe on the morrow of the termination of the Lend-Lease agreement.[55]

Tribune even managed to play Cassandra amidst the jubilation over the founding of the WFTU 'whose constitution', the paper warned, 'is framed with more regard to joint political demonstrations than to detailed work on an international scale'.[56] Commenting on the rise of communist parties in Europe *Tribune* wrote on 12 October 1945, 'The Communists have remained fundamentally dictatorial and "Russian" . . . The chief task of the Communist in West Europe is to prevent any development regarded as undesirable by the Soviet Union.'[57] *Tribune*'s columns were open to anti-Soviet writers like Arthur Koestler and George Orwell, who wrote in the autumn of 1945:

We are told *now* that any frank criticism of the Stalin régime will 'increase Russian suspicions', but it is only seven years since we were being told (in some cases by the same newspapers) that frank criticism of the Nazi régime would increase Hitler's suspicions . . . The first step towards decent Anglo-Russian relations is the dropping of illusions. In principle most people

---

[52] *Tribune*, 20 July 1945.
[54] *Tribune*, 24 Aug. 1945.
[56] *Tribune*, 14 Sept. 1945.

[53] *Tribune*, 10 Aug. 1945.
[55] *Tribune*, 7 Sept. 1945.
[57] *Tribune*, 12 Oct. 1945.

would agree to this: but the dropping of illusions means the publication of facts, and facts are apt to be unpleasant.[58]

In 1946, *Tribune* kept up its criticisms of Soviet and communist action in Eastern Europe. The paper accused the 'Communist-directed Security Corps in Poland' of murdering their political opponents.[59] Michael Foot accused the Russians of interference and intimidation in Bulgarian, Polish, and Yugoslavian politics while in East Germany, he added, 'by a mixture of intimidation, terror, censored propaganda and despicable tricks the Communists have achieved control of all life in the Russian zone'.[60]

A report from Berlin by the German-speaking Labour MP, Patrick Gordon Walker, supported Foot's charge. Gordon Walker claimed that Berlin's police—'entirely under Communist control'—were harassing social democrats in their homes.[61] The plight of social-democratic parties in Soviet-occupied Europe continued to be a running feature in *Tribune*'s pages, and to a lesser extent in those of the *New Statesman*, during the years between the war's end and the final sundering of Europe around the time of the Berlin blockade. On 7 June 1946, *Tribune* called for greater help for European democratic socialist parties.

The future of Britain as a Socialist State and the future of democratic socialist parties in Europe are interdependent. Labour's victory last year sounded the reprieve for many parties which seemed faced with the alternative of surrender to American economic imperialism or to Russian totalitarianism [and to] a Communist Party growing in strength and irrevocably tied to Russia.[62]

The significance of this steady, almost weekly, drip of anti-Soviet news and comments in the first twelve months after the war's end lay in the fact that of all the left-wing journals, *Tribune* was the one most widely read by trade-unionists. Its influence, Bill Jones has written, was considerable amongst 'working class socialists'.[63] Those amongst them who placed hope, if not faith, in continuing the positive, friendly wartime relations with the Soviet Union perhaps could discount *Tribune*'s hostility to the Soviet Union and communism as mere journalism, but there was other evidence that beneath the grandiose declarations of friendship at the WFTU

[58] *Tribune*, 16 Nov. 1945.
[60] Ibid.
[62] *Tribune*, 7 June 1946.

[59] *Tribune*, 1 Feb. 1946.
[61] *Tribune*, 5 Apr. 1946.
[63] Jones, *The Russia Complex*, p. ix.

conference in Paris, difficult problems confronted those who saw trade-unions as being a bridge between East and West.

UNFRATERNAL DELEGATIONS?

Even the small change of international trade-unionism—the exchange of fraternal delegations—presented problems for the British metal unions. On his visits to Britain during the war, Kusnetsov, the secretary of the Russian trade-union confederation, had urged the AEU to send a delegation to the Soviet Union. Tanner, who avoided meeting the Russian on his visit to Britain in 1944, did not respond. This led an irritated Kusnetsov, in November 1944, to complain publicly in Moscow about the AEU leader 'not replying to our letters', adding that Tanner 'would be well advised to alter his position'. Kusnetsov's remarks were published in the Russian trade-union paper, *Trud*, and he went on to mock the British trade-union leader: 'When our delegation visited the Metro-Vickers work in Manchester, union activists asked us when they could begin to exchange delegations. They ought to put the question to Tanner as well.'[64]

Tanner's reticence over an AEU visit to the Soviet Union can be interpreted in more than one way. Either it is evidence that already before the war's end he was aloof, perhaps even hostile, to the Soviet Union. This in contrast to all his public statements of admiration for Russia, and his embrace of the creation of the WFTU and the need for co-operation with Russian trade-unions. Or he was shrewd enough to realize, based on his experiences in the 1920s of dealing with the Russians, that reasonable relations with the Soviet trade-unions were best maintained through a prudent guarding of distance. To send a politically mixed delegation of no-nonsense AEU members to report on all they saw in the Soviet Union might not turn out in quite the way that Kusnetsov desired.

One important British union delegation did leave for Russia in the summer of 1945. It was from the Iron and Steel Trades' Confederation (ISTC), the first visit by industrial unionists as opposed to TUC representatives, since the war's outbreak. The report of the ISTC visit was printed as a pamphlet, and widely

---

[64] *Trud*, 30 Nov. 1944 (IMFA). *Trud*'s report on Tanner's refusal to reply to Kusnetsov's invitation was translated into German for Ilg.

circulated. Today it makes anodyne reading. Much of it was technical, a description of steel-making in the Soviet Union, a diary of all the steel plants visited, and constant emphasis on the terrible destruction wrought by the Germans.

The ISTC report paid tribute to the Russians as 'a kindly, tolerant and friendly people'.[65] The delegation poked its nose here and there, observing with interest the safety standards which appeared higher than in an equivalent British plant. The food in works canteens, it was noted, 'lacked variety' none the less 'the workers seemed to be healthy and adequately fed'.[66] The British steelworkers, while warning that 'Russia is such a land of contrasts and contradictions that a visitor can come back with any impression he likes and most suited to any previously conceived notions he may have had,'[67] had plenty of admonitions about aspects of Russian industrial life and union organization that they felt uneasy about.

They were unhappy with the Stakhanovite movement. 'This is a system which creates a privileged class at the expense of those not able to reach the output levels of their stronger and quicker-witted fellow workers.'[68] They were not sure about the trade-unions. 'It was plain that the union officials were as much concerned about increasing production as the management', and they noted that in one plant the office of the works' union chairman was of

second importance only, in size and in the quality of its furnishings, to that of the Managing Director's [sic]. Whether this is a sign of the union's authority, or a sign that the trade-union official is simply part of the managerial set-up, is a question that could only be answered by someone with more time to examine it than we had.[69]

'There is no question of striking', noted the report, 'because this is illegal,' while 'a few less slogans about the virtues of Stalin would not do Russia any harm'.[70] The delegation recorded the view that the Russian people 'ardently want peace, and are looking to the British people to help them secure it'.[71] At the same time the Russians were

sensitive to criticism . . . because they have been told for so long that they

[65] ISTC Report of visit to Soviet Union, Oct. 1945. (ISTC).
[66] Ibid.   [67] Ibid.
[68] Ibid.   [69] Ibid.
[70] Ibid.   [71] Ibid.

are the most socially advanced country in the world and that in the outside capitalist countries the workers are a poor exploited downtrodden mass . . . This complete ignorance of the conditions existing in other countries is to some extent being dispelled, particularly amongst those who during the war have had opportunity to travel outside Russia. But it will take a very long time to do it, unless the rigid censorship existing in Russia is relaxed and the people who have visited other countries are allowed to freely and publicly draw comparisons without exposing themselves and inviting the displeasure of the authorities with all the serious risks such a step would entail.[72]

These extracts highlight criticisms or reserves in what, taken overall, was a positive report by British trade-unionists who repeatedly stressed their desire for friendly relations with their opposite numbers in Russia. It is not a report that could or would have been written three years later once the Cold War had broken out when the ISTC was in the vanguard of anticommunist unions. But the delegation's refusal to shut their eyes to issues that struck them as trade-unionists—the ban on strikes, the Stakhanovism, the identification of union with management—made the ISTC report fascinating reading to other trade-unionists. Ilg of the IMF, for example, had it translated into German. It was the first thorough insight into Russian trade-unionism once the wartime obligations of uncritical support for the Soviet Union had been lifted.

Writing of those who came to admire Soviet industrial development in the previous decade, Freda Utley, who lived in Russia in the 1930s, remarked on their lack of knowledge about industrial life: 'Communists and fellow-travellers, many of whom had never seen the inside of a factory or power station, journalists and authors, school teachers and "intellectuals" of all kinds, came on conducted tours of the Soviet Union and worshipped at the shrine of the machine.'[73] The importance of the British steelworkers' report was that it was cast in a very different mould. This was not just because of the intimate knowledge of steel and iron production that all the British delegates enjoyed but because they were experienced trade-unionists who enjoyed explaining to Russian steelworkers how many weeks' or days' wages an equivalent British steelworker would need to buy a coat, or a pair of shoes. Such discussions, such comparisons, however friendly or amicable, were not to the

[72] ISTC Report of visit to Soviet Union, Oct. 1945. (ISTC).
[73] Freda Utley, *Lost Illusion* (London, Allen and Unwin, 1949), 164.

advantage of the Soviet Union. They were far removed from the high politics of WFTU debates, or the great speeches of Anglo-Soviet trade-union friendship in the Albert Hall or the Hall of Columns in Moscow. But if more and more delegations came from British trade-unions then more and more issues such as those raised by the ISTC delegation would arise. Yet membership of the WFTU brought with it friendly relations and implied reasonable access for union delegations from Britain and other Western countries.

The publication of the ISTC report in December 1945 was received very badly in the Soviet Union. The Russian trade-unions attacked the 'prejudiced report . . . which distorts the true state of affairs in the USSR'.[74] In Moscow, the *New Times* published two long letters from Russian steelworkers attacking the delegation's report.[75] Radio Moscow broadcast a statement from Ernest Thornton, the general secretary of the Australian Federated Ironworkers' Association: 'When I read the false judgements of the members of the British Metalworkers' delegation, I cannot but feel grief at such lack of honesty.'[76] Thornton, a communist, had also made a trip to the Soviet Union but his report, which stressed 'the heroism of these men whom I met in the USSR', was couched in acceptable terms.[77]

The return visit by Russian steelworkers as guests of the ISTC did nothing to dispel the tensions created by the British trip to the USSR. The ISTC invited the Russians to come in the spring of 1946 but the Soviet delegation did not arrive until June the following year. The ISTC extended every courtesy. The Russians were taken to see Karl Marx's grave, Windsor Castle, and the East Ham Co-op.

What the Russians wanted was a mass meeting to 'convey greetings from the workers of the USSR and their thanks for the British workers for the contributions they had made to the rebuilding of Stalingrad'.[78] Three or four years previously, Russian trade-union delegations bearing such messages had been enthusiastically greeted by thousands of workers. In the summer of 1947, the

[74] Radio Moscow, 2 Jan. 1946.
[75] Bělina to Ilg, 22 Jan. 1946.
[76] Ibid.
[77] See Robert Murray and Kate White, *The Ironworkers: A History of the Federated Ironworkers' Association of Australia* (Sydney, Hale and Iremonger, 1982), 156.
[78] Report of the visit of the USSR Delegation (ISTC, 1947).

ISTC organized a meeting in Ebbw Vale, a centre of left-wing trade-unionism. Only sixteen people turned up to hear the Russians. It was, noted the ISTC official responsible for the arrangements, 'an absolute flop'.[79]

The host union tried to make amends with a better organized and publicized meeting the following week in Middlesborough which produced a turnout of 150. Long gone were the days when 5,000 enthusiasts filled the Albert Hall to greet a Russian trade-union delegation with shouts of 'Long live Stalin!', when the Red Flag flew over factories producing tanks for Russia, and 64,000 people came to Wembley Stadium to hail the Red Army. Sixteen in Ebbw Vale, 150 in Middlesborough: twenty-four months after the war's end, and before the Cold War's shadow had time to lengthen such miserable turnouts indicated the lack of interest or enthusiasm amongst rank-and-file steelworkers for the Russian trade unions.

On their return to the Soviet Union, the Russians criticized their British hosts. The ISTC executive was told 'the attacks by the Confederation' do not 'augur well for the success of any future delegations from the Russian trade-unions or for the promotion of good feeling between the workers in the two countries'.[80]

[79] Report of the visit of the USSR Delegation (ISTC, 1947).
[80] Ibid.

11

The Politics of German Unions After the End of Nazism

TRADE unions were seen as an essential part of a democratic Germany once the war ended. The Atlantic Charter laid down as one of the war aims 'the object of securing, for all, improved labour standards, economic advancement and social security'.[1] On 10 June 1945, the Soviet High Command in Germany issued its second general order which called for the setting up of 'free trade-unions'.[2] Britain's Field Marshal Montgomery also addressed himself to the German people. 'You may have Trade Unions', he wrote in a draft of a personal proclamation on 15 July 1945.[3]

The generals might ordain but it was military officers and civilian functionaries who were responsible for seeing the orders carried out. The British sent 25,000 civilians, the last great outpouring of proconsular staff in Britain's history, to help restore and rebuild Germany in a way that corresponded to the decisions of Tehran, Yalta, and Potsdam. The Americans sent fewer—7,000 civilian

---

[1] For the full text of the Atlantic Charter see Hugh Thomas, *Armed Truce: The Beginnings of the Cold War 1945–1946* (London, Hamish Hamilton, 1986), 556. Other documents setting out the Allied policy, objectives, and interventions on the trade-union question in Germany are to be found in Herman Weber and Siegfried Mielke (eds.), *Quellen zur Geschichte der deutschen Gewerkschaftsbewegung im 20. Jahrhundert vi. Organisatorischer Aufbau der Gewerkschaften 1945–1949* (Cologne, Bund Verlag, 1987), 123–81, 997–1035.

[2] Order No. 2 of the Soviet Military Administration in Germany, 16 June 1945, in *Dokumente und Materialen zur Geschichte der Deutschen Arbeiterbewegung* (henceforth DMDA) edited by the Institute for Marxism-Leninism of the Central Committee of the Socialist Unity Party of Germany, i. *May 1945—Apr. 1946* (Berlin, Dietz, 1959), 12. The use of the adjective 'free' when applied in German labour-movement terminology dates back to the 19th c. and was used to distinguish socialist unions from Christian unions. See Helga Grebing, *Geschichte der deutschen Arbeiterbewegung* (Munich, Nymphenburger Verlagshandlung, 1966), 103. After the founding of the International Confederation of Free Trade Unions in 1949, the adjective, especially in English and French, was used to identify non-communist unions. See Barbara Barnouin, *The European Labour Movement and European Integration* (London, Pinter, 1986), 19.

[3] Montgomery is quoted in Nigel Hamilton, *Monty: The Field Marshal 1944–1976* (London, Hamish Hamilton, 1986), 570.

advisers in all—but they too enjoyed advising, decreeing, or consenting to plans for reshaping Germany. Indeed many of the accounts written in English of this period in German history are by British or American participants who recorded their experiences. The British historian, Hugh Thomas, in his section on Germany, which is the hinge of his book, *Armed Truce: The Beginnings of the Cold War 1945–1946*, has written a detailed account without citing one source or book in German, so copious are the archives, memoirs, and histories available in English.[4] American historians who have written on US involvement in the post-war German unions have also produced analyses without using German sources.[5]

The politics of the German labour movement in the period immediately following the war's end are worth examining from the point of view of German workers and trade-unionists seeking to establish their rights and develop their role after the collapse of Nazism. This approach is not to discount the central importance of the decisions and interventions of the Allies, nor to plead that reference to German sources makes for better history. The German side of the development of the German labour movement between 1945 and 1948 has not been much told in English.[6] The division of Germany was always the most obvious expression of the Cold War in Europe and as Fritz Stern has written, 'For over a century, "the German Question", in all of its guises, has had a decisive bearing on the history of the world.'[7] The German labour movement played a part in this and illuminates the origins of the Cold War.

[4] Thomas, *Armed Truce*, 323–51. I am not suggesting that Lord Thomas, a gifted Europeanist, avoids German-language sources, but English-language archives and personal accounts are so numerous that it is possible to write an interesting and scholarly account of post-war Germany without reading anything in the German.

[5] R. Radosh, *American Labor and United States Foreign Policy* (New York, Random House, 1969), is one example. Carolyn Eisenberg also wrote her oft-cited 'Working Class Politics and the Cold War: American Intervention in the German Labor Movement, 1945–1949', *Diplomatic History*, 7 (Autumn 1983) quoting only from English-language texts.

[6] There are two important exceptions. One is William Graf whose *The German Left Since 1945* (London, Oleander Press, 1976) has been followed by contributions on the problems of the post-war German Left in his articles in the *Socialist Register* and elsewhere. In many ways the former German Democratic Republic is better served for English readers through the works of Martin McCauley, *Marxism-Leninism in the German Democratic Republic: The Socialist Unity Party* (London, Macmillan, 1979), and *The German Democratic Republic Since 1945* (London, Macmillan, 1983).

[7] Fritz Stern, *Dreams and Delusions: The Drama of German History* (London, Weidenfeld, 1988), 4.

To give the initial legitimation to trade-unions led to many more issues, each of them increasingly complicated. What kind of trade-union organization—centralized, or based on industrial, regional, political, religious, or craft unions? Each of the Allies had functioning models in their own countries of all these forms of trade-union organization. Who would run the new unions? Pre–1933 trade-unionists? Those who had been in exile? Or those who had proved their commitment through illegal activity or imprisonment under the Nazi régime? Would social democrats and communists sink their pre–1933 differences? Could the unions be independent of political parties not just in a formal organizational sense but in terms of political orientations and overall policy demands? What demands would they adopt and how should the Allies react to them?

Should the reborn German unions adopt collective bargaining in the American sense of leaving the running of industry to its owners and managers, or would they seek wide-scale public ownership as seemed to be the pattern in Britain, or might they pick up the thread of codetermination which had been developed under the Weimar Republic? Could they organize beyond towns or defined regions and, above all, could workers from the different occupation zones meet and develop policy or choose leaders? What relations would be permitted with unions in other countries or with the World Federation of Trade Unions or the international trade secretariats such as the International Metalworkers' Federation? Answers to these questions represented an arena of political division between German trade-unionists and a source of potential conflict with the Allied military administrations.

Many German and non-German historians of this period have tended to place the main responsibility for key decisions in the hands of the Allies. That view was first put forward in the late 1940s by Matthew Kelly who wrote, 'The labor movement in Germany today is . . . to a considerable degree the product of the expressed or implied policy of the Allies.'[8] This continues to be the dominant line expressed by later historians.[9] The theory of Allied responsibility is the common assumption shared by both historians

---

[8] Matthew Kelly, 'The Reconstruction of the German Trade Union Movement', in *Political Science Quarterly*, 64 (March, 1949), 29.
[9] See Michael Fichter, *Besatzungsmacht und Gewerkschaften*, (Opladen, Westdeutscher Verlag, 1982), 274.

who regard the role of the Western Allies as broadly positive[10] and those for whom the main aim of the Allied, especially American activities in the labour field was 'to restore capitalism in postwar Germany' and 'inhibit indigenous social radicalism'.[11]

The view that British trade-union leaders were central in determining the post-war shape of German unions is put forward by Gary Busch: he emphasizes a visit in November 1945 by TUC leaders who 'suggested the creation . . . of a single united national centre including both social democratic and christian union and made up of thirteen nationwide industrial unions'.[12] Carolyn Eisenberg goes further. Arguing mainly from American diplomatic sources she concludes that 'US officials undertook a far-reaching campaign to gain control of German labor', and that the 'American government' sought 'to determine the leadership, structure and program of the German working class organization'.[13]

Of course under the Yalta and Potsdam agreements the American, Soviet, British, and French military authorities had almost unlimited power in their respective zones, and as Stalin remarked, 'whoever occupies a territory also imposes on it his own social system'.[14] But the developments concerning German trade-unions owed far more to specifically *German* labour-movement practice and theory and, above all, to differences between social democrats and communists arising from German traditions and recent history. Germany was the key to Europe. Its economic might, its military power, its political and theoretical analyses had dominated continental Europe since the middle of the nineteenth century. After the First World War, Keynes wrote: 'On the prosperity and enterprise of Germany the prosperity of the Continent mainly depends',[15] and his observation was no less true after 1945. The twelve years of Hitlerism and the destruction of the war gave the impression that this old Germany had vanished, leaving a *tabula rasa* upon which the victors could inscribe any design they wished.

---

[10] See e.g. Michael Balfour and John Mair, *Four Power Control in Germany 1945–1946* (Oxford, Clarendon Press, 1956), 240 ff.

[11] Eisenberg, 'Working Class Politics', 283.

[12] G. Busch, *The Political Role of International Trade Unions* (London, Macmillan, 1983), 52.

[13] Eisenberg, 'Working Class Politics', 284.

[14] M. Djilas, *Conversations with Stalin* (London, Davies, 1962), 105.

[15] J. M. Keynes, *The Economic Consequences of Peace* (London, Macmillan, 1919), 14.

Yet any close examination of the first two years of trade-union activity in Germany after 1945 shows that, from the labour movement's perspective, far from German history being made afresh, themes that dominated labour-movement debate in the Weimar period were especially those that aroused most passions after 1945.

During the Nazi period the organizations had been suppressed but the traditions, ideas, and many of the personnel remained alive. For German labour the twelve years of Nazism had been more like a terrible storm that uproots and destroys but it is possible to seek shelter (even, horribly paradoxical as it may seem, in the very heart of the storm—in the Third Reich by being imprisoned), or to bend before the wind, waiting for more clement times. As Gordon Craig insists, 'hatred of the régime never faltered' amongst the German working class.[16] Research by German historians indicates that political opposition, the maintenance of left-wing hopes, was much more widespread than would appear from the accounts which depicted Nazi totalitarianism annihilating all opposition. In fact, the Nazi classification of some trade-union activists as 'unworthy' of service in the German army saved many who otherwise might have died in military action.[17]

The embers of working-class politics were still there. But of course Germany at the end of the Second World War was quite different from the Germany of 1918. Here the effect of twelve years of Nazi rule was crucial. Unlike in 1918 there was no experience of revolutionary or socialist-orientated working-class activity at the moment of the war's end. Those who looked or still look for a missed revolution in 1945—or as a minimum consider the moment to have been 'a possible first stage in an original continent-wide

---

[16] *New York Review of Books*, 16 July 1987.

[17] See H. Erstens and H. Pelger, *Gewerkschaften im Widerstand* (Hanover, Verlag für Literatur und Zeitgeschehen, 1967); Gerhard Beier, *Die illegale Reichsleitung der Gewerkschaften 1933–1945* (Cologne, Bund Verlag, 1981); A. Ulrich, (ed.), *Hessische Gewerkschafter im Widerstand 1933–1945* (Giessen, Anabas-Verlag, 1985). English accounts are in A. Merson, *Communist Resistance in Nazi Germany* (London, Lawrence and Wishart, 1985) and M. Balfour, *Withstanding Hitler*, (London, Routledge, 1988). In the 1950s, in the West German metalworkers' union, there were at least 20 union officials who were declared *unwürdig* (unworthy) for military service after 1933 and in consequence passed the war in factories where they kept alive a kernel of trade-union memory. (Conversation with Werner Thönesson, former IG Metall official, Geneva, 6 Nov. 1986.)

revolutionary development'[18] ignore the absence of an anti-nationalist, tested, angry, and self-confident proletariat based in factories, that had so shaken Europe at the end of the previous war. A German worker had to be over 30 to have had direct personal experience of open labour-movement activity directed against employers or the state.

Of these there were thousands who flocked to the unions. By mid–1947, there were 4.5 million members of trade-unions in Germany. As the Allied armies arrived in 1945, thousands of former labour-movement activists—social democrats and communists—came out of concentration camps and prisons. Thousands who had lain low and survived the war now sought to resume activity. Several hundred who had gone into exile, notably the Ulbricht group of German communists who had been in Moscow, returned to pick up the threads of political activity.

The power of the Allies, it is necessary to stress, was restrictive in several key areas. Neither as workers, nor in the sense of wider citizenship, were Germans allowed full rights to determine their own destiny. Bargaining on wages, working time, or workplace conditions was prohibited. If anything, the ban on such bread-and-butter work increased the focus on political issues and economic policy questions. The unions, in particular, did debate and decide upon organizational forms and policies which gave a clear indication of what the German people, or at least its working class, wanted by way of a future society.

The economic background to the political developments in the years 1945–47 contained its own contradictions. Compared with its pre-war economic strength, German industry appeared ruined. In 1946, the western zones of Germany were only producing 32 per cent of their 1938 output, a figure that moved up to 37 per cent in 1947.[19] It was these figures, combined with the visible misery of destroyed housing and transport and scanty food availability that justifiably allowed the depiction of a 'Germany in chaos' that became the usual language of those arguing for economic assistance

---

[18] F. Claudin, *The Communist Movement from Comintern to Cominform* (New York, Monthly Review Press, 1975), 621.

[19] Werner Abelhauser, *Wirtschaft in Westdeutschland 1945–1948: Rekonstruktion und Wachstumbedingungen in der amerikanischen und britischen Zone* (Stuttgart, Deutsche Verlags-Anstalt, 1975), 15.

from the US in 1947.[20] Yet despite all the bombing, the core of German industry remained relatively unscathed. Only 10 per cent of steel plants and coal mines had been completely destroyed. At the end of the war, German factories were found to have better stocks of materials than British factories.[21] Germany's peak wartime inventory of machine tools—the key to industrial manufacturing—stood at 2,150,000 compared with 740,000 in Britain.[22]

As soon as fighting stopped, German metalworkers tried to get civilian production started again. Materials of all sorts were missing but the desire to produce was not. The Adler typewriter factory in Frankfurt tried to set up a production line for bicycles to meet demand.[23] The theme of productionism became a post-war German obsession much as it had been in America and Britain during the war. In the Opel factory at Rüsselsheim, the works council chairman, a communist, told workers at a factory meeting in February 1946: 'Before, the might of the trade-union lay in the slogan: Stop the Works! Today the slogan has to be "Keep the Wheels" turning where it is possible.'[24]

Here the German workers ran into the muddle of Allied economic policy. It is perhaps unfair to talk of a unified Allied economic policy as each of the four occupying powers had its own policy. Furthermore, it is impossible to talk of an economic policy divorced from a political settlement as the question of ownership, control, output, planning, reparations, and trade were all conditional on what political system would either be imposed on or emerge within Germany. 'The compromise of Potsdam', wrote Basil Davidson who visited and wrote on Germany in the post-war years, 'broke down for reasons of basic policy. No common foundations for a new German society were laid. Separatist action took the place of unified developments.'[25]

The Morgenthau plan for the pastoralization of Germany did not

---

[20] See Irving Brown's report in Ch. 6. Victor Gollancz's book *In Darkest Germany*, published early in 1947, painted a picture of 'devastation and misery' according to the *New Statesman* (25 Jan. 1947).

[21] Douglas Botting, *In the Ruins of the Reich* (London, Unwin, 1986), 96.

[22] C. Barnett, *Audit of War* (London, Macmillan, 1986), 60–1.

[23] Angela Jacobi-Bettien, *Metallgewerkschaft Hessen 1945 bis 1948*, (Marburg, Verlag Arbeiterbewegung und Gesellschaftswissenschaft 1982), 45.

[24] Ibid. 339

[25] Basil Davidson, *Germany, What Now?* (London, Muller, 1950), 174.

survive long but the demand for reparations did. Reparations seemed the obvious answer to the question of how the Germans should repay some of the damage done to the rest of Europe while dismantling of key industries and factories would prevent the revival of a German war machine. To avoid the mess of financial transfers that had caused such chaos after the First World War the Allies determined on different methods of reparations. For the Allies, in Alec Cairncross's summing up, reparations 'should take the form of payment in kind, either through removals of plant, etc., or out of current production, or alternatively should consist of labour services by prisoners of war or other workers detained in the receiving country. Loot and slavery, the traditional forms of reparation, had returned to favour.'[26]

For the Western Allies, reparations made little economic sense. (The first come, first served, large-scale transfer of scientific knowledge and key personnel which was undertaken by all four occupying powers did not fall within the formal reparations policy.) At the end of May 1946, the British Chancellor of the Exchequer, Hugh Dalton, told the cabinet that the United Kingdom had received less than £2 million from Germany in reparations since the war ended but that Britain expected to pay £131 million to feed and administer Germany in 1946. The month before, General Clay, the US military governor, had suspended the dismantling of factories in the American zone for transfer to Russia but it continued apace in the Soviet, French, and, on a reduced level, the British zones. Prominent visitors from England and America expressed concern about the barriers created to resumed economic activity in Germany. In August 1946, Lord Beveridge deplored the blowing-up of harbours and docks in Hamburg which stopped German fishermen from bringing in herring to feed the population, while a few months later the former US president, Herbert Hoover, noted that European production would not pick up until a healthy Germany could make its contribution, so interwoven was the European economy with that of Germany. He pleaded for a relaxation of controls over German industry and an end to the policy of dismantling.[27]

[26] Alec Cairncross, *The Price of War* (Oxford, Blackwell, 1986).
[27] Lord Beveridge's impressions are in K.-J. Ruhl (ed.), *Neubeginn und Restauration* (Munich, DTV, 1982), 331; Hoover's visit and report are in Wolfgang Benz, *Von der Besatzungsherrschaft zur Bundesrepublik: Stationen einer Staatsgründung 1946–1949* (Frankfurt, Fischer, 1984), 128.

The latter policy was deeply resented by German trade-unionists. Oskar Schultze, a pro-Western metalworkers' leader in Bremen, protested at a meeting with German-speaking metal-trade-unionists from Austria and Switzerland: 'The most important thing is to provide Germany with the necessities of life . . . An increase in production is naturally not possible when the necessary machines are being dismantled.'[28]

In the Soviet zone, the dismantling policy was much more severe. 1,200 plants alone were dismantled in a fortnight prior to the Potsdam meeting.[29] Soviet dismantling was carried out on a vast scale. Taking 1936 as a base from which to start, the Russians dismantled and transferred from their zone 45 per cent of the iron industry, 60 per cent of the electrical industry, 40 per cent of the metal industry and 50 per cent of all machinery.[30]

Was there an alternative to reparations? If reparations were seen as a punishment the answer was 'no'. Nor if, from the Soviet point of view, reparations were considered a kind of short cut to technological modernization, particularly through the transfer of machine tools. However, if the object of reparations was to prevent the resurgence of German industrialism harnessed to military aggressiveness, then clearly there were other policies available. One such was put forward by the German unions almost as soon as they reconstituted themselves from 1945 onwards. The unions sought a radical reform of economic relations through nationalization of the key industries and banks, production only for civilian use, central planning of credit allocation and investment decisions, industrial democracy through codetermination (*Mitbestimmung*), and the creation of major consumer and distributive co-operatives.[31] In the view of works' council delegates in Darmstadt, meeting in April 1946, such economic democracy, particularly the introduction of full codetermination at the supra-firm or industry level as well as at the workplace level, where worker representatives would sit

---

[28] *Protokoll der Konferenz mit Vertretern der deutschen und der österreichischen Metallarbeitergewerkschaften, May 24–26, 1947* (IMFA).

[29] Cairncross, *Price of War*, 200.

[30] J. Nettl, *The Eastern Zone and Soviet Policy in Germany 1945–1950* (Oxford, Clarendon Press, 1951), 205.

[31] For a summary of trade-union demands for economic reorganization see Horst Thum, *Mitbestimmung in der Montanindustrie. Der Mythos vom Sieg der Gewerkschafter* (Stuttgart, Deutsche Verlags-Anstalt, 1982), 19–30, and E. Schmidt, *Die verhinderte Neuordnung 1945–1952*, 53 ff.

alongside management taking decisions on investment, production, prices, and hiring and firing, would constitute a 'method for the democratic reconstruction of the economy and [offer] the best guarantee that monopoly capitalism can never again use its economic might to rearm in secret and finance reactionary and fascist parties.'[32]

But the unions' desire for major reorganization of economic relations met with opposition on the part of the Western Allies. The British were willing, in principle, to accept a nationalization of the coal and steel industries as Bevin repeatedly made clear during 1946,[33] but ran into two problems. Firstly, there was no German government to assume ownership of the major Ruhr industries. Both the Russians and the French insisted on forms of internationalization of the Ruhr, and resisted Bevin's proposal to make the regional government of North Rhine-Westphalia the vesting authority for the coal industry. Secondly, and more importantly, the Americans made very clear following the merger of the British and American zones at the beginning of 1947 that they would oppose any nationalization measures. By mid–1947, Attlee was telling Bevin, 'If the British were to commit themselves to socialization of the Ruhr coal industry this might seriously prejudice the chances of additional American assistance for Germany.'[34]

Had the Labour government taken more radical steps soon after the war's end to support German trade-union demands for economic reform, the Americans would have been presented with a *fait accompli* in the key industrial region of the Ruhr. However, any Labour government wish to support German trade-union demands for nationalization also had to run the gauntlet of 'a British Control Staff who were by no means convinced of its wisdom' as Michael Balfour, himself a senior civilian adviser with the British occupation forces, observed.[35] Alfred Dannenberg, an English-speaking metal-union leader in Lower Saxony in this period recalls that the British officials responsible for economic policy in the British zone 'were a

[32] Quoted in Anne Weiss-Hartmann, *Der freie Gewerkschaftsbund Hessen 1945–1949*, (Marburg, Verlag Arbeiterbewegung und Gesellschaftswissenschaft, 1978), 180.
[33] See Thum, *Mitbestimmung*, 28 and A. Bullock, *Ernest Bevin: Foreign Secretary* (London, Heinemann, 1983), 341.
[34] Bullock, *Ernest Bevin*, 429.
[35] Balfour and Mair, *Four Power Control*, 154.

pretty conservative lot'.[36] As it was the absence of a Labour policy towards Germany in 1945 and 1946 aimed at putting into effect the democratic-socialist ideas—especially in the field of public owner-ship and industrial democracy—which the German labour move-ment had argued for,[37] left the future economic organization of Germany in the hands of those who did know what they wanted and had the power to obtain their desired ends.

For the Americans this was the reconstruction of a private-enterprise-based system in which trade-unions would play a role similar to that of unions in the United States, as collective-bargaining agents functioning in a free market democracy. Not only did the American military government reject major national-ization proposals but General Clay also refused any extension of codetermination rights as laid down in the proposed constitutions for the regional governments in Hesse and Bremen even though these had been endorsed in referendums.[38]

THE POLITICS OF GERMAN UNIONS AFTER 1945

The need for organizational unity in the trade-union movement was taken for granted by all in 1945, but the form of that unity, and the leadership of a united trade-union movement, remained open to question. So, too, would be the political and economic demands of the trade unions. In formal terms the unions were to be independent of any party, for that was the minimum precondition of unity. Yet that did not mean the unions would give up political demands or restrict themselves to economic issues. The group of exiled German trade-unionists in London published a leaflet in September 1944 which was dropped by Allied aeroplanes over Germany. It announced that 'a united German trade-union confederation' would join with socialist and other democratic parties in seeking the common aims of a democratic transformation of state and society, economic security, and social justice.[39]

[36] Alfred Dannenburg interview (Geneva, Mar. 1987).

[37] This is discussed in W. Paterson, 'The British Labour Party and the SPD 1945–52' in W. Albrecht (ed.), *Kurt Schumacher als deutscher und europäischer Sozialist*, (Bonn, Friedrich-Ebert Stiftung, 1988), 95–112. On Labour Party hostility to SPD ideas in the 1940s see Anthony Glees, *Exile Politics in the Second World War* (Oxford, Clarendon Press, 1978).

[38] Weiss-Hartmann, *Freier Gewerkschaftsbund Hessen*, 179–201.

[39] 'Wiederaufbau deutsche Gewerkschaften: Eine Vorlage der Landesgruppe

A stronger line was taken by social-democratic and communist inmates of Buchenwald, some of them to be prominent in political life after 1945. In their *Buchenwald Manifesto* published in April 1945 they argued that 'social crises can only be brought to an end through a socialist economy. Germany can only be rebuilt economically along socialist principles.'[40] Their last point was common ground to all on the Left. Capitalism was seen as dead and buried in the ruins of the Third Reich. Prominent SPD trade-unionists from the Weimar era, such as Fritz Tarnow, returned from exile in Sweden to announce: 'The era of free private and capitalist control of production is over.'[41] Hans Böckler, the leader of the trade-unions in the British zone, after proclaiming in March 1946, 'We no longer have class enemies in front of us,' declared that the only questions to be settled were the details of a post-capitalist economy: 'Should it be full nationalization or the creation of social control based on factory co-operatives?' he asked.[42]

Hans Brummer, a right-wing SPD metal-union leader from Stuttgart, told a metal-union conference in August 1946 that no sensible person believed that the German economy could be rebuilt along 'pure private capitalist principles'.[43] The theme of rebuilding Germany's economy along non-capitalist lines was common amongst more than left-wing spokespersons in the first two years after the war. The 1947 Ahlen programme of the Christian Democratic Union called for 'a new social and economic order' no longer based on 'capitalist striving after profit'.[44] Karl Arnold, the CDU head in North Rhine-Westphalia told his regional government in June 1947: 'The capitalist economic system has collapsed on account of its own laws.'[45]

deutscher Gewerkschafter in Grossbritannien', in P. Altmann (ed.), *Hauptsache Frieden. Kriegsende, Befreiung, Neubeginn 1945–1949: Vom antifaschistischen Konsens zum Grundgesetz* (Frankfurt, Röderberg-Verlag, 1985), 86.

[40] *Buchenwalder Manifest*, 13 Apr. 1945, in Ruhl (ed.), *Neubeginn und Restauration*, 175.

[41] Quoted in Theo Pirker, *Die blinde Macht: die Gewerkschaftsbewegung in der Bundesrepublik* (Berlin, Olle und Walter, 1979), 54.

[42] Quoted in Schmidt, *Die verhinderte Neuordnung*, 61.

[43] *Protokoll vom ersten ordentlichen Verbandstag des Industrieverbandes Metall Württemberg-Baden*, 10–11 Aug. 1945. Archives of Industriegewerkschaft Metall für die Bundesrepublik Deutschland (IG Metall) Frankfurt (henceforth IGMA).

[44] *Das Ahlener Programm* (Feb. 1947). The CDU programme was printed as a pamphlet by the metalworkers' union in Frankfurt (IGMA).

[45] Quoted in Jürgen Kocka, '1945. Neubeginn oder Restauration', in C. Stern and H-A. Winkler (eds.), *Wendepunkte deutscher Geschichte* (Frankfurt, Fischer, 1979), 148.

So there were two points of common ground—on trade-union unity and on building a post-capitalist economy—in the labour movement at the war's end. The important pre-war issues that so bitterly divided social democrats from communists—the call for a revolutionary overthrow of capitalism and for the creation of communist-led, Soviet-orientated unions—seemed therefore to have disappeared.

The overlap between SPD members and trade-unionists is not possible to quantify in the immediate post-war period but it is reasonable to assume that at the end of 1946 of the 600,000 members of the SPD most were also amongst the 1.2 million trade-unionists in the three Western zones. Two-thirds of the SPD members in 1946 had belonged to the party before 1933.[46] The overlap between party and trade union in the pre–1933 era had been very marked. Over half the SPD group of deputies in the 1933 Reichstag had been trade-union officials. The incidence of pre–1933 activists was also marked in other left-wing groups in the Western zones. Of the 1,152 members of the *Antifa* (anti-fascist) movement in Brunswick in 1945, 91 per cent were aged between 31 and 63 and two-thirds had belonged to political parties or unions before 1933.[47] The same was true of the German Communist Party (Kommunistische Partei Deutschlands—KPD) in the Western zones. In the KPD in North Rhine-Westphalia, 36 per cent of the party's members were 50 or over, and 45 per cent aged between 36 and 50.[48]

Leadership and political activism in the trade-unions in the months after 1945 tended therefore to be the preserve of the middle-aged. This was also true for both the KPD and the SPD. In the latter's case, there was also an infusion of Marxists unwilling to join the KPD. Members of breakaway left-wing groups who had split from the SPD before 1933 in opposition to its cautiousness now rejoined the SPD. Otto Brenner, the metalworkers' leader in Hanover had been in the SAP (Sozialistische Arbeiter Partei— Socialist Workers' Party) along with Willy Brandt but they now joined the SPD. Wolfgang Abendroth, a radical intellectual close to the left wing in the trade-unions returned to work (until 1947) in the Soviet zone but joined the SPD. He recalled that for him the memory of 'Stalin's terror was the key factor . . . Many leading SPD

---

[46] P. Kulemann, *Die Linke in Westdeutschland nach 1945* (Hanover, Soak Verlag, 1978), 32–3.
[47] Ibid.   [48] Ibid.

members in the Western zones were from small splinter groups or even the Communist Party'.[49]

In the Western zones, leadership was provided by Kurt Schumacher, the former SPD Reichstag deputy who before 1933 had been most vigorous and full of contempt in his opposition to the Nazis, and least willing to contemplate conciliation or compromise with fascism. A journalist who had lost his arm in the First World War, and who had taken part in the 1918 revolution, Schumacher came to prominence with the power of his attacks on the Nazis between 1930 and 1933. They returned the compliment by imprisoning him in Dachau. Strongly anti-Stalinist, Schumacher refused contact with KPD prisoners in the concentration camp. Lewis Edinger's biography of Schumacher seeks to explain his dominance in post-war SPD politics in terms of his personality and will as well as his position as a senior SPD representative whose suffering at the hands of the Nazis conferred extra status.[50]

Schumacher's major contribution however arose not only from his personal prestige and iron determination but from his formulation, within a few weeks of the war's end, of a policy for the SPD that was coherent, in the tradition of the party, and provided ideological guidelines to help answer many of the key questions of the moment. It is necessary to look in some detail at the SPD policy as defined by Schumacher in the course of the second half of 1945, because the trade-unionists organizing the new unions, most of them loyal SPD veterans, could hardly avoid being influenced by the official SPD position on key issues of what attitude to take towards the occupying powers, especially the Russians, and to other political parties, particularly the Communist Party.

Schumacher's 'Political Guidelines for the SPD', circulated in August 1945, are forthright in their opposition to communism in the political, organizational, economic, and national spheres. Insisting that 'modern democracy can only function in a state with competing political parties [*Parteienstaat*]'. Schumacher denounced the German communists as 'inseparable from one of the victorious

---

[49] Wolfgang Abendroth, *Ein Leben in der Arbeiterbewegung* (Frankfurt, Suhrkamp, 1976), 199. Opposed as he was to Stalinism, Abendroth declined ever to be considered an anticommunist. (I am grateful to Frau Lisa Abendroth for comments on her husband's politics.) On 1930s Marxists joining the SPD see Graf, *The German Left*, 64.

[50] Lewis Edinger, *Kurt Schumacher: A Study in Personality and Political Behaviour* (Stanford, Calif., Stanford University Press, 1965).

powers. The KPD is tied to Russian national and imperial state interests and its foreign policy objectives.'[51]

He mocked the 'surprising conversion to democracy' of the communists and dismissed as a tactical manœuvre the statement from the KPD that Germany would not go down the same road as the Soviet Union because such a path did not correspond to 'present conditions of development': Schumacher seized on the word 'present', arguing that later on (i.e. once they had won power) the KPD would revert to being a dictatorial party.[52]

Two further points separated Schumacher's elaboration of SPD politics from the communists. Firstly, he gave vent to a German nationalism—a democratic and socialist nationalism, but a German nationalism all the same: 'As German social democrats we are not British, nor Russian, nor American, nor French. We are the representatives of the German working people and hence the German nation.'[53] He refused to accept the concept of German collective guilt declaring that 'the German people have the undeniable right to stand up and express themselves';[54] in addition he refused to accept the eastern borders of Germany as final, for which, in due course, he was denounced in the Polish press as 'an imperialist like Hitler'.[55]

Secondly, he put forward an economic programme based on the wide-scale socialization of privately owned firms. This he contrasted scornfully, in the summer of 1945, with the position of the communists which was based, in accordance with Popular Front policy, on an acceptance of a private sector and of free-market activity. 'Socialists cannot support a free market and private ownership,' he wrote: the Communists' economic policy could be summed up in the slogan ' "*Enrichissez vous*!" ["Get rich!"]' while for German socialists the economy could only be rebuilt on the basis of planning.[56]

---

[51] Kurt Schumacher, 'Politische Richtlinien für die SPD', Aug. 1945, in Altmann, *Hauptsache Frieden*, 118–19.

[52] Ibid.

[53] Quoted in H. Ritzel, *Kurt Schumacher* (Hamburg, Rowohlt, 1972), 48.

[54] Schumacher, 'Richtlinien', in Altmann, *Hauptsache Frieden*, 118–19.

[55] *Dziennik Zachodi*, 1 Feb. 1947, quoted in Edinger, *Kurt Schumacher*, 237. A united Germany was a theme common to the Left. See e.g. the KPD leader, Wilhelm Pieck, in Jan. 1946: 'It is the iron will of the Communists. . . to ensure the unity of Germany.' Quoted in P. Brandt and H. Ammon, (eds.), *Die Linke und die nationale Frage* (Hamburg, Rowohlt, 1981), 74.

[56] Schumacher, 'Richtlinien'. Schumacher, whose contact with the outside world

A final line was drawn between the commitment to democracy of socialists and communists. In the guidelines for the SPD Schumacher wrote: 'Democracy is inseparable from the concept of socialism . . . Socialism is of itself democratic, and as the struggle for the spiritual, political, and economic liberation of the masses it is the fight for freedom and justice against oppression and violence. Socialism that is dictatorial in word or act is not socialism.'[57] So in the confusion of Germany in the summer of 1945, Schumacher's guidelines served not just to stiffen SPD resolve against merger or unity with the communists but to establish the SPD as the party of democracy, of German interests, and as the more left-wing of the two competing workers' parties. At a time when millions of German workers were looking for political direction, Schumacher set out to cultivate four separate groups, all of them represented in the trade-unions.

Firstly, the anticommunism appealed to the pre–1933 tradition of the SPD. Secondly, the nationalism appealed to the millions of refugees from the East (in German they were (and are) called the *Vertriebene*—those expelled or driven out) and to those opponents of Hitler in Germany sickened at the barely disguised Vansittartism in many of the statements and suggestions from Western politicians, soldiers, and journalists.[58] Thirdly, Schumacher's anti-Russian remarks found an echo amongst those, especially women, who had experienced rough treatment at the hands of Soviet troops as they marched towards Berlin and amongst others horrified at the crude and inefficient dismantling of hundreds of German factories, with much of the machinery left to rust on sidings as the Russians had no means to transport it back to the Soviet Union.[59] Finally,

---

had stopped in 1933, goes on to compare the 1945 economic policy of the KPD to the Soviet NEP (New Economic Policy) of the 1920s which, in his view gave rise to unacceptable disparities of wealth as well as sanctioning greed as the main motor of individual economic activity.

[57] Schumacher, 'Richtlinien'.

[58] Sir Robert Vansittart must be the only British diplomat whose name has entered the German language thanks to his wartime racial fulminations against the German people. See entry under *Vansittaritismus* in Meyer's *Geschichte Taschen-Lexikon*, vi. (Mannheim, 1982), 167. Bevin said of Germans: 'I tries 'ard, but I 'ates them.' Quoted in Bullock, *Ernest Bevin*, 90.

[59] See Wolfgang Abendroth, *Sozialgeschichte der europäischen Arbeiterbewegung*, (Frankfurt, Suhrkamp, 1965), 177, on the growth of anti-Russian feeling, and Cairncross, *Price of War*, 203, on Russian dismantling.

the call for a planned, socialized economy held the allegiance of the Marxists and younger left-wingers who had opted for the SPD.

The importance of Schumacher's guidelines lay in the fact that they were put forward and were broadly accepted so soon after the fall of the Nazi régime. SPD activists who argued for different policies, including joint work leading to a fusion with the communists, or for less radical economic policies, or for a more friendly outlook towards the Russians, could not make headway against Schumacher's programmatic policy laid down so soon after the war's end.

In the last months of 1945, Schumacher and his version of SPD politics imposed themselves on the party. He made a point of cultivating trade-unionists. The metal-union leaders in Lower Saxony, Otto Brenner and Alfred Dannenberg, called on him and found him to be an 'impressive and powerful personality'.[60] In October 1945 in Hanover, Schumacher's home ground, a conference of the party was held. It was not a formal party congress, but present were representatives of the SPD from all the Western zones and from the exiled groups, and, most significantly, a delegation led by Otto Grotewohl, who, with Russian backing, had set up a central committee of the SPD in Berlin, still very much seen as the capital of Germany. Schumacher successfully argued that there could be no national party leadership until a full party congress was held, and it was agreed to acknowledge his leadership in the three Western zones leaving Grotewohl responsible for the SPD in the Soviet zone. Grotewohl was an advocate of unity with the communists and SPD delegates from Hamburg and Kiel also described in positive terms how they were working closely with the KPD. But Schumacher expressly refused a merger. 'The recipe for a unity party that the Communists propose would place the SPD under communist leadership. A social democratic party under communist leadership would however be a communist party.'[61] Even those who were in favour of an eventual merger with the communists were cautious as the following statement from the SPD in Heidelberg in December 1945 suggests.

We are ready to work with all democratic parties and in particular the

---

[60] Dannenberg interview.
[61] Kurt Schumacher, *Programmatische Erklärungen*, 5 Oct. 1945, in Ruhl, *Neubeginn und Restauration*, p 209.

Communist Party. We honestly believe in a longlasting union with the Communists but we would warn against getting married in a rush. As the poet says: 'Check everything, before eternal binds are made.' Before the final fusion, certain questions have to be cleared up. For example, we cannot decide to commit ourselves to only one side as far as foreign policy is concerned.[62]

Schumacher's opposition to communism, the KPD, and the Soviet Union was permanent. An analysis of his major post-war speeches shows that half of them were devoted to critical analyses or attacks on communism, or the Soviet Union.[63] He opposed the merger of the SPD and KPD to form the Socialist Unity Party (SED) in the Soviet zone in 1946. In turn, he became the object of attacks by communists, some even going so far as to suggest that he had not been in Dachau.[64] His fierce opposition to unity politics did not cost him political popularity. He was overwhelmingly elected party leader at the SPD congress in May 1946 and his leadership never came under serious challenge. His political line was endorsed by voters. In local and regional elections in the three Western zones in October 1946, the SPD outpolled the KPD by a factor of four to one. In the only electoral test between the SPD and SED (Sozialistische Einheitspartei—the merged socialist-communist party in the Soviet zone)—for seats in Berlin's city parliament in October 1946—the SPD obtained 48.7 per cent to the SED's 19.8 per cent. Even in the Soviet sector of Berlin, the SPD outpolled the SED by 43.6 per cent to 29.8 per cent.

For SPD members in the unions, Schumacher's politics— democratic, anticapitalist, hostile to communism, and the Soviet Union—set the tone and reflected their own attitudes. The insistence after 1945 that unions should be free of formal party links did not diminish the loyalty that SPD trade-unionists felt towards their party, nor alter the overall acceptance of the party leadership as the political representative of the wider interests of the German working class and the German people. At the SPD congress in Hanover in May 1946, Hans Böckler, head of the trade-unions in

[62] P. Merz, *Dokumente zur Geschichte der Arbeiterbewegung in Heidelberg 1845–1949* (Heidelberg, IG Metall, 1986), 269.

[63] Edinger, *Kurt Schumacher*, 327.

[64] Ritzel, *Schumacher*, 38–41. Schumacher's difficulties in persuading Western and Eastern European socialists to accept the SPD's credentials are covered in Rolf Steininger, *Deutschland und die Sozialistische Internationale nach dem Zweiten Weltkrieg* (Bonn, Archiv für Sozialgeschichte, Verlag Neue Gesellschaft, 1978).

the British zone, declared his complete agreement with the proposals of the SPD. 'Our [the trade unions'] plans and intentions are identical with those proposed yesterday [by the SPD's economic spokesman].'[65]

To understand the political outlook of the majority of the German trade-union movement as it stood in 1945 and 1946, the statements from Schumacher, speaking for the reborn SPD, are a good guide. If Churchill's Fulton speech announced the Cold War to a world audience, Schumacher's 'political guidelines', written nine months earlier in July 1945, made outright opposition to political unity with the communists and opposition to the Soviet Union the foundation stones of the post-war German non-communist Left. In the Soviet zone meanwhile, a mirror image of the same process was taking place with the trade-unions at the centre of the struggle for political control.

TRADE UNIONS IN THE SOVIET ZONE

Order Number 2 from the Soviet military commander, issued on 10 June 1945, permitted the establishment of political parties and trade unions in the Soviet Zone. The Western Allies, and those Germans anxious to rebuild a labour movement in the Western zones, faced a problem in that the Russians forced the pace of internal political developments to which those in the West had to respond. In the Soviet zone, the Russians were first with a functioning trade-union, first with a functioning mass party of the Left—the Socialist Unity Party (SED)—and first with a series of reforms in land ownership and economic control which corresponded to some extent with the demands of the Left since 1933 and especially after 1945. The Russians shaped the agenda for political development in their zone, and as the Allies and the Germans agreed on the need to maintain Germany—the *Reich* as it is continually referred to in German in this period—as an economic and, in due course, a political entity, what happened in the Russian zone became the standard to which others would have to react.

For Soviet historians, writing up to the mid–1980s, the communist parties after the war wanted to carry on with the policy laid

[65] *Protokoll der Verhandlung des SPD-Parteitags vom 9–11 Mai 1946*, 145 (IGMA).

down by the seventh congress of the Communist International and build broad antifascist coalitions which would have as their aim 'the defence of democratic rights and freedoms'.[66] Communist parties rejected 'sectarian and radical leftwing proposals for an immediate move towards a socialist revolution', and instead proposed a thorough democratization of society run by 'progressive and democratic' administrations 'of a provisional character'.[67] In due course this would lead to a 'relatively peaceful transition to socialism' but in the meantime such administrations would not have 'a direct socialist character'.[68]

Within that framework, how did the trade-unions in the Russian zone develop after 1945? Documents and memoirs from the former German Democratic Republic trace the growth of the unions in the Soviet zone in the two years after May 1945. By the middle of 1946, the East German unions had already adopted the organizational structure and political line that they would henceforth hold; indeed, the pattern of control was laid down by the autumn of 1945. As trade-unionists in the West—working with greater handicaps—tried to relaunch unions, they could see a united union getting bigger and stronger in the East. They could also see under whose control it had fallen.

For the communists the question of having a single union incorporating all political tendencies had long since been settled. In 1934 the underground Communist Party in Germany had been instructed to change its trade-union policy and henceforth support 'the revival of a united trade-union federation'.[69] By 1945 of course this was common ground between those rebuilding the unions irrespective of political orientation. The first appeal, issued in Berlin, to create unions had a majority of social-democratic signatures plus that of Jakob Kaiser, leader of the pre–1933 Christian unionists, but later accounts, written during the era of communist rule of East Germany, of the founding of the Freier Deutscher Gewerkschaftsbund (FDGB), stress that it came into being 'on the initiative of communist trade-unionists' who 'worked

[66] Boris Ponomarev (ed.), *Die internationale Arbeiterbewegung. Fragen der Geschichte und der Theorie*, vi (Moscow, Progress Publishers, and Berlin, Dietz, 1985), 48.

[67] Ibid.

[68] Ibid.

[69] Merson, *Communist Resistance in Nazi Germany*, 157.

closely with the Soviet Army'.[70] The preface to a collection of memoirs of the first years of the FDGB insisted on how, from the moment of liberation, there was

constant help from the Soviet Union, especially the Soviet trade-unions. Our Soviet comrades brought us the teaching of Marxism-Leninism and made it possible for us to get to know about the experiences of unions in building the socialist society in the Soviet Union and to use this information for our own trade-union activities.[71]

Three aims can be seen in the implementation of trade-union policy in the Soviet zone: First, to stamp out any spontaneous grass-roots working-class organization; second, to ensure that amongst the communists it was those who had been in Moscow during the Nazi era who were in overall control; third, to find German communists to run the unions whose acceptance of democratic centralist-party discipline could be relied upon. With ease, all three tasks were swiftly accomplished. The factory committees created spontaneously in the eastern parts of Germany in the wake of the advancing Red Army were dissolved on the orders of the Soviet military administration. Walter Ulbricht, the driving force in the KPD behind the figurehead leadership of 69-year-old Wilhelm Pieck, made clear his determination to stamp out any grass-roots activity by German communists, who unlike him and the KPD leadership, had not spent most of the years since 1933 in Moscow. Writing to Georgy Dimitroff, Ulbricht reported that:

We have shut down the spontaneously opened Communist Party offices, the peoples' committees, the committees of the Free Germany Movement, and the committees of the July 20th Movement which previously had been operating illegally and are now functioning in public. We have told the comrades that they must focus all their energy and activities on works councils, local administration committees, and so forth.[72]

Who were these 'comrades' that Ulbricht refers to, and why was he so certain that they would follow his peremptory instructions? The key figures were middle-aged German communists who had proved

[70] *Geschichte: Lehrbuch für Klasse 10*, the former German Democratic Republic's official school history book for 16-year-olds (Berlin, 1983), 53.

[71] E. Lehmann, (ed.), *Aufbruch in unsere Zeit: Erinnerungen an die Tätigkeit der Gewerkschaften von 1945 bis zur Gründung der Deutschen Demokratischen Republik*, (Berlin, Tribüne Verlag, 1975), 6.

[72] W. Ulbricht to G. Dimitroff, 17 July 1945 in Ulbricht (ed.), *Zur Geschichte der deutschen Arbeiterbewegung* ii. *1933–1946* (Berlin, Dietz, 1963), 458.

their loyalty to the Communist Party and the varying instructions issued from Moscow in the 1920s and 1930s. To say that they were tested KPD functionaries with experience going back to the Weimar era needs further qualification. As Wolfgang Abendroth, himself a Marxist militant in Weimar, pointed out, communists who had party functions in 1933 were those who had risen to office in the party or its unions after 1924, that is, after the revolutionary period of upheavals between 1918 and 1923; they were not those who had leadership experience in a period of 'historical change'; nor, writes Abendroth, did KPD functionaries have a direct connection with workers through leadership in the workplace: 'Most were unemployed and spent their time in party offices.'[73]

One example is Fritz Apelt, born in 1893, originally a locksmith, who had been an active communist since 1920. Apelt worked in Moscow during the 1920s for Profintern—the Red trade union International. Apelt spent the years 1935–45 in Moscow, and was given the key post of editor of the trade-union daily newspaper upon his return to Berlin. Two of the signatories to the appeal of 15 June 1945, calling for a unified trade-union movement, were Hans Jendretzky who had first joined the German metalworkers' union in 1912 and who had been a communist activist since the 1920s, and Paul Walter, born in 1891, and a long-standing communist. Roman Chwalek, head of the railway workers' union in the Soviet zone, had spent the last three years of the Weimar republic as secretary of the communist Revolutionäre Gewerkschaftsopposition (Revolutionary Trade Union Opposition—RGO). He had been interned in a concentration camp, and later formally sentenced to a term of imprisonment. At the end of the war he was living quietly in a Berlin suburb. As soon as Ulbricht arrived back to open up the KPD organization in Berlin Chwalek reported to him and was instructed to begin forming a trade-union. He sought out communist colleagues he knew and trusted from Weimar days.[74]

Yet there was no communist triumphalism in the early days of the trade-unions in the Soviet zone. Restraint and organizational

---

[73] Abendroth, *Ein Leben*, 147. See also Frank Deppe, *Jürgen Kuczynski Gespräch* (Marburg, Verlag Arbeiterbewegung und Gesellschaftswissenschaft, 1984), 76, on the lack of contact between communists and employed workers in the late 1920s and 1930s.

[74] See Lehmann, *Aufbruch*, for these and further details on communist union leaders in 1945.

co-operation with other political tendencies were the hallmarks of the opening period. But there were signs that the new union movement should look eastwards, and invoke the example of Soviet Russia and Leninist norms. For example, after the 10 June order permitting the creation of trade unions, the 'preparatory committee for the creation of a free, united trade-union' met with a Soviet general on 13 June 1945 to be given 'the greetings of the Russian trade-unions'.[75] Two days later the committee published its appeal to create a new union. An examination of the language of this appeal provides the first, small evidence of the future course of the new union.

The appeal of 15 June 1945 was a condemnation of the Nazi era and called for 'the creation of new, free trade-unions bringing together all tendencies in a united struggle for the complete destruction of fascism and the creation of new democratic rights for manual and office workers': in addition, the appeal urged workers to rid their factories of Nazis, to get energy, transport, and food production moving again and urged the education of workers into the 'spirit of anti-fascism and democratic progress'.[76]

The demands and tone were thus relatively general and the appeal was endorsed by SPD as well as communist trade-unionists. But hidden in the rosy universalism of the appeal were sectarian thorns. In its paragraphs of historical analysis, the appeal focused on the failure of the ADGB (Allgemeiner Deutscher Gewerkschafts-bund—the pre–1933 social-democratic trade-union federation) to stand up to Nazism. The ADGB is not mentioned by name but its clumsy, bureaucratic attempt to preserve some kind of existence by conciliating Hitler is described as 'the blackest day in the history of the labour movement'.[77] This attack, without any corresponding criticism of KPD, Profintern, or Communist International third-period 'class against class' politics in the years before 1933, became a constant refrain in communist articles, resolutions, and speeches in the months after the launch of the unions in the Soviet zone.

This process can be seen unfolding in the appeal issued by the FDGB[78] committee in the province of Brandenburg, which stated

[75] Ibid. 16.

[76] *Aufruf des Vorbereitenden Gewerkschaftsausschusses für Gross-Berlin*, in DMDA, 33–4.

[77] Ibid. For a summary of the ADGB's behaviour in 1933 see W. Kendall, *The Labour Movement in Europe* (London, Allen Lane, 1975), 105.

[78] The decision to use the name Freier Deutscher Gewerkschaftsbund for the

that up to 1933, 'the ability of the trade-unions to fight had been paralysed by the policy of the then leadership of the ADGB'.[79] The Brandenburg proclamation was published in the Berlin paper, *Deutsche Volkszeitung*, in August 1945, which suggests that even by that early date the communists were worried about former ADGB leaders once again picking up the reins of trade-union organization. To brand them as contributing to Hitler's rise to power would keep them in their place.

In this Brandenburg appeal there is also a small but significant shift of emphasis by comparison to the Berlin appeal issued two months previously. Whereas the latter referred to the destruction of Hitler's tyranny by the 'Allies', the Brandenberg appeal gently glossed history in declaring 'thanks to the victory of the Red Army we can come together in free trade-unions'.[80] References to the Red Army being responsible for Hitler's defeat without any mention of the Western Allies become the norm in KPD and trade-union statements from now on. Further evidence of the KPD's determination to exercise control in the unions can be seen in a delegate conference in Saxony held on 15 September 1945. Laying down the next tasks of the trade-unions the conference called for elections in the unions to be held 'according to the principles of democratic centralism'; further, there should be no room for former trade-union officials 'who in the past have proved themselves untrue to the principles of the modern trade-union movement and therefore to socialism': such officials 'can find no place in the leadership of the new free trade-union movement'.[81]

In August 1945, the first education material to train union officials in the Soviet zone was produced and a little later the Soviet authorities provided sufficient newsprint to publish a daily newspaper for the unions; its editor was a communist.[82] By the autumn of 1945, the KPD had opened special schools to train communist

union(s) that arose in the Soviet zone in 1945 appears to have come about spontaneously before it was formally adopted at the FDGB's launch congress in Feb. 1946.

[79] *Aufruf des Vorbereitenden Gewerkschaftsausschusses der Provinz Branden-burg*, 7 Aug. 1945, in DMDA, 94–7.

[80] Ibid.

[81] *Entschliessung der Delegiertenkonferenz des FDGB der Provinz Sachsen*, 15 Sept. 1945, in DMDA, 163.

[82] H. Ahrendt (ed.), *Geschichte des FDGB: Chronik 1945–1982* (Berlin, Tribüne Verlag, 1982), 11–18.

trade-union officials[83] while at a meeting on reconstruction in Halle, a speech by Walter Ulbricht 'was accepted as the basis of union activity'.[84] In December 1945, Ulbricht emphasized the need for special care in choosing trade-union officials. Above all he warned against SPD union officials 'who talk about the leading role of the Social Democrats'.[85]

A united trade-union broadly orientated to KPD perspectives was an important power-base in the struggle for influence and control of the working class. For Ulbricht it was the key organizational question in the run-up to the first FDGB congress planned for February 1946. Wolfgang Leonhard, who had been trained at the Comintern school, and who returned with the Ulbricht group to help establish the KPD in 1945, recalls how KPD officials were told to switch around their union membership cards in order to maximize communist votes.[86]

During the period just prior to the congress, when factories in Berlin were electing delegates, Leonhard saw Ulbricht at work in the KPD headquarters with other trade-union specialists from the party's central committee. Ulbricht was giving orders on the phone to KPD factory representatives to get party members to vote exclusively for communists even if this meant breaking an agreement for a joint slate with an equal number of SPD members. Leonhard noted this exchange between Ulbricht and a party official:

'Tell everybody! Vote only for Communists, only for Communists. This is the moment that counts!'

'The comrades don't want to do this. They say they've made an agreement with the Social Democrats to have a union committee based on parity between them and us so our people should vote for the Social Democrats as well.'

'There is absolutely no question of that. Make it quite clear. They should vote only for Communists.'

A few minutes later, writes Leonhard, the party official returned to report:

[83] See McCauley, *Marxism-Leninism in the German Democratic Republic*, 19.
[84] Lehmann, *Aufbruch*, 163.
[85] *Deutsche Volkszeitung*, 19 Dec. 1945, in DMDA, 342.
[86] Wolfgang Leonhard, *Die Revolution entlässt ihre Kinder* (Cologne, Kiepenheuer und Witsch, 1981), 380. A shortened version of Leonhard's book, omitting references to trade-union work, is available in English—*Child of the Revolution* (London, Ink, 1979).

'The comrades are unhappy. They say that if we don't keep our agreement with the Social Democrats we will destroy all unity.'
'Unity will be all the stronger the more Communists we have in the leadership of the FDGB. You tell them that!' was Ulbricht's reply.[87]

The hard and politically uncompromising work of Ulbricht, Chwalek, and other communists during the second half of 1945 paid off. At the first congress of the FDGB, its official launch, held in Berlin, 9–11 February 1946, the 1,019 delegates confirmed in their posts the communists from the various preparatory committees and those communists already in place in provisional leaderships of industrial and regional unions. Originally there were about 530 communist delegates to 250 social democrats but a further 180 Social Democrats who had been invited as guests were given delegate credentials to even up the party balance. One delegate at the congress, Otto Suhr, a SPD union leader from Berlin, criticized 'the election system whose results had to be corrected by such means'.[88]

Not only was the FDGB leadership communist, despite the contrived boost to the number of SPD delegates at the congress, but the organizational form was firmly along Soviet lines. The FDGB was set up as a highly centralized federation with industrial unions such as the metalworkers or transport workers dependent on the central body for their finances—the industrial unions received back only 15 per cent of their contributions for their own purposes.[89] From the communists' point of view, the importance of establishing the FDGB under communist control by February 1946 was underlined a month later when a poll carried out amongst SPD members in Berlin showed 85 per cent voting against an immediate merger with the KPD.[90] The KPD–FDGB link was emphasized by

[87] Leonhard, *Die Revolution entlässt ihre Kinder*, 380.

[88] Quoted in a report from an American observer at the congress, 862. 504/2. 1546 (DSNA).

[89] *Geschäftsbericht des freien deutschen Gewerkschaftbundes Gross-Berlin 1946* (Berlin, FDGB), 428 ff. (IGMA).

[90] The merger poll of 32,500 SPD members in West Berlin rejected by 82% to 12% the proposal to merge the two parties, but by 62% to 23% endorsed the idea of an 'alliance which will guarantee co-operation and exclude fraternal strife'. As McCauley has written this result showed 'that the will to co-operate was still extraordinarily strong but time was needed to iron out the differences'. McCauley, *The German Democratic Republic Since 1945*, 28. Communist insistence on a fusion in 1946 produced the same counter-reaction as Lenin's insistence on a split a quarter of a century earlier.

Ulbricht's presence at every session of the launch congress. Echoing what had now become the communist position, delegates urged the swiftest possible merger between the SPD and KPD in the Soviet zone which would 'be a glowing example to the entire German working class'.[91]

By early spring 1946, the Soviet zone in Germany had a functioning, centralized trade-union federation, formally independent of party political control, and uniting communists and social democrats with Christian and other pre–1933 trade-union tendencies. But the FDGB, whatever its formal status proclaimed, was firmly in the hands of communists whose loyalty was to Ulbricht and those German communists who had returned from Moscow on the heels of the Red Army. When the SPD and KPD merged to form the Socialist Unity Party (SED) the FDGB adopted as its symbol the SED's unity handshake logo. The closeness between the SED and the FDGB was given an important impetus in September 1946 when the SED, adopting the Soviet Union's form of political organization, made the enterprise rather than a local area, the organizing centre of party activity.[92] An observer from Switzerland, attending the FDGB's second congress in Berlin in April 1947, noted that the FDGB 'is completely in the hands of the SED'.[93] This position is shared by the German Democratic Republic labour historian, Albert Behrendt, who, describing political relations in 1947, writes of 'the trade-unionists in the Soviet occupation zone under the leadership of the Socialist Unity Party'.[94]

[91] *Entschliessung für die Schaffung einer einheitlichen Arbeiterpartei*, FDGB Congress, Feb. 1946, in DMDA, 494–5.

[92] See McCauley, 'East Germany', in McCauley (ed.), *Communist Power in East Europe 1944–1949* (London, Macmillan, 1977), 67.

[93] *Bericht der Gewerkschafts-Delegation nach Deutschland für die internationale Föderation der Verbände des Personals öffentlicher Dienste*, 1 May 1947 (IMFA).

[94] Albert Behrendt, *Die Interzonenkonferenzen der deutschen Gewerkschaften* (Berlin, Tribüne Verlag, 1959), 44.

12

The Organization of German Metalworkers After 1945

As one by one the towns and cities of Western Germany were occupied by the Allies in the spring of 1945, the workers in factories formed works' councils and sought to establish trade-union organization. In February 1945, a provisional trade-union committee was set up in Aachen and news of its existence and programme was broadcast on the Allied-controlled radio. In March, a similar body was set up in Cologne. In most cases, the instigators had been union officials in the Weimar period. In Frankfurt, Willi Richter, a metalworker and former regional head of the ADGB, had been the link between a group of pre–1933 trade union officials during the Nazi era. In April 1945, he wrote to the American occupying forces in Frankfurt suggesting that pre–1933 officials be entrusted with rebuilding the trade-unions.[1] In Stuttgart trade-unionists had approached the French military authorities before the end of April 1945 to announce their intention of restarting union activities and on 11 May 1945 the Württemberg Trade Union Federation was launched. At its head were Markus Schleicher, former vice-president of the pre–1933 woodworkers' union, and Hans Brümmer, former Stuttgart secretary of the pre–1933 metalworkers' union.[2]

Eberhard Schmidt in his influential *Die verhinderte Neuordnung*, bemoans the swift arrival in leadership positions of elderly SPD stalwarts whose outlook had been formed in the Weimar Republic.[3] For young radical academics writing in the late 1960s, men like Willi Richter, who was 51 in 1945, or Hans Brümmer, who was 59, must have seemed ancient. Yet it is difficult to see who else could have provided the leadership other than the pre–1933 generation.

[1] A. Jacobi-Bettien, *Metallgewerkschaft Hessen 1945 bis 1948*(Marburg, Verlag Arbeiterbewegung und Gesellschaftswissenschaft, 1982), 173.
[2] F. Opel and D. Schneider, *90 Jahre Industriegewerkschaft, 1891 bis 1981* (Cologne, Bund Verlag, 1981), 347.
[3] E. Schmidt, *Die verhinderte Neuordnung 1945–1952* (Frankfurt, Europäische Verlag, 1970), 48–51.

In April 1945, as the American troops took control of Essen, Richard Riegel, a communist metalworker, decided on his own initiative to call a meeting of workers in his factory. He recalls telling an apprentice to pass the word that a factory meeting would be held at 8 a.m. one morning. 'But what is a factory meeting?' asked the young worker.[4]

No one under 30 had any experience of trade-union or political activity based on open and publicized opposition to what employers and government laid down. Workers returned to the only organizational forms which they remembered, had experienced, or had been told about—works' councils in factories, mines, and steel plants, and trade-unions acting above the workplace level. In the industrial city of Bochum, 83 per cent of the works'-council members elected in steel and metal plants in 1945 had been born before 1905;[5] 63 per cent of them had belonged to the pre–1933 SPD-orientated metalworkers' union, DMV, and only 1.3 per cent had been active in the pre–1933 communist RGO.[6]

Workers turned to those leaders, at all levels, who had a record of trade-union activity prior to 1933, or those, like Otto Brenner in Lower Saxony or Willi Richter in Hesse, who had been involved in clandestine anti-Nazi activities during the Hitler era. Those elected to leadership positions in the first weeks of the Allied arrival in Western Germany remained, and were confirmed in office thereafter. Richter, for example, was confirmed as head of the Hesse trade-union federation in August 1946 with 177 votes against 36 for a communist opponent.[7] The leadership of the trade-unions in Hanover elected in May 1945 had to resubmit themselves and their proposed constitution for reconfirmation at union meetings in November, in accordance with orders from the British occupation authorities. The men and the rules agreed upon in May were not altered in any way six months later.[8]

With the exception of a small group of younger men who came with the American and British armies in the spring of 1945 the bulk

---

[4] P. Altmann, *Hauptsache Frieden* (Frankfurt, Röderburg-Verlag, 1985), 142.

[5] M. Wannöffel, 'Gewerkschaftlicher Neubeginn und Gewerkschaftspolitik in Bochum nach dem zweiten Weltkrieg' (thesis, Bochum University, 1982), 94,

[6] Ibid.

[7] A. Weiss-Hartmann, *Der freien Gewerkschaftsbund Hessen* (Marburg, Verlag Arbeiterbewegung und Gesellschaftswissenschaft, 1982), 101.

[8] F. Hartmann, *Geschichte der Gewerkschaftsbewegung nach 1945 in Niedersachsen*, (Hanover, Göttingen University, 1972), 39.

of emigré trade-unionists were unable to return until early 1946 or even later. Normal postal traffic with Germany was not re-established until March 1946. The thread running through some accounts of the rebirth of German trade-unions, that the US military government sought 'to promote a congenial leadership' by 'assisting the fortunes of Markus Schleicher . . . and Willi Richter',[9] does not give sufficient emphasis to the fact that most if not all those who later came together to form the West German trade-union confederation, the Deutscher Gewerkschaftsbund (DGB), were already accepted universally as union leaders by midsummer 1945.

Political affiliation at this early stage was not so determinant. At the factory meeting in Essen, for example, the communist Riegel was elected chairman of the newly formed works' council and he went on to become a member of the five-strong executive committee of the Essen trade-union council—a committee which was carefully balanced with two social democrats, two communists, and a christian democrat.[10] The same story was repeated all over Germany. Works' council elections were paralleled by the rebuilding of a town- or city-wide trade-union with both workplace and geographical union building taking place under the guidance of pre–1933 union activists or officials.

EINHEITSGEWERKSCHAFT

There was one crucial difference with the pre–1933 situation. That was the decision to form unions incorporating all political tendencies. Much has been written on the significance of the principle of the *Einheitsgewerkschaft* (united union). For Wolfgang Abendroth, who, until his death in 1986, occupied the kind of place as a radical historian-cum-political-activist that in Britain would be associated with an E. P. Thompson or, earlier, an R. H. Tawney, the creation of a trade-union incorporating all political tendencies was the 'most positive achievement'[11] of German labour after

---

[9] C. Eisenberg, 'Working Class Politics and the Cold War: American Intervention in the German Labour Movement', in *Diplomatic History*, 7 (Autumn, 1983), 289.

[10] Altmann, *Hauptsache Frieden*, 143.

[11] Wolfgang Abendroth, 'Das Erbe des Widerstandes: Einheitsgewerkschaft', in A. Ulrich (ed.), *Hessische Gewerkschafter im Widerstand* (Giessen, Anabas-Verlag, 1985) (ed.), 310–317.

1945, a view shared by most historians of the post-war German trade-union movement.[12] In comparison with the trade-unions of 1933, split as they were into socialist-, communist-, Christian-, and company-orientated organizations, the agreement on a united union in 1945 was considerable progress.

Almost automatically, the principle of 'one factory, one union'[13] became so established that it was taken for granted. The more important debate and decision concerned union organization above the level of the workplace. What kind of an *Einheitsgewerkschaft* was desired—highly centralized with finance, functionaries, and policies controlled by the leadership, or a federation of separate industrial unions, each an *Einheitsgewerkschaft* in its own right but otherwise autonomous? In German, the term *Einheitsgewerkschaft* is taken as a concept to mean a union including all political tendencies with sole representational rights in a workplace or industry. But the principle of *Einheit*—unity—was also applicable to the overall form of union organization, and *Einheitsgewerkschaft* can also be taken to mean one union for all workers in all industries, all sectors, everywhere. It will be necessary in the following discussion to keep the concept of *Einheitsgewerkschaft* (industrial unions including all political tendencies) separate from the idea of one united general union for all workers.

At first sight a centralized, general *Einheitsgewerkschaft* appears to be the model closest to communist ideas on trade-union organization, and that view was advanced by AFL American labour advisers to General Clay the military governor of the American zone.[14] Yet the strongest advocates of a centralized trade union were the SPD trade-union leaders in the British zone led by Hans Böckler, all of whom had been strongly anticommunist under Weimar.[15] One problem that divided the trade-unions before 1933 —the division along political or religious lines—had been resolved,

[12] See H. Grebing, *Geschichte der deutschen Arbeiterbewegung* (Munich, Nymphenburger Verlagshandlung, 1966), 272, and Gerhard Beier, 'Einheitsgewerkschaft: zur Geschichte eines organistorischen Prinzips der deutschen Arbeiterbewegung', in Gerhard Beier, *Geschichte und Gewerkschaft* (Frankfurt, Otto Brenner Stiftung, 1981), 315–56.

[13] 'In jedem Betrieb, auf jeder Baustelle, nur eine Gewerkschaft' in *Einheitsgewerkschaft*, July 1945 (journal of the German group in the French Confédération Générale du Travail), 6.

[14] See F. Gannon, *Joseph D. Keenan* (Lonham, Md., University Press of America, 1984), 76.

[15] See Schmidt, *Die verhinderte Neuordnung*, 37–40.

but another remained, and that was the split between manual workers (*Arbeiter*), office workers (*Angestellte*), and civil servants (*Beamter*), the latter category in Germany extending to public servants such as teachers and postal workers as well as civil servants. Böckler and the other advocates of a centralized *Einheitsgewerkschaft* sought to overcome these divisions by incorporating all employees in one organization. Böckler's vision was ambitious. Had it been put into effect, German workers would have had a powerful trade-union organization at a key early stage in post-war German history.

This was one reason that led the British occupation authorities to discourage Böckler. They withheld permission for further union organization above the workplace level until the Germans agreed to drop the idea. A TUC delegation, including Jack Tanner, the engineers' president, visited Germany in November 1945, and told Böckler that the British would not support his idea for a centralized *Einheitsgewerkschaft*. During and immediately after the war's end the TUC had only had the most superficial consideration of trade-union policy in Germany, and there was intensive briefing by government officials in London and by the British military government labour experts, prior to and during the trip. Indeed, the TUC delegation spent three days in Germany before even meeting any German trade-unionists. The principal objective from the government side was to secure TUC endorsement of the existing policy on trade-union organization based on a cautious development of workplace-elected officers gradually coming together in separate unions.[16] Contrary to the widespread myth that the TUC suggested the form of industrial relations and trade-union structures eventually developed in West Germany, there is no written or oral evidence from the period laying down any specific blueprint from the TUC. What drove the TUC to its opposition to Böckler's general union was neither organizational, nor even finally political, unease with the idea. Rather the TUC's approach appeared to be determined by its English analysis of the German character. The TUC delegation sent a letter to Böckler on 27 November 1945 making clear their position:

[16] Rolf Steininger has exhaustively investigated the TUC's approach to German labour developments, 1944–46, in *England und die deutsche Gewerkschaftsbewegung 1945–1946* in (Bonn, Archiv für Sozialgeschichte, Verlag Neue Gesellschaft, 1978), 41–118.

We are disturbed about your desire to have one Trade Union . . . Even if this desire comes from the workers we feel it will mean in practice that all effective power will ultimately reside in a small group of men at the top. Although arrived at by a different path, this will be the same position as when the Nazis took power. Once again the rank and file will wait for orders from the centre . . . And we feel that if the workers are too far removed from the centre (as they may well be in one huge Trade Union) they will lose interest and merely obey orders . . . the great weakness of the German Trade Unionists is this tendency in the German people to blindly obey instructions from Headquarters. We, therefore, as representatives of a great Trade Union Movement, which sincerely desires to see a real democracy in Germany, ask you to modify your plan so that a small number of Unions shall have complete autonomy over the industrial affairs of their members.[17]

As with the Labour government's lack of support for the SPD's call for a socialized economy, the TUC also disappointed the hopes of the German trade-unionists for a far-reaching, all-embracing trade-union federation. Böckler and his colleagues accepted the TUC advice, and at the end of 1945 let drop their concept of a powerful, mass trade-union organization representing all workers irrespective of job, trade, or industry. In that sense, the TUC, like the Labour government (and Party) acted against the wishes of German working-class leaders in 1945. It was not by imposing an elderly SPD leadership on the unions that the British, as an occupying power, curtailed radicalism, but by a straightforward political rejection of the demands put forward by Böckler, and those veteran German union leaders.

Hopes that in the French zone where the Labour Division of the French military authorities was much influenced by the CGT, itself a relatively centralized general union, might support the development of a general *Einheitsgewerkschaft* came to nothing. The French dismissed the idea as 'a left-over from national-socialist mysticism'.[18] They had a point. The German Labour Front was one of the Nazi organizations dissolved as soon as Germany was occupied. The writers of the Buchenwald Manifesto had called for the transformation of the Labour Front into a democratic body.[19]

[17] TUC letter to Böckler, 27 Nov. 1945, printed ibid. 113.
[18] 'Le Syndicalisme en zone française', in *La Révue de la zone française*, 6,7 (April, May 1946) quoted in Johannes Kolb, *Metallgewerkschaften in der Nachkriegszeit* (Frankfurt, Europäische Verlagsanstalt, 1970), 77.
[19] K.-J. Ruhl (ed.), *Neubeginn und Restauration* (Munich, DTV, 1982), 177.

This was also the suggestion made by Fritz Tarnow, a former ADGB president, in exile in Sweden, but his view was not shared by the majority of German trade-unionists in exile in Sweden.[20] The German Labour Front was so much a symbol of Nazi and employers' control that to call for its transformation was unrealistic. No one could dispute the democratic credentials of Böckler but the centrally controlled union he wished to create, although entirely an independent trade-union organization, was clearly a reminder of the central control associated with fascism.

Those who harboured hopes that something might be salvaged of the idea of one big union were also to be disappointed. The WFTU came down decisively in favour of industrial unions. A delegation led by Sir Walter Citrine but including a Russian representative and the Left-leaning Louis Saillant, himself still a secretary of the French CGT—a centralized confederation—toured Germany in February 1946. The delegation rejected the idea of a centralized union as 'unwise' and called for the development of industrial unions, each being financially autonomous.[21] The WFTU recommendation, following on the TUC's rejection, was crucial in burying the putative development of a centralized union in the Western zones at the beginning of 1946. Critics of WFTU activity in Germany[22] have not acknowledged the service of the WFTU in endorsing the idea of autonomous industrial unions which soon proved an anticommunist bulwark.

Johannes Kolb in his pioneering research into the organization of metalworkers after 1945 is emphatic that it was the occupation authorities—an extra-German force—who prevented the creation of a general *Einheitsgewerkschaft*,[23] and both the TUC and WFTU opposed the idea. However, later and more detailed research into local and regional development of unions in 1945 and 1946 calls for a modification of that judgement and leads to a conclusion that German workers themselves were unsure about the wisdom of one big union. The general *Einheitsgewerkschaft* was a creation of the

[20] Dieter Günther, *Gewerkschafter im Exil: Die Landesgruppe deutscher Gewerkschafter in Schweden von 1938–1945* (Marburg, Verlag Arbeiterbewegung und Gesellschaftswissenschaft, 1982), 129.
[21] *Report of the Commission of the WFTU to Investigate Conditions in Germany*, Feb. 1946.
[22] See e.g. P. Taft, *The AFL from the Death of Gompers to the Merger* (New York, Harper, 1959), 348–9.
[23] Kolb, *Metallgewerkschaften in der Nachkriegszeit*, 53.

first hour to serve immediate needs—the common social struggle to keep basic services functioning, cope with the refugee problem, chase Nazis out of administrative positions, maintain food provision, and restart production especially in the mines. But in many areas the metalworkers, and especially the transport workers, responsible for rail and water traffic, had already insisted on developing industrial unions. In Hamburg, the metalworkers had begun creating their own autonomous structure by November 1945. In a meeting with the TUC delegation, Hamburg union leaders had rejected Böckler's concept, telling the TUC leaders, 'We want independent, separate trade unions which will be nevertheless linked together at the top level'.[24] Meanwhile in Hesse and Baden-Württemberg the greater part of organization from mid–1945 onwards was along recognizably industrial lines.[25] In Munich, a separate metalworkers' union was launched in June 1945 and it became the dominant union in Bavaria.[26]

So German workers themselves cannot be said to have been unanimously in support of a centralized trade-union structure. German workers, notably outside the Böckler-dominated Ruhr region, shared with the occupation authorities and the WFTU the responsibility for the development of post-war industrial unionism in West Germany. The metalworkers, in particular, were keen on industrial unionism. True, in Lower Saxony, a general *Einheitsgewerkschaft* was created in the summer of 1945, and managed to survive late into 1946 before its members were divided up into industrial unions. Even there the metal-union official, Alfred Dannenberg, recalls that he and Otto Brenner, both pre–1933 metalworkers, clung to their belief that an autonomous metalworkers' union was needed. 'Brenner and I were quite clear. We wanted a metal union. Our tradition was industrial unionism. We did not want to make a fuss while everyone was talking about a general union but we were quite definitely in favour of an industrial union.'[27]

[24] Franz Spliedt quoted in Steininger, *England und die deutsche Gewerkschaftsbewegung 1945–1946* (Bonn, Neue Gesellschaft, 1978), 108. On Hamburg metal union see F. Opel and D. Schneider, *90 Jahre Industriegewerkschaft 1891 bis 1981* (Cologne, Bund Verlag, 1980), 349.

[25] Jacobi-Bettien, *Metallgewerkschaft Hessen*, 90.

[26] See *90 Jahre Gewerkschaft Metall München 1891–1981* (Munich, IG Metall, 1981), 75.

[27] Dannenburg interview.

According to Dannenberg, even Böckler, the champion of the general union principle, later expressed doubts as to whether it would have been practicable.[28] Moreover, the alternative of industrial unions was not as such an Allied, TUC, or WFTU proposal. Since before the First World War the bulk of SPD trade-unionists had been organized along industrial lines. The 1922 congress of the ADGB had agreed in principle to a reorganization along industrial lines. Between 1925 and 1930, in accordance with this policy, a quarter of the ADGB's affiliates had agreed to merge with bigger unions.[29]

The fear expressed by the military authorities[30] that an all-embracing *Einheitsgewerkschaft* was more vulnerable to communist take-over (and the FDGB in the Soviet zone was very much such an *Einheitsgewerkschaft*) than industrial unions cannot be proved. But an examination of union elections confirms that in the three Western zones, if left to a free vote, the German workers, especially the metalworkers, at both works' council and union level, opted to be represented and led by members of the SPD. In this they were returning to pre–1933 traditions. The last full elections for works' councils in the Weimar republic held in 1931 had shown SPD-orientated ADGB union candidates winning 83.6 per cent of all works'-council seats as against 3.4 per cent for the communists.[31] Overall communists were in a minority amongst union leaders at factory, town, and regional level in the Western zones. The areas of Germany occupied by the Western Allies tended to be the more conservative, Catholic parts of the former Reich while the Russians held Protestant Saxony and dominated in Berlin where the left-wing of the SPD and the KPD had been at its strongest before 1933. According to Peter Lösche, the 'trade-union districts of the Ruhr area, with its high percentage of unskilled workers, always belonged to the right wing of the Socialist labour movement'.[32]

---

[28] Ibid.

[29] Kurt Schönhaven, *Die deutschen Gewerkschaften* (Frankfurt, Suhrkamp, 1987), 64 ff.

[30] See Field Marshal Montgomery and British administrators quoted in Schmidt, *Die verhinderte Neuordnung*, 35.

[31] J. Moses, *Trade Unionism in Germany from Bismarck to Hitler 1869–1933* ii. *1919–1933* (Totowa, NJ, Barnes and Noble, 1982), Appendix 12.

[32] Peter Lösche, 'Stages in the Evolution of the German Labour Movement', in A. Sturmthal and J. Scoville (eds.), *The International Labor Movement in Transition* (Urbana, University of Illinois Press, 1973), 117.

Moreover those refugees driven from their homes by the Red Army who had been able to obtain employment were not likely to vote for communist candidates in union elections.

Amongst American historians there is considerable debate about the extent to which right-wing and left-wing officials (the left-wingers being those associated with the CIO and the New Deal, and the right-wingers being strongly anticommunist and AFL-orientated) in the American military government were able to influence or control union leadership by seeking to emphasize 'bottom-up' workplace unionism aimed at producing radical leadership as opposed to those who supported the creation of regional and zonal 'top-down' structures in which veteran officials would predominate.[33] Two clear factions emerged in the American military government. One was the left-wing 'grass-roots' faction grouped around Mortimer Wolf. Opposed to them was the Porter–Rutz group, so called after two officials, Paul Porter and Henry Rutz, who promoted the case of the older Weimar officials. Yet the antithesis between grass-roots, hence left-wing unionists, and those whose credentials dated from before 1933—the Manichean difference between rank-and-file activists and full-time bureaucrats dear to some writers on union affairs—is, in this case, a false one.

As Angelika Jacobi-Bettien concludes at the end of her extremely detailed study of the growth of metal-union organization in Hesse between 1945 and 1948: 'After 1945 there was an extraordinarily close connection between the . . . factories and the unions . . . the works councils acted as the trade-union organ in the factory, carrying out their tasks in co-operation with local trade-union bodies and being responsible to the latter.'[34] Franz Hartmann, the historian of the rebirth of trade-unions in Lower Saxony, writes that typically, the local trade-union official and works'-council chairman were one and the same person.[35] The delaying tactics and antiradicalism of the occupation authorities cannot be seen to be decisive in terms of promoting SPD candidates at the expense of communists. Responsibility in the choice of union leaders after 1945 lies firmly with the workers themselves.

---

[33] The most thorough account of the struggles between the different factions in the US military government is to be found in M. Fichter, *Besatzungsmacht und Gewerkschaften* (Opladen, Westdeutscher Verlag, 1982).

[34] Jacobi-Bettien, *Metallgewerkschaft Hessen*, 313–14.

[35] Hartmann, *Geschichte der Gewerkschaftsbewegung*, 19.

In addition to some appointed and elected positions in the metal unions, communists predominated in the coal mines of the Ruhr, but really only there. The importance of coal as the chief source of energy to get European industry moving again cannot be over-estimated. But whatever their inclination to elect communists to works' councils in the mines, the miners themselves were hardly in a fit state for a serious political-industrial challenge. Apart from chronic shortages of food, the average age of the miners was a relatively high 43; of the returning soldiers who were directed to work in the mines, 50 to 60 per cent deserted. There was an absenteeism rate of 30 per cent as miners took time off to forage for food.[36] So while reports back to Washington or London could speak of the alarm at the strength of communist influence in the mines, the reality was a confused, hungry, mining workforce beset by absenteeism and workers who simply disappeared rather than work in the pits.

In the British zone the control of the Böckler group which was dominated by the SPD, though it included some KPD members, never faced serious challenge. In the steel plants around Bochum, the SPD comfortably controlled the majority of works' councils.[37] In Hesse, Willi Richter led the executive committee for the Hesse trade-union federation which was entirely composed of SPD members. In Hamburg, SPD and KPD members in the metal union did oppose each other but Wilhelm Petersen, who had been head of the metalworkers' union between 1920 and 1933, re-emerged as leader of the Hamburg metal union in 1945. In an election for the union leadership in March 1946 he got 116 votes against 74 for a KPD candidate.[38] In Hanover, where the metalworkers' union under the energetic leadership of the former SAP activist, Otto Brenner, formed the core of the union organization in the area, the SPD was also in control. Of 250 factories organized by the metal union, Alfred Dannenberg recalls only one which had communist leadership in the works' council.[39]

In most Hesse metal factories the SPD outstripped the KPD in works'-council elections by a factor of between 7 and 10 to 1.[40] Mortimer Wolf, who headed the Labour Relations Branch of the

---

[36] M. Balfour and J. Mair, *Four Power Control in Germany 1945–1946* (Oxford, OUP, 1956), 149.

[37] M. Wannöffel, 'Gewerkschaftspolitik in Bochum', 93–7.

[38] Kolb, *Metallgewerkschaften in der Nachkriegszeit*, 38.

[39] Dannenburg interview.

[40] Jacobi-Bettien, *Metallgewerkschaft Hessen*, 241–76.

American military government, observed in February 1946 that in works'-council elections (which he wrongly described as 'shop steward elections'), 'only a handful of Communists were being selected'.[41] This point was echoed by Wolf's political foe, the AFL's Joe Keenan, who wrote in mid–1946: 'The Communists have practically no influence in the trade-unions of Western Germany which are controlled mostly by leaders who have fought against the Nazis and are now pledged to a democratic Germany.'[42]

There is of course an important difference between pre–1933 and post–1945 rivalry between the SPD and KPD for influence and control of German labour. Before 1933 the struggle was expressed in terms of divergent world views, signified by loyalty to competing international organizations, intermittently based on the creation of directly competing unions, and usually couched in language that was polemical and abusive. For a while after 1945 none of these conditions obtained although this did not mean that SPD–KPD rivalry had been eradicated. But it did appear in a new and less virulent form.

The fratricidal *Brüderkampf* of Weimar was over but the SPD trade-unionists made sure that they emerged as the dominant force in the trade-unions. This process started from the very hour that the Nazis lost power. The SPD leadership of the unions was also endorsed massively in workplace and union elections. The political course of the SPD as a party was set by Schumacher in the summer of 1945. It was one of hostility to the Soviet Union and opposition to political unity with the communists. But in the immediate tasks of physical survival and elementary reconstruction these problems hardly impinged on the unions. It was only when the issues beyond those of day-to-day existence and organization came on to the union agenda that the divergence of socialist and communist views would surface. One such issue was international affiliation.

INTERNATIONAL LINKS

In their appeal from London in the autumn of 1944, the exiled German trade-unionists in Britain called upon the international trade-union movement to help in the rebuilding of Germany and

[41] Wolf quoted in Eisenberg, 'Working Class Politics', 288.
[42] Keenan, no date, but written between Apr. and Sept. 1946, quoted in Gannon, *Keenan*, 77.

urged the involvement of the post-war German unions in the ILO.[43] In the first months after the war that appeal went unheeded as the organizational form and rebirth of German unions was determined by German workers, pre–1933 activists and union officials, and the military authorities. One simple reason for this was the ban on mail and visits to Germany. With few exceptions, exiled German trade-unionists in Britain, Sweden, or America were unable to return, or even to write to their colleagues before the spring of 1946. Contact with trade-unionists outside Germany was all but impossible.

The visit by the British TUC delegation in November 1945 was dismissed by Fritz Tarnow as a patronizing if well-meaning attempt to impose 'the English model of unions' on Germany.[44] His views were endorsed by Wilhelm Petersen, the metalworkers' leader from Hamburg in the British zone, who complained about the lack of experience among British officers, 'most of whom hadn't the faintest notion of trade-unionism and those who did wanted to create unions along English lines without any consideration for German views'.[45]

In the spring of 1946, the ban on postal traffic with Germany was lifted, followed shortly by the removal of travel restrictions, though in the latter case the military authorities exercised considerable control through the issuing of entry permits to the different zones; moreover road, rail, and air transport was still limited and uncertain. Who could take advantage of these facilities? As German speakers the Swiss trade-unionists became an important point of contact with the German unions. The Swiss trade-union federation, especially its biggest affiliate, the metalworkers' union, had seen eye to eye with the ADGB before 1933, and was anxious to see a solid social-democratic trade-unionism develop in Germany.

There was more to this than ideological solidarity. Two-thirds of Switzerland's trade was with Germany and it had been raw materials from Germany that had maintained the Swiss economy during the war. For Switzerland, 'Germany was by far the most important trading partner', wrote a Swiss trade-union economist in

---

[43] 'Wiederaufbau Deutscher Gewerkschaften: Eine Vorlage der Landesgruppe deutscher Gewerkschafter in Grossbritannien', in Altmann (ed.), *Hauptsache Frieden*, 87.

[44] Fritz Tarnow, 'Wiederaufbau der deutschen Gewerkschaften', in *Gewerkschaftliche Rundschau für die Schweiz* (Oct. 1946), 422.

[45] W. Petersen letter to K. Ilg, 30 May 1947 (IMFA).

1946.[46] The Swiss unions had emerged stronger at the war's end with a 30-per-cent increase in membership, while unemployment had dropped from 77,000 in 1939 to 14,500 in 1945. For Konrad Ilg, as president of the Swiss Metalworkers and a leading socialist member of the Federal parliament, the economic growth of Germany was essential for his own country's future prosperity.

As early as May 1945, in the Swiss metal-union journal, he was urging the swiftest return to international free trade, and arguing against protectionism.[47] Like his productionist colleagues in the British metal unions, Ilg championed growth, increased output, and trade. For him, this meant German industry had to be restored to full capacity as soon as possible. He used his pre-war contacts with Ernest Bevin to beg the British Foreign Secretary to remove Swiss companies from an export black-list on which they appeared because of their war-time activity. 'Switzerland depends on foreign trade more than any other country. It was for this reason that it was necessary for us to increase our trade with Germany from mid 1940 to 1944, in order to avoid large scale unemployment,' he wrote to Bevin.[48] As soon as postal traffic was re-established with Germany, Ilg was in contact with pre–1933 metal-union leaders. He arranged for food and clothing parcels to be sent to the families of German union leaders, an initiative taken up by the AFL, which in October 1946 began sending CARE packages to selected trade-union officials. The gratitude of the Germans for this charity was genuine, though as the AFL's official historian notes there was 'never enough'[49] for the many thousands of union officials in the American, let alone the hungrier British and French zones. Of more enduring importance was political contact with like-minded trade-unionists from outside Germany. Whereas the WFTU's Louis Saillant, the TUC's Walter Citrine, and the AFL's Joe Keenan or Irving Brown had to work through interpreters, and to have all written material laboriously translated, the IMF's Ilg felt at home and was confident that his political instincts would be shared by his German correspondents.

This was confirmed when Paul Weh, head of the metalworkers in

[46] E. Wyss, 'Die Wirtschaft der Schweiz im Jahre 1945', in *Gewerkschaftliche Rundschau* (April 1946), 210.

[47] *Schweizerische Metallarbeiter Zeitung*, 16 May 1945.

[48] Ilg to Bevin, 23 Aug. 1945 (IMFA).

[49] Taft, *The AFL from the Death of Gompers*, 358.

Cologne, wrote to Ilg in May 1946 expressing the hope that the German metalworkers could again be members of the IMF.[50] In September 1946, Ilg told the British engineering and metal unions of his contacts with Germany. He said that the metal unions 'were developing very well. What the German metalworkers now expect from us is not financial support, but moral support in their hard struggle to set up a free trade-union movement . . . to keep them from . . . Russia's influence.'[51] For Ilg there was a 'great vacuum existing in Central Europe which could not be advantageous, nor can it continue indefinitely'.[52] He urged the British to make contact with the German metal unions and lend their support.

Ilg's contacts were with Germans in the three Western zones and he did not seek contacts with the FDGB metalworkers in the Soviet zone. The WFTU had encouraged meetings between the unions in the four zones, with the promise that a united German union federation could apply for membership of the WFTU. At the first inter-zone union conference in Mainz in November 1946, the WFTU's general secretary, Louis Saillant, expressly urged the Germans not to join the international trade secretariats but to come into the WFTU as a united all-German federation. Ilg had this information from the Stuttgart metal-union leader, Hans Brummer,[53] and it would have stiffened his attitude towards the WFTU prior to the crucial December 1946 meeting between the WFTU and the international trade secretariats which signalled the end of any real hope of integrating the secretariats into the WFTU.

Already by the end of 1946, the German metalworkers, independently of Ilg and the WFTU, had sought to re-establish contact abroad within the framework of industrial-union internationalism. In the autumn of 1946, Wilhelm Petersen, head of the metalworkers' union in Hamburg, and soon to become the president of the metal union for the British zone, had written to the 'English Metalworkers' Union' in London describing the Germans' strength, their intention to 'form a uniform metalworkers' union' in the British zone, and expressing the 'desire strongly to co-operatee with the workers of all countries in the battle for the aims and tasks

[50] P. Weh to Ilg, 29 May 1946 (IMFA).
[51] Minutes of IMF British Section, 28 Sept. 1946 (IMFA).
[52] Ibid.
[53] H. Brummer to Ilg, 6 Dec. 1946.

of international workers'.[54] Petersen's letter found its way to Lincoln Evans, the British steelworkers' leader, and secretary of the British section of the IMF, and a correspondence developed between them. At the founding meeting of the metalworkers' union for the British zone in February 1947, Petersen told delegates that the new German metal union should 'become not just a strong but the strongest member of the International Metalworkers' Federation.'[55]

The orientation of the pre–1933 metal-union officials towards the British and the IMF was to be expected but the major new factor was the existence of functioning metalworkers' organizations in the Soviet zone in which the controlling presence of communists and an orientation towards the WFTU were marked. From the beginning of 1947 onwards there were occasional meetings between metal representatives from the Western and Soviet zones. But far from this process leading ineluctably to unity, each meeting seemed to throw up significant points of division between the communist trade-unionists from the Russian zones and the SPD unionists from the Western zones. The metal-union meetings ran parallel with the inter-zone conferences of the union federations. Two detailed studies of the latter, one by the (ex) German Democratic Republic historian, Albert Behrendt,[56] and a later study by Sylvia Pfeifer,[57] underline the fundamental cleavage between the two political groupings. Their opposition was expressed in the traditional method of bureaucratic manœuvre in which neither side wished to be held responsible for a breakdown. So while agreements on generalizations were reached, anything concrete such as the form of organization or voting for an all-Germany federation was never put to a divisive vote, and anything truly contentious was put off to a following meeting or referred to a working party.[58]

For the German metal-union leaders one divisive issue was their relations with metalworkers outside Germany. At their inter-zone

[54] W. Petersen letter to the 'English Metalworkers' Union', 9 Oct. 1946 (IGMA).

[55] *Protokoll über den ersten Verbandstag der Industrie-Gewerkschaft Metall für die Britische Zone und Land Bremen 20–1 Feb. 1947 (IGMA).*

[56] A. Behrendt, *Die Interzonenkonferenzen der deutschen Gewerkschaften* (Berlin, Tribüne Verlag, 1959).

[57] Pfeifer, *Gewerkschaften und Kalter Krieg, 1945 bis 1949* (Cologne, Pahl-Rugenstein, 1980).

[58] Details ibid. 144–8, 176, 179–85.

meeting in Mannheim, 20–1 February 1947, Brümmer, from the American zone, put forward a list of principles to govern relations between the metal unions in the different zones. The sixth of his eleven headings was 'Cultivation of friendly relations with the IMF'. This was countered with a proposal from the FDGB metal-union representative calling for 'the German metalworkers union to establish relations with the WFTU'.[59] Brümmer argued that the question of relations with the WFTU was a matter for the union federation while the industrial (metal) union could agree to join the international trade secretariat.[60]

So one dividing line between socialist and communist leaders of the German metalworkers was being drawn around the question of affiliation to the IMF. It was a marginal theme barely noticed at the time, yet decisions about the organizations to which a union would affiliate are ultimately statements about the union's political line. From the moment they were able to establish postal and other links with unions outside Germany, the elected leaders of metalworkers in the three Western zones opted unequivocally for a resumption of contacts with the IMF and Ilg. As Wilhelm Petersen wrote to Ilg in May 1947, 'Since the interzone committee for metalworkers has been set up it must be possible for the German metalworkers to be again accepted into the IMF.'[61]

The reintegration of German metal unions into the IMF took a further step forward when Ilg invited representatives of the metal unions in the Western zones to a meeting in Switzerland in May, 1947. He also invited Austrian metal-union leaders, including Karl Maisel, the leading figure in the re-established Austrian trade-union movement. As well as being president of the combined metal-workers' and mineworkers' union, Maisel was the Minister of Social Security in the government which, under the watchful eyes of the Russians, was endeavouring to steer Austria along a path both socialist, in terms of wide-scale state control of the economy, and democratic, in terms of respecting political, cultural, and personal freedoms.[62] That Maisel, despite pressing duties in Austria, took

---

[59] Kolb, *Metallgewerkschaften in der Nachkriegszeit*, 98.

[60] Ibid.

[61] Petersen to Ilg, 30 May 1947 (IMFA).

[62] For details of Maisel's career see A. Magaziner, *Ein Sohn des Volkes* (Vienna, Europaverlag, 1977). For a critical evaluation of Austrian unions after 1954 see Gene Sensenig, *Österreichisch-amerikanische Gewerkschaftsbeziehungen 1945 bis 1950* (Cologne, Pahl-Rugenstein, 1987).

time to come to this pan-German meeting of metal-union leaders is evidence of the importance the IMF retained in the minds of union leaders emerging from the dark years of the Nazi Reich. Both the Germans and the Austrians reported to Ilg that the communists were 'not very powerful', and that, in Austria's case, 'the Socialists have won an overwhelming majority in the union'.[63]

Relieved that he did not have to disguise his feelings as when speaking in front of British or Scandinavian unions, Ilg burst out against his two preferred enemies, communist Russia and the WFTU.

I can hardly believe that the Russians will stop being a dictatorship in the coming years . . . Bolshevism is based on the ruthless use of force . . . and the Russians are possessed by an appetite for power. They do not see or consider things as we do. So it will be extremely difficult to have friendly relations with them.[64]

Ilg outlined to them the failure of the IMF and other international trade secretariats to come to terms with the WFTU. This point was taken by Wilhelm Petersen, the leader of the metalworkers in the British zone, who told Ilg that the Germans had not heard these criticisms of the WFTU before. At the same time his colleague, Oskar Schultze from Bremen, revealed a source of anti-WFTU feeling amongst the Germans. This was the resentment they felt that Saillant, and other WFTU leaders, arrived heading WFTU delegations which paternalistically lectured the Germans on what trade-union organizational form and policies they should adopt, on top of their failure to stand up to Hitler's takeover. For the Austrians, Maisel expressed concern about the WFTU's hostility to the international trade secretariats, and promised to report this on his return to Vienna, as well as the news 'that the "Iron International" is being rebuilt': his Austrian colleague, Dominik Hummel, told the meeting that Austrian trade-unionists did not have much confidence in the WFTU 'because it is exhausting itself with political demands'.[65] Criticism of the WFTU's 'political' orientation was exactly what Ilg hoped to hear. He offered the alternative of the International Labour Organization which 'in contrast to the WFTU provides a possibility of discussing international questions such as

[63] *Konferenz mit Vertretern der deutschen und der österreichischen Metallarbeitergewerkschaften*, Vitznau, 24–6 May 1947 (IMFA).
[64] Ibid.   [65] Ibid.

wages and conditions, production and trade. Participation in the ILO conferences would establish the position and the independence of the German unions.'[66]

However the immediate priority for the Germans and Austrians was to rejoin the IMF. As Maisel explained: 'Although we are only a small country we consider it very important to be members of the IMF',[67] while Petersen summed up the sense of humiliation felt by German union leaders at having continually to seek the approval of the representatives of the occupying powers before undertaking any initiatives: 'As a conquered land it means a great deal to us to have international contacts where we are not considered as defeated people but where we feel we are dealing with colleagues. We believe we can work more effectively in the IMF than is possible in the WFTU.'[68] The Germans reported on their meeting with Ilg and the Austrians at the next inter-zone meeting of the metal unions which met 11–12 June 1947 in Frankfurt. The meeting took place only a week after General Marshall's Harvard speech and so before the Marshall Plan became a great dividing line between socialist and communist union representatives, and at a time when there were still faint hopes that some accommodation between the international trade secretariats and the WFTU could be reached at the executive committee of the WFTU, being held in June 1947 in Prague. Accordingly the German metal-union leaders, including those from the Soviet zone, sent a message calling for 'co-operation on an international trade-union basis [as] a necessary condition for [the] successful reconstruction' of Germany and asked to be invited as guests to the IMF Congress due to be held in Copenhagen in August 1947.[69]

The announcement and initial discussions on the Marshall Plan did not have any dramatically negative impact on relations between SPD and communist metal-union leaders. The description of the Marshall Plan as an imperialist and aggressive act only followed the policy decisions that were made in Moscow leading to the forced and reluctant withdrawal of the Polish and Czechoslovak governments from the Marshall Plan discussions and their participation in

---

[66] *Konferenz mit Vertretern der deutschen und der österreichischen Metallarbeitergewerkschaften*, Vitznau, 24–6 May 1947 (IMFA).
[67] Ibid.   [68] Ibid.
[69] Petersen to Ilg, 18 June 1947 (IMFA).

the launch of Cominform in September.[70] The first post-war congress of the IMF took place immediately after Moscow's instructions to Prague and Warsaw to boycott the Marshall Plan, but before the gathering of communist parties in Poland in September to announce the all-out campaign against the Western powers. For the first time since 1945, representatives of German metal unions could attend an international labour movement gathering in a foreign country.

Five Germans, three from Western zones, and two from the Soviet zone came to the IMF Congress in Copenhagen. They sat as observers, in contrast to their Austrian colleagues who took part as delegates. In his opening speech Ilg praised the pre–1933 German metal union, challenged those ready to criticize the German metalworkers to remember the Hitler–Stalin pact, 'an agreement between Moscow and Berlin . . . concluded in the first place in order to conquer Poland', claimed that it was impossible to imagine 'how the world is ever to be built up again with Germany in the condition it is in at the present', and finally opined that 'if the German metalworkers union is revived, it should be admitted to the International Metalworkers' Federation once again'.[71] Ilg was rebuked by British and Belgian delegates who expressed doubts about readmitting the Germans while public opinion in their countries was still hostile to Germany, and the issue did not surface again at the Congress. The leader of the Belgian metalworkers, Gailly, posed two questions to the Germans: 'Does the German nation recognise the grave responsibility it bears as a result of the events of recent years?' and 'Can the German people give us the necessary guarantee for the future? At the present moment this does not seem to be the case.'[72]

This shocked and disappointed the Germans, who had spent two hard years rebuilding their unions. Anti-Germanism and anti-fascism remained the dominant discourse in Western Europe. As long as the victorious powers failed to resolve the question of Germany the chances of consolidating organizational gains inside the country, or winning acceptance and recognition abroad, must have seemed dim indeed to the German union leaders. If only anti-Germanism could be displaced, and if only antifascism could be

---

[70] See F. Fejtö, *Histoire des démocraties populaires* (Paris, Seuil, 1965), 182–3.
[71] Proceedings IMF 1947 Congress, 31.
[72] Ibid. 50.

superseded, how much easier, it must have seemed, for Belgian, British, and other trade-unionists to accept once again their German brothers as full members of the international trade-union movement.

The IMF Congress in Copenhagen was the first and last time that metal-union representatives from both Western and Eastern zones sat together at an international union meeting outside Germany. For the American- and British-zone metalworkers, Hans Brümmer of Stuttgart reported optimistically on the 'friendly' reception of the Germans and urged his colleagues 'to prove through trade-union work and actions that we are worthy to become members of the IMF'.[73] A sharply different line was taken by Paul Peschke, president of the metal union for the Soviet zone outside Berlin. In an interview with the Danish communist newspaper, *Land og Folk*, he dismissed the IMF as 'not a real international federation', attacked Ilg's hostility to the WFTU, and added that the Copenhagen congress was 'a symbol of disunion'; the IMF had been taken over by 'wolves pretending to be shepherds'.[74]

The president of the Danish metalworkers replied angrily the next day in the Danish social-democratic paper accusing Peschke of misreporting the congress.[75] The Dane's anger was all the greater as the Danish metalworkers had defended the WFTU at the IMF Congress, and it had been the Danish leader who had insisted that IMF entry into the WFTU on acceptable terms was still a desirable goal. So Peschke's intemperate attack in the Danish communist paper only served to confirm Ilg's warnings, repeated at all IMF meetings since 1945, that co-operation with trade-unions in areas now controlled by the Soviet Union would be neither easy nor fruitful.

This took place in August 1947, before the WFTU split over the Marshall Plan, before the launch of Cominform, before the beginning of the public anticommunist crusade in the West. From the moment the German metal-trade-unionists had been able to establish communications with unionists outside Germany they sought to reconnect in one way or another with the IMF. There is no evidence that they were manipulated into so doing by American or British union or military government representatives. On the contrary, independent relations with Ilg allowed the Germans to complain about the heavy-handedness of the Anglo-Saxon ap-

---

[73] *Gewerkschafts-Zeitung*, 1 Sept. 1947.
[74] *Land og Folk*, 5 Aug. 1947.
[75] *Social-Demokraten*, 6 Aug. 1947.

proach to the rebuilding of German unions. But if participation in the IMF allowed the Germans to feel that they were beginning the process of establishing a post-Hitler period in which they could be accepted as members of the international community, it also pointed up the division between the policies and outlook of the social democrats who controlled the metal unions in the Western zones and the communists in charge in the East. The divisions everywhere in Europe between social-democratic or Labour and communist trade-unionists grew much greater from the summer of 1947 onwards. In Germany, the British- and American-zone unions merged in November 1947, a move which was criticized by the Soviet-zone representatives as foreclosing a German-wide federation. But by then the latter's formation seemed an even more distant prospect with not even an agreement on whether the all-German body would be based on independent industrial unions—the western view, or a single centralized body—the communist proposition.[76]

By early 1948 the emergence of two camps—to use a Zhadanovism—was clear to see. In Berlin, the UGO (Unabhängige Gewerkschaftsorganization—Independent Trade Union Organization) a breakaway group from the FDGB, social-democratic in orientation and supported by the Western occupying powers and the AFL, had established itself and was demanding to be recognized, alongside the FDGB, for the workers it represented.[77] The January 1948 inter-zone meeting saw the Western representatives putting forward a set of political principles which any new all-German federation should adopt. These included a commitment to free elections, unions to be independent of party control, and the state to respect individual freedom and other norms of liberal democracy. The communists replied with their demands that the new federation should call for state planning and the nationalization of banks, and, in an evident reminder of the language used in Weimar Germany, insisted that the new union should be a *Kampforganization* (a fighting organization).[78]

[76]   Pfeifer, *Gewerkschaften und Kalter Krieg*, 176.

[77]   Formed with Western support at the end of 1947, the UGO quickly became popular. In FDGB elections in April 1948, the UGO won two-thirds of the votes in the Western sectors of Berlin and, despite considerable obstacles, 40% in East Berlin. See ibid. 223–4, and Eisenberg, 'Working Class Politics', 297–8.

[78]   Ibid. 179–85.

Hostility to the West, muted during the first two years of manœuvring, was now developing rapidly. In February 1948, the Soviet-zone metal union publicly accused the IMF of sabotaging the

formation of a metal trades department of the WFTU . . . Behind such action can be seen the hand of Mr. Brown, the agent in the service of the AFL's leaders who support American monopoly capitalism. Brown has been smuggled into the IMF secretariat by Konrad Ilg . . . German metalworkers will stand by the WFTU and reject the splitting tactics of Brown and Ilg.[79]

Great publicity was given to this attack on Ilg in the trade-union papers of the Soviet zone and to make sure their Western colleagues received the message, the statement was mailed to the metal unions in the British zone. East German trade-union attacks on the attitude of their Western homologues towards the Marshall Plan became more and more shrill. The fused British and American zones were described as being on their way to becoming 'an American colony',[80] and that 'union officials in the West are ready to work for dollar imperialism'.[81] In May 1948, the Soviet-zone metal-union journal sharpened its attack on the IMF and Ilg's 'splitting tactics'; if the Western-zone metal unions joined the IMF it would 'erect a barrier to an all-German metalworkers' union',[82] while their 'activities under the pressure of capitalist occupation powers were promoting the tearing apart of Germany'.[83]

The regression to the language of the 1920s was merely the outward sign of the inward collapse of real moves or even aspirations for trade-union unity from the autumn of 1947 onwards. But it was on the issue of international affiliation that all hopes of unity finally collapsed. The metalworkers in the West, by now merged into a single industrial union for the three zones, arranged a meeting in June 1948 with Ilg, Evans from Britain, Gailly from Belgium, and Irving Brown to discuss affiliation to the IMF. Representatives of the Soviet-zone metalworkers turned up but before they were admitted to the meeting they were asked to withdraw their public statements attacking Ilg and the IMF. They

[79] Peschke to British zone IG Metall, 11 Feb. 1948 (IGMA).
[80] *Der Metallarbeiter*, Mar. 1948.
[81] *Tribüne*, 27 Mar. 1948.
[82] *Der Metallarbeiter*, May 1948.
[83] *Tribüne*, 14 June 1948.

refused to do this and the breach was final.[84] The West German metal union was readmitted as a member of the IMF in October 1948.

[84] 'Neiderschrift der Konferenz mit dem Exekutiv-Komitee des Internationalen Metallarbeiter-Bundes und den Industriegewerkschaften Metall der amerikanischen, britischen, franzözischen Zone und der unabhängigen Gewerkschaftsopposition Berlin', 13 July 1948 (IGMA).

13

The Divisions in the French Unions

AT first sight France fits neatly enough into the conventional narratives and analyses of the origins of the Cold War. The wartime unity leading to a tripartite government of communists, socialists, and christian democrats founders on the rocks of the Truman Doctrine, the Marshall Plan, and the launch of Cominform in 1947. First, the Truman Doctrine in March; then, the expulsion of the communist ministers from government in May, followed by the socialist acceptance and communist rejection of the Marshall Plan. In September 1947, the French communists are accused of reformism and parliamentary cretinism by Zhadanov at the founding meeting of Cominform in Poland. In November, a wave of major strikes hits France. They are repressed by socialist ministers helped by workers willing to maintain production. In December 1947, the principal trade-union confederation, the Confédération générale du Travail (CGT) splits, and the Force Ouvrière confederation is launched.[1]

The split in the CGT has been seen as a benchmark. It was the first post-war split in a trade-union of a major country, taking place against the background of the accelerating American–Soviet conflict. In the view of many historians the development of French

[1] There are numerous studies of this period. Philip Williams, *Politics in Post-War France* (London, Longman, 1954) remains a good general introduction. R.W. Johnson, *The Long March of the French Left*, (London, Macmillan, 1981), Neil Nugent and David Lowe, *The Left in France*, (London, Macmillan, 1982), and Edward Mortimer, *The Rise of the French Communist Party* (London, Faber, 1984), all have good chapters on the period, especially as it concerns left-wing parties and trade-unions. Annie Lacroix-Riz, *La CGT de la libération à la scission de 1944–1947* (Paris, Éditions sociales, 1983), and Alain Bergounioux, *Force ouvrière* (Paris, Seuil, 1975), are detailed studies of French labour in the 1940s. Jean Lacouture's biography *Léon Blum* (Paris, Seuil, 1977), and the second vol. of his life of de Gaulle (Paris, Seuil, 1985), have excellent accounts of the period. Georgette Elgey's *La République des illusions* (Paris, Fayard, 1965), remains a vivid, scholarly account. Irwin Wall, *L'Influence américaine sur la politique Française 1945–1954* (Paris, Balland, 1989), is based on a thorough examination of the American, mainly diplomatic archives covering post-war France. The political passions of the French Left in the years immediately after the Liberation are well captured in Simone de Beauvoir's 2-vol. novel, *Les Mandarins* (Paris, Seuil, 1954).

trade-unionism is seen as dependent on international factors. For some the main issue was the defence of democracy against a Soviet-inspired, communist strategy aimed at creating the kind of tension, chaos, and political instability seen in Prague in February 1948;[2] others prefer to emphasize the role of the United States in seeking the relegation of left-wing economic and social policies.[3]

The forty months between the liberation of Paris and the split of the CGT are amongst the richest, most packed political periods in the history of France. In addition to the CGT itself which had 5.5 million members at the time of its first congress in April 1946, two new giant political formations entered politics: the christian-democratic Mouvement Républicaine Populaire (MRP), and the French Communist Party, Parti Communiste Français (PCF). The latter of course was not strictly a post-war creation, but with its 160 deputies, and 25 per cent of the vote, its ministers in government, its press and intellectuals, and its new institutional presence in so many corners of French society, the massive PCF that emerged from the Resistance fundamentally changed the political landscape. Although the French socialists, the Section Française de l'Internationale Ouvrière (SFIO), seemed overshadowed by their communist comrade-rivals, they too were more present than before the war. Socialist membership doubled to 345,000 in 1946.[4]

Looming over all parties was the formidable figure of de Gaulle whose prestige, authority, and ambition made him a critical part of post-war political processes. De Gaulle was a political institution in himself. His Rally of the French People—Rassemblement du Peuple Français (RPF)—which he launched in the spring of 1947 won 40 per cent of the votes in municipal elections in November 1947.

Another new political factor was the heritage of the Resistance which, once de Gaulle had restored a functioning state by the end of 1944, bestowed authority on a new generation of political leaders like Georges Bidault of the MRP, Guy Mollet in SFIO, and the trade-unionist, Louis Saillant. The latter, in 1947, was carrying

---

[2] Williams described the expulsion of communists from the French government in 1947 as France's 'battle of Prague', *Politics in Post-War France*, 20.

[3] Johnson, *The Long March*, 29–32.

[4] See Williams, *Politics in Post-War France*, 68. From 1948 onwards the SFIO declined in membership, electoral support, and political stature. Writing of the socialists in the 1950s, Williams described 'an ageing bourgeois party, sadly lacking in dynamic energy', Ibid. 71. But for the period 1945-7, the socialists were not yet so moribund.

name cards in which he was identified thrice—as chairman of the National Council of Resistance, as a member of the Executive Bureau of the CGT, and as general secretary of the WFTU.

If the political landscape of France was overfilled with novel topography its inhabitants, the French people themselves, were called to the polls thirteen times for nationwide governmental or municipal elections, or constitutional referendums, between May 1945 and the split in the CGT in December 1947. Each occasion was a moment of political debate prior to the vote. Each result provoked recriminations and altered to some extent the political balance in the country. Despite sharing membership of the governments up to May 1947 most of these polls had the communists and socialists in opposition to each other in the search for electoral endorsement. The percentage of voters for the PCF was relatively stable at between 25 and 28 per cent, while SFIO scored around 23 per cent.

For the trade-unions, this endless round of elections, government changes, and the reawakening of turbulent political life called for responses. The communists in the CGT leadership generally sought to enlist the CGT in support of positions favoured by the PCF, such as endorsing the inclusion of CGT candidates in a common Resistance list in the 1945 municipal election, a move opposed by the socialists. The decision of the CGT leadership in 1945 to allow members to participate fully as political candidates or to hold office in political parties underlined the political difference between those like Benoît Frachon, the joint general secretary, who sat on the Political Bureau of the PCF, and his socialist colleagues in the CGT leadership such as Oreste Capocci, head of the white-collar federation of the CGT, who was a member of the SFIO executive committee, or Albert Glazier, a CGT national secretary who was elected a socialist deputy in October 1945.

If the CGT moved into politics, the political parties of the Left moved into industry. Maurice Thorez, the PCF leader and his fellow communist ministers were as one with their comrades in the CGT leadership in urging higher production while the SFIO decided to set up party branches in factories. The nationalizations meant that many workers now found themselves employees of the state rather than of private capital. The Renault car firm, much of the aircraft industry, the coalmines, the Bank of France, the four main deposit banks, and Air France were taken into public ownership in 1945. In 1946 this was followed by the nationalization of gas, electricity, and the major insurance companies. Under Thorez's ministerial guidance, all public employees and civil servants were given full trade-union rights to organize, elect representatives, and go on strike.

DE GAULLE, THOREZ, BLUM

The relationship between de Gaulle and the Communists is one of the most fascinating in twentieth-century French history. How they used one another, in war and in peace, in domestic and in international relations! By supporting de Gaulle's Free French movement in London and Algiers, and by accepting de Gaulle's authority once he arrived in Paris, the communists achieved the breakthrough to government status, and a broader national acceptability.[5] For his part, de Gaulle's embrace of communists, giving them ministerial posts in North Africa, and then in liberated France, secured his flanks against political attacks from the Left, and the most vigorous of the Resistance fighters. De Gaulle also used the Soviet Union in order to bolster French status, and his own prestige *vis-à-vis* Roosevelt and Churchill. The signing of a Franco-Soviet Treaty with Stalin in December 1944 asserted the independence of French foreign policy.[6] Later on, in the second half of 1947, it seemed almost as if de Gaulle and the communists needed each other, not just as linked objects of mutual vilification, but as specific reference points which defined and justified their respective positions—de Gaulle to save France from communism, the communists to protect democracy from a dictatorial general.[7] The wave of strikes in November 1947 which coincided with de Gaulle's RPF winning 40 per cent of the vote in local elections are often depicted as communist-instigated at the behest of the Kremlin.[8]

---

[5] For a contemporary assessment see Maurice Edelman, *France: The Birth of the Fourth Republic* (London, Penguin, 1944). H-C. Giraud's *De Gaulle et les communistes i: L'Alliance, juin 1941-mai 1943* (Paris, Albin Michel, 1988), suggests that de Gaulle had a secret agreement with Stalin as early as 1941 and this governed his relationships with the communists, including those in the underground CGT, and vice versa.

[6] See Charles de Gaulle, *Mémoires de guerre : Le Salut 1944–1946* (Paris, Plon, 1959), 68–80.

[7] See Jean Lacouture, *De Gaulle*, ii. 310.

[8] See A. Bullock, *Ernest Bevin: Foreign Secretary* (London, Heinemann, 1983), 486–487.

There were plenty of domestic reasons for the strikes, but if Stalin did expect any advantage from the industrial action, it was more likely to be a return of de Gaulle to power than a communist takeover. This indeed would probably have been Stalin's preferred outcome. De Gaulle's profound, ineradicable hostility to American and British dominance in European and global affairs would have seriously perturbed the American-led model that Washington was hoping to impose on the world. De Gaulle back as head of the government, while keeping France clearly in the Western camp, would have refused to subordinate his vision of a leading and autonomous France to the plans of Acheson, Kennan, and others present at the creation of the Cold War. This surely would have suited Stalin's interests far better than social insurrection with the impossible aim of putting communists in power.

Patriotism, a strong French state, and, if anti-Americanism is too strong a word, then deep suspicions about Anglo-Saxon designs, were all attributes of both de Gaulle and the communists. In his memoirs the General is warm about Thorez, who 'rendered service to the public interest', and who 'encouraged workers to produce as much as possible whatever the cost. Was this simply political tactics? The question did not concern me. It was enough that France was being served.'[9] The communists had discovered the advantages of being a national party during the Popular Front era,[10] and their French nationalism also fitted in well with de Gaulle's exalted idea of French destiny. Thorez's office was decorated with the national flag and communist papers bore names like *La Patriote* and *La Marseillaise*. When Churchill came to visit Paris in November 1944, he told de Gaulle that he had expected to confront insurgent crowds; instead he found order and reasoned discussion. 'Your revolutionaries are just like our Labour Party people!' he told de Gaulle.[11]

The appearance of communist strength also needs to be questioned despite the presence of communists in government, their large block of deputies, and their widely circulated press. R. W. Johnson asserts that 'one Frenchman in four was now a communist'[12] which presumably is based on the 25 per cent vote received by

[9] De Gaulle, *Le Salut*, 101.
[10] See Mortimer, *Rise of the French Communist Party*, chs. 6 and 7.
[11] De Gaulle, *Le Salut*, 51.
[12] Johnson, *The Long March*, 36.

the PCF in this period. Instead of marvelling at the 25 per cent of the vote the PCF obtained, one might ask in what other country would being rejected by three out of four voters be hailed as opening the way to power? Is it in order to dramatize the events of 1947, to make a titanic struggle of world significance out of a badly run, half-supported general strike, that some historians have painted the power and position of the French communists in such vivid hues?[13] Was it so likely that the events of 1939–41, when the PCF refused to support the war and painfully had to justify the Hitler–Stalin pact, had been entirely eradicated from French memory? Hugh Thomas writes that such was the power of the communists that the 1939–41 period 'was caused to be forgotten',[14] but forgotten by whom? Certainly not by the socialists. In March 1945, Léon Blum's book, *A l'échelle humaine* (*On the Human Scale*) was published. It was reprinted twenty times in that year alone, becoming one of the best sellers in liberated France. At the book's heart lay a devastating attack on the French communists, especially on their behaviour between 1939 and Hitler's attack on Russia.

Blum, the leader of the socialists since 1920, and the Popular Front premier, had been arrested by the Vichy authorities and placed on trial accused of being responsible for the defeat in 1940. More than 250 observers attended the trial in the winter of 1942. His Ciceronian indictment of Pétain's role in supporting conservative military thinking in the 1930s and his speeches in defence of republican democracy from the dock made him a champion of liberty speaking out from the heart of Nazi-dominated Europe. From there he sent a peace message to French communists. In 1940, Thorez had called Blum 'warlike, with long and crooked fingers, a police informer',[15] but two years later Blum told his Vichy judges:

It is impossible to defend republican freedom in France by excluding the working masses and the part of their leadership orientated toward communism . . . There have been differences between them and me but that is no longer important and I erase them completely from my memory. Let

---

[13] See e.g. Hugh Thomas, *Armed Truce* (London, Hamish Hamilton, 1986), 364–374. Henry Pelling also considers that the French Communist Party 'threatened to supplant the shaky democratic regime . . . set up before the end of the war'. Pelling, *Britain and the Marshall Plan* (London, Macmillan, 1989), 7.

[14] Thomas, *Armed Truce*, 366.

[15] Quoted in J. Lacouture, *Léon Blum*, 437.

us not forget that, as we speak, the Soviet Union is fighting in the war, the same war we were fighting two years ago, against the same enemy. Let us not forget that in the occupied zone of France, the Communist Party is providing a big, a very big share of the hostages and victims. I saw in a newspaper the other day, in a list of hostages, the name of Timbaud. I knew him well. He was an official of the metalworkers' union in Paris. I often met him and [politically] we fought each other. Now he has been shot, going to his death singing the Marseillaise, the Marseillaise of Hugo 'winged but still singing as the bullets fly'. That is how Timbaud, and many like him, went to their deaths. That is all I have to say about the Communist Party.[16]

It was a defiant performance, all the more so from a Jew whose fate, despite his status, could not be guaranteed. With Thorez in the safety of Moscow, here was his socialist rival in France, praising the heroism of the French communists and welcoming the Soviet Union's entry into the war. Before he was taken to captivity in Germany, Blum also endorsed General de Gaulle as the leader of wartime, resisting France and told his Socialist Party comrades to show support for de Gaulle while maintaining and renewing the party organization.

If Blum had praised the bravery of the communists in the Resistance, his comments on them in *A l'échelle humaine*, which appeared in March 1945, came as a great shock. The text had been completed in December 1941 and was highly critical of third-republic institutions and the French bourgeoisie. But an equally condemnatory message in the book concerned communism and the Soviet Union, and the events of 1939 and 1940. His most bitter remarks were reserved for Stalin, whose treaty with Hitler in 1939, wrote Blum, 'had betrayed the peace' while the French Communist Party 'in remaining stubbornly faithful to Stalin, had betrayed France'.[17] Blum accused the PCF of following orders from Moscow, and therefore the French communists were 'not an internationalist party but clearly a foreign nationalist party'.[18] Blum's words from 1941 froze the tentative discussions about unity between communists and socialists which were taking place in early 1945. Recalling the Popular Front period, Blum wrote that the Socialists had suffered because of their identification with the

[16] Quoted in J. Lacouture, *Léon Blum*, 475–6.
[17] Léon Blum, *A l'échelle humaine* (Paris, Gallimard, 1945), 104.
[18] Ibid. 106.

Communist Party. Public opinion had not understood 'the clear distinction between Socialism and Communism even though they represented completely separate forms of working class theory and action'.[19]

So the end of the war in France was marked by a polemic about the nature of French communism from the leading French socialist. The PCF responded with a long denunciation of Blum's book written by Florimond Bonte, a member of the PCF's Central Committee, and a former editor of L'Humanité. Bonte's pamphlet *A l'échelle de la nation: Réponse à l'auteur de 'A l'échelle humaine'* (*At the Level of the Nation: A Reply to the Author of 'On the Human Scale'*) was published as a pamphlet in June, 1945.[20] The debate between Blum and Bonte on the behaviour of communists, socialists, and the French authorities between 1939 and 1941 shows the mutual denunciations already under way in left-wing politics in 1945. Under Blum's guidance, the socialists refused any merger with the communists at the Socialist Party conference in August 1945. The election of the apparently more left-wing schoolteacher of English, Guy Mollet, as the Socialist Party's general secretary at the party congress in 1946 did not produce a change in the anti-merger policy laid down by Blum. In fact, Mollet was elected on a sectarian wave which was critical of the actions of communist ministers in government, the communist propagation of wage restraint, and denunciations of strikes. Thus the communists as a governing party of France found themselves under a twin attack from the anticommunist Blum, who represented the pre-war socialists, and the Marxist Mollet, who represented the younger Resistance militants of SFIO eager for a swifter march to pure socialism.

DIVISIONS IN FRENCH TRADES UNIONISM

On the surface, the CGT emerged from the war a united body. But this was deceptive. Founded in 1895, highly centralized, and with the same general secretary, Léon Jouhaux, since 1909, the syndicalist claims of its key constitutional statement, the 1906 Charter of Amiens, stressed the CGT's role as an instrument of

---

[19] Ibid. 107.
[20] Florimond Bonte, *A l'échelle de la nation* (Paris, PCF, 1945).

social and economic transformation. The Charter, while acknowledging the need for the CGT to ameliorate the lot of workers
through wage increases and reduced working time, described its
main task as preparing for the complete emancipation of the
working class through the overthrow of capitalism by means of a
general strike. This double duty, one of daily work, one of future
upheaval and emancipation, allowed the CGT, in theory and
rhetoric at any rate, to present itself as an instrument of reform and
revolution at one and the same time. Unlike in Britain, where
workers identified principally with their individual union, and only
distantly with the TUC, the CGT in France was the union whose
card members carried. The Charter of Amiens also precluded CGT
involvement with political parties and enjoined its members not to
bring their political beliefs into the union.[21] Jouhaux, writing in
1920, explained the CGT's 'inevitable separation . . . from all
political control' in the context of keeping the unions 'distant from
all parliamentary quarrels'.[22]

The split between the socialists and communists in France in
1920 was far more than a parliamentary quarrel but the principle
of keeping a very clear separation between trade-union organization and activity orientated towards, or under the control of, a
political party was erected into a totem by the CGT leadership. The
1906 injunction to maintain the CGT free from external political
control became, after 1920, and most especially after 1945, a
constant point of reference in the contest with communist activists
in the union.

The first formalized rupture in the CGT took place in 1921,
following the political split between socialists and communists. The
revolutionary syndicalists who were expelled set up a rival trade-
union confederation, the Confédération Générale du Travail
Unitaire (CGT-U) which held its first congress in 1922, thus
launching institutional processes which drove the two union
confederations further apart and the CGT-U closer to the communists. Attitudes on what position to take towards the rival union

---

[21] There are several studies of the CGT in its period. Dolléans, *Histoire du
mouvement ouvrier*, ii. *1871–1936* (Paris, Colin, 1939), remains the classic account.
Léon Jouhaux wrote two books, *Le Syndicalisme et la CGT* (Paris, Sirene, 1920) and
La CGT: Ce qu'elle est, ce qu'elle veut (Paris, Gallimard, 1937). René Mouriaux, *La
CGT* (Paris, Seuil, 1982), is a good overall account, taking the CGT's history to the
1970s.
[22] Jouhaux, *Le Syndicalisme et la CGT*, 140.

internationals, the French occupation of the Ruhr, and the fact that the French Communist Party increasingly drew its leadership from CGT-U militants, deepened the divide. By 1924, as Edward Mortimer has written, 'it was hard to say whether the party had won control over the CGT-U or vice versa'.[23]

Many of the communists who were to be involved in the process leading up to the 1947 split were already in leadership positions in the Communist Party or the CGT-U by the mid–1920s, as were their opposite numbers in the CGT and the SFIO. Others expelled from the young Communist Party included the revolutionary syndicalist, Pierre Monatte, whose Marxist but anti-Stalinist writings had some impact in shaping a leftist anticommunism from 1945 onwards.[24] The politics and personalities of the different Lefts in France were not freshly minted after 1945. Another controversial topic in the history of the post–1945 disputes— financial help for opposing factions from non-French sources—also had precedents from a quarter of a century previously. The Russians subsidized their supporters while Jouhaux received financial help from the ILO, whose director-general was Albert Thomas, the wartime socialist labour minister with whom Jouhaux had closely worked.[25]

The split in the CGT, which lasted from 1921 until 1935, measurably weakened trade-union organization in France. In 1934, fewer than 750,000 French workers carried union cards, two-thirds with the CGT and one-third with the CGT-U. As in other countries the two rivals for leadership and representation of the working class opposed each other until the shock of Hitler's takeover forced some rethinking. The most important and lasting organizational development in this period had been the continuing integration of the leadership of the CGT-U with that of the PCF. CGT-U leaders entered as a group into the leadership of the party and the CGT-U congress in 1929 recognized the leading role of the PCF.[26] The

[23] Mortimer, *Rise of the French Communist Party*, 97.

[24] On Monatte see Philippe Robrieux, *Histoire intérieure du parti communiste* (Paris, Fayard, 1980–4), 198–201. There are also useful biographical sketches of leading French communists, including CGT leaders, in vol. iv (1984).

[25] See Mortimer, *Rise of the French Communist Party*, 92, for Soviet financial help, and M. Fine, *Towards Corporatism: The Movement for Capital-Labor Collaboration in France 1914–1936* (Madison, University of Wisconsin Press, 1971), 333, for Thomas's support for Jouhaux.

[26] Mouriaux, *La CGT*, 67.

PCF, for its part, based its organization on factory cells, so when the tidal wave of left-wing unity of the Popular Front era swept all before it the communists were extremely well placed to increase their organization, and influence.

The four years of the Popular Front (1934–38) were, and remain, extremely important in the history of the French Left, especially of the trade-union movement.[27] The CGT and CGT-U merged in 1935. Union membership increased from 750,000 to 5 million. There was an electoral pact between communists and socialists leading to the Popular Front government under Léon Blum. A general strike and factory occupations in 1936 led to laws providing the forty-hour week, paid holidays, and workplace delegates. The aircraft industry was nationalized. For the purposes of this study two points are worth stressing. During the period between 1934 and 1938 it was not that French workers changed and identified with the revolutionary programme of the PCF, rather it was French communism that changed and identified itself with the pragmatic needs of French workers. Secondly, the unity inside the CGT, although it provided an immense magnet drawing workers into the union, thus enhancing the power and authority of CGT representatives, was a unity of convenience rather than whole-hearted fusion based on a commonality of ideology, vision, and purpose.

If the CGT sought to show a common profile in its domestic action and demands, the question of international policy and its attendant loyalties and affiliations remained divisive. One issue was the policy of non-intervention in Spain, and then the Munich agreement. Jouhaux's, and hence the CGT's, active participation in the ILO was another cause of division as was the question of which international federation the unified CGT should belong to. In 1935, the communists suggested a joint affiliation to Profintern and the International Federation of Trade Unions but Jouhaux, a vice president of the IFTU, insisted on staying with the Amsterdam international alone.[28]

[27] The literature on the Popular Front is extensive. Works already cited cover the period well. See, especially, Edward Mortimer's discussion of the PCF becoming a national party over those four years. Alain Prost, *La CGT à l'époque du Front populaire* (Paris, Seuil, 1964) provides a detailed account.

[28] See B. Georges *et al.*, *Léon Jouhaux dans le mouvement syndical français* (Paris, Presses Universitaires de France, 1979), 144. The issue disappeared when Profintern stopped functioning.

On these, as on other issues, the communists from the CGT-U did not bring the differences to a head and generally gave way. But whatever the various subjects which occasioned the divisions it was clear enough that the fissure was straightforwardly between communists, and non-communists. Although the latter maintained a majority in the unified CGT executive, the communists won control of the major industrial federations representing the metal, railway, textile, and building workers. The metalworkers, for example, expanded from 40,000 in 1935 to 800,000 in 1938, and the metal federation's secretary, Ambroise Croizat, was a communist deputy. Jouhaux's control of the executive rested on a complicated system of election which gave considerable weight to the departmental, that is, geographical, organizations of the CGT. For the most part, the surge of membership and authority of the unified CGT from 1936 onwards benefited the former CGT-U leaders. The importance of the political differences and struggles inside the CGT in the Popular Front era is that to a large extent they prefigure the differences a decade later, from 1944 to 1948. The same arguments, the same personalities, and the same accusations were to be heard again and again.

While 1935 and 1936 showed the value of including communists in the Popular Front movement it did not resolve the problem of the political division between the two standard-bearers of the Left. The CGT was unified on paper and its outward unity was central to its success under the Popular Front, but no one inside the CGT had any illusions that the the question of the communist–socialist relationship had been resolved. To maintain their identity the anticommunists launched their own weekly journal, *Syndicats*, to counter the influence of the communist trade-union weekly, *La Vie ouvrière*. In 1937, the latter sold 100,000 copies against 60,000 for *Syndicats*. Jouhaux, who kept a distance from the hardline anticommunists grouped around *Syndicats* (true to his embrace of the *union sacrée* in 1914, Jouhaux supported French rearmament and was opposed to the Munich agreement, unlike the pacifist Syndicats group) was none the less determined that the policies and the leading personalities from the pre-unified CGT would remain dominant in the unified CGT. On the ground, too, there were campaigns against the growing influence of the communists. The SFIO tried to organize factory groups and charged the communists with being *mouscoutaires*, following Moscow's orders, and forcing employers to engage in 'Stalinist hiring practices'.[29] The debate broke into the open as early as 1937 when Jouhaux had to intervene to prevent communists taking over certain departmental unions. The word 'colonialization' began to be used by anticommunists to describe what they denounced as the undue influence of the PCF.[30] The revived and unified CGT lasted as long as the Popular Front governments did. Impressive as the gains and growth of the unified CGT had been, the wider political problem of creating a solid and enduring left-wing government was beyond the reach of the parties of the day. Suspicion of communist motives and national loyalty remained deep. The CGT was a testing ground for joint work but it seemed as if the communists were continuing to operate as a faction, influenced, even guided from outside, and seeking to place their activists in as many key positions as possible. The communists could argue that their younger, more militant leadership corresponded better to the needs of the day, and removing supporters of Munich or opponents of sending arms to Spain was no more than the latter deserved. The experience of the CGT in the Popular Front era can be seen as throwing into sharper relief, rather than resolving, the question of communist–socialist relations in the trade-unions.

The defeat in November 1938 of the CGT general strike against the Daladier government's harsh economic austerity programme, which proposed the abolition of the forty-hour week and other gains from 1936, only worsened relations between communists and non-communists in the CGT. Membership sank in 1939 from 5 million to around 2 million as employers settled scores and dismissed union activists. The government at the same time ejected trade-unionists from the public boards to which they had gained admittance after 1936. Several hundred CGT militants, mostly communists, were imprisoned after fights with police who were evicting strikers. It was a period of revenge by reactionary French employers and public authorities after the concessions they had been forced to make three years previously.[31]

The recriminations broke along the line of communists and non-

[29] Quoted in Henry Chapman, 'The Political Life of the Rank and File: French Aircraft Workers During the Popular Front, 1934–1938', in International Labor and Working-Class History (1986), 13–31.
[30] Georges et al., Léon Jouhaux, 205.
[31] See Guy Bourdé, La Défaite du Front Populaire, (Paris, Maspero, 1977).

communists. The Syndicats group issued an appeal for 'constructive trade-unionism, free of political interference', while the communists called for full parity in the CGT's leadership, hinting that Jouhaux should accept the former CGT-U leader, Benoît Frachon, as joint general secretary, a move Jouhaux contemptuously rejected. As CGT membership slumped, the political infighting worsened. The circulation of the communist *La Vie ouvrière* increased to 200,000 while the anticommunist *Syndicats* went up to a weekly sale of 100,000. Was it simply anticommunist venom or keen political premonition which led René Belin, leader of the Syndicats group to mention 'rumours suggesting that the Soviets will get together with Hitler' in his paper in January 1939?[32] At the beginning of 1939 it was a serious insult to make such a suggestion and it bode ill for future unity within the CGT.

In some ways, the Syndicats group foreshadowed the anticommunist Résistance Ouvrière (later Force Ouvrière) group which emerged after 1944 inside the CGT. Belin and some of his other Syndicats associates became completely discredited because of their participation in the Vichy government, whereas the trade-unionists associated with Résistance Ouvrière, while being just as opposed to communism as the pre–1939 Syndicats group, were able, as their name suggests, to enter post-Liberation politics with a proud record of anti-German activity. The question of how one had behaved under Pétain, was of course the great dividing point in France after the end of the war, and so comparisons between Syndicats and Force Ouvrière are otiose. The point was that the unified post–1935 CGT had within it irreconcilably opposing politics organized around publicly known groups. Had the specific events in 1939, or the Hitler–Stalin pact and then the invasion of Poland not forced the issue it was difficult to see the CGT not splitting again once the Popular Front governments had disappeared.

In September 1939 the CGT under Jouhaux immediately endorsed the government's declaration of war. The communists, after initially pledging their support in a war against Hitler, were left on the hook of loyalty to Moscow's pronouncement that it was an imperialist war which communists must oppose. During the period of the phoney war, it seemed as if the French government took more seriously the internal war against communists than the

---

[32] *Syndicats*, 12 Jan. 1939.

business of dealing with the enemy across the Rhine. Communist trade-unionists were interned, deputies arrested, and their papers closed down. The CGT leadership moved against their communist *confrères* who were dismissed from the executive. Frachon went into hiding. The PCF leader, Thorez, fled to Moscow. In effect, at the end of 1939, the CGT was once again split into communist and non-communist sections.

14

External Interference in French Labour

ONCE the Germans were at war with the Soviet Union, the split CGT rediscovered the virtues of unity. Jouhaux had remained hostile to Vichy and, like Blum, had praised the courage of communist militants as well as endorsing de Gaulle's leadership. He sought out Frachon to propose the reintegration of the communists into the CGT on the pre-war basis. The so-called Perreux Agreement of April 1943 was important because it allowed the reunited CGT to be represented in the National Council of Resistance and to stake a claim to posts in de Gaulle's provisional government based in Algiers.[1] Was this unity better rooted than that which existed between 1935 and 1939? With Belin, the animator of the Syndicats group, discredited because of his participation in the Vichy administration, did this mean a softening of differences between communists in the CGT and their pre–1939 rivals? With Jouhaux taken to Germany as a prisoner in 1943, not to return until May 1945, nine months after Frachon moved into the CGT headquarters in Paris, was the way now open to accept communist leadership of the unified CGT?

Whatever hopes there were for an affirmative answer to these questions, the divisions inside the reunified CGT between communists and non-communists were soon to be as acute after the Liberation as they had been in the years before the Soviet Union's entry into the war. It is worth stressing the distinction between the Liberation, which for most of France was an accomplished fact by the autumn of 1944, and the European war's end, nine months later. The restoration of the state's authority, based on an enhanced Popular Front programme, was the priority for the communists. Their sense of duty was orientated towards securing maximum support for the successful prosecution of the war in which the Red Army, and the Soviet Union under Stalin, were performing so prodigiously.[2]

[1] R. Mouriaux, *La CGT* (Paris, Seuil, 1982), 86. M. Edelman, *France: The Birth of the Fourth Republic* (London, Penguin, 1944), 57.
[2] See E. Mortimer, *The Rise of the French Communist Party 1920–1947*, 323–7.

If this meant that the PCF now definitively buried any lingering desire for a Leninist seizure of power, its line none the less corresponded to the mood of the moment, especially amongst industrial workers who, as in 1936, flocked into the CGT. The rise by communists into positions of control inside the CGT after September 1944 was helped in several instances by their rivals. The purge of any officials who could be accused of collaborating with Vichy was carried out under the guidance of Oreste Capocci, a prominent SFIO member, who headed the white-collar federation of the CGT. In this post-Liberation period, the socialists were more radical in their general political line than the more cautious PCF, and Capocci went about his task with a zeal worthy of Robespierre.[3]

Two other factors helped the communists' rise in the CGT. Several prominent non-communist CGT leaders prior to 1939 now went into full-time politics and became ministers in the provisional government. Others, such as Jouhaux's lieutenant, Louis Saillant, who had worked in the Resistance during the war, had now moved much closer to communist positions.[4] Secondly, the CGT failed in its attempt to merge with the Catholic trade-union, the Confédération Française des Travailleurs Chrétiens (CFTC). The CFTC leaders had played a prominent role in the Resistance. The CFTC had called, jointly with the CGT, for a general strike in August 1944 as troops neared Paris, and the CFTC's leader sat on the Council of National Resistance alongside the CGT representative. At the war's end the CFTC, like the new Christian-democratic

[3] Mouriaux, *La CGT*, 88, and A. Bergounioux, *Force ouvrière* (Paris, Seuil, 1975), 29. Cappoci paid a price for his 1944 purges 4 years later when FO militants refused to elect him to the executive at FO's first constituent congress.

[4] Saillant also had family connections to the PCF. His father had been expelled from the CGT in 1921 because of his adherence to a revolutionary position, and Saillant grew up in Valence under the influence of Pierre Sémard, later leader of the CGT-U railway workers. Saillant's wife came from a prominent communist family. The war thrust Saillant into posts of high influence. He succeeded Bidault as chair of the Council of National Resistance and, of course, became WFTU general secretary in Sept. 1945 with the backing of the Soviet and the communist unions. In the autumn of 1944 he is reported to have said that he was the most important man in France after de Gaulle, though as the source for that remark is Jouhaux one has to be careful in accepting it. Saillant contributed to *Résistance ouvrière* in 1945, and never joined the PCF, so it is inaccurate to mark him down, as do several American historians, as a communist. None the less he depended on communist support to sustain his personal position and to buttress his genuinely held views on the importance of unity, and to maintain the politics of the democratic revolution called for by the Council of National Resistance.

party, the MRP, with which it was closely associated, supported policies of wide-scale nationalization, trade-union rights, and social welfare.[5]

The presence of the CFTC, with about 1 million members, as a rival organization to the CGT has to be considered in any assessment of CGT and Communist Party power in this period. CFTC lists attracted considerable support in elections for social-security committees in 1947. This encouraged anticommunists in the CGT in their view that PCF control of the trade-union was not popular with members, and CFTC members played an important role in the strike movement of November and December 1947 by refusing to accept CGT and communist calls to strike.

The most important opposition to the stronger communist presence in the CGT was not external however but was found within the CGT's own ranks. In the middle of 1943, the first issue of *Résistance ouvrière* appeared as the journal of the non-communists in the CGT. It was expressly designed to counter the influence of the communist-controlled *La Vie ouvrière*. The guiding force in *Résistance Ouvrière* was Robert Bothereau, a member of the CGT executive committee since 1933, and an assistant general secretary of the CGT under Jouhaux since 1940. To begin with, Résistance Ouvrière was the home of a loose grouping of non-communists including SFIO activists, revolutionary syndicalists, the loyal followers of Jouhaux, and those like Saillant who wanted the CGT to become a permanent and accepted body with established political rights in the economic and social spheres. The pages of *Résistance ouvrière* in 1945 carried articles by Saillant and others, including Albert Camus, arguing their respective positions. Bothereau himself published a short history of French trade-unions in April 1945. It described the divisions of the 1920s and 1930s. The book was aimed at the millions of new CGT members. In it Bothereau made clear his opposition to communist dominance in the CGT. 'Our trade-unions jealously maintain their independence and generally refuse to be placed under the aegis of a political party . . . any attempt by a political party to take over the union inevitably results in the mass of trade-unionists leaving the union,

---

[5] Henri Hamon and Pierre Rotman, *La Deuxième Gauche. Histoire intellectuelle et politique de la CFDT* (Paris, Seuil, 1984), 23–5.

and becoming unorganized, or turning to free and independent organizations.'[6]

The origins of Résistance Ouvrière lay in providing a home to those elements in the CGT outside the PCF. It was a non-communist rather than an anticommunist grouping. At what point did it become the rallying point for a more virulent anticommunism? For Alain Bergounioux, the difference between communists and socialists on what attitude to take towards the referendum in November 1945 was the moment of division.[7] Annie Lacroix-Riz proposes the socialists' opposition in the summer of 1946 to the wage demands of the CGT, and their endorsement by the PCF, as the moment when the two tendencies moved into mutual open opposition.[8] In August 1946, Blum accused the PCF of 'taking over the control of the trade-union movement'.[9]

For others, the division dates from the first meeting of the CGT's national committee (a larger body than the executive) in September 1945 at which a communist majority was visible in votes on issues such as formally making Benoît Frachon the joint general secretary with Jouhaux. 'For the first time since the liberation', wrote one of Jouhaux's supporters, 'a vote has clearly split our movement into a majority and a minority. Yesterday's majority [i.e. Jouhaux and the non-communists] has become today's minority . . . Two different conceptions [of trade-unionism] can now begin to oppose each other.'[10]

Yet the hunt for a precise moment when the division can be said to be clear, or a single most important cause, seems sterile. Since 1920 the two opposing organizational and political forces in the French working class had been struggling for control of the trade-union movement. The political changes after the Liberation, and the participation of the PCF as a constitutional and moderating force in the government altered the way the communists in the CGT conducted their business, but there was no cease-fire in the battle between them and their opponents for control of the CGT. In terms of organized, institutional presence the creation of the Résistance

[6] Robert Bothereau, *Histoire du syndicalisme français* (Paris, Presses universit-aires de France, 1945), 39.

[7] See Bergounioux, *Force ouvrière*, 34.

[8] A. Lacroix-Riz, *La CGT de la libération à la Scission de 1944–1947* (Paris, Éditions sociales, 1985), 124–7.

[9] *Le Peuple*, 6 Aug. 1946.

[10] R. Deniau, in *Résistance ouvrière*, 44 (Sept. 1945).

Ouvrière movement in the war, and its continuing activities afterwards shows that the CGT was far from united even if in formal terms it enjoyed a unified structure after 1945.

Résistance Ouvrière changed its name to Force Ouvrière in December 1945. Thus six months after the war's end, and arising from internal forces inside the French trade-union movement, the nucleus of a non-communist CGT with determined leadership, an effectively written paper as an organizing tool, and even a resounding name was already in place. The previous quarter-century of French trade-union existence had shown how the CGT was liable to split along the line of communism and non-communism. After 1945 the CGT was again unified but not united. The crisis that led to the third split in the CGT since 1920 burst out in the last months of 1947 but before then serious differences had arisen. These differences, in addition to the institutional presence of the Force Ouvrière, suggested that the CGT with a communist dominance, if not formal control at many leadership levels, was a far more fragile body than its impressive membership and wide-ranging presence suggested.

In February 1947, the American embassy reported back to Washington of the 'insoluble crisis growing out of the conflict between wages on one side and prices and public finance on the other'.[11] The crisis of inflation, an ever-declining franc, and inadequate purchasing power had been simmering since the Liberation. It was a challenge which all, but especially the left-wing parties, preferred to avoid rather than to face, and thus to enforce unpopular decisions. Ever since 1945, the communists had thrown themselves into what Frachon dubbed 'the Battle of Production', and the PCF and communist CGT leaders became productionists as ardent as their comrades across the Channel. As a result, and with the advantages of centralized planning and allocation from the greater state involvement in industry, the period according to Alan Milward 'was one of vigorous growth'.[12]

Yet the industrial growth, some of the credit for which belonged to the national economic loyalty of the PCF, did not bring benefit to workers. Nearly all the indices of social amelioration were negative.

[11] Caffery to State, 16 Feb. 1947, 851. 504/2–164 (DSNA).
[12] A. S. Milward, *The Reconstruction of Western Europe 1945–1951* (London, Methuen, 1984), 11.

In 1946, eighteen months after the liberation of Paris, the average weight of a textile worker in the city was 20 pounds less than in 1939.[13] Infant mortality was up on pre-war levels. Despite wage rises of up to 50 per cent after the Liberation, the purchasing power of workers never remotely caught up with the rise in prices— especially the cost of food upon which, in 1946, a worker with two children had to spend up to 80 per cent of his wages in order to maintain a minimum calorific intake for his family.[14]

Like Britain, France had to turn to the United States for financial help, sending Léon Blum on a long mission to America in 1946 to secure a loan. Then as the dollar-gap widened inexorably in 1947[15] France became even more desperate for external financial aid, and thus increasingly open to the proposals in the Marshall Plan. The efforts to increase production for which the communists in the PCF, and the CGT, can rightly take much credit did not directly benefit their members. During the course of 1947, writes one French historian:

Industrial production was back at 1938 levels; France had shown her vitality, productivity at work was increasing and the economy was becoming more flexible. The workers however knew that the working week had increased from 40 to 45 hours between the autumn of 1944 and 1947, that their purchasing power, eaten away by continually rising prices, was 25 per cent to 50 per cent less than before the war and had fallen by 30 per cent since the Liberation.[16]

Against this sombre economic background the outbreak of strikes by different sections of the French working class was hardly surprising. The first major wave of strikes was in May 1945 centred on the industrial regions around Lyons. There, in the second city of France, after a march through the centre, strikers occupied the Préfecture, protesting against rising prices. The PCF's central committee discussed the Lyons strike after hearing a detailed report on it but communist newspapers, and La Vie ouvrière, censored all reference to this important example of working-class discontent. The line instead was set by an editorial in L'Humanité under the

---

[13] Lacroix-Riz, La CGT 1944–1947, 66.

[14] Ibid. 60.

[15] The French trade deficit with the United States went from $649 million in 1946 to $956 million in 1947. See Millward, Reconstruction of Western Europe, 26.

[16] Jean-Pierre Rioux, La France de la Quatrième République 1944–1952 (Paris, Seuil, 1980), 120.

heading 'Who is Sabotaging Production?'[17] Small-scale strikes continued throughout 1945, notably amongst local government workers who felt most directly the government's attempts to hold down wages.[18]

1946 opened with a strike by Paris printworkers. The communist Minister of Labour denounced the strikers. In a radio broadcast he virtually accused them of having been collaborators during the war. His intervention helped prolong the dispute, and left the printworkers federation in the hands of anticommunists in April 1946.[19]

The first post-war congress of the CGT in April 1946 brought into the open the opposition to the communist domination of the CGT. Calls for secret ballot votes instead of raised hands at mass meetings were rejected. Although Jouhaux was confirmed as joint general secretary, the voting system was changed to give effective control to the handful of big industrial federations thus sweeping away the rights of the departmentally based unions. The style of the congress alarmed some. 'The slogans, the salvoes of applause, the delirious ovations had nothing to do with previous congresses of the CGT', remarked Raymond Patoux, head of a departmental union in the provinces.[20] Bothereau, the leader of Force Ouvrière in the CGT, presented the opposition's case.

For some trade-unionism is a means of obtaining political power and, once that power is obtained, a method of keeping it. For others, trade-unionism represents an economic power which on the whole should keep its distance from political power. Our comrades cannot see the rise to power in all levels of the movement of trade-union activists obedient to Communism without some concern. The movement risks being at the service of a single party.[21]

Pierre Monatte, one of the founders of French communism in the 1920s but now an independent Marxist active in the printworkers' union, wrote a pamphlet in May, 1946, *Where is the CGT Going*. In it he concluded: 'From now on the CGT is nothing more than an annexe of the Communist Party.'[22]

---

[17] Lacroix-Riz, *La CGT 1944–1947*, 83–88.
[18] Ibid. 91.
[19] Bergounioux, *Force ouvrière*, 47.
[20] Quoted in Jean-Louis Validire, *André Bergeron, une force ouvrière* (Paris, Plon, 1984), 56.
[21] *Force ouvrière*, 11 Apr. 1946.
[22] Pierre Monatte, *Où va la CGT?* (Paris, privately published pamphlet, 1946).

From the CGT leadership's point of view, far worse followed in July 1946. A rank-and-file organized strike of postal workers was condemned by the communist leadership of the CGT postal workers' federation. The membership repudiated this call for a return to work, and supported the strike committee. Once the strike was settled, largely on rank-and-file terms, the strike committee, followed by about half the membership, formed itself into a rival union, declaring that 'nothing more can be done with the [CGT] postal workers federation. It has to be abandoned to its political colonizers.'[23]

During the dispute, the non-communist strike committee had been supported by Force Ouvrière, and afterwards the breakaway postal workers' union was strongly backed by SFIO. The significance of this dispute lies in the fact that it was, in miniature, what happened to the CGT a year later, and demonstrated that in organizational, and political terms a split in a CGT federation was sustainable.

The postal workers' strike in the summer of 1946 marked an important turning-point in the fortunes of the CGT. After the strike there was an increase in the now open polemic about communist domination of the CGT, and the communist leadership's unwillingness to sanction action by the base. In August 1946, the leaders of the CGT in Dijon, loyal to Frachon, sought to persuade railway workers, who had gone on strike in protest over the lack of food supplies, to return to work. The workers ignored these instructions, and this small railway workers' dispute turned into a strike covering all CGT members in Dijon. Aferwards one of the participants expressed his discontent: 'There is an unhealthy gap between the base and the leadership of the [railway workers'] federation. The base is at its wit's end and believes the federation is not carrying out its obligations to its members . . . there are not provocateurs, nor agents of capital amongst the staff, just people who are fed up.'[24]

In these circumstances, an opening was provided for the SFIO to try and weaken the links between the CGT leadership and the PCF. The SFIO leadership, hitherto aloof from trade-union questions, now sought openly to gain influence within the CGT. Blum wrote a

---

[23] *Le Postier Syndicaliste*, Dec. 1946, quoted in Bergounioux, *Force ouvrière*, 52.
[24] Quoted in Lacroix-Riz, *La CGT 1944–1947*, 185.

strong attack on the handling of the postal workers' strike, bringing into play themes he had advanced in *A l'échelle humaine* the year previously. Why had the postal workers' strike gone so wrong?

The cause is clear. It is the takeover of the control of the French trade-union movement by the French Communist Party. In a country like France, where the working class is politically divided, the control by one party of the trade-union movement is bound to introduce the fatal germs of division and the germs of division are the germs of indiscipline . . . The Communist Party has obliged the trade-union organization to follow its line in purely political action. It has even obliged it to support its position against that of the other party of the working class.[25]

Blum's intervention has to be seen against a wider political background. Firstly, the SFIO had refused to make a left-wing coalition with the PCF after the elections in June 1946, insisting on the continuation of the tripartite government with the MRP's Bidault as prime minister. From now on, despite the sharing of ministerial portfolios, the communists and socialists would be much more openly at odds with each other. Secondly, the forthcoming SFIO congress in August 1946 would be the occasion of left-wing activist criticism against socialist ministers for the moderation of their coalition politics.

Blum's tactics were obvious enough. From on high, he could loftily criticize PCF control of the CGT as injurious to the principles of trade-unionism while at the same time giving a green light to rank-and-file socialist activists in any of their activities which might embarrass communist officials. The socialist head of the white-collar workers' federation in the CGT, Capocci, urged the non-communists to organize with energy:

Up to now, too many of them, either out of a sense of unity or from fear of being insulted and hurt . . . have kept quiet and become discouraged; such an attitude will not promote unity because sooner or later disillusioned workers will leave us as they left the CGT-U, because it has been taken over [by the PCF]. It is not a question of organizing a split . . . or of simple anticommunism . . . but of no longer obeying a political line.[26]

The summer of 1946 saw the spread of the 'Friends of *Force ouvrière*' which now became a card-carrying grouping inside the

[25] *Populaire*, 6 Aug. 1946.
[26] *Force ouvrière*, 13 June 1946.

CGT. André Bergeron, then a 24-year-old printworker, already active in the pre-war CGT, recalled:

After the CGT congress [in April 1946], I was convinced that a split was inevitable. I joined the 'Friends of FO' and became secretary of the FO group which we created in the area around Belfort in June, 1946. I worked hand in hand with the local Socialists and the workplace Socialist committees. We started publishing a journal, *Fraternal Links*, but ran out of money.[27]

To their dismay the communists, now in control of the CGT, found themselves confronted with the rhetoric and calls to arms of their CGT-U days, while they felt obliged to act and sound like the reformists, conciliators, and compromisers they had so denounced in the 1920s and early 1930s. The extent to which SFIO took seriously its chances of regaining control of the CGT with a leftist or anticommunist policy is impossible to judge. But it is the socialists who, from the spring of 1946 onwards, were the active opponents of communist control of the CGT.

The employers had satisfactory relations with the CGT, and the newly formed employers' federation co-operated with the CGT leadership in 1946 and 1947. It is to the socialists and the workers grouped around *Force ouvrière* that one should look when seeking a more important cause for the split in the CGT than French capital or American imperialism. Frachon himself identified very clearly that the threat to PCF control of the CGT came from the socialists rather than from any other direction. Replying to Blum's criticism of the communist handling of the postal workers' strike and the socialists' denunciation of the PCF control of the CGT, Frachon expressed his fears:

This brutal intervention by the leader of a party in the life of the CGT is not at all normal . . . I believe the reason for this intervention can be found in the section of his article where he says the 'working class is politically divided.' Does Léon Blum want the CGT to have a Socialist orientation as is the case in some Western European countries? Or, if that is impossible, is he prepared to have several CGTs, one of which is Socialist?[28]

By the end of the summer in 1946, the picture for the CGT leadership was indeed alarming. They had no policy to channel the

---

[27] Validire, *Bergeron*, 61.
[28] *L'Humanité*, 7 Aug. 1946.

rank-and-file discontent save endless appeals to loyalty to the CGT and continuing exhortation to produce. The socialists were openly proclaiming the need for the CGT to lose its communist orientation. Force Ouvrière was organizing with vigour what, in any language, could be the nucleus of a rival CGT. An important federation, that of the postal workers, had split away. Outside the CGT the catholic CFTC and smaller leftist trade-union organizations were using language, putting forward claims, or supporting minor strikes all of which laid claim to the militant heritage of the communist activists of the CGT-U.

1947: STRIKES AND THE SPLIT

Most of the strikes up to 1947 were in white-collar occupations such as the civil servants who went on strike at the Ministry of Finances in September 1946. The loyalty of industrial workers to the CGT and the PCF was in contrast to the discontent, and anti-CGT feelings cultivated by all manner of non-communist labour activists amongst white-collar workers and civil servants. Yet this is further evidence of the lack of strategy for an effective post-war policy by the PCF. With their eyes focused on that central pillar of Marxist strength—the industrial proletariat—the communists were unable to offer a more flexible trade-union practice to cope with the increase in trade-union organized wage-earning categories outside industry.

Moreover, the passage from being employed by a private employer, a traditional capitalist, to being employed by the state also demanded new thinking about trade-union representation. Thorez had affected a great reform in securing employment and trade-union rights for all civil servants. Thanks to Thorez trade-union organization amongst French civil servants increased dramatically. They repaid him by joining Force Ouvrière, and becoming its strongest section.

The well-known strike by Renault workers, themselves employees of the state, in April 1947, which was first condemned by local CGT leaders, and then taken over by the national leadership as they realized the depth of feeling amongst their members, was not the beginning of a wave of industrial action culminating in the great strikes of November and December 1947, but rather another stage in a series of strike protests clearly visible since May 1945. Whatever the demagogic or organizational powers of the Trotskyists held to be responsible for setting off the Renault strike, there can be no doubt that had it been an isolated, one-off stoppage the CGT would have exerted sufficient discipline to re-establish order. But the Renault dispute, the first serious expression of industrial action in the manufacturing sector, and one moreover in the suburbs of Paris, the heart of PCF territory, reflected already well-established discontent with the CGT line.

It coincided with a major defeat for the CGT's prestige in the elections to committees to run workers' social-security funds in which the CGT and the CFTC presented rival lists. The CGT claimed 6 million members but only obtained 3.3 million votes. The Catholic CFTC obtained 1.5 million votes, and the vote was seen as a major expression of protest against the CGT's line. In some areas, workers expressly transferred known CGT communists to the bottom of the list, a further public humiliation for the PCF members in the CGT leadership.[29]

Other events were pressing on the PCF ministers, notably their unease at having to share governmental responsibility for the increasing brutality of French military action to restore its empire[30] but it was the strike of the Renault workers that provided the occasion for their dismissal from the government, the decisive moment in the history of the fourth republic. Since the middle of 1946, socialist ministers in government had preached austerity and had been dismissive of rank-and-file discontent even as SFIO activists were at the heart of stirring up anti-government trouble. The socialists therefore were in the government and opposed to it, a luxury social democrats have often afforded themselves, usually to the profit of their opponents, but this was not a habit known to a Leninist party like the PCF. Thorez perhaps hoped he could play the same card by supporting the Renault strikers, once it had been

---

[29] Lacroix-Riz, *La CGT 1944–1947*, 219.

[30] After the revolt by nationalists in Madagascar in March 1947, the French army slaughtered 89,000 blacks to demonstrate the firmness of French colonial rule. The communist presence in the government endorsing such reprisals was uncomfortable, to say the least. French military activity in Indochina to restore imperial rule was also on the rise early in 1947. None the less, no communist minister resigned on either issue. See Rioux, *La France de la Quatrième République*, 165, and Mortimer, *Rise of the French Communist Party*, 356.

endorsed by the CGT, while remaining in government along with the three other communist ministers.

However the socialist prime minister, Ramadier, did not apply socialist rules to his communist partner-rivals. The Renault strike was for pay increases in breach of the government imposed wage freeze. Ramadier made support for the wage policy a question of confidence in the National Assembly. When the PCF ministers refused to vote with their colleagues he dismissed them from government. While it was true that internationally by May 1947 the split between West and East was firming up with the announcement of the failure of the Moscow foreign ministers' conference (especially Stalin's rejection of French claims over Germany) following hard on the announcement of the Truman Doctrine, it is no accident that the expulsion of the communists from government lay essentially in a dispute about who represented, and exercised influence over, the working class.

Despite the office enjoyed by the PCF ministers, and their contribution to the reforms achieved in French economic and social relations between 1944 and 1947, the communists lacked an applicable theory to define their role in a pluralist society in which they were not the controlling party. As the chances of electoral majority receded, and they were never realistic, and as the hopes of fusion with the socialists were rejected by the latter, the communists clung all the more strongly to their positions in the CGT.

Here at least, inside the working class, of the working class, they could assert their claim to be part of national society, and so the PCF, irrespective of parliamentary vicissitudes, would be permitted to play a leading role in post-war France. However, precisely because France was a pluralist society, precisely because the war had been fought to restore liberal-democratic rights, the exact equivalence between a party and a national trade-union centre was open to all sorts of internal and external pressures for which democratic centralist training and habits were not the best preparation.

The identification of the PCF and the CGT leadership was too glaring. Instead of being a source of strength for the PCF in government, the communist dominance of the CGT encouraged and excited anticommunism of a powerful, effective kind because it was based on working-class needs and theory. By the time the PCF was able openly to endorse CGT rank-and-file demands, it was too late. The seeds of the split, already contained in the past history of the CGT, had been sown at the moment the Germans were driven out of France, and thereafter were brought to life as much by communist behaviour as by socialist and other anticommunist agitation.

Although the summer of 1947 saw a rash of strikes in mining, electricity, railway, and other industrial sectors—strikes this time endorsed by the PCF and effectively led by Frachon—none of them were seen as threatening the government's authority. About 1.2 million workers took part in the strikes in the second quarter of 1947, about half as many as the numbers participating in the so-called insurrectionary strikes in November and December.[31]

The CGT and the employers' federation met and concluded a wage agreement in August 1947 which was hailed in *Le Monde* as showing that 'instead of fighting each other . . . employers and union mutually recognise each other's existence and rights'.[32] At the same time Thorez was willing to welcome the Marshall Plan,[33] whose announcement had been warmly greeted by Jouhaux. The activities of the socialist ministers and SFIO activists in the CGT continued to be orientated towards making as much trouble as possible for the CGT communists. The government sought to freeze the agreement between the CGT and the employers' federation, and instituted price rises, including one of 135 per cent for bread, which further increased working-class discontent. It was almost as if the SFIO was pressing the CGT to a crisis, looking for an explosion that would allow the CGT to burst apart to the discredit of the communists. In October, the CGT initially moved to put down a strike by Paris transport workers organized by a group of 'autonomous' activists who accused the CGT of lacking a commitment to 'the principle of trade union independence' but then found, as at Renault, a majority of workers followed the strike call and so the CGT switched its instruction and placed itself at the head of the strikers.[34]

The turbulence amongst rank-and-file workers was evident to all

[31] Lacroix-Riz, *La CGT 1944–1947*, 252.
[32] *Le Monde*, 3–4 Aug. 1947.
[33] The Sept. 1947 issue of *Cahiers du communisme* declared: 'France like England must not refuse American aid but, as our comrade Thorez has made clear, its independence must be jealously maintained.'
[34] *Le Monde*, 13 and 14 Oct. 1947.

in the second half of 1947 but the central development that changed the face of French trade-unionism was the Soviet attack on the Marshall Plan and the enforced call to arms imposed on the French communists at the meeting in Poland which gave birth to Cominform in September 1947. It was clear from the events of the summer that the ousting of the communist ministers, far from weakening communist strength over the CGT, permitted Frachon to endorse popular discontent. Communists could once again organize strikes and criticize government decisions. Despite the propaganda efforts of *Force ouvrière* the position of the non-communists in September 1947 was no stronger than in late 1946 or April 1947, at the time of social security elections. The CGT was willing to play a corporatist role as is shown by its agreement with the employers in the summer.

From this position of relative strength, the communists in the CGT were sacrificed on the altar of the new line emerging from Moscow. In its analysis of what had taken place, *Le Monde* noted that henceforth the Communist Party would be in opposition, as the meeting in Poland had declared war on 'the Socialists and Blum' and the PCF would now be obliged 'openly to defend the USSR's foreign policy'.[35]

The strikes that broke out in the autumn of 1947 were a continuation of the wage disputes, and protests against the lack of food and high prices, but they were given a political twist by the condemnation of the Marshall Plan by CGT communists. The images of violence that surrounded the strikes, including the sabotage of express trains leading to twenty deaths and the use of the army and riot police to break picket lines, has tended to remain their lasting legacy. Walter Kendall, for example, calls them 'wildly adventurist political strikes' while for Anthony Carew the Communists 'now adopted insurrectionary tactics in a bid to defeat the government and block the Marshall Plan'.[36] And yet during this period the most the CGT could mobilize was 3 million workers— 2 million according to some estimates—out of a working population ten times the latter number. The list of demands put forward by the CGT was much the same as in previous months, and not so

---

[35] Ibid. 7 Oct. 1947.
[36] W. Kendall, *The Labour Movement in Europe* (London, Allen Lane, 1975), 57. A. Carew, *Labour under the Marshall Plan* (Manchester, Manchester University Press, 1987), 34.

different to those advanced by rank-and-file strikers in 1946 and in the first ten months of 1947.[37]

Despite hysterical scenes in the National Assembly, CGT officials kept negotiating with the socialist Minister of Labour, Daniel Mayer, during the course of the strikes. Strikes in mines and metal-industry factories stopped production but not national life. Attempts to cut electricity supplies and the running of the Métro in Paris were thwarted by the authorities.[38] If this was an insurrection, it had little preparation, and no chance of success. For an adventure it was backed by a large number of French workers with a long list of genuine grievances.

This is not to deny the important new political element, the shrill anti-Americanism and the opposition of the communists to the Marshall Plan, but the introduction of politics into the considerations of the opposing tendencies in the CGT was hardly an innovation by the end of 1947. What the strike did, however, was to harden up the opposition to the communist control of the CGT. In many areas, workers refused to follow the orders of the CGT, insisting on a secret ballot before going on strike. Their views ignored, some of them then sought to cross picket lines as did members of the CFTC. Verbal, and in some cases, physical violence between pro-Frachon CGT officials and their Force Ouvrière rivals reached heights unknown since the class-against-class hatreds of the late 1920s. Frachon sought to bypass the CGT leadership by setting up a national strike committee, a move which infuriated Jouhaux.[39]

The latter however believed that the final climb-down by the CGT communist leadership in the face of the determination of the government, especially the socialist Minister of the Interior, and the widespread reports of disaffection from the base at the disastrous handling and politicization of the strike would open up the possibility, for the first time since 1945, of ousting or severely reducing the communist dominance in the CGT. This view was

---

[37] See 'Les grandes grèves de Novembre-Décembre 1947', in Benoît Frachon, *Au rythme des jours*, (Paris, Éditions sociales, 1973), 259–77. *Le Monde* reported almost daily on major demonstrations and strikes against cuts in rationing in Sept. 1947.

[38] There are numerous accounts of the Nov.–Dec. 1947 strikes. A good one is in G. Elgey, *La République des illusions* (Paris, Fayard, 1965), 341–73.

[39] B. Georges *et al.*, *Léon Jouhaux dans le mouvement syndical français* (Paris, Presses universitaires de France, 1979), 332.

expressed at a national conference of FO activists in November when they appealed to workers not to leave but to join the CGT and fight inside it for FO policies.[40]

There is nothing like a badly defeated strike of major proportions to bring out the differences, and worse, between opposing groups inside a trade-union. If, from the perspective of decades later, the strike wave at the end of 1947 appears less than overwhelming, that was not how it seemed at the time to socialists caught between the possibility of either the communists or de Gaulle securing absolute power, or enough to create a much more authoritarian state. De Gaulle's RPR had won 40 per cent of the vote in municipal elections in November 1947, winning control of several cities and towns hitherto controlled by the PCF. In Blum's words the situation called for defensive action on two fronts: 'Defence of Socialism and democracy against Communism: Defence of democracy and the Republic against Gaullism.'[41] By the autumn of 1947, the external factor of the now open contest between the Soviet Union and United States forced choices on the French trade-unionists in the CGT. As Saillant put it in the debate in the CGT executive at which the decision to reject Marshall Aid was decided: 'If I have to decide between capitalism and the Soviet Union, then for my part I am with the USSR.'[42] The final choice however was not made at the level of leaders such as Saillant, Jouhaux, Frachon, or Bothereau, nor expressed in such grandiose terms. When Force Ouvrière organized a national conference of 250 activists in the middle of December 1947, a week after the end of the strike, the intention of Jouhaux was to urge his followers to stay inside the CGT, and try to win control from the communists.[43] But the representatives from the provinces were so angry at the conduct of the strike, so bitter at the insults and violence they had suffered, so full of the wrongs they felt had been perpetrated by Frachon and the communists in the CGT since the Liberation, that they cast aside the temporizing suggestion that a dossier about communist violence be prepared and, with a large majority, called instead for a clean break.[44] On 19 December 1947, Jouhaux and the other four Force Ouvrière

---

[40] *Le Monde*, 11 Nov. 1947.
[41] Léon Blum, quoted in Bergounioux, *Force ouvrière*, 77.
[42] Ibid. 85.
[43] Georges *et al.*, *Léon Jouhaux*, 333–4.
[44] *Le Monde*, 20 Dec. 1947.

members of the CGT executive submitted their resignation to Frachon. For the third time in its history the CGT was split.

THE INFLUENCE OF THE AMERICAN FEDERATION OF LABOR

The question remains how decisive was the American role in the split of the CGT? The influence of the United States, through the AFL's Irving Brown or via its own agents, is taken as a given in most accounts of the period. Yet a great deal of the evidence is either based on statements or memoirs produced some time after 1947, or tends to conflate diplomatic and other activities from 1948 onwards—once the split was consummated—with the presumption that support for the breakaway Force Ouvrière confederation after its birth was the same as being its creator. More detailed studies have not confirmed this *post hoc, propter hoc* view that FO owed its creation directly to American political or financial support,[45] but as we have seen, this correction does not yet appear to have worked its way into more general accounts of the period.

The forces leading to the split of December 1947 were internal to the French labour movement, and were the result of pressures that pre-dated the WFTU, Marshall Aid, or AFL activities in Europe after 1945. Jouhaux, the French trade-unionist who had the most access to the Americans in his triple role as a prominent office-holder in the CGT, the WFTU, and the ILO no doubt was told that AFL support would be forthcoming if a split took place. He visited

---

[45] See Jacques Kantrowitz, 'L'Influence américaine sur Force ouvrière: Mythe ou réalité?', in *Revue française de science politique* 28, (1978), 717–21. Steven Burwood, in his 'American Labor, French Labor and the Marshall Plan: Battle-grounds and Crossroads' (Paper presented to the 9th North American Labor History Conference, Detroit, Oct. 1987), is critical of the Marshall Plan 'as a powerful boost to the French ruling class' but concludes that as far as the split in the CGT was concerned: 'It was the domestic dynamics of French society, French politics and of French industrial relations which proved the strongest influence on . . . the labor movement in France.' Irwin Wall, in his *L'Influence américaine sur la politique française 1945–1954* (Paris, Balland, 1989), 10, also asserts that 'at no moment were French trade-unionists going to take orders from Washington while, in essence, the shape of the labour movement conformed to its previous history'. An opposite view, powerfully argued, can be found in Lacroix-Riz, 'Autour d'Irving Brown: l'AFL, le Free Trade Union Committee, le Département d'État et la scission syndicale française (1944–1947)', in *Le Mouvement social*, 190 (1990). Prof. Lacroix-Riz considers that the split in the CGT was orchestrated and financed by the USA to ensure that a split, divided, French working class would not effectively oppose the vast economic ambitions of the USA regarding Western Europe.

both Moscow and New York in the autumn of 1947 where the views of both sides on the Marshall Plan were made clear. Yet Jouhaux, of all the founders of the FO, was the least enthusiastic for the split, and had to be almost pushed into endorsing it by the anticommunist militants from the base, few, if any, of whom would have heard of the AFL, let alone met Irving Brown.

American contacts with the CGT had been well established by the American embassy staff soon after the Liberation, and were a continuation of relations already made with CGT representatives in exile in London and Algiers. In June 1945, the American Embassy arranged for Joe Keenan, the AFL labour affairs official in the American military government in Germany, to meet with the communist general secretary of the CGT miners' union to discuss how to increase coal production in French pits. The relations between the AFL's Keenan and the communist CGT official were amicable, and the CGT miners' leader promised to work through the American Embassy to keep Keenan informed about CGT ideas on stepping up coal production.[46] CGT officials of different tendencies had regular contacts with the embassy staff. Paris hosted the founding congress of the WFTU in 1945, and with the new federation's headquarters located in the French capital, Paris was very much the centre of international trade-union politics and activity.

It therefore comes as a surprise to see the uncertainty in the reports to Washington on what was happening inside the French labour movement. For example, the embassy in Paris reported in September 1945 that 'strikes in various occupations', and 'political conflict in which [the] French Confederation of Labour may assume a leading part' would shortly break out: in fact, the very opposite happened and the communist leadership of the CGT sought to damp down all industrial conflict until mid-1947.[47]

By the middle of 1946, the embassy had swung over to reporting left-wing, almost Trotskyist remarks critical of the 'CGT's refusal to support strikes and other direct action to improve living conditions'.[48] US diplomats were also in contact with a small, extreme left-wing group inside the CGT which was opposed to both the communists, and the Jouhaux-led reformist wing which it

[46] Caffery to State, 25 June 1945, 851. 504/6–2545 (DSNA).
[47] Caffery to State, 7 Sept. 1945, 851. 504/9–745 (DSNA).
[48] Caffery to State, 20 May 1946, 851. 504/5–2046 (DSNA).

accused of 'soft pedalling anti-Communist' organization and propaganda.[49]

Clearly, the American Embassy was an open house for elements of every political hue in the CGT.[50] After the postal workers' strike in the summer of 1946, Jouhaux, in talks with an embassy official, 'privately expressed his intention to trip up [the] Communist Party majority at [some] future date'.[51] But at the beginning of 1947, Jefferson Caffery, the American ambassador, played down the strike of Paris printworkers, and asserted that 'contrary to . . . alarmist accounts . . . in [the] foreign press, both Gov[ernmen]t and CGT authorities emphasize that there is no unusual or really critical labor crisis or any present political crisis warranting serious concern at the present time'.[52]

What these extracts (which are not usually published in the accounts of those who prefer Caffery's stronger denunciations of the communists in the CGT,[53]) suggest is that the American Embassy was fulfilling its professional role of trawling for information with no very clear idea of the exact balance of forces, or orientation inside the CGT. If the full-time labour experts in the US Embassy in Paris had such difficulties in predicting developments inside the CGT, why should it be assumed that the forays of Irving Brown—the AFL representative who, it should be remembered, was dashing around all the other European countries as well as travelling to America to report to his chiefs—were so decisive?

What then was the role of the AFL in the period between the Liberation of Paris and the split in the CGT? Accounts by participants written some years after the event were in no doubt that the AFL's financial and political support was crucial. In 1952, Benoît Frachon wrote: 'Irving Brown began distributing

---

[49] Caffery to State, 20 May 1946, 851. 504/5–2046 (DSNA).

[50] Considerable detail of the trade-union reporting by the US Embassy in Paris is provided in Wall, *L'Influence américaine sur la politique française*, 145–70. On the questionable reliability of the analysis of French politics provided by the US ambassador, Jefferson Caffery, see Milward, *The Reconstruction of Western Europe*, 116, 117.

[51] Caffery to State, 6 Aug. 1946, 851. 504/8–646 (DSNA).

[52] Caffery to State, 16 Feb. 1947, 851. 504/2–1647 (DSNA).

[53] See e.g. Caffery's statement, 'The long hand of the Kremlin is increasingly exercising power, or at least influence, in all European countries, largely through its principal lever, the French Communist Party and its fortress, the CGT', quoted in P. Weiler, *British Labour and the Cold War* (Stanford, Stanford University Press, 1988), 99.

dollars to those working for a split in 1946 . . . He financed *"Force Ouvrière"*'.[54] A few months later, in 1953, George Meany, the AFL leader, claimed in a speech at the National Press Club in Washington that the AFL had helped split the CGT, and many years later Meany told his biographer: 'We financed a split in the Communist-controlled union in France.'[55]

When the communist Frachon and the anticommunist Meany both make the same claim, the reaction is to take it as a given fact. Victor Reuther, who although no friend of the communist CGT was hostile to the AFL's pretensions to control US labour's foreign policy, also asserted in his memoirs that the AFL's Irving Brown 'encouraged, with American funding, the withdrawal of non-Communists from the CGT . . . what cannot be questioned is that even that small split could not have been organized without encouragement from certain Americans and the cost of it heavily underwritten by US government funds.'[56] As CIO representative in Paris from 1950 onwards Reuther was certainly aware of US financial support for non-communist unions in France and Italy.

But the CIO's Reuther, like the AFL's Meany, and the CGT's Frachon were making their charges and counter-charges to fight the battles of the 1950s and back-projecting the external American support for Force Ouvrière after its creation to the period prior to the split in December 1947. They are making American financial aid a major cause for the CGT splitting and Force Ouvrière coming into being. Yet the only sum of money that researchers have been able to trace was $25,000 sent in 1947 via Jay Lovestone's Free Trade Union Committee and the International Ladies' Garment Workers' Union. Early in 1946, Irving Brown demanded $100,000 to support non-communist groups in the CGT, but he was allocated only $1,000.[57] These amounts are not insignificant, but spread over the several dozen organizers working under the Force Ouvrière umbrella, or when divided up into the thirty-four departments where Force Ouvrière had a measurable presence in 1947, even $25,000 did not go far.

[54] *L'Humanité*, 6 Nov. 1952.
[55] For Meany in 1953 see Burwood, 'American Labor, French Labor and the Marshall Plan'. For the later claim see A. Robinson, *George Meany and His Times* (New York, Simon and Schuster, 1981), 135.
[56] V. Reuther, *The Brothers Reuther* (Boston, Houghton Mifflin, 1976), 338.
[57] Wall, *L'Influence américaine sur la politique française*, 152, and Carew, *Labour Under the Marshall Plan*, 65.

The CGT communists were more concerned about AFL political support for non-communist groups inside France. Their concern surfaced in the autumn of 1946 after the AFL announced its intention of opening an office in Paris. Irving Brown had been based in Paris since 1945 but the AFL now proposed to set up a formal, publicly recognized office in opposition to the WFTU. In a long article in *La Vie ouvrière* in October 1946, Benoît Frachon denounced this proposal to set up an AFL office whose activities would consist 'of anti-Soviet provocation, of attacks against the WFTU, and of efforts to divide the working class'.[58]

The CGT leader's language against Brown ('an agent of reactionaries . . . working with the debris of the Vichy régime against trade union unity . . . intervening cynically in our national life as if acting in a conquered country'[59] was strong enough, as was his accusation that Brown 'intended to support his "arguments" with a large amount of dollars': but Frachon did not specify any case in which Brown had already financially aided anti-CGT groups.[60] Brown had reported back to the AFL as early as December 1945 on the anticommunist leanings of Bothereau's Force Ouvrière group but was dismayed to note that Bothereau and his friends were 'reluctant to accept aid that will compromise them in the struggle in the CGT'.[61] The most detailed investigation by a historian friendly to the CGT on the question of AFL attempts to suborn CGT trade-unionists prior to the split in December 1947 has come up with no more than allegations by a communist railway-union leader that Brown offered one of the railway-union officials 'a bag of dollars, a car, a chauffeur and so forth on condition that he became an agent of Truman'.[62]

[58] *La Vie ouvrière*, 25 Oct. 1946.
[59] Ibid.
[60] Ibid.
[61] Quoted in R. Radosh, *American Labor and United States Foreign Policy* (New York, Random House, 1969), 314. Radosh notes Brown's appeals for money and the transfer of funds via the Jewish Labor Fund but does not show how or to whom the money was given. Bothereau's cautious and politically intelligent refusal to allow Force Ouvrière to be compromised was typical of his political sensitivity.
[62] Lacroix-Riz, *La CGT 1944–1947*, 326. Brown doubtless appeared the potential source of much largesse as he travelled in style contacting CGT members hostile to communism, and distributed dollars, to pay for meals and hotel expenses, to his contacts. Ben Rathbun's forthcoming biography of Irving Brown may finally reveal the exact nature of Brown's relationship with US government agencies after 1945 and the extent of his financial disbursements to anticommunist French unionists prior to 1948. I am grateful to Mr Rathbun for conversations on this point.

The AFL had given funds to French trade-unions after the war but these were given centrally to the CGT itself. In his report to the CGT congress in 1946, the CGT treasurer noted: 'Since the Liberation, the American trade-unions in the CIO and AFL have sent us 32 million francs. Between now and October 1946, the Americans have agreed to send us 206,818 dollars or 23 million francs. They have also agreed to send 75,000 dollars' worth of food.'[63]

American trade-union finance sent centrally to the CGT was therefore acceptable in 1945 and 1946 but the arrival of Brown and the orientation of the AFL's involvement in France towards a purely anticommunist policy altered the attitude of the CGT, or at least of its communist leadership, to the question of finance from the United States. The translation and distribution in France of the anti-WFTU publications of the AFL, and the presence of Brown at meetings of CGT federations not controlled by communists, at which he put forward the AFL's vision of trade-unionism, were doubtless activities that Frachon, Saillant, and other CGT leaders found intolerable, but France was now restored to democracy, and Brown's activities were perfectly legal. Jouhaux asked the AFL not to press the matter of opening an office in Paris, and Brown set up the AFL's European bureau in Brussels instead.[64]

Annie Lacroix-Riz stresses what she calls the 'discreet visit' of Jouhaux to the United States at the end of October 1947, following which, she has argued, the issue of a split came into the open inside the CGT.[65] Jouhaux went to New York as an official and well-publicized representative of France to attend the general assembly of the United Nations. Whatever private discussions he had with American union leaders in an interview with the Washington correspondent of *Agence France Presse* (AFP), he publicly re-affirmed his opposition to American desires to see a separation between communists and non-communists in the CGT. 'As long as I am alive the CGT will not be split. It would be a catastrophe for the working people of France and I will oppose such a move with all my might,' he declared, predicting that socialists and communists would unite with the CGT as in 1935, in opposition to what he called the 'apprentice dictator', de Gaulle.[66]

---

[63] Quoted in Validire, *Bergeron*, 94.
[64] Georges *et al.*, *Léon Jouhaux*, 321.
[65] Lacroix-Riz, *La CGT 1944–1947*, 325.
[66] J. Davidson, *Correspondent à Washington* (Paris, Seuil, 1954), 194, and *Le Monde*, 5 Nov. 1947.

The events of November and December 1947 were of course to overwhelm Jouhaux's oft-stated desire to stay inside a unified CGT. But his statement to the AFP suggests that, despite AFL wooing, he was not ready to lead a split. In discussing external responsibility for the split in the CGT it is necessary to distinguish between the general cleavage in international affairs on one hand, and the specific activities of the AFL on the other. As far as the former was concerned, the communist CGT leadership, including the non-communist Saillant, sided very clearly with the Soviet position against the Marshall Plan. Thus they could be depicted, for the first time since 1944, as seeking to act against the direct national economic interests of France, and the alleviation of the poverty and shortages affecting both industry and, more directly, workers and their families. Against that monumental shift in position, the propaganda and dollars of the AFL were small change.

Even after the split it was the French government, in the person of the socialist Minister of Labour, which most helped the newly born Force Ouvrière confederation by releasing to it 40 million francs, blocked since 1944 in the frozen accounts of the labour fronts set up by Vichy, as well as making offices available in many towns and cities.[67] As important as the financial aid was the political support of the Western trade-union organizations. The TUC along with most other West European unions sent fraternal delegates to the founding congress of Force Ouvrière in April 1948.[68] Jouhaux and Bothereau took part in the London conference called to support the Marshall Plan the previous month. None the less, Jouhaux can hardly have found favour with the AFL and Irving Brown when, in April 1948, he successfully persuaded the first congress of Force Ouvrière to apply for membership of the WFTU.[69] The move may have been insincere, a tactic to display to members of the CGT Jouhaux's continuing commitment to world trade-union unity, but as membership of the WFTU had been the issue which the AFL had defined since 1945 as the key test for its vision of trade-unionism, the decision of Force Ouvrière to seek WFTU membership reinforces the view that the AFL's influence was less than the claims later made by Frachon and Meany. At the

[67] Bergounioux, *Force ouvrière*, 1–93.
[68] TUC Int. C'ttee Minutes, 20 Apr. 1948.
[69] Ibid.

founding congress, the CIO, and not the AFL, was represented by a fraternal delegate.[70]

Although the Force Ouvrière confederation has received American union and government financial support ever since 1948[71] this did not secure Force Ouvrière compliance with AFL policy positions, notably in the 1950s over the issue of decolonialization.[72] The basic anticommunism and anti-Sovietism of Force Ouvrière, although identical in many ways with that of the AFL, stem from French labour history, theory, and practice. At best, the AFL acted as an occasional nursemaid once Force Ouvrière was born but did not beget the new organization. Force Ouvrière is a child of France, not of the United States.

[70] Ibid.

[71] In Nov. 1985, *Libération* revealed that Force Ouvrière was receiving funds amounting to $830,000 for 1984–1985 from the US government's National Endowment for Democracy. The revelations caused a small scandal in France, though curiously the CGT condemned the newspaper coverage—rather than the receipt of funds—as an outside attempt to interfere in internal French matters. See *International Labour Report* (Manchester) Feb. 1986. Along with the PCF, the CGT was long accused by French investigators of receiving hidden subsidies from the Soviet Union, see G. Busch, *The Political Role of International Trade Unions* (London, MacMillan, 1983), 58.

[72] See Kantrowitz, 'L'Influence américaine sur Force ouvrière'.

15

The Lessons of 1945

THE international politics of the labour movement continues to have contemporary political resonance. In many industrialized countries, the trade-unions, especially those in the manufacturing (i.e. principally metal) sector became weaker in the 1980s as unemployment, anti-union laws, new production processes, and a culture of individualism attacked the unions' presence and power in the workplace and society generally. Yet in the same decade, newly formed unions (whose main strength lay in metal industries) in countries as different in their geographical location, internal politics, and cultural tradition as Poland, South Africa, and South Korea arrived and transformed existing political and economic relationships in those countries. The reunification of Germany and the end of the division of Europe came about, in part, as a result of processes launched by Polish workers in 1980 when they formed their then 10-million-strong union, Solidarity. The Polish union removed definitively whatever lingering claims that ruling communist parties had to exercise dictatorial power in the name of the working class.

Elsewhere—in Latin America, in Turkey, in Malaysia—unions presented challenges to established authority, and were a factor to be taken into consideration in the political development of many states.Added to this was a growing understanding of the internationalization of finance and production which led to an increased discussion of international labour questions, despite the perceived weakness of unions in many northern countries.[1] In Europe, the moves towards a single integrated market in the European

---

[1] An introduction to some of these themes can be found in Mike Press and Don Thompson (eds.), *Solidarity for Survival: Trade Union Internationalism* (Nottingham, Spokesman, 1989); Ronaldo Munck, *The New International Labour Studies* (London, Zed, 1988); and in Peter Waterman (ed.), *For a New Labour Internationalism* (The Hague, 1984). See also Geneviève Bibes and René Mouriaux, *Les Syndicats européens à l'épreuve* (Paris, Presses de la fondation nationale des sciences politiques, 1990), and Kim Moody, *An Injury to All: The Decline of American Unionism* (London, Verso, 1988).

Economic Community have rekindled interest in the transfrontier relationships of trade-unions in Europe.[2]

Overhanging all these developments are the continuing divisions in the world labour movement stemming from the split in the WFTU and the divisions in national unions after 1945 that have been examined in this book. Few writers who analyse the problem do so without referring to the WFTU split, and there has been continuing discussion about it amongst historians of the post-war labour movement. It remains a sensitive subject for many. Clive Jenkins, the white-collar British union leader devoted a chapter in his autobiography to 'Unions and Intrigues in the USA' and considered that the 'World Federation of Trade Unions, founded in party post-war amity, was split from the outside (the British Trades Union Congress played a sorry, junior partner's role in this). Some of the international trade-union secretariats, by declining to have some of their functions integrated into the new World Federation, helped to precipitate the crisis and fissure.'[3]

In this study I have sought to argue three main points. The first is that the Cold War was not external to the trade-union movement but grew from existing political divisions that resurfaced as soon as the fighting stopped in 1945. The major split of the world trade-union movement (leaving to one side the problem of Christian unions) took place in 1920. The WFTU's attenuated existence after 1945, especially its failure to incorporate the international trade secretariats, was due in large part to the division not having healed over by 1945. Secondly, the trade-unions' international experience and institutional memory dating back to the 1920s were the main source for the elaboration of labour-movement thinking and policy after 1945. The picture of union leaders as puppets on the end of strings controlled by policy-makers in Washington or London is no longer acceptable. One historian of the Labour Party makes the accusation against Ernest Bevin that he 'was not at all equipped intellectually for the position of Foreign Secretary' as he lacked

---

[2] See Denis MacShane, 'British Unions and Europe' in Ben Pimlott and Chris Cook (eds.), *Unions in British Politics*, 2nd edn. (London, Longman, 1991).

[3] Clive Jenkins, *All Against the Collar. Struggles of a White-Collar Union Leader* (London, Methuen, 1990), 65. Jenkins' comment on the WFTU shows the enduring hold that a certain interpretation of post-war international labour history has. For a recent American debate on international labour politics see Paul Garver, 'Beyond the Cold War: New Directions for Labor Internationalism', and Tom Kahn, 'Beyond Mythology: A Reply to Paul Garver', in *Labor Research Review* 7 (Spring 1989).

'practical experience of foreign affairs and international relations'.[4] Of course, Bevin possessed neither a D.Phil. nor a Cambridge education, but his travels abroad, and work with foreigners in international organizations between his trip to the United States in 1916 and the war's outbreak in 1939, amount to a more thorough grounding in foreign affairs than is given to many a foreign minister or, for that matter, to labour historians who write on international affairs.

It may be reasonable to criticize the Labour government's foreign policy after 1945 but to patronize or to condescend to Bevin is as wrong historically as it was unprofitable in political dealings with him when he was alive. On the contrary, Bevin, like his friends in the AFL in Washington, had a clear, if obsessive, idea of the Soviet Union and of communism, and it was their vision that was imposed on or became conflated with government and diplomatic policy after 1945. Many regretted the anticommunism of Western trade-unions but as the response of the metal unions from different countries as early as October 1945 showed, the suspicions and fears of communist and Soviet intentions existed at an early stage. To suggest that this policy arose from the Cold War as it developed from 1947 onwards, or that it was earlier created by government officials and then slipped into trade-union thinking by manipulative outsiders is no longer a thesis that can be sustained on the evidence available.

The third issue is the division of responsibility for the post-war shape of the trade-unions in continental Europe. The claim that the Americans imposed leaders and policies on the German trade-unions and organized the split in the French CGT is still widely disseminated. Daniel Cantor and Juliet Schor, in their book, *Tunnel Vision: Labor, the World Economy and Central America*, wrote that in France, 'the AFL financed a split in the communist-led union [and] chose the leaders of the breakaway group' while 'in Germany, the AFL's European representatives actually selected the leaders and organizations that would receive preferential treatment for the Allied military authorities, with scarcely a nod to the wishes of the German workers'.[5] Cantor and Schor make their allegation to introduce a general thesis about the role of American trade-unions

[4] John Saville, *The Labour Movement in Britain* (London, Faber, 1988), 98.
[5] D. Cantor and J. Schor, *Tunnel Vision: Labor, the World Economy and Central America* (Boston, South End Press, 1987), 35–7.

in supporting anticommunist labour organizations and policies in various parts of the world in the 1950s and thereafter. But their case, and that of others who criticize US international union policy is weakened by the attempt to erect a model of an all-powerful AFL intervening in Europe after 1945 to select labour leaders or to split unions at will.

The reality is more complex, and the evolution of French and German trade-unionism after 1945 is based mainly on national traditions and politics. To transfer the blame to the United States is a way to avoid asking harder questions about the nature and limits of labour-movement organization and theory as it stood in Europe in the months after the war's end. Such transference also discourages the posing of similar questions about the internal politics of third-world countries where union movements have been an area of political contestation in recent years. Reducing the developments in the world's labour movements since 1945 to the issue of external American—or, from an anticommunist perspective, Soviet—interference can provide a simple global picture in which villainy is clearly identified: but at the same time is skirted the more important question about the continuing supremacy of national identity as being the chief determinant in the organization and actions of unions at home, and in terms of labour's international relations.

Instead of seeing the WFTU falling victim to global power politics, diplomatic chicanery, or the Cold War it would be better to admit that it was set an impossible task—that of expressing international working-class interests at a moment when these were being most effectively asserted in the national context. The WFTU was created at a moment of history when the conditions were not there to sustain its continuing existence. In 1945 and 1946, unions were reaching the peak of their identification with national interests. French communists were no less patriotic than their American confrères. CGT leaders wrapped themselves in the Tricolore with all the fervour of American trade-unionists waving the Stars and Stripes at their conventions in the same period. Of course, the Soviet representatives in the WFTU sought to use their membership to advance Soviet interests, but the British, American, French, and Dutch union leaders equally defended and promoted their countries' positions or interests.

The American historian, Peter Weiler, has argued that the TUC gained from WFTU membership because this stopped attempts to set up a purely communist-dominated international. The Russians, argues Weiler, 'could after all have founded a new international on their own terms, with most European trade-union movements following their lead'.[6] For Weiler, the Cold War between the unions developed because the wartime friendship with the Soviet Union and the suspension of the pre–1941 fights between socialists and communists created a new 'united front [which] tended to work to the benefit of the Communists; only a return to total anticommunism allowed their growing influence to be checked'.[7] While this may have been true in France—and even here important qualifications are needed—the evidence of the metal unions in Europe does not bear out Weiler's assertion. For the British, Benelux, and Nordic metal unions, and for the CIO unions in the United States, there is no significant communist threat to the existing leadership after 1945. And had Stalin tried to set up a purely Soviet-led international after 1945, the evidence from the meetings of the IMF is that he would have simply brought forward by two or three years the split that took place.

If anything, the Russians were concerned not to allow the WFTU to become the expression of democratic-socialist values. The extension of public ownership, the creation of welfare states, and the presence of the Left in governments created a very different Western Europe from the pre-war states ravaged by fascism and bankrupt capitalism. Only a tiny handful of carefully picked Soviet representatives were allowed to participate in WFTU meetings. But international trade-unionism supposes contacts and knowledge about the internal workings of the economy and production methods of affiliated countries. If the WFTU were to evolve from a body of occasional meetings in which high politics were discussed into being a vibrant, effective representative of working-class interests, it might well ask questions about social, economic, and political relations in the Soviet Union that Stalin would prefer not to be asked.

[6] Peter Weiler, 'The British Trades Union Congress and World Politics in 1945' (unpublished paper presented to North American Labor History Conference, 1985). I am grateful to Dr Weiler for sending me this paper as well as for many useful discussions on the WFTU. Although I disagree with some of his conclusions, all students of the origins of the Cold War and the international labour movement are in his debt.
[7] Ibid.

Here is how a historian writing recently in Russia sums up Stalin's dilemma:

The war against Nazism revealed the contradiction between the 'victorious people' and the 'victorious' state. In 1944–1945, millions of Soviet people broke loose from the 'iron curtain' that Stalin had been creating from the late 1920s and saw a different life. They returned home realizing that our society had to be made democratic . . . For Stalin, [it was necessary] to curb contacts between a victorious people with an awakened consciousness and liberated Europe.[8]

Thus for the Soviet leadership, only a return to total antisocialism would guarantee an isolation of both Russia and the Eastern European states from the contamination of democratic-socialist values.

That is the importance of the fight over the international trade secretariats such as the International Metalworkers' Federation. In an inchoate and often conservative way, they represented part of the values of democratic socialism which Stalin, following in Lenin's footsteps, so despised. They had to be dissolved and brought under centralized control. At the level of interstate relations, the Russians sought coexistence after 1945, whereas the Americans and British, keen to protect and extend liberal capitalism (for the Americans), and imperial interests (for the British) were opposed to the politically destabilizing and anticapitalist impact of accepting the Soviet Union as a global partner. But at the microcosmic level of union activities, the wartime unity gave way to the contest between two visions of social organization—centralist or pluralist—a contest exemplified by the international trade secretariat question.

In this study, the International Metalworkers' Federation has been used as a kind of prism through which to examine part of the history of labour internationalism in the first half of the twentieth century. At best, the international industrial secretariats were marginal players in the processes of labour and union development in the European countries up to 1950. Their importance arises at the moment when unions enter the international field and seek to make links of an enduring transfrontier character. At moments of

---

[8] V. Kuznechevsky at a round-table conference on Soviet–Yugoslav post-war relations at the Institute of Slavonic and Balkan Studies, USSR Academy of Sciences, Moscow. Quoted in *Moscow News*, 2 July 1989.

fluidity, such as existed after the Second World War, the international trade secretariats become more important, possibly even decisive, players. Their desire for autonomy and independence within the WFTU was the first obstacle on which the new world international foundered.[9] It was an obstacle the Russians had to overcome as Leninist democratic-centralist concepts of state-controlled trade-unionism were not compatible with the pluralist traditions of European democratic socialism. Any future development of world union organization will have to respect this autonomy and plurality.

If the international secretariat question was the submerged rock that ripped out one of the sides of the WFTU, the more visible reef on which the organization came to grief was the question of the Marshall Plan. Clearly the Marshall Plan had political consequences. Equally important was the way the Marshall Plan was linked to the question of productionism, the contribution that unions believe they can and should make to developing the productive forces in society in a way that does not unfairly exploit the producers, while helping to increase the store of national wealth. The metal unions are organizations of producers. The more production, the stronger the metal unions. They are also interested in the terms of production, the conditions in terms of wages, hours, safety questions, and the nature of control in the workplace. But wages, hours, and related conditions take second place to the need to produce, as a guarantor of employment, as a basis for union strength, and as a contribution to the material development of society. The Soviet Union's hold on the imagination of people in the 1930s was based, in part, on its industrialization, even if the terrible costs of that process or, in the longer term, the economic cul-de-sac that mass production divorced from a market economy entails were well hidden from most observers. The wartime achievements of the two capitalist democracies—America and Britain—in terms of production, full employment, and increased social rights, showed that models other than the Soviet one could result in the desired ends of labour.

[9] A recent detailed study of another international trade secretariat, the International Union of Foodworkers, confirms this view. Peter Rütters in his *Chancen internationaler Gewerkschaftspolitik* (Frankfurt, Otto Brenner Stiftung, 1989), 41, writes that 'neither Cold War politics, nor the AFL's influence were determinant' in the IUF's debates and its decision to reject incorporation into the WFTU on the terms acceptable to the Russians.

The Marshall Plan offered the capital to extend further the wartime achievements. Certainly, the extension of production was carried out on capitalist, often authoritarian, managerial terms.[10] But the health and material standards of workers in Western Europe under the Marshall Plan contrast favourably with their equivalents in Eastern Europe who had a Stalin Plan of industrial development imposed on them.[11] If American economic largesse was preferred to Soviet planning, is this to be read as further proof of the pro-capitalist inclinations of the post-war union leaders? James Hinton has argued that Labour leaders, 'by their obsessive anticommunism', intensified 'the pressures leading to the Cold War and the division of Europe'.[12] The problem is that the anticommunism of the political and union leaders in Britain in 1945 was rooted in bitter experience and memory of the antisocialism of Leninism and Stalinism, which had had such deleterious effects on working-class organization and unity after 1920. Based on knowledge and experience, most leaders of the labour movement decided that life under communism was perhaps more to be feared than life under parliamentary capitalism. This attitude was not peculiar to the leadership. Victor Serge, who lived through the early years of Soviet Russia, considered that elsewhere in Europe the masses of 'canny workers' were 'ridden by fear of revolution' because the only one that succeeded, the Russian one, 'had suffered too much famine, waged too much terror, and strangled too much freedom in its early years'.[13]

The anticommunism of labour leaders in 1945 did not emerge from malignant, right-wing personalities but was based on a quarter of a century of disappointed observation of the Soviet experiment. In addition, for those experienced in international labour questions, the deep suspicions of Russian splitting tactics in

[10] A. Carew, *Labour under the Marshall Plan* (Manchester, Manchester University Press, 1987), has details.

[11] See P. Wiles, 'Wages and Incomes Policies', and K. Bush, 'Retail Prices in Moscow and Four Western Cities in March 1979', in L. Schapiro and J. Godson (eds.), *The Soviet Worker: Illusions and Realities* (London, Macmillan, 1981). For more recent complaints about living standards and primitive working conditions see Jonathan Steel, 'Soviet Unions Set Out on Road to Solidarity', in the *Guardian*, 10 July 1989.

[12] James Hinton, *Protests and Visions. Peace Politics in Twentieth-Century Britain* (London, Hutchinson, 1989), 148.

[13] Victor Serge, *Memoirs of a Revolutionary* (Oxford, Clarendon Press, 1963), 173.

the 1920s and 1930s, as well as the memory of Stalin's abrupt changes of line, created reservations. Consistent evidence of a new opening of the Soviet leaders in the direction of democratic socialism would be needed before sufficient trust could be established to soften these suspicions. That evidence was not forthcoming after 1945 despite the grandiloquent words and noble intentions of the WFTU.

The question then remains, what was the contribution of the trade unions to that process and era known as the Cold War? One of the basic historiographical debates about the Cold War is when exactly to place its start.[14] To answer that question from the perspective of the unions it may be helpful to have a definition of the Cold War. Take that of Fred Halliday from his *The Making of the Second Cold War*. He lists six characteristics which define a Cold War. Apart from a mutual military build-up these include:

1. A particularly intense propaganda campaign . . . in which each side sought maximally to denigrate each other.
2. Polemics and mutual denunciation replaced compromise and negotiated agreement.
3. Conflict between capitalism and communism found expression in the third world.
4. There was a tightening of controls in the communist and capitalist camps.
5. All other conflicts were viewed in the context of this overriding one.[15]

If the modern term, 'third world' is replaced with, 'China, India, and the colonies', Halliday's definition fits with considerable acuity the international relations between trade-unions in the 1920s and 1930s, especially the rivalry between Profintern and the Western union internationals such as the International Metalworkers' Federation. If the Cold War is seen only as an expression of interstate relations then it can be said to get under way some time in mid–1947. But if it is considered as a conflict between political ideologies and systems of social organization then as far as the unions are concerned it was already under way from the moment Lenin declared war on democratic socialism and set out to split the

[14] This is discussed in J. L. Gaddis, *The Long Peace: Inquiries into the History of the Cold War* (Oxford, OUP, 1989). See also his *The United States and the Origins of the Cold War* (New York, Columbia University Press, 1972).

[15] F. Halliday, *The Making of the Second Cold War* (London, Verso, 1983), 8–9.

existing socialist trade-union movement. This Cold War in the
labour movement dating back to the quarter of a century prior to
1945 had the most far-reaching impact on the development of
political, economic, and social organization after 1945 in the three
European countries examined in this book.

In Britain, for example, after 1945, communists, left-wing
democratic socialists, and right-wing Labour ministers, their
advisers, and the trade-union leaders sensed that foreign relations
would play their part in the evolution of domestic policies. Foreign
relations, not just in the classic diplomatic sense but across a wide
economic, financial, and ideological front. In the discussions on the
dollar shortage, on the relations between the Communist Party and
the Labour Party, on the best way to maintain production, and on
what the role of trade unions in post-war society should be, the
reference points were often international.

A reading of diplomatic archives alone shows the TUC operating
a parallel foreign policy with close relations to the Labour Foreign
Office. Yet the oscillation over policy was influenced by information and events from outside Britain. This affected all unions and to
focus only on the TUC—despite the richness of its leading
personalities, and the availability of material in various archives—
is to misread the British trade-union movement which is more
heterogeneous and less confederated than a superficial glance at the
all-embracing nature of the TUC might indicate.

The passage of Britain's key metalworkers' union, the AEU, from
pro-Soviet leftism to pro-Marshall-Aid anticommunism in just
three years shows that forces other than a desire to blend in with
the dictates of Bevin's foreign policy were at work and must be
taken into consideration if the roots of the Cold War are to be
uncovered. These forces can be summed up simply. A new
concept—productionism allied to full employment, and rising
social welfare under political democracy, replaced an old model—
the abrupt overthrow of capitalism, and the institution of centrally
directed industrial growth. The change in perception of the Soviet
Union from heroic military ally to bullying occupying power was
under way already by 1946. It became a dominant Western theme
after Churchill's Fulton speech. But another reason is more
important for the loss of charm of Stalin's Russia for trade-
unionists in Britain. Most of the reports coming out of Russia
depicted the social, workplace, and political conditions of Russian

workers to be primitive, repressed, and without any of the rights enjoyed by their British sisters and brothers. The collapse of Russia as a model was under way well before the growth of anti-Sovietism became the norm. The United States, which hardly featured in British labour-movement discourse prior to 1939, now became the source of capital and technological know-how if the productionist society emerging in Britain was to be maintained without Stakhanovite compulsion or impoverishment to sustain capital formation.

The role of British communists was crucial in this regard. They are held, correctly, to have supported productionism at least until the middle of 1947. Economically therefore they were at one with their Labour colleagues in this period of the interstate Cold War's prehistory. But politically the communists decided to make a challenge very early on with their bid for affiliation. This united the left and the right wings in the Labour Party and trade-unions, and awakened the memories, spirit, and language of the 1920s and 1930s. In this process, clear parallels with events in Germany, France, the Nordic countries, and the rest of continental Europe could be seen. Britain was not a case apart in the immediate post-war period. The European-wide rejection by Socialist, Labour, and Social Democratic Parties of communist demands for fusion in late 1945 and early 1946 is one of the keys to understanding how the Cold War arose. These decisions were taken within a context of European political discourse with little evidence of the United States playing any interventionary role. Harold Laski's anticommunism was more influential in Britain (and elsewhere in Europe) than George Meany's.

Linked to this was the dispersed, often contradictory thinking and actions of the Left within the labour movement as a whole. The radical changes introduced by the Labour government did not fundamentally alter key aspects of British society. At home, manufacturing industry was left in the hands of private capital and its managers. Abroad, Labour Britain's first charge appeared to be maintaining its colonial possessions other than the Indian subcontinent which was no longer governable from Westminster. There was no return to the 1930s but neither was the opportunity taken to reform the processes of education, administration, and production, which were left in the hands of a conservative group, able to solve some key welfare problems from the past but lacking in the vision needed to prepare Britain for the future.

That said, equally lacking was a convincing analysis and coherent programme of action from the Left in Britain taken as a whole. The insistence of the Communist Party on maintaining its separate identity, its loyalty to Soviet foreign policy, and its insistent claim to represent more authentically than Labour the real interests of the working class placed it in the category of opposition to be isolated. Yet without an organized linkage to the mass of economic producers —the working class—left-wing politics tended to be multi-directional, and vacillating as the Keep Left group and other left-wing forces showed. In politics at all levels, ideas find difficulty in existing independently of the organization that puts them forward. Some of what the Communist Party suggested made sense. But the Party's institutional existence linked to the Soviet Union of Stalin meant that what it said was considered with suspicion, if not hostility. The Communist Party thus acted as a block to the elaboration of an effective alternative policy to that pursued by Attlee, Bevin, and Morrison but was not strong enough to force through its own ideas.

The period between 1945 and 1947 was one of growing political estrangement in the British Left reflecting a similar process in France and Germany. When it arrived, the Marshall Plan therefore did not impose its political agenda on Europe but rather came as economic help to European, including British, social democracy which had already rejected communism and the Soviet Union on ideological, and, equally importantly, on economic grounds.

In Germany, the domestic roots of the Cold War as far as the labour movement is concerned must be seen within the context of political memories and traditions of the inter-war years. On the political front, Schumacher and the SPD leadership made clear in the summer of 1945 the unyielding opposition of their concept of social democracy to communism. On the organizational front, the return to specifically German labour-movement institutions— notably the works' councils linked to industrial unions—was well under way by the end of 1945. The powerful forces in favour of the *Einheitsgewerkschaft* principle worked to strengthen whichever were the dominant political tendencies in the respective zones, while the WFTU's endorsement of industrial unionism buried whatever hopes there had been of one big general union. But industrial unionism conformed to the thrust of German trade-union organizational development prior to 1933. It cannot be said to have been externally defined and then imposed upon German workers by the Allies.

On the leadership front, those leaders whose credentials were proven prior to 1933 quickly re-established themselves. Ballots of either union leaders or votes on policies were held continually at various levels after the German surrender. The endorsement in the Western zones of either the SPD leadership or their policies from the middle of 1945 onwards is consistent. Despite Ulbricht's manœuvres to ensure communist domination in the FDGB, the arrival of communists in the Soviet Zone in leadership posts to some extent reflected their genuine popularity. The Soviet zone included Berlin and Saxony, the centre of left-wing socialist and communist working-class support before 1933. One of Ilg's colleagues, the Swiss secretary of the postal workers' trade-union international, travelled in the Soviet zone in November 1947, and contrasted the support of the Soviet military administration in providing offices, education centres, food, cigarettes, and drinks for union meetings with the attitude of the Western occupying powers which was not so friendly to the unions.[16]

Clearly the presence of the occupying forces of the Soviet Union and the Western powers in their respective zones favoured the activities of trade-unionists who were not openly hostile to the politics of Russia, America, Britain, and France. But German workers took up positions, supported leaders, or sought to elect representatives on the basis of their own judgement. The Russian ban on all free elections in the Soviet zone after 1946, or General Clay's refusal to accept the referendum vote on codetermination showed that the occupying powers were far from happy with the freely expressed views of the German people in the political or economic field.

Some of this was due to the occupying powers' estimation of their own domestic politics.[17] According to Louis Wiesner, who worked as political adviser to the State Department's representative

[16] F. Gmür, *Report on Germany* (Postal, Telegraph, and Telephone International, Berne, Dec. 1947).

[17] For an analysis arguing that Soviet policy in East Germany was related to the factional struggles between Zhadanov and Malenkov in post–1945 Russia see G. Ra'anan, *International Policy Formation in the USSR: Factional 'Debates' During the Zhadanovschina* (Hamden, Conn., Archon Books, 1983).

in Germany, Robert Murphy, the impact of the 1946 congressional elections (which returned a Republican majority in the House of Representatives), and the anti-union Taft-Hartley Act, passed over President Truman's veto in 1947, made General Clay 'more anti-Soviet and anti-labor'.[18] More than 200 US Congressmen visited Germany in 1947. Clay told his staff that in order to secure necessary appropriations for his military government 'he had better not show any favoritism to "socialistic elements" or "socialistic experiments" '.[19] Doubtless this corresponded to Clay's own inclination—he retired to become a banker and leading republican —but lacking was any political support for the aims of the SPD or their trade-unions from the ideological allies, notably in Britain.

This was recognized at the time by *The Economist* which, in October 1946, urged more positive support for the SPD's policies. In so doing, argued *The Economist*,

Britain would stand out in the eyes of Germany, and of all Europe, as taking a positive lead in economic reconstruction and that Social Democrats everywhere would be delivered from the sense of frustration which has possessed them, the sense of being ground between the millstones of Communism and American capitalism with the prospect of finding a middle way more suitable to the political inheritance and present circumstances of West Europe.[20]

The failure of the Labour government or Party in Britain to support or endorse the wide-reaching reforms desired by Schumacher and Böckler in 1945 and 1946, which were aimed at creating a durable democratic-socialist Germany, was an important reason for the restoration of a liberal-capitalist Germany in the three Western zones. The American trade-unionists were no better. According to a friendly observer in Berlin, AFL and CIO officials went

to Berlin on lightning visits, [went] in to see Clay, usually not taking the trouble to get thoroughly briefed in advance, presented the familiar

---

[18] L. Wiesner to D. Horowitz (International Labor Division, State Department) 28 Jan. 1949, 862. 504/1–2849 (DSNA). The political struggle, and internal union differences on how to respond to the passage of federal and state anti-union legislation in the United States in 1946 and 1947, develop in parallel with the elaboration and adoption of administration policies directed against the Soviet Union. Taft-Hartley did to left-wing trade-unionism domestically what the AFL was seeking to do internationally.

[19] Ibid.

[20] *The Economist*, 26 Oct. 1946.

German union grievances in the most general terms [and] listened respectfully while Clay . . . explained the complexities of meeting their demands . . . Nothing in writing has ever emerged from Clay's office after such conversations, and the labor leaders have never attempted to follow up on their 'successes' in the way they would if engaged in collective bargaining at home.[21]

For the British, the main internal political reason for their dilatory attitudes towards German socialists was the lack of any wider European vision. Bevin and the Labour leadership were anti-European and still orientated towards a global role. They were unable to shake off an imperial legacy and replace it with a more realistic estimation of Britain's place in the post-war world. As Ritchie Ovendale has written, Bevin wanted an English-speaking alliance and 'he made it clear to the Americans and the Commonwealth that he did not want Britain as part of Europe'.[22] The TUC, apart from rejecting Böckler's all-embracing *Einheitsgewerkschaft*, played little relevant role, leaving the making of German policy to the government. The American trade-unionists were more energetic but their ideological vision was shaped by a driving hostility to left-wing ideas associated, however unfairly, with communism, and so the arguments from the German labour movement for widespread socialization evoked no response from American union representatives for whom such ideas were far removed from their own experiences and ideology.

A democratic and socialist Germany however was no more acceptable to Stalin than it was to the Western Allies. He wanted to ensure not just a militarily safe Germany but an ideologically safe one as well. Once it became clear that Germans in the Soviet zone would vote for the SPD in preference to the KPD or even the SED, Stalin closed down the options for permitting independent political activity in the labour movement in the Eastern zone. For Washington, London, Paris, and Moscow, a demilitarized, democratic Germany with socialized economic relations was unacceptable, and the Germans themselves had not the strength, nor, on the Left, the internal unity needed to force through an alternative policy. The

---

[21] Wiesner to Horowitz, 28 Jan. 1949.

[22] Ritchie Ovendale, *The English-Speaking Alliance: Britain, the United States, the Dominions and the Cold War, 1945–1951* (London, Allen and Unwin, 1985), 284. See also Michael Newman, *Socialism and European Unity: The Dilemma of the Left in Britain and France* (London, Junction Books, 1983), 124–5.

latter point, the disunity of the labour movement, a disunity stemming from internal rivalries dating back to before 1933, is the German contribution to the failure to make a different Germany from the two that emerged after 1948.

Disentangling the share of responsibility to attribute to Germans and that which belongs to the military governments for the final post-war settlement in Germany is an exercise that will engage historians for a long time.[23] What can be said, as far as the trade-union movement is concerned, is that German factors, German traditions, German personalities, and German memories played a greater role in the shaping of the trade-union movement than has previously been allowed for in most accounts published in English, irrespective of the political outlook of the writer concerned.

Internationally, the German (and Austrian) metalworkers desired to reconnect with metalworkers in other countries as soon as possible. They sought to do this by rejoining the organization which they helped to found, the International Metalworkers' Federation. Like their British and Scandinavian colleagues they wanted to enjoy a double affiliation—to the WFTU which would group the world's national trade-union centres including the Soviet Union, and to an independent industrial trade-union secretariat which would maintain the links between autonomous industrial unions. By chance, the secretary of the International Metalworkers' Federation was a German-speaker from neutral Switzerland who had been very sympathetic to the pre–1933 German metalworkers' union. He appears to have played a more significant role than either British or American union representatives in reforging the links of international trade-unionism, along the lines of pre–1933 hostility to communism and the Soviet Union, than has previously been acknowledged.

On the international level, the metalworkers of the Soviet zone were not prepared to co-operate with their West German colleagues except within the framework of the WFTU, an organizational attitude which, when compared with the more catholic desire of Western zone trade-unionists to participate in both the WFTU and the IMF, contradicted the formal position of the communist

---

[23] For a discussion of differing German historical interpretations of the German labour movement's problems, and possibilities immediately after 1945 see K. Schönhaven, *Die deutschen Gewerkschaften* (Frankfurt, Suhrkamp, 1987), 198–216.

expression of willingness to work democratically with all anti-fascist forces. The legacy of the split German labour movement between 1919 and 1933 hung heavily over the survivors who set to work in 1945.

In France, the split in the CGT in 1947 was, in many ways, the direct descendant of the split in the Socialist Party at Tours in 1920 and in the CGT in 1921. A quarter of a century was a fleeting passage of time to Jouhaux and Blum, politically active since the previous century, and not so very long to Thorez and Frachon who had held leadership positions since their twenties. The opportunism, contradictions, political careerism, and seeming lack of principle evident in the SFIO—evident especially to those impressed by the sturdy solidity of the Labour Party in the same period—has relegated this unhappy party to the status of being an appendage to its more menacing communist rival in the 1940s. Yet, within a few percentage points, the SFIO obtained the same electoral score as the PCF, its ministers were able, its theoreticians impressive, and it had a leader in Blum whose moral authority was of the highest, all the more so as he placed himself above any personal ambition for office.

The communists both increased and lost influence due to their post-war politics. They increased influence because of their positive, enthusiastic commitment to rebuilding the French economy and supporting increased social welfare. But they lost it as they ignored or downplayed legitimate grievances of workers. This loss was exploited by their opponents, all seasoned trade-unionists, without external prodding. In many of his writings, Léon Blum drew a distinction between the conquest and the exercise of power. He applied this distinction to his Popular Front administration but it was even more applicable to the PCF after the Liberation. They neither conquered power, nor were they certain in the exercise of the power allocated to them. Neither the PCF nor the CGT had a strategy, based on worked-out theory, for operating in the mixed economy and in the partly socialized state that came into being after the Liberation. They could not reject the model of the USSR that had been so important beforehand, and did not have their own conception despite Thorez's hazy references to national roads to socialism.[24]

[24] See P. Spriano, *Stalin and the European Communists* (London, Verso, 1985), 276.

But no more did the SFIO and the non-communists in the CGT. Their rhetoric on trade-union independence was a handy stick with which to beat the communists but the whole thrust of Popular Frontism to which they subscribed had been to seek institutional power from and within the state. This, however, was only possible on an enduring basis, if the working class was united, and represented by a single dominant party and allied unions working closely together within a framework of electoral democracy. Once the formal programme of Popular Frontism had been carried out in France—and, in terms of nationalizations, welfare, and labour rights, this was largely the case by 1946—the lack of further commonly agreed programmatic demands encouraged the reintroduction of the political question about which should be the dominant party of the Left, and who controlled the trade-unions. In this hiatus, the urgent demands of the working class for an improved standard of living became more pressing. The communists had no answer to this problem, while it provided agitational possibilities for their opponents. Marshall Aid, and the Soviet rejection of it, clarified the field and provided the occasion for fresh position taking alongside American or Soviet allies. But the opposing tendencies were already in place and in the CGT had forced two splits already in 1921 and 1939. The rivalry and incompatibility between communism and socialism was the main reason for the split in the CGT. The interstate Cold War, as it developed in 1947, was the occasion—not the reason—for it to take place when it did.

The history of the political struggle in the trade-union movement after 1945 suggests common European trends, values, and differences that made co-operation between communist and democratic-socialist unions impossible to realize. Trade unions were the main organizational sphere in which these two currents of the Left had sought to coexist. But coexistence was not easy to achieve as the lack of democracy inherent in communism was not compatible with democratic socialism. Trade-union internationalism, despite its rhetoric and the trappings of its conferences, was not able to draw together unions in a way that enabled them to let go of their national traditions, national demands, and national political culture, nor could it overcome this fundamental incompatibility between communism and democratic socialism. Differences of personality and organizational power within national unions, as well as interstate differences between the Soviet Union and the West, all played their part. But as Basil Davidson, a contemporary participant in the struggles of the wartime Resistance, has written:

The absolute demands of the liberation fight [was] that democracy should prevail, and be seen to prevail . . . [The] resistance did in fact achieve by 1945 one of the greatest democratizing insurrections of European history. And this achievement stood foursquare within the tradition which has linked, and which still links, anti-authoritarian and anti-colonial ideas and aspirations with the belief that freedom, the rule of law, is a supreme good in itself.[25]

That commitment to freedom and the rule of law was not part of communist ideology. As far as the labour movement is concerned, the underlying reason for the Cold War lies not in inter-government rivalries, territorial or economic differences, or domestic politics, though all played their part. It is simply and bleakly that the practice of Soviet communism was unacceptable to the working people of Europe for it demanded a price in loss of freedom that they were not prepared to pay. Leninism and Stalinism dragged down in their wake the values and hopes of a humane, united, democratic Left, and the chances of building a post-war Europe that was socialist and democratic.

[25] Basil Davidson, *Special Operations Europe: Scenes from the Anti-Nazi War* (London, Grafton, 1987), 303–4. Davidson is writing about Italy but his comments also apply to France and to other occupied countries in Europe.

Bibliography

ARCHIVAL SOURCES

1. Government

National Archives, Washington DC
  State Department (Record Group 59).
  Labor Department (Record Group 174, Secretaries of Labor).
  Defense Department (OSS).

Public Records Office, London
  Cabinet (CAB 128, Labour Cabinet minutes, and CAB 129, Labour Cabinet memoranda).
  Labour Ministry (LAB 13, Overseas Labour Department).

2. Trade Unions

Europe

Amalgamated Engineering Union National Committee reports 1944–48 (AEU, London).

Industriegewerkschaft Metall für die Bundesrepublik Deutschland minutes, summaries of meetings and correspondence of British- and American-zone metal unions 1945–8 (IG Metall, Frankfurt-am-Main).

International Metalworkers' Federation Congress, Central Committee minutes, papers and correspondence 1893–1948. IMF correspondence, circulars, and national report files 1920–48 (IMF, Geneva).

International Transport Workers' Federation reports and correspondence 1920–48 (ITF, London).

Iron and Steel Trades Confederation Executive Council minutes 1945–48 (ISTC, London).

Trades Union Congress International Committee minutes 1940–8 (TUC, London).

World Federation of Trade Unions reports and Executive Committee and Bureau minutes 1945–49 (International Confederation of Free Trade Unions, Brussels, and TUC, London).

United States

American Federation of Labor archives 1900–48 (Washington DC).

Congress of Industrial Organizations papers 1935–46 (Wayne State University, Detroit).

United Auto Workers of America correspondence and minutes 1935–48 (Wayne State University, Detroit).

United Steel Workers of America Executive Council minutes 1940–48
  (USWA, Pittsburgh).

PRIVATE PAPERS

John Brophy Papers (Catholic University, Washington DC).
James Carey Papers (Wayne State University, Detroit).
Richard Deverall Papers (Catholic University, Washington DC).
Konrad Ilg Papers (IMF, Geneva).
Philip Murray Papers (Catholic University, Washington DC).
Walter Reuther Papers (Wayne State University, Detroit).
Victor Reuther Papers (Wayne State University, Detroit).
Jack Tanner Papers (Nuffield College, Oxford).

PUBLISHED SOURCES

Labour Party Conference Report, 1940–48.
Trades Union Congress Annual Report, 1940–48.
International Metalworkers' Federation Congress Report and Secretary's
  Report 1893–1947.
Geschäftsbericht des Freien Deutschen Gewerkschaftsbundes Gross-Berlin
  1946.
Geschäftsbericht des Industriegewerkschaft Metall für die britische Zone
  und das Land Bremen 1947–48.
Proceedings of the Second Congress of the Communist International, i
  (London, New Park, 1977).

DOCUMENT COLLECTIONS

Dokumente und Materialen zur Geschichte der Deutscher Arbeiterbe-
  wegung i. May 1945-April 1946 (Berlin, Dietz, 1959).
KOCH-BAUMGARTEN S., and RÜTTERS P., Zwischen Integration und
  Autonomie: Der Konflikt Zwischen den internationalen Berufsse-
  kretariaten und dem Weltgewerkschaftsbund um den Neuaufbau einer
  internationalen Gewerkschaftsbewegung 1945 bis 1949 (Cologne,
  Bund Verlag, 1991).
MERZ P., Dokumente zur Geschichte der Arbeiterbewegung in Heidelberg
  1845–1949 (Heidelberg, I. G. Metall, 1986).
Occupation of Germany: Policy and Progress 1945–1946. (Washington
  DC, United States Government Office, 1947).
RUHL H-J., (ed.), Neubeginn und Restauration. Dokumente zur Vorges-
  chichte der Bundesrepublik Deutschland 1945–1949 (Munich, DTV,
  1982).

Weber H., and Mielke, S. (eds.), *Quellen zur Geschichte der deutschen Gewerkschaftsbewegung im 20. Jahrhundert: Organisatorischer Aufbau der Gewerkschaften 1945–1949* (Cologne, Bund Verlag, 1987).

NEWSPAPERS, MAGAZINES, AND UNION JOURNALS

AEU Journal
AFL Federationist
Cahiers de Communisme
CIO News
Economist
Force ouvrière
Gewerkschaftliche Rundschau für die Schweiz
Gewerkschafts-zeitung
L'Humanité
IMF Review
International Labour Review
Labor Action
Land og Folk
Labour Monthly
Machinist
Man and Metal
Der Metallarbeiter
Le Monde
New Statesman
New York Times
Le Peuple
Populaire
Résistance ouvrière
Schweizerische Metallarbeiter Zeitung
Social-Demokraten
Steelabor
The Times (London)
Tribune (Berlin)
Tribune (London)
La Vie ouvrière
WFTU Information Bulletin

BOOKS, PAMPHLETS, ARTICLES

Abelhauser, W., *Wirtschaft in Westdeutschland 1945–1948: Rekonstruktion und Wachstumbedingungen in der amerikanischen und britischen Zone* (Stuttgart, Deutsche Verlags-Anstalt, 1975).

ABELOVE, H., BLACKMAR B., DIMOCK P., and SCHNEER J. (eds.), *Visions of History* (New York, Pantheon, 1984).

ABENDROTH, W., *Sozialgeschichte der europäischen Arbeiterbewegung* (Frankfurt, Suhrkamp, 1965).

—— *Ein Leben in der Arbeiterbewegung* (Frankfurt, Suhrkamp, 1976).

—— *Die Aktualität der Arbeiterbewegung* (Frankfurt, Suhrkamp, 1985).

ADDISON, P., *Now the War Is Over* (London, Jonathan Cape, 1985).

AHRENDT, H. (ed.), *Geschichte des FDGB: Chronik 1945–1982* (Berlin, Tribüne Verlag, 1982).

ALBA, V., *Politics and the Labor Movement in Latin America* (Stanford, Calif., Stanford University Press, 1968).

ALBRECHT, W. (ed.), *Kurt Schumacher als deutscher und europäischer Sozialist* (Bonn, Friedrich-Ebert Stiftung, 1988).

ALLEN, V., *Power in Trade Unions* (London, Longman, 1954).

—— *Trade Unions and Government* (London, Longman, 1960).

ALTMANN, P. (ed.), *Hauptsache Frieden* (Frankfurt, Röderberg-Verlag, 1985).

ANDERSON, P., 'Communist Party History', in R. Samuel (ed.), *People's History and Socialist Theory* (London, Routledge and Kegan Paul, 1981).

ARNESEN, E., 'Crusades against Crisis: A View from the United States on the "Rank and File" Critique and other Catalogues of Labour History's Alleged Ill', in *International Review of Social History*, 33 (1990).

AZÉMA, J-P., PROST A., and RIOUX J-P., *Le Parti communiste des années sombres 1938–1941* (Paris, Seuil, 1986).

BADSTÜBNER, R., and THOMAS S., *Entstehung und Entwicklung der BRD: Restauration und Spaltung 1945–1949* (Cologne, Pahl-Rugenstein, 1979).

BALFOUR, M., *Withstanding Hitler* (London, Routledge, 1988).

BALFOUR, M., and MAIR J., *Four Power Control in Germany 1945–1946* (Oxford, Clarendon Press, 1956).

BARNARD, J., *Walter Reuther and the Rise of the Autoworkers* (Boston, Little Brown, 1983).

BARNETT, C., *Audit of War* (London, Macmillan, 1986).

BARNETT, R., *The Alliance: America-Europe-Japan, Makers of the Postwar World* (New York, Simon and Schuster, 1983).

BARNOUIN, B., *The European Labour Movement and European Integration* (London, Francis Pinter, 1986).

BAUCHARD, P., *Les Syndicats en quête d'une révolution* (Paris, Buchet/Chastel, 1972).

BEHRENDT, A., *Die Interzonenkonferenzen der deutschen Gewerkschaften* (Berlin, Tribüne Verlag, 1959).

BEIER, G., *Die illegale Reichsleitung der Gewerkschaften 1933–1945* (Cologne, Bund Verlag, 1981).

—— *Geschichte und Gewerkschaft* (Frankfurt, Otto Brenner Stiftung, 1981).

—— *Schulter an Schulter, Schritt für Schritt: Lebenslauf deutscher Gewerkschafter* (Cologne, Bund Verlag, 1983).

BENDINER, B., *International Labour Affairs* (Oxford, OUP, 1987).

BENZ, W., *Von der Besatzungsherrschaft zur Bundesrepublik: Stationen einer Staatsgründung 1946–1949* (Frankfurt, Fischer, 1984).

BERGOUNIOUX, A., *Force ouvrière* (Paris, Seuil, 1975).

BERNSTEIN, I., *Turbulent Years: A History of the American Workers 1933–1941* (Boston, Houghton Mifflin, 1971).

BIBES, G., and MOURIAUX, R., *Les Syndicats européens à l'épreuve* (Paris, Presses de la Fondation nationale des sciences politiques, 1990).

BIRCH, R., *A Wage Based on Human Needs* (London, Communist Party, 1946).

BIRCHALL, I., *Workers Against the Monolith: The Communist Parties Since 1943* (London, Pluto, 1974).

BLOOMFIELD, J., *Passive Revolution. Politics and the Czechoslovak Working Class 1945–1948* (London, Allison and Busby, 1979).

BLUM, L., *A l'échelle humaine* (Paris, Gallimard, 1945).

—— *Les Devoirs et les tâches du socialisme* (Paris, Éditions de la liberté, 1945).

BONNEL, V., 'Radical Politics and Organized Labor in Pre-Revolutionary Moscow 1905–1917', in *Journal of Social History* 3 (1978).

BONTE, F., *A l'échelle de la nation* (Paris, Éditions du Parti communiste français, 1945).

BORKENAU, F., *The Communist International* (London, Faber, 1938).

BORNSTEIN, S., and RICHARDSON, A., *War and the International: A History of the Trotskyist Movement in Britain 1937–1949* (London, Socialist Platform, 1986).

BOTHEREAU, R., *Histoire du syndicalisme français* (Paris, Presses universitaires de France, 1945).

BOTTING, D., *In the Ruins of the Reich* (London, Unwin, 1986).

BOURDÉ, G., *La Défaite du Front populaire* (Paris, Maspero, 1977).

BRANCIARD, M., *Syndicats et partis: Autonomie ou dépendance N 1879–1947* (Paris, Syros, 1982).

BRANDT, P., and AMMON, H. (eds.), *Die Linke und die nationale Frage* (Hamburg, Rowohlt, 1981).

BRANDT, W., *Links und frei: Mein Weg 1930–1950* (Hamburg, Hoffman, 1982).

BRANSON, N., *History of the Communist Party of Great Britain 1927–1941* (London, Lawrence and Wishart, 1985).

BRAUNTHAL, J., *History of the International* i. *1864–1914*; ii. *1914–1943* (London, Nelson, 1966–67); iii. *1943–1968* (London, Gollancz, 1980).

BRETT, T., Gilliat, S., and POPE, A., 'Planned Trade, Labour Party Policy and US Intervention: The Successes and Failures of Post-War Reconstruction', in *History Workshop* 13 (1982), pp 130–42.

BROOKS, R., *Clint: A Biography of a Labor Intellectual* (New York, Atheneum, 1978).

BULLOCK, A., *Life and Times of Ernest Bevin* i (London, Heinemann, 1960).

—— *Ernest Bevin: Foreign Secretary* (London, Heinemann, 1983).

BURNHAM, J., *The Struggle for the World* (New York, Day, 1947).

BURRIDGE, T., *British Labour and Hitler's War* (London, Deutsch, 1976).

BUSCH, G., *Political Currents in the International Trade Union Movement* (London, Economist Publications, 1980).

—— *The Political Role of International Trades Unions* (London, Macmillan, 1983).

CAIRNCROSS, A., *Years of Recovery: British Economic Policy 1945–1951* (London, Methuen, 1985).

—— *The Price of War* (Oxford, Blackwell, 1986).

CALDER, A., *The People's War: Britain 1939–1945* (London, Granada, 1971).

CALHOUN, D., *The United Front, the TUC and the Russians 1923–1927* (Cambridge, CUP, 1976).

CANTOR, D., and SCHOR, J., *Tunnel Vision: Labor, the World Economy and Central America* (Boston, South End Press, 1987).

CAREW, A., 'The Schism within the World Federation of Trade Unions: Government and Trade Union Diplomacy', in *International Review of Social History* 24/3 (1984).

—— *Labour Under the Marshall Plan* (Manchester, Manchester University Press, 1987).

CARR, E. H., *A History of Soviet Russia*, 14 vols. (London, Macmillan, 1950–78).

—— *Twilight of the Comintern 1930–1935* (New York, Pantheon, 1982).

CARRILLO, W., *The Truth About the Events in Spain: An Open Letter to Joseph Stalin* (Berne, IMF 1939).

CAUTE, D., *The Great Fear: The Anti-Communist Purge under Truman and Eisenhower* (New York, Simon and Schuster, 1978).

—— *The Fellow Travellers* (London, Yale, 1988).

CAUX, L., DE *Labor Radical: From the Wobblies to the CIO, a Personal History* (Boston, Beacon Press, 1970).

CAVE BROWN, A., and MACDONALD, C., *On a Field of Red: The Communist International and the Coming of World War II* (New York, Putnam, 1981).

CHAM, E., and FISERA, V. (eds.), *Socialism and Nationalism* 3 vols. (Nottingham, Spokesman, 1979).

CHAPMAN, H., 'The Political Life of the Rank and File: French Aircraft Workers During the Popular Front 1934–1938', in *International Labor and Working-Class History*, 30 (1986).

CITRINE, W., *What is the TUC Doing?* (London, TUC, 1935).

—— *I Search for Truth in Russia* (London, Routledge, 1936).

—— *In Russia Now* (London, Hale, 1942).

CITRINE, LORD, *Two Careers* (London, Hutchinson, 1967).

CLARKE, P., GOTTLIEB, P., and KENNEDY, D. (eds.), *Forging a Union of Steel: Philip Murray, SWOC, and the United Steelworkers* (Ithaca, NY Cornell University Press, 1987).

CLAUDIN, F., *The Communist Movement from Comintern to Cominform* (New York, Monthly Review Press, 1975).

CLEGG, H., *A History of British Trade Unions Since 1889* ii. *1911–1933* (Oxford, OUP, 1985).

COATES, K., and TOPHAM, T., *Trade Unions in Britain* (Nottingham, Spokesman, 1985).

COATES, W. AND Z., *History of Anglo-Soviet Relations* 2 Vol. (London, Lawrence and Wishart, 1958).

COCHRAN, B., *Labor and Communism: The Conflict that Shaped American Unions* (Princeton, NJ, Princeton University Press, 1977).

COHEN, S., *Rethinking the Soviet Experience: Politics and History Since 1917* (New York, OUP, 1986).

COLE, G. D. H., *A History of Socialist Thought*, 5 vols. (London, Macmillan, 1953–60).

COT, J-P., and MOUNIER, J-P., *Les Syndicats américains: Conflit ou complicité* (Paris, Flammarion, 1977).

COURTOIS, S., 'Construction et déconstruction du communisme français', in *Communisme*, 15–16 (1987).

CROUCHER, R., *Engineers at War 1939–1945* (London, Merlin Press, 1982).

DAVIDSON, B., *Germany, What Now?* (London, Muller, 1950).

—— *Special Operations Europe: Scenes from the Anti-Nazi War* (London, Grafton, 1987).

DAVIDSON, J., *Correspondent à Washington* (Paris, Seuil, 1954).

DAVIS, M., 'Why the US Working Class is Different', *New Left Review* 127 (1980).

DEIGHTON, A., *The Impossible Peace: the Division of Germany, and the Origins of the Cold War* (Oxford, Clarendon Press, 1990).

DELPERRIE DE BAYAC, J., *Histoire du Front populaire* (Paris, Fayard, 1972).

DEPPE, F., *Jürgen Kuczynski Gespräch* (Marburg, Verlag Arbeiterbewegung und Gesellschaftswissenschaft, 1984).

DETJE, R. (AND AUTHORS' COLLECTIVE), *Von der Westzone zum Kalten Krieg: Restauration und Gewerkschaftspolitik in Nachkriegsdeutschland* (Hamburg, VSA, 1982).

DEUTSCHER, I., *Stalin*, (London, Penguin, 1961).

—— *Marxism, Wars and Revolutions* (London, Verso, 1984).

DEVIN, G. (ed.), *Syndicalisme. Dimensions internationales* (Paris, Erasme, 1990).

DEWAR, H., *Communist Politics in Britain: The CPGB from its Origins to the Second World War* (London, Pluto, 1976).

DJILAS, M., *Conversations with Stalin* (London, Davies, 1962).

DOLLÉANS, E., *Histoire du mouvement ouvrier* ii *1871–1936* (Paris, Colin, 1939).

DONOVAN, R., *Conflict and Crisis: The Presidency of Harry S. Truman 1945–1948* (New York, Norton, 1977).

DORPALEN, A., *German History in Marxist Perspective: The East German Approach* (London, Tauris, 1985).

DRAPER, T., *American Communism and Soviet Russia* (New York, Viking, 1960).

DUBOFSKY, M., and TYNE, VAN, W., *John L. Lewis: A Biography* (New York, Quadrangle Books, 1977).

—— *Labor Leaders in America* (Urbana, University of Illinois Press, 1987).

DURBIN, E., *New Jerusalems* (London, Routledge, 1985).

EDELMAN, M., *France: The Birth of the Fourth Republic* (London, Penguin, 1944).

EDINGER, L., *Kurt Schumacher: A Study in Personality and Political Behaviour* (Stanford, Calif., Stanford University Press, 1965).

EISENBERG, C., 'Working Class Politics and the Cold War: American Intervention in the German Labour Movement 1945–1949', in *Diplomatic History*, 7 (Autumn, 1983).

ELGEY, G., *La République des illusions* (Paris, Fayard, 1965).

ERSTENS, H., and PELGER, H., *Gewerkschaften in Widerstand* (Hanover, Verlag für Literatur und Zeitgeschehen, 1967).

FEJTÖ, F., *Histoire des démocraties populaires* (Paris, Seuil, 1952).

FICHTER, M., *Besatzungsmacht und Gewerkschaften* (Opladen, Westdeutscher Verlag 1982).

FILTZER, D., *Soviet Workers and Stalinist Industrialization* (London, Pluto, 1986).

FIMMEN, E., *Labour's Alternative* (London, Labour Publishing Co. 1924).

FINE, M., *Towards Corporatism: The Movement for Capital-Labor Collaboration in France 1914–1936* (Madison, University of Wisconsin Press, 1971).

FISCH, G., and KRAUSE, F., *SPD und KPD 1945–1946: Einheitsbestrebungen der Arbeiterpartien* (Frankfurt, Marxistische Blätter, 1978).

FONER, P., *History of the Labor Movement* 6 vols. (New York, International Publishers, 1956–82).

FONTAINE, A., *Histoire de la guerre froide* (Paris, Fayard, 1965).

FOWKES, B., *Communism in Germany under the Weimar Republic* (London, Macmillan, 1984).

FRACHON, B., *Au rythme des jours* (Paris, Éditions sociales, 1973).

FRANCK, D., *Jahre unseres Lebens 1945–1949* (Hamburg, Rowohlt, 1983).

FROW, E. and R., *Engineering Struggles: Episodes in the Story of the Shop Stewards' Movement* (Manchester, Working Class Movement Library, 1982).

GARBAN, P., and SCHMID, J., *Le Syndicalisme suisse: Histoire politique de l'Union syndicale 1880–1980* (Lausanne, Éditions d'en bas, 1980).

GADDIS, J., *The United States and the Origins of the Cold War* (New York, Columbia University Press, 1972).

—— *The Long Peace: Inquiries into the History of the Cold War* (Oxford, OUP, 1989).

—— 'The Emerging Post-Revisionist Synthesis on the Origins of the Cold War', in *Diplomatic History*, 7 (Summer 1983), 171–90.

GALENSON, W. (ed.), *Comparative Labor Movements* (New York, Prentice Hall, 1952).

GALLACHER, W., *The Case for Communism* (London, Penguin, 1949).

GANNON, F., *Joseph D. Keenan: Labor's Ambassador in War and Peace* (Lanham, Md., University Press of America, 1984).

GARVER, P., 'Beyond the Cold War: New Directions for Labor Internationalism', in *Labor Research Review* 8 (Spring 1989).

GAULLE, C. DE, *Mémoires de guerre: Le Salut 1944–1946* (Paris, Plon, 1959).

GEORGES, B., TINANT, D., and RENAULD, M-A., *Léon Jouhaux dans le mouvement syndical français* (Paris, Presses universitaires de France, 1979).

GIMBEL, J., *The American Occupation of Germany: Politics and the Military 1945–1949* (Stanford, Calif., Stanford University Press, 1968).

—— *The Origins of the Marshall Plan* (Stanford, Calif., Stanford University Press, 1976).

GIRAUD, H-C., *De Gaulle et les communistes* i. *L'Alliance, juin 1941–mai 1943* (Paris, Albin Michel, 1988).

GLEES, A., *Exile Politics During the Second World War* (Oxford, Clarendon Press, 1978).

—— *The Secrets of the Service: British Intelligence and Communist Subversion 1939–1951* (London, Jonathan Cape, 1987).

GODSON, R., *American Labor and European Politics: The AFL as a Transnational Force* (New York, Crane Russack, 1976).

GOLDBERG, A., *AFL-CIO: Labor United* (New York, McGraw Hill, 1956).

GOLDEN, C., and RUTTENBERG, H., *Dynamics of Industrial Democracy* (New York, Harper, 1942).

GOLLANCZ, V., *In Darkest Germany* (London, Gollancz, 1947).

GOMPERS, S., *Labor in Europe and America* (New York, Harper, 1910).

GOTTFURCHT, H., *Die internationale Arbeiterbewegung* (Cologne, Bund Verlag, 1966).

GOULDEN, J., *Meany* (New York, Atheneum, 1972).

GRAEDEL, A., *Hommage à Conrad Ilg* (Berne, Swiss Metalworkers' Union, 1954).

GRAF, W., *The German Left Since 1945* (London, Oleander Press, 1976).
—— 'Anti-Communism in the Federal Republic of Germany', in *The Socialist Register 1984* (London, Merlin Press, 1984).
GREBING, H., *Geschichte der deutschen Arbeiterbewegung* (Munich, Nymphenburger Verlagshandlung, 1966).
GÜNTHER, D., *Gewerkschafter in Exil: Die Landesgruppe deutscher Gewerkschafter in Schweden von 1938–1945* (Marburg, Verlag Arbeiterbewegung und Gesellschaftswissenschaft, 1982).
HALLIDAY, F., *The Making of the Second Cold War* (London, Verso, 1983).
—— 'Three Concepts of Internationalism', in *International Affairs* 64/2 (1988).
HAMILTON, N., *Monty: The Field Marshall 1944–1976* (London, Hamish Hamilton, 1986).
HAMON, H., and ROTMAN, P., *La Deuxième Gauche: Histoire intellectuelle et politique de la CFDT* (Paris, Seuil, 1984).
HARMAN, C., *The Lost Revolution: Germany 1917–1923* (London, Bookmarks, 1982).
HARBUTT, F., *The Iron Curtain: Churchill, America, and the Origins of the Cold War* (New York, OUP, 1986).
HABERL, O. N., and NIETHAMMER, L. (eds.), *Der Marshall-Plan und die europäische Linke* (Frankfurt, Europäische Verlagsanstalt, 1986).
HARMON, J., *The International Metalworkers' Federation* (Washington DC, United States Department of Labor, 1959).
HARRIES, M. and S., *Sheathing the Sword: The Demilitarisation of Japan* (London, Heinemann, 1989).
HARRIS, H., and LICHTENSTEIN N. (eds.), *Industrial Democracy Past and Present* (New York, CUP, 1991).
HARTMANN, F., *Geschichte der Gewerkschaftsbewegung nach 1945 in Niedersachsen* (Hanover, Göttingen University, 1972).
HAWES, S., and WHITE, R. (eds.), *Resistance in Europe 1939–1945* (London, Penguin, 1976).
HEMMER, H-O., and SCHMITZ, K. (eds.), *Geschichte der Gewerkschaften in der Bundesrepublik Deutschland* (Cologne, Bund Verlag, 1990).
HINTON, J., *Labour and Socialism: A History of the British Labour Movement 1867–1974* (Brighton, Harvester, 1983).
—— *Protests and Visions: Peace Politics in Twentieth Century Britain* (London, Hutchinson, 1989).
HIRSCH, F., and FLETCHER, R., *The CIA and the Labour Movement* (Nottingham, Spokesman, 1977).
HOBSBAWM E., *Revolutionaries* (London, Quartet, 1977).
—— *The Age of Empire* (London, Weidenfeld, 1987).
—— *Worlds of Labour* (London, Weidenfeld, 1984).
HOBSON, C. (ed.) *International Metalworkers' Federation* (Birmingham, Hudson, 1915).

HOLTHOON, F. VAN, and LINDEN, M. VAN DER, *Internationalism in the Labour Movement 1830–1940* 2 vols. (Leiden, E.J. Brill, 1988).

HORNER, A., *Incorrigible Rebel* (London, Macgibbon and Kee, 1960).

HOROWITZ, D., (ed.), *Corporations and the Cold War* (New York, Monthly Review Press, 1969).

HOSKING, G., *A History of the Soviet Union* (London, Collins, 1985).

HOWE, I., *Socialism and America* (New York, Harcourt, 1985).

HOWE, I., and WIDDICK, B., *The UAW and Walter Reuther* (New York, Random House, 1949).

HUSTER, E-U. (and authors' collective), *Determinanten der westdeutschen Restauration 1945–1949* (Frankfurt, Suhrkamp, 1972).

HUTT, A., *British Trade Unionism: A Short History*, 4th edn. (London, Lawrence and Wishart, 1952).

ISAACSON, W., and THOMAS, E., *The Wise Men* (New York, Simon and Schuster, 1986).

ISSERMAN, M., *Which Side Were You On? The American Communist Party in the Second World War* (Middletown, Conn. Wesleyan University Press, 1982).

JACOBI-BETTIEN, A., *Metallgewerkschaft Hessen 1945 bis 1948* (Marburg, Verlag Arbeiterbewegung und Gesellschaftswissenschaft, 1982).

JEFFEREYS, J., *The Story of the Engineers* (London, Lawrence and Wishart, 1945).

JENKINS, C., *All Against the Collar. Struggles of a White-Collar Union Leader* (London, Methuen, 1990).

JENKINS, M., *Bevanism, Labour's High Tide* (Nottingham, Spokesman, 1979).

JOHNSON, R., *The Long March of the French Left* (London, Macmillan, 1981).

JOLL, J., *The Second International 1889–1914* (London, Routledge, 1974).

JONES, B., *The Russia Complex: The British Labour Party and the Soviet Union* (Manchester, Manchester University Press, 1977).

JOUHAUX, L., *Le Syndicalisme et la CGT* (Paris, Sirene, 1920).

—— *La CGT: Ce qu'elle est, ce qu'elle veut* (Paris, Gallimard, 1937).

KAHN, T., 'Beyond Mythology: A Reply to Paul Garver', in *Labor Research Review*, 8 (Spring 1989).

KAMPELAMN, M., *The Communist Party versus the CIO* (New York, Praegar, 1957).

KANTROWITZ, J., 'L'influence américaine sur Force ouvrière: Mythe ou réalité?' in *Revue française de science politique*, 28/4, (1978).

KASSALOW, E. (ed.), *National Labor Movements in the Postwar World* (Evanston, Ill., Northwestern University Press, 1963).

KEERAN, R., *The Communist Party and the Autoworkers' Union* (Bloomington, Indiana University Press, 1980).

KELLY, M., 'The Reconstruction of the German Trade Union Movement', in *Political Science Quarterly* 64, (March, 1949).

KENDALL, W., *The Revolutionary Movement in Britain 1900–1921* (London, Weidenfeld and Nicolson, 1969).
—— *The Labour Movement in Europe* (London, Allen Lane, 1975).
KENNAN, G., *Memoirs 1925–1950* (Boston, Little Brown, 1967).
KEYNES, J., *The Economic Consequences of Peace* (London, Macmillan, 1919).
KLEHR, H., *The Heyday of American Communism: The Depression Decade* (New York, Basic Books, 1984).
KLUGMAN, J., *History of the Communist Party of Great Britain 1921–1924* (London, Lawrence and Wishart, 1969).
KOLB, J., *Metallgewerkschaften in der Nachkriegszeit* (Frankfurt, Europäische Verlagsanstalt, 1970).
KOLKO, J. AND G., *The Limits of Power* (New York, Harper, 1972).
KRIEGEL, A., *Les Internationales ouvrières 1864–1943* (Paris, Presses Universitaires de France, 1964).
—— *Aux origines du communisme français* (Paris, Flammarion, 1969).
KUCZYNSKI, J., *The Condition of Workers in Great Britain, Germany and the Soviet Union 1932–1938* (London, Gollancz, 1939).
KULEMANN, P., *Die Linke in Westdeutschland nach 1945* (Hanover, Soak Verlag, 1978).
LACOUTURE, J., *Léon Blum* (Paris, Seuil, 1977).
—— *De Gaulle* ii. *Le politique* (Paris, Seuil, 1985).
LACROIX-RIZ, A., *La CGT de la Libération à la scission de 1944–1947* (Paris, Editions sociales, 1983).
—— *Le Choix de Marianne. Les relations franco-américaines de la Libération aux débuts du Plan Marshall 1944–1948* (Paris, Éditions sociales, 1985).
—— 'Autour d'Irving Brown: l'AFL, le Free Trade Union Committee, le Département d'État et la scission syndicale française 1944–1947' in *Le Mouvement social* 190 (1990).
LAQUEUR, W., *Europe Since Hitler* (London, Penguin, 1985).
LASKI, H., *The Secret Battalion* (London, Labour Party, 1946).
—— *Trade Unions in the New Society* (New York, Viking, 1949).
LEFRANC, G., *Les Expériences syndicales internationales* (Paris, Aubier, 1952).
—— *Le Syndicalisme dans le monde* (Paris, Presses universitaires de France, 1977).
LEHMANN, E. (ed.), *Aufbruch in unsere Zeit: Erinnerungen an die Tätigkeit der Gewerkschaften von 1945 bis zur Gründung der Deutschen Demokratischen Republik* (Berlin, Tribüne Verlag, 1975).
LENIN, V., *Lenin on Trade Unions* (Moscow, Progress Publishers, 1970).
LEONHARD, W., *Die Revolution entlässt ihre Kinder* (Cologne, Kiepenheuer und Witsch, 1981).

LEWIN, L., *Governing Trade Unions in Sweden* (Cambridge, Mass., Harvard University Press, 1980).

LICHENSTEIN, N., *Labour's War at Home: The CIO in World War II* (Cambridge, CUP, 1982).

LICHTHEIM, G., *A Short History of Socialism* (London, Fontana, 1975).

LIEBERMAN, S., *Labour Movements and Labour Thought, Spain, France, Germany and the United States* (New York, Praeger, 1986).

LINDEMANN, A., *The Red Years: European Socialism versus Bolshevism 1919–1921* (Berkeley, University of California Press, 1974).

—— *A History of European Socialism* (New Haven, Conn., Yale University Press, 1983).

LOGUE, J., *Towards a Theory of Trade Union Internationalism* (Göteborg, Göteborg University, 1980).

LORWIN, L., *The International Labor Movement* (New York, Harper, 1953).

LORWIN, V., *The French Labour Movement* (Cambridge, mass., Harvard University Press, 1954).

LOSOVSKY, A. (ed.), *Führer durch die Sowjetgewerkschaften für Arbeiterdelegationen* (Moscow, Verlagsgenossenschaft ausländischer Arbeiter in der UdSSR, 1937).

—— *Die rote Gewerkschafts-Internationale* (Frankfurt, ISP Verlag, 1978).

LOUIS, P., *Histoire du mouvement syndical en France 1789–1941* 2 vols. (Paris, Valois, 1947–8).

LOVESTONE, J., *People's Front Illusion* (New York, Workers' Age Publishers, 1936).

MACSHANE, D., *Solidarity: Poland's Independent Union* (Nottingham, Spokesman, 1981).

MACSHANE, D., PLAUT, M., and WARD, D., *Power: Black Workers, Their Unions and the Struggle for Freedom in South Africa* (Boston, South End Press, 1985).

MCCAULEY, M. (ed.), *Communist Power in East Europe 1944–1949* (London, Macmillan, 1977).

—— *Marxism-Leninism in the German Democratic Republic: The Socialist Unity Party* (London, Macmillan, 1979).

—— *The German Democratic Republic Since 1945* (London, Macmillan, 1983).

—— *The Origins of the Cold War* (London, Longman, 1983).

MCCORMICK, T., *America's Half-Century: United States' Foreign Policy in the Cold War* (Baltimore, Johns Hopkins University Press, 1989).

MCGUFFIE, C., *Working in Metal* (London, Merlin Press, 1985).

MCSHANE, H., *No Mean Fighter* (London, Pluto, 1978).

MAGAZINER, A., *Ein Sohn des Volkes* (Vienna, Europaverlag, 1977).

MAHLEIN, L., *Gewerkschaften international im Spannungsfeld zwischen Ost und West* (Frankfurt, Nachrichten-Verlag, 1984).

MAHNKE, G. AND STROTHMAN, F., *'Wir wollten mehr als die Trümmer beseitigen'* (Frankfurt, Otto Brenner Stiftung, 1989).

MAHON, J., *Harry Pollit* (London, Lawrence and Wishart, 1976).

MAIER, C., 'The Politics of Productivity: Foundations of American International Economic Policy after World War II', in *International Organization*, 31 (Autumn, 1977), 607–33.

MANLEY, M., *A Voice at the Workplace: Reflections on Colonialism and the Jamaican Worker* (London, Deutsch, 1975).

MARQUAND, D., *The Unprincipled Society* (London, Fontana, 1988).

MARTIN, R., *Communism and the British Trade Unions 1924–1933: A Study of the National Minority Movement* (Oxford, Clarendon Press, 1969).

MERSON, A., *Communist Resistance in Nazi Germany* (London, Lawrence and Wishart, 1985).

MEYNAUD, J., and SALAH BEY, A., *le Syndicalisme africain* (Paris, Payot, 1963).

MIDDLEMAS, K., *Politics in Industrial Society: The Experience of the British System Since 1911* (London, Deutsch, 1979).

—— *Power and the Party: Changing Faces of Communism in Western Europe* (London, Deutsch, 1980).

—— *Industry, Unions and Government* (London, Macmillan, 1983).

MILNER, S., 'The International Labour Movement and the Limits of Internationalism: The International Secretariat of the National Trade Union Centres 1901–1913', in *International Review of Social History* 33/1 (1988).

MILWARD, A., *The Reconstruction of Western Europe 1945–1951* (London, Methuen, 1984).

MONETA, J., *Le PCF et la question colonial* (Paris, Maspero, 1971).

MONTGOMERY, D., *Workers Control in America* (Cambridge, CUP, 1980).

—— *The Fall of the House of Labour* (Cambridge, CUP, 1987).

MOODY, K., *An Injury to All. The Decline of American Unionism* (London, Verso, 1988).

MOORE, J., *Japanese Workers and the Struggle for Power 1945–1947* (Madison, University of Wisconsin Press, 1983).

MORGAN, K., *Labour in Power 1945–1951* (Oxford, OUP, 1984).

MORTIMER, E., *The Rise of the French Communist Party 1920–1947* (London, Faber, 1984).

MORTIMER, W., *Organize: My Life as a Union Man* (Boston, Beacon, 1971).

MOSES, J., *Trade Unionism in Germany from Bismarck to Hitler* (Totowa, NJ, Barnes and Noble, 1982).

MOURIAUX, R., *La CGT* (Paris, Seuil, 1982).

MUNCK, R., *The New International Labour Studies* (London, Zed, 1988).

MURRAY R., and WHITE, K., *The Ironworkers: A History of the Federated*

Ironworkers' Association of Australia (Sydney, Hale and Iremonger, 1982).

NETTL, J., *The Eastern Zone and Soviet Policy in Germany 1945–1950* (Oxford, Clarendon Press, 1951).

NEWMAN, M., *Socialism and European Unity: The Dilemma of the Left in Britain and France* (London, Junction Books, 1983).

NICHOLSON, M., *The TUC Overseas: The Roots of Policy* (London, Allen and Unwin, 1986).

NORTHEDGE, F., and WELLS, A., *Britain and Soviet Communism: The Impact of a Revolution* (London, Macmillan, 1982).

NUGENT, N., and LOWE, D., *The Left in France* (London, Macmillan, 1982).

OLLE, W. (ed.), *Einführing in die internationale Gewerkschaftspolitik* (Berlin, Olle und Wulter, 1978).

OPEL, F., *Der deutsche Metallarbeiter-Verband während des ersten Weltkrieges und der Revolution* (Cologne, Bund Verlag, 1980).

OPEL, F., and SCHNEIDER, D., *75 Years of the Iron International* (Geneva, IMF, 1968).

—— *90 Jahre Industriegewerkschaft, 1891 bis 1981* (Cologne, Bund Verlag, 1981).

OVENDALE, R., *The English-Speaking Alliance: Britain, the United States, the Dominions and the Cold War 1945–1951* (London, Allen and Unwin, 1985).

OVERESCH, M., *Deutschland 1945–1949* (Düsseldorf, Droste, 1979).

PELLING, H., *A History of British Trade Unionism* (London, Penguin, 1976).

—— *Britain and the Marshall Plan* (London, Macmillan, 1989).

PERLMAN, M., *Labor Union Theories in America* (New York, Row, Peterson, 1958).

—— *The Machinists* (Cambridge, Mass., Harvard University Press, 1961).

PFEIFER, S., *Gewerkschaften und kalter Krieg, 1945 bis 1949* (Cologne, Pahl-Rugenstein, 1980).

PIMLOTT, B., *Labour and the Left in the 1930s* (London, Allen and Unwin, 1986).

—— *Hugh Dalton* (London, Jonathan Cape, 1985).

—— *The Political Diaries of Hugh Dalton 1918–1940 and 1945–1960* (London, Jonathan Cape, 1986).

PIMLOTT, B., and COOK, C. (eds.), *Trade Unions in British Politics* (London, Longman, 1982).

PIRKER, T., *Die blinde Macht: Die Gewerkschaftsbewegung in der Bundesrepublik* 2 vols. (Berlin, Olle und Walter, 1979).

POLLARD, R., *Economic Security and the Origins of the Cold War, 1945–1950* (New York, Columbia University Press, 1985).

PONOMAREV, B. (ed.), *Die internationale Arbeiterbewegung: Fragen der*

Geschichte und der Theorie 6 vols. (Moscow, Progress Publishers and Berlin, Dietz, 1978–85).

POOLE, M., *Theories of Trade Unionism: A Sociology of Industrial Relations* (London, Routledge, 1981).

PORTELLI, H. (ed.), *L'Internationale socialiste* (Paris, Éditions ouvrières, 1983).

PORTNOY, S., *Henryk Erlich and Victor Alter: Two Heroes and Martyrs for Jewish Socialism* (New York, Jewish Labor Bund, 1990).

PRAVDA, A., and RUBLE, B., *Trade Unions in Communist States* (London, Allen and Unwin, 1986).

PREIS, A., *Labor's Giant Step: Twenty Years of the CIO* (New York, Pathfinder Press, 1964).

PRESS, M., and THOMPSON, D. (eds.), *Solidarity for Survival: Trade Union Internationalism* (Nottingham, Spokesman, 1989).

PRICE, J., *The International Labour Movement* (London, OUP, 1945).

PROST, A., *La CGT à l'époque du Front populaire* (Paris, Seuil, 1964).

RA'ANAN, G., *International Policy Formation in the USSR: Factional 'Debates' During the Zhadanovschina* (Hamden, Conn., Archon Books, 1983).

RADOSH, R., *American Labor and United States Foreign Policy* (New York, Random House, 1969).

REUTHER, V., *The Brothers Reuther and the UAW* (Boston, Houghton Mifflin, 1976).

RIOUX, J-P., *La France de la Quatrième République* (Paris, Seuil, 1980).

RITZEL, H., *Kurt Schumacher* (Hamburg, Rowohlt, 1972).

ROBERTSON, A., *The Bleak Midwinter 1947* (Manchester, Manchester University Press, 1987).

ROBINSON, A., *George Meany and His Times* (New York, Simon and Schuster, 1981).

ROBRIEUX, P., *Histoire intérieure du parti communiste 1920–1982*, 4 vols. (Paris, Fayard, 1980–4).

ROTHWELL, V., *Britain and the Cold War 1941–1947* (London, Jonathan Cape, 1982).

RUPNIK, J., *Histoire du parti communiste tchécoslovaque* (Paris, Fondation nationale des sciences politiques, 1981).

RUSSIN, S. (ed.), *Democracy Under Fire: Memoirs of a European Socialist: Adolf Sturmthal* (Durham, NC, Duke University Press, 1989).

RÜTTERS, P., *Chancen internationaler Gewerkschaftspolitik: Struktur und Einfluss der Internationalen Union der Lebens- und Genussmittelarbeiter-Gewerkschaften* (Frankfurt, Otto Brenner Stiftung, 1989).

SAMUEL, R., 'Class Politics: The Lost World of British Communism', in *New Left Review* 165 (Sept. 1987).

SAVILLE, J., 'Ernest Bevin and the Cold War 1945–1950', in *The Socialist Register 1984* (London, Merlin Press, 1984).

—— *The Labour Movement in Britain* (London, Faber, 1988).

SCHAPIRO, L., *The Communist Party of the Soviet Union* (London, Eyre and Spottiswoode, 1970).

SCHAPIRO, L., and GODSON, J., *The Soviet Worker: Illusions and Realities* (London, Macmillan, 1981).

SCHEVENELS, W., *45 Years IFTU* (Brussels, International Confederation of Free Trade Unions, 1955).

SCHMID, J., *Le Syndicalisme suisse* (Lausanne, Éditions du Bas, 1980).

SCHMIDT, E., *Die verhinderte Neuordnung 1945–1952* (Frankfurt, Europäische Verlag, 1970).

SCHNEER, J., *Labour's Conscience: The Labour Left 1945–1951* (London, Unwin, 1987).

SCHÖNHAVEN, K., *Die deutschen Gewerkschaften* (Frankfurt, Suhrkamp, 1987).

SCHULZE, P., *Gewerkschaftskampf von unten: Amerikanische Automobilarbeiter im New Deal* (Frankfurt, Campus, 1987).

SCIPES, K., 'Trade Union Imperialism in the US Yesterday: Business Unionism, Samuel Gompers and AFL Foreign Policy', in *Newsletter of International Labour Studies* 40–1, (1989).

SENSENIG, G., *Österreichisch-amerikanische Gewerkschaftsbeziehungen 1945 bis 1950* (Cologne, Pahl-Rugenstein, 1987).

SERGE, V., *Memoirs of a Revolutionary* (Oxford, Clarendon Press, 1963).

SMITH, J. (ed.), *The Papers of General Lucius D. Clay 1945–1949* (Bloomington, Indiana University Press, 1974).

SPRIANO, P., *Stalin and the European Communists* (London, Verso, 1985).

STEININGER, R., *England und die deutsche Gewerkschaftsbewegung 1945–1946* in (Bonn, Archiv für Sozialgeschichte Verlag Neue Gesellschaft, 1978).

—— *Deutschland und die Sozialistische Internationale nach dem Zweiten Weltkrieg* (Bonn, Neue Gesellschaft, 1979).

STERN, C., and WINKLER H-A. (eds.), *Wendepunkte deutscher Geschichte* (Frankfurt, Fischer, 1979).

STERN, F., *Dreams and Delusions: The Drama of German History* (London, Weidenfeld, 1988).

STONE, I., *The Truman Era 1945–1952* (Boston, Little Brown, 1972).

STRACHEY, J., *The Theory and Practice of Socialism* (London, Gollancz, 1936).

STURMTHAL, A., *The Tragedy of European Labour* (London, Gollancz, 1944).

STURMTHAL, A., and SCOVILLE J. (eds.), *The International Labor Movement in Transition* (Urbana, University of Illinois Press, 1973).

TAFT, P., *The AFL in the Time of Gompers* (New York, Harper, 1954).

—— *The AFL from the Death of Gompers to the Merger* (New York, Harper, 1959).

TAFT, P., *Organized Labor in American History* (New York, Harper, 1964).

——— *Defending Freedom: American Labor and Foreign Affairs* (Los Angeles, Nash, 1973).

TAWNEY, R., *The American Labour Movement and Other Essays* (London, Macmillan, 1955).

THERBORN, G., 'The Coming of Swedish Social Democracy' in E. Collotti (ed.), *L'Internazionale Operaia e Socialista tra le due guerre* (Milan, Feltrinelli, 1985).

THOMAS, H., *Armed Truce: The Beginnings of the Cold War 1945–1946* (London, Hamish Hamilton, 1986).

THUM, H., *Mitbestimmung in der Montanindustrie: Der Mythos vom Sieg der Gewerkschafter* (Stuttgart, Deutsche Verlags-Anstalt, 1982).

TOUCHARD, J., *La Gauche en France depuis 1900* (Paris, Seuil, 1977).

ULBRICHT, W. (ed.), *Zur Geschichte der deutschen Arbeiterbewegung* 6 vols. (Berlin, Dietz, 1959–66).

ULRICH, A. (ed.), *Hessische Gewerkschafter im Widerstand 1933–1945* (Giessen, Anabas-Verlag, 1985).

UTLEY, F., *Lost Illusion* (London, Allen and Unwin, 1949).

VALIDIRE, J-L., *André Bergeron, une force ouvrière* (Paris, Plon, 1984).

WALL, I., *L'Influence américaine sur la politique française 1945–1954* (Paris, Balland, 1989).

WATERMAN, P., 'Some Reflections and Propositions on Workers and Internationalism', in *Newsletter of International Labour Studies* 30–1 (1986).

——— 'The New Internationalism', Institute of Social Studies, The Hague, Working Paper 37, (1984).

——— (ed.), *For a New Labour Internationalism* (The Hague, Institute of Social Studies, 1987).

WATT, D.C., *Britain Looks to Germany* (London, Wolff, 1965).

WEE H., VAN DER *Prosperity and Upheaval: The World Economy 1945–1980* (London, Penguin, 1987).

WEILER P., 'The United States, International Labor and the Cold War: The Break-up of the World Federation of Trade Unions', in *Diplomatic History* 5/1, (Winter, 1981).

——— *British Labour and the Cold War* (Stanford, Calif., Stanford University Press, 1988).

——— 'British Labour and the Cold War: The Foreign Policy of the Labour Governments 1945–1951', in *Journal of British Studies* 26 (Jan. 1987).

WEISS-HARTMANN, A., *Der freie Gewerkschaftsbund Hessen 1945–1949* (Marburg, Verlag Arbeiterbewegung und Gesellschaftswissenschaft, 1978).

WERTH, A., *France, 1940–1955* (London, Hale, 1955).

WILLIAMS, P., *Politics in Post-War France* (London, Longman, 1954).

WILSON, G., *Unions in American National Politics* (London, Macmillan, 1979).

WINDMULLER, J., *American Labor and the International Labor Movement* (Ithaca, NY,Cornell University Press, 1954).

—— 'International Trade Union Movement', in R. Blancpain (ed.), *International Encyclopaedia for Labour Law and Industrial Relations* (Deventer, Kluver, 1987).

WOHRLE, A., *Ein Leben in der Organisation* (Frankfurt, IG Metall, 1983).

WOLFE, A., *America's Impasse: the Rise and Fall of the Politics of Growth* (Boston, South End Press, 1981).

WORLD FEDERATION OF TRADE UNIONS, *La Fédération syndicale mondiale 1945–1985* (Prague, WFTU, 1985).

WRIGHT, A., *Socialisms, Theories and Practices* (London, OUP, 1986).

YERGIN, D., *Shattered Peace: The Origins of the Cold War and the National Security State* (London, Penguin, 1980).

YOUNG, J., *Britain, France and the Unity of Europe 1945–1951* (Leicester, Leicester University Press, 1984).

Anon., *In Memoriam Edo Fimmen* (London, International Transport Workers' Federation, 1952).

Anon., A New Era: The Philadelphia Conference and the Future of the ILO (Montreal, ILO, 1944).

DISSERTATIONS AND PAPERS

BURWOOD, S., 'American Labour, French Labor, and the Marshall Plan: Battlegrounds and Crossroads', (paper presented to the 9th North American Labor History Conference, Detroit, Oct. 1987).

GRANGE, S., 'Those Bloody Reds: Ernest Bevin's Public Vision of Communism and British Foreign Policy 1945–1950' (Masters Dissertation, Michigan State University, 1983).

JACQUES, M., 'The Emergence of "Responsible" Trade-Unionism: A Study of the "New Direction" in TUC Policy 1926–1935' (Ph.D. thesis, Cambridge, 1977).

KRIER-BECKER, L., *Edo Fimmen* (Unpublished manuscript in International Transport Workers Federation archives, London).

SCHWARTZ, M., 'Soviet Policy and the World Federation of Trade Unions 1945–1949' (Ph.D. thesis, Columbia University, 1963).

VOŠAHLÍKOVÀ, P., 'Tschechoslowakische Gewerkschaftsbewegung nach dem zweiten Weltkrieg und die Teilnahme der Sozialdemokraten daran' (Paper presented at the Internationale Tagung der Historiker der Arbeiterbewegung, Linz, 1990).

WEILER, P., 'The British Trades Union Congress and World Politics in

1945', unpublished Paper presented to North American Labor History Conference, October 1985.

WANNÖFFEL, M., 'Gewerkschaftlicher Neubeginn und Gewerkschafts-politik in Bochum nach dem zweiten Weltkreig' (doctoral thesis, Bochum University, 1982).

Index